In Women's Experience

In Women's Experience

Edited by

Patricia L. Munhall, ARNP, Ed.D., PsyA, FAAN

Associate Dean of Graduate Program
Director of the Center for Nursing Science
School of Nursing
Barry University
Miami, Florida

National League for Nursing Press • New York
Pub. No. 14-2612

The poem on page 359 was reprinted by permission. Rainer Maria Rilke, *The Possibility of Being.* Copyright 1957 by New Directions Publishing Corporation.

Copyright © 1994
National League for Nursing
350 Hudson Street, New York, NY 10014

ISBN 0-88737-610-X

This book was set in Garamond by Publications Development Company, Crockett, Texas. The editor and designer was Allan Graubard. The printer was Clarkwood Corp. The cover was designed by Lauren Stevens.

Printed in the United States of America.

Acknowledgments

*G*ratitude swells within me when I think of those who made this volume possible. At last, a book of phenomenological studies *and* on women!

To the authors—Cathy Appleton, Carolyn Brown, Diane Cope, Geri L. Dickson, Ellen Goldschmidt Ehrlich, Carol Germain, Sarah Selen Lauterbach, Dula F. Pacquiao, and Zane Robinson Wolfe—a most warm thank-you.

To Max van Manen for his inspiration, and to Allan Graubard, Editorial Director, National League for Nursing Press, for his encouragement, patience, and genuine enthusiasm for this project.

To all the women whose very being makes this book relevant. Thank you for sharing your joys, frustrations, sadness, and enormous strength. My hope is that this book gives to other women, as much as it has given to me, meaning and a renewed appreciation for women's *being*.

P.L.M.

Prologue

*T*oday, as I write this, it is Sunday, October 3, 1993. *The New York Times Magazine* is running an article entitled, "Are Women's Hearts Different?" I know they're different. The article states:

> . . . men experience "textbook" cases of angina and other *heart-disease symptoms because the textbooks were written to describe men's symptoms. (p. 61)*

As were the textbooks on psychology, sociology, politics, and history. This is not new knowledge, but there is, finally, not only a growing recognition of the lack of information about women, but an impetus to correct what could be misleading. This book of women's interpretations of experience is one such example, among a growing body of literature.

Another section of today's paper, *The New York Times Book Review,* attests to this. Clarissa Pinkolan Estes' *Women Who Run with the Wolves* has been on the best-seller list for 50 weeks. This book is a narrative on how "myths and folk tales can enable women to understand their psyches" (p. 34). Twenty weeks on the best-seller list is John Gray's *Men Are from Mars, Women Are from Venus.* Another book to explain our differences. On the paperback list, Deborah Tannen's *You Just Don't Understand,* which discusses the different languages men and women speak, has been on the best-seller list for 124 weeks! Like this book, it is about coming to understand.

New books continue to appear, written about some facet of women's experiences. This book, *In Women's Experience,* is part of a post-modern recognition that women are not like men, nor are they inferior or deviant because they are different. Instead, they are *marvelously* different.

Let me tell you how this particular book came to be. In the summer of 1992, in Jacksonville, Florida, I was one of many women researchers participating in a summer workshop on phenomenology, as a way of coming to know. We were all academic "types" and, true to form, an idea was conceived over dinner. I call these women "the Philadelphia contingent": Carol Germain, Zane Robinson Wolfe, and Susan Langer. We talked about doing a book on women's experiences based on phenomenological perspectives. The focus seemed to be midlife experiences and, not too coincidentally, that's where we were all temporally situated.

After the summer workshop, Allan Graubard, Editorial Director, National League for Nursing Press, expressed immediate enthusiasm about the project and we began discussing Volumes Two and Three! With that encouragement, I began to seek out other academic women who were interested in this approach and might participate in this effort to understand the meaning of being a woman in different situations.

A Florida group was formed, consisting of Cathy Appleton, Carolyn Brown, and Diane Cope. The Philadelphia group first enlarged to include Sarah Steen Lauterbach and then expanded into the tri-state area with the addition of Dula Pacquiao from New Jersey and Ellen Ehrlich and Geri Dickson from New York.

We all agreed to follow a similar interpretation of phenomenology as depicted by Max van Manen (1990). With this approach, our senses were opened to the appearance of the experience in whatever form it took. We also became aware of what was concealed.

Each chapter is a narrative in some form, using many women's voices. This book tells the way women live "things"—the way they describe their lives and interpret their experiences. In this way, the many narratives are authentic and faithful to the experience of women.

Since that summer, chapters have gone back and forth. The authors of individual chapters, while residing in their own work, wanted, upon deeper reflection, to add more to their chapters. The process was lively.

I was the most fortunate of the group. I received the drafts of the chapters and grew in my own sensitivity to the experiences described. Also, I became aware of the threads of thoughts, perceptions, and values that transcend a specific experience and that women seem to share.

I would like to mention a few. One is strength. Women are indeed strong. They are living multiple roles in one life. They are caring and caretakers. They are experiencing the vicissitudes of maturing and growing. They grieve their losses and struggle with conditions that society still maintains as appropriate. They wish to be both caring and powerful. They receive mixed messages from those around them and often sacrifice self for others. That part is not good for them. They often suffer in silence but, more and more, they have begun to talk with one another and, in this process, to deconstruct myths and theories.

In the company of other women, they find the comfort of support from friends and sometimes even from strangers. There is a relational perspective with the world that enables the families, children, friends, and parents of these women to experience their loyalty and support. This does not always happen nor is it the story of every woman.

The stories here are in progress. The experiences are not necessarily connected. Not everyone has had these experiences in the same circumstances, but we all know someone who has—and that someone may be ourselves. Thus, we see ourselves *and* other women in these pages. In our natural proclivity for attachment, understanding the meaning of experience is a beginning.

I love these women whose writing craft has been motivated by a desire to understand the meaning of our lives, sometimes by sharing their sorrows and triumphs as revealed in a particular experience. Life is not a series of dissected experiences, so what we learn about these women is that, in some way, they maintain a continuity of spirit. The spirit of women is rhythmical. Feeling weak, strong, then weak—the counterpoint continues. Through our common bonds and through our understanding of being women, we are there to reach out, in strength and weakness, in turn.

Women comfort, care for, and nurture other women and men. Through the process of understanding, as it is offered to readers of this book, women hear each other even as they listen and speak.

Such listening and speaking are not small feats and they have powerful consequences. Women can see and understand beyond behavior and appearance. They can grasp the underlying meaning of experience—what women's words and behavior intend, propose, and dispose. What is the meaning? This is the question these authors address. Via the synchrony of women's rhythmical patterns of give and take, of meaning and sharing meaning, mutual explorations of possibility come to light. The women who contributed to these pages are engaged in an existential way of being with choices. They are constructing new ways of being. They are composing the contextual meaning of women *being*.

REFERENCES

van Manen, M. (1990). *Researching lived experience.* New York: SUNY Press.

Henig, R. (October 3, 1993). "Are Women's Hearts Different?" *New York Times.*

Preface

*T*his book is guided by the philosophy of phenomenology. There are different interpretations of this philosophy, but the primary theme guiding this book resides in one question: What is the meaning of being human? Because the book is focused on women, the question must then be phrased: What is the meaning of being a woman? Researchers who ask such questions are dealing with extraordinary complexity. Paradoxically, the answers to these questions can be best found in everyday, concrete experience. Many phenomenologists reason that, to understand what it is like to be a human being, we must seek to understand a human being in experience. That is where we find humans.

In this book, we say we wish to understand women in experience. This means that, in order to understand women, we find women in experience within a context of some sort. We simply cannot understand women by comparing them to some "thing" or by merely theorizing or conceptualizing. We must hear women speak of their experience if we are to understand their meanings and perceptions. Their descriptions and interpretations come from living in the everyday world—in a body; in time, space, and place; in a situated context.

A phenomenological perspective is one of enlargement. It makes us thoughtful of the consequential and the inconsequential, the significant and the taken-for-granted. This perspective questions the foregone conclusions, assumptions, and norms. Phenomenological reflection attempts to liberate us from what we believe we know so well, from the way we take the world for granted. Phenomenology has the potential of emancipating us from our own presuppositions.

The essence of our interest in a particular experience is found in opening up and keeping open to all emerging possibilities, as they appear or as they are concealed.

To hear women speak, the authors in this volume have begun their work in silence. The question they are asking has taken up residence within them. In this way, they have remained open to different variations and to appearances whenever and wherever they appear. The major task is to construct (and, in this way, perhaps desconstruct) a possible interpretation of the nature of a human experience (in this book, a woman's experience). The major aim is understanding, and we aim toward understanding because we seek to answer that extraordinary question: What is the meaning of being? Of being a woman?

Women's experiences were studied for this book by following Max van Manen's (1990) way of inquiry. The researcher uses personal experience as a starting point, obtains experiential descriptions from women and from literature, reflects on essential themes, and synthesizes the material back into a whole—a narrative or a text. When studying women in experience, I began a journal; I noted when I saw and heard the experience in films, at conferences, during conversations. Once I turned my attention to it, I began to see the experience and find its essences everywhere. All becomes grid for phenomenology.

This kind of study is not linear nor is it method-driven. It is scientific and it asks that its investigators be creative, attentive listeners; that they reside with the material collected; that they reflect on what emerges and write about it. Self and others must understand what it means to be human in certain experiences, sometimes and in some ways.

This book represents phenomenological study of post-modern women in their situated context. There is no pretense to generalize; that is not the purpose of such study. However, the notion of "resonance" should be an outcome. Does the description sound familiar or, if not familiar, possible for someone else? Differences occur in perception, depending on different situated contexts. Even then, differences emerge, and that is fine. That is all part of our story.

To be specific, each chapter of this volume is about women's experience. Readers might first read the text, which is written from a phenomenological perspective. For each chapter, a small section entitled "About the Study" will offer additional insight. Then there will be some references. Lastly, there is a short personal note, "About the Author," that will be of "human" interest. This, in its own way, is an attempt to eliminate distance between the reader and the text.

How does one arrange such chapters—in what order and with what intent to give meaning to such ordering? How can categorizing into sections be done when women do not live this way; when things simply happen?

For this first volume, the chapters appear in the alphabetical order of the authors' last names. Each author challenges us by examining and revisiting normative commitments, biased interpretations, and unquestioned assumptions. Women's hearts *are* different.

PATRICIA L. MUNHALL

Miami, Florida
March 1994

Contents

Editor and Contributing Author

Patricia L. Munhall, ARNP, EdD, Psy A, FAAN
Professor and Associate Dean of Graduate Program
Director of the Center for Nursing Science
School of Nursing
Barry University
Miami, Florida

Contributing Authors

Cathy Appleton, ARNP, CS, PhD
Interim Graduate Program Director
Florida Atlantic University
College of Nursing
Boca Raton, Florida

Carolyn Brown, RN, PhD
Associate Professor
School of Nursing
Barry University
Miami, Florida

Diane Cope, PhD, RN
Visiting Assistant Professor
Florida Atlantic University
Boca Raton, Florida

Gerri L. Dickson, RN, PhD
Assistant Professor
New York University
New York, New York

Ellen Goldschmidt Ehrlich, MEd, EdD, RN
Assistant Professor
College of Mount Saint Vincent
Riverdale, New York

Carol P. Germain, EdD, FAAN
Associate Professor
School of Nursing
University of Pennsylvania
Philadelphia, Pennsylvania

Sarah Steen Lauterbach, EdD, RN
Assistant Professor
School of Nursing
LaSalle University
Philadelphia, Pennsylvania

Dula F. Pacquiao, EdD, RN
Assistant Professor
Department of Nursing
Kean College
Union, New Jersey

Zane Robinson Wolfe, PhD, RN, FAAN
Professor
School of Nursing
LaSalle University
Associate Director of Nursing for Research
Albert Einstein Medical Center
Philadelphia, Pennsylvania

1

Caring: In Women's Experience

Cathy Appleton

There are four ways to write a woman's life: the woman herself may tell it, in what she chooses to call an autobiography; she may tell it in what she chooses to call fiction; a biographer, woman or man, may write the woman's life in what is called a biography; or the woman may write her own life in advance of living it, unconsciously, and without recognizing or naming the process. (Heilbrun, 1988, p. 11)

What is caring like in women's lives? From the autobiographies of 12 women, the experience of caring comes forth with profound and astonishing veracity. Each woman, an autobiographer, tells what caring is like and its meaning in her life. As researcher and biographer, I weave the themes of this study into one phenomenologically written description of *Caring: In Women's Experience*.

No record has been more poignant than the narratives from these women, who willingly and with deep commitment told me about the joy, sorrow, and pain of caring; of living selfishly and selflessly in caring; of the beauty and blissfulness of caring; and of the anger and depression caring creates. They told me about the work of caring: its burdens, conflicts, and risks; of good, caring people; and of their hopes and dreams for a future where caring becomes empowered in the world.

These women lead diverse lives. The majority are professionals; a few are retired, actively engaged in pursuing avocations. They are married and single, with and without children. They live in extended, blended, and nuclear families. Their cultural backgrounds vary as does the time they have lived their lives. Some of these women are young adults, others are middle-aged, and two are entering the seventh decade of life.

Regardless of their age, race, culture, or family situation, their descriptions of caring define their uniqueness as individuals and as women. Their lives reflect a consciousness about themselves and the meaning caring has for them as women. Like flowers in a bouquet wild and conventional, exotic and prosaic, bold and unobtrusive, these women inspire and astonish us with their candid, moving autobiographical essays.

As Heilbrun (1988) acknowledges, "Unconsciously and without recognizing or naming the process, women may write their own life in advance of living it" (p. 11). Lillian, who "never really thought about caring," finding it a rather "strange thing for her to think about," imparts a life of caring, cultivated from a deep and profound love of self, others, and the world. Thinking about caring is a rather "strange thing" in that, when Lillian wants to do something, especially for someone, she's doing it because she wants to do it, not because she has to do it—"I love them."

In contrast, Elena told me caring is something that "I think about a lot." Finding it fascinating how the meaning of caring changes in her life from experience and through culture, Elena says, "The older I get, the more caring is projected outward toward friends, family, and my profession."

"The coming of age portends all the freedoms men have always known and women never—mostly the freedom from fulfilling the need of others" (Heilbrun, 1988, p. 130). Margaret knows that caring entails, in part, fulfilling the needs of others. In an effort to have the freedoms Heilbrun writes of, Margaret has released herself from relationships with men who totally rely on her to take care of "the mechanics of living together," such as the cooking, grocery shopping, cleaning, and laundry. Margaret establishes relationships that are mutually satisfying and reciprocal in nature. Margaret has found with men of her generation that working out "the mechanics of living together" is always "a bone of contention." She would rather be single and finds deeply gratifying her relationships with friends, colleagues, and family.

Francene experiences what Margaret avoids with men of her generation: The responsibility of taking care of the daily activities of living together. She prepares dinner and does the grocery shopping for an extended family, in addition to the major care of her daughter. Francene feels she has the "burden of caring for the family" because she is the oldest daughter and female. This automatically make her responsible for the mechanics of daily living, illness, and holidays. While working to develop a professional career, caring in Francene's life "is a part of daily living." She feels this is especially true for "women, who have so many responsibilities that, if they didn't care, nothing would get done."

Taking a part in whatever discourse is essential to action and having the right to have that part matter are, according to Heilbrun, a description of power (1988, p. 18). Gerda says caring is "being treated seriously" and having things that are important to her "validated by the other person's interest in them." Gerda enjoys woman friends and feels friendships with women are typified by a regard for one another that is holistic, genuine in consideration for the other person, and simply not selfish. While this has been Gerda's experience of women friends, she does consider her husband a friend and depicts him as a man who understands her and is able to express his understanding in caring. Gerda says, "He listens, is patient, sustains an incredible attitude of affection and love for me," and doesn't let differences get in the way of their relationship.

Gabrielle told me, "I'm better at caring for, than being cared for." Not knowing whether it's a female phenomenon that women tend to be more nurturing, she says, "I'm not real good about people caring for me, but I'm much better about caring for them." While growing up, Gabrielle received from her parents messages about caring that perhaps have affected her choices. "My parents always said, you have to be able to take care of yourself and, as a woman functioning in the world, you have to be able to support yourself and be independent. You shouldn't have to have somebody take care of you."

Having what she calls "a track record" of her family's hurting her, Sylvia describes caring in her life as a sense of connectedness—"an unfelt energy between people that exists when you let all barriers down and you tell the truth." Sylvia finds, through what she calls her "disharmonious, chaotic, screaming and yelling" formative experience, that harmony and disharmony characterize the wholeness of human nature. In spirituality, she finds a way to care about and for herself. She told me this becomes primary in caring about anyone or anything else in life.

Maxine's experience informs her that caring is a process of "moral development." For her, "Caring is in the act of giving." Maxine told me that, in the act of caring, there doesn't have to be a reciprocal response in order for caring to matter. In giving, "Caring is self-sufficient."

Sylvia believes people need someone to listen to them. She says, "If we don't have people at home who listen, we need to look for people outside our family. There are so many problems that are very complex, we cannot solve them alone." Concerned about families, schools, and communities, Sylvia comments about a lack of values and knowledge of caring in the world. She directs her efforts to create schools and communities where caring is learned and experienced.

Natalie finds caring to be lacking outside of the family and inside organizations. "The system does not recognize the potential of the whole person, especially women," she reports. Although Natalie and her colleagues care about and for each other, this personal and localized caring does not extend into the policy and governance of the organization. The dynamics of organizations stem from a viewpoint that values the contribution and potential of people defined largely from a male perspective about what caring means. Natalie is concerned that organizations ground methods of evaluation and a structure of reward in a perspective that does not recognize the whole person. She understands that these organizational practices will never be caring for women.

Dorothy finds it difficult to get something you want in the political arena that men have shaped and where men hold most decision-making positions. She believes that men have needs different from those of women and that she will develop with that difference in mind. She cares for and about things in her work life that are not necessarily compatible with the "male viewpoint." Caring organizes her life in such a way that her methods of interacting are considered somewhat unconventional in the workplace. Dorothy talks about the glass ceiling in her professional work. She told me, "A woman can only get to a certain level," and firmly stated she was not trying "to parrot what's been written or give a textbook observation." Her personal view comes from the kind of workplace that she has experienced for 25 years.

Coming away from a volunteer experience with a completely different outlook about the meaning of unconditional caring, Elizabeth told me, "We all have to function together." Interestingly, Elizabeth spoke of the different outlook she developed when she volunteered to help in a soup kitchen. "I was just fascinated because that is really hands-on caring and hard work." Elizabeth's commitment as a volunteer extends to church and community. As the chairperson of a board of directors and as a member of community groups, Elizabeth gives freely of her time in caring.

The volume of transcripts generated from the narrative descriptions reflects five essential themes that express caring in these women's experience as: (1) the work of helping; (2) caring on both sides: living the conflict; (3) finding out what matters in life: taking the risk; (4) incredibly good people: the bread of God; and (5) empowering caring in our lives: a mission.

Generally speaking, in each essential theme, caring exists for these women as:

- *Affection*—love, respect, acceptance of uniqueness and diversity;

- *Communication* —sensitivity, honesty, openness, directness, consolation, listening, dialogue;
- *Knowing* —valuing, thinking, perceiving, believing;
- *Sharing* —emotions (such as joy or sorrow), ideas, information, beliefs, and/or customs;
- *Moral development* —responsibility, duty, obligation, charge, custody, burden, accountability;
- *Interaction* —making an effort, taking time, responding to a need, being there.

Challenged by the task to convey what these women described to me, I wove the essential themes with literature, poetry, philosophy, psychological and social theory, and women's autobiographies and biographical sketches. According to Janeway (1975):

Reviewing books is a good exercise for a writer of books if only because it involves an exercise in role-reversal. A writer-reviewer turns into a reader for a while and must think analytically about processes which are largely unconscious when one is writing: how to communicate experience as fully as possible, how to produce an intended emotion, how to use the instruments of language and literary device to create a simulacrum of reality which will seem plausible and moving to the reader. Beyond this, reviewers know that many nascent ideas, not yet solid enough for full, coherent expression in an independent form, will first come to light by attaching themselves to the world and ideas of others. A bell rings there, an echo resonates in ones's own mind. (p. 215)

So it is with bells and echoes that I write about women's experience of caring.

THE WORK OF HELPING

Helping stems from the responsibility to care, and from caring about ourselves and others. Like a string that runs through pearls, hiding behind what can be seen by the naked eye, caring, the work of helping another, is primary in women's lives. Evident in the process of caretaking and caregiving, women take care of, and give care to, others. When this is their lifelong experience, women have times when these activities become a burden. This is not to suggest that women's experience of caring is devoid of reciprocation and mutuality; it's not. But caretaking and caregiving never seem to cease in women's lives.

When women are there *for* and *with others*, they support, comfort, and empower them. Women derive benefit from their caring. Not limiting their relationships to solely caretaking activities, women get back what they give in caring. Mutually beneficial and reciprocal in expression, mature caring is a process of giving and taking for women in relationships grounded in respect and regard for one another.

As this book will show, these themes of caretaking and caregiving, of feeling the burden of caring, and of mature caring lie at the heart of the controversy involving caring and gender, science, and women's experience. At the core of the women's movement to create a context of social change is women's experience of caring.

Caretaking and Caregiving

Caretaking and caregiving are part of women's daily life, especially for women who believe they have the sole responsibility for caring. Francene finds, living in an extended family, that her life entails taking care of and giving care to all the family members. It also means taking care of the grocery shopping, meals, and laundry for her husband and child while she works at developing a professional career.

Because the members of Francene's extended family speak different languages, she feels responsible for the communication among all the family. Peace keeping, by virtue of caring for several family members, becomes a caretaking function. Francene feels she's responsible for keeping "a certain degree of harmony" within the family, beyond the day-to-day mechanics of living.

By and large, women experience caring for the family in the home; they perform activities of caretaking and caregiving, including management of a family unit and a house, in addition to helping individual members to grow and develop. In most cases, children are the family members who are the concern of women's caretaking and caregiving. Frequently, however, after the children are grown, women are called on to care for aging parents.

Dorothy, for example, has children who are grown and have children of their own. For Dorothy, caring means "doing for others, administering to them physically and spiritually." Dorothy's caring now centers more around her mother than herself. With respect to her children's ages, Dorothy tries not to do the same kind of caring for them that she used to do. She finds this "very hard" for a mother at any time in any generation.

Doing for others by administering to them physically and spiritually has been a part of Dorothy's life. She's the oldest of three children and thinks that, perhaps, the role of the oldest nurtures the activity of taking care of siblings. She remembers taking care of her younger brother when he was small. Now Dorothy spends considerable time caring for her mother, whose frail condition becomes progressively worse.

As a mother, Maxine says, there is "lots of giving out," but as an adult it is a reciprocal process. She speaks of caring in her life as "going both ways." Caring is nurturing, understanding, and meeting the needs of the other person. As a caregiver, Maxine is the person who takes care "when others don't yet know how or are unable to take care of themselves." Her children require the majority of her caregiving, although her caregiving also extends to individuals in her profession with whom she works as a director.

Maxine offers a unique description of the nature of a parent's relationship to children. She told me a story about the birth of her first child. Her father came to visit and told her, "You know, Maxine, your child is not your own."

Maxine concurs; she doesn't own her children. "They are in my life for a time, but come to me helpless, and caring is the response to that need." The quality of caring and the perspective about children that Maxine refers to is beautifully described by Kahlil Gibran:

Your children are not your children.
They are the sons and daughters of Life's longing for itself.
They come through you but not from you,
And though they are with you they belong not to you.

You may give them your love but not your thoughts,
For they have their own thoughts.
You may house their bodies but not their souls,
For their souls dwell in the house of tomorrow, which you
*   cannot visit, not even in your dreams.*

You may strive to be like them, but seek not to make them
*   like you.*
For life goes not backward nor tarries with yesterday.
You are the bow from which your children as living arrows
*   are set forth.*

The archer sees the mark upon the path of the infinite, and
He bends you with His might that His arrow may go swift
*   and far.*
Let your bending in the archer's hand be for gladness;
For even as He loves the arrow that flies, so He loves also the
*   bow that is stable.*
                    Kahlil Gibran (1951, pp. 17-18)

Maxine told me she cares for her children if only for a fleeting time.

Women, particularly women with children, find they still do the majority of caretaking and giving in families and in the home setting. Although this exists in varying degrees, from women's perspective and experience, women feel responsible for taking care of and giving care to their families. The marketing ploy, "You've come a long way, baby," initially used to promote Virginia Slims cigarettes, and later adopted by middle class "feminist" agendas, perhaps excludes women's sense of responsibility for caring for others, which seems to have remained constant in their lives.

For example, in Elena's life, caring is "basically doing everything for everybody." Elena tells me that she is a caring person, and, correspondingly, part of caring for her is concern for others. Meeting the needs of her family and assisting others, she attributes to gender and culture. She told me that in her culture, "Women are supposed to be taking care of everything, whether they work fulltime or stay at home."

Elena distinguishes between taking care of, as caring, and caring in general. She claims that, in caring, another level of bonding and interaction occurs with family or friends. Elena says that she takes care of her daughter by taking her to school, making sure she does her homework, or getting whatever she needs. But she also cares for her daughter by spending time with her, reading, playing games, talking, or just doing something fun together. With friends, caring is more of an experience of talking and "being there" for one another, not necessarily taking care of their needs.

When women care about themselves, family, friends, work, community, or the future, they care for these things by taking care of and giving care to them. It becomes a process of "taking care of and giving to what you care for." Women derive an array of feeling in this activity that ranges from joy and satisfaction to anger and resentment.

Emily Dickinson (1877) captured this role of women's caring poignantly by writing of a woman's response to the need of another for caring:

They might not need me—yet they might—
I'll let my Heart be just in sight—
A smile as small as mine might be
Precisely their necessity—

Such is women's perspective of the caretaking and caregiving role.

Feeling the Burden of Responsibility

When women take on the day-to-day responsibilities of caring for and about "everything and everyone," resentment, anger, frustration, and fantasies of fleeing appear. Caretaking and caregiving can become an "overwhelming and all-consuming" experience for women.

For example, Francene says she feels as if she has "the burden of caring for the family" because she is the oldest and a female, which makes her automatically responsible for special events and holidays, in addition to the mechanics of living. This includes shopping for gifts and preparing food, not to mention the planning and arranging. She claims that if she doesn't do it, "no one else cares as much" as she does, and they'll let it go.

The burden of caring can best be illustrated by diverse perspectives. Francene told me that if I asked her family about this, "They would probably say that I want to do it, that I like expressing my caring"—which she does, although she wishes her family would help.

There are times when women do not want nor are they able to meet the daily responsibilities of caring for "everyone and everything." Francene clearly communicates this in her description of wanting and asking for help when she doesn't feel like caring for her family, and not receiving what she needs. "I guess I am responsible for what I care about; it's hard when you're the only one who cares about a situation. It's like banging your head against the wall."

The burden of caring, particularly during illness and at death, takes its toll on women. Women frequently choose to assist loved ones, easing the hardship that comes with ill health and dying. Gabrielle told me that she took care of her mother for the last five years of her life with her father at home. This was the "most direct, intensive experience" she had with caretaking and giving in her life. She found herself doing things that she never thought she could or would do. "I was giving her injections, and catheterizing her four or five times a day."

Even though it took a toll on her, Gabrielle's caring for her mother reflected a deep devotion and a desire to help in any way possible to make her mother's illness and eventual death comfortable and peaceful. Initially, moving back into her parents' house was very difficult; Gabrielle had lived on her own for two decades. Despite finding the majority of her time spent in taking care of her mother, and eventually her father, who needed support in the face of her mother's declining health, Gabrielle did not want to give up her job, which she loved. Wanting to keep a piece of her life for herself, Gabrielle commuted long distances to and from her place of employment. Keeping her job meant hours on the road, but it provided her a time and space for herself.

The intensity of this prolonged situation left an indelible mark on Gabrielle. She expressed no regrets for having done it and felt a sense of peacefulness about her choice to help her mother. Yet she also experienced the overwhelming, arduous, and all-consuming demands that caretaking and caregiving entailed. "It was as if as soon as I let down, I became overwhelmed," she told me. Hardest of all was her own realization of the toll her mother's illness and eventual death had taken on her: "That was the hardest thing for me to deal with."

Mother in gladness, Mother in sorrow,
Mother today, and Mother tomorrow,
With arms ever open to fold and caress you
O Mother of Mine, may God keep you and bless you.
                    W. Dayton Wedgefarth
                    (cited in Alexander, 1956, p. 49)

Today, Gabrielle laughs about relatives who continually suggest she needs a man to take care of. "Oh, sure. Just what I need," she tells me. "I wasn't quite sure that I could ever get through that period but I did. It's amazing what you can do, that you don't think you have the strength to do."

Gabrielle's choice for herself, her mother, and her father came from her "desire to give back for the thirty-some years that they've been there for me." She did so even in the face of her father's initial discouragement of the arrangement, and told me, "I'm glad I did it."

Mature Caring or Selfishness?

In maturity, when caring becomes a reciprocal process, such as with spouses, adult family members, lovers, and good friends, it is experienced as a mutual expression of "being there" for one another. Maturity in caring conveys support, comfort, and empowerment to women.

Gerda describes it as "looking beyond what is of interest to you in a person, or for that matter what is of interest to you in anything you do." For Gerda, maturity in caring goes "beyond what is immediately useful" or advantageous to the person. For women, "that's real caring."

Often, women discover later in life that caring is directed outward, toward endeavors that are truly enjoyed or perhaps perceived as needed in the world. Lillian's life now, as she described it to me, is an example of "real caring." Caring as something a woman directs her thoughts to is "strange to think about" for Lillian, and may very well symbolize mature caring that becomes embodied as authentic caring in women's experience.

Dorothy spoke about "a real good kind of caring," the kind "where you don't let selfish needs override the caring." Dorothy explains: "It's when I don't let my needs get in the way." For her part, Lillian told me about selfishness and mature caring:

> As I've matured, my caring has changed. I think when I was a younger woman, I was very busy, extremely busy finding out who I was. Caring ability comes when you know who you are and where you are and that you're happy with yourself. When you're young, you're busy establishing yourself, economically, psychologically, and physically. You're busy creating your life. I think caring happened when I married and I realized I do care for somebody else.

When Lillian was a young woman and before she married, she wanted to be successful. The things she wanted to do, she says, "were rather selfish things, selfish in that they were not for others." She was caring for herself and interested in herself, wanting to be the best she could possibly be, but she says, "I was doing it for me. I think it was purely selfish."

Now Lillian is in a career where she knows that what she does has tremendous therapeutic benefit for people. She still wants to be the best, but likes the way she has matured and the person she has become. She feels that "you" have to be selfish in order to find "yourself" and until "you" can come to terms with yourself. "Without that persistence and drive of being selfish, you wouldn't get anywhere."

Today, Lillian doesn't think very much about herself. She's actively engaged in a busy career of doing something that benefits others. She tends her garden, cares with her husband, and enjoys her friends and life.

CARING ON BOTH SIDES: LIVING THE CONFLICT

Women have gained the freedom both to have children and to pursue careers, but society and institutions have not adapted to a world where women are in the workplace to stay. (Skolnick, 1991, p. 9)

Family First, Career Second?

The sense of being pulled in multiple directions because women care about family and careers is described as the conflict in caring—caring on both sides. Caring for family and career requires a life expertise in how to balance all things at all times. For some women, caring for family precludes placing a career first. Maxine says her primary work is parenting and only secondarily does she work at a career in the theater. She told me that there are times and situations where she feels like a second-class citizen because she has decided to place family in the forefront of her life and career at the periphery.

According to Mayeroff (1971), devotion is essential to caring. Women commit themselves to family or career by and large without knowledge of the foreseeable future. Their decisions about what they will be devoted to entail obstacles and difficulties that eventually women must overcome through a willingness to exercise their will.

When Dorothy started out in life, she made decisions herself, especially to get married and have children. After she married, she subsequently made the decision not to stay on in a career. These were her decisions and hers alone. "Life," she told me, "didn't make these decisions for me."

To a certain extent, Dorothy has been able to engage her desires throughout her life. She always had a great inner desire to be adventuresome, but was not able to do everything she had hoped for. Dorothy thinks her sights were larger than her drive to accomplish them, and admits to always having altruistic desires, but acknowledges she hasn't reached a point where she's "willing to sublet the house, put everything in storage, and go off to the unknown, inasmuch as I have a tremendous interest in this life."

Dorothy says that her caring is probably very much on her own terms, and concludes that caring is something "you develop yourself; you fulfill caring for yourself." Dorothy eventually resumed her career, but "developed caring for herself" primarily around a life devoted to a family.

Career First, Family Second?

Women, caring for career and family, find that cultural and professional expectations are "at odds." Sylvia tells me she won't separate her home from her professional life because if she does, she's "denying her needs." Referring to the multiple roles women play at home, at work, and in society, she says:

> We are creating very superficial relationships. Being a mother and worker is a very hard task because we have to take care of our children and sometimes we feel we need more time with them. When I was an administrator, I provided this type of support to my colleagues. When I came to this county [the United States], I noticed that the responsibility is different because no matter what you have to be at work, first is work, and second is your home.

In this country, Sylvia experiences people using excuses rather than telling the truth about their need to take care of their families. This happens, she believes, out of fear of reprisal from administrators and contributes to a double standard in society.

For Sylvia, the double standard develops into what she calls "role playing," or playing one role at work and another role at home. This split bodes ill for women like Sylvia, who believe that it epitomizes how professional and cultural expectations of women are at odds in the world. Denying the reality of problems at home and work introduces stress into women's lives and disregards their multiple responsibilities.

Weedon's (1987) social analysis of the family in American culture alleges that the social institutions women enter preexist them. If this is true, then Naisbitt and Aburdene's (1985) observation seems reasonable: by sheer numbers alone, women are changing the world of work for other women. But what exactly is the nature of these changes? Do women immediately experience them as a release from conflict when they care for both career and home?

Sylvia finds the professional work environment demanding when she must dedicate herself to a career and nurture a family. The overriding value for productivity requires great personal sacrifice for her and her women colleagues. In an effort to be clear about women with careers, Sylvia is not suggesting that she doesn't have colleagues and friends with whom she shares and collaborates professionally. On the contrary, she enjoys these relationships immensely. But she finds the administrative philosophy, organizational structure, and personnel policies and procedures lacking in concern for a precious resource—human beings in general and women in particular.

Sylvia is not alone in her experience of the workplace for women, where there is a lack of understanding and of a perspective of the whole person. Natalie describes the same experience. She deliberately attempts to connect with the other women, to come to know their experiences of the work environment, but finds the identical contextual phenomenon that Sylvia described. Natalie particularly notes the incongruencies existing among her beliefs, her experiences, and the nature of caring translated into the practices of the organization in which she is employed.

According to Naisbitt and Aburdene (1985), women are changing the workplace and demanding "a whole range of goods and service" in the places they work (p. 204). Admitting that women's wages continue to suffer in relationship to men's, Naisbitt and Aburdene also believe that women have been integral to changes such as flex-time, daycare, relocation policy, and parental leave, all of which entered the workplace recently.

For women, who traditionally have been assigned roles that involve major responsibility for helping others, the massive migration from home to the workplace presents conflicts in caring for family and career. Some change in corporate policy, organizational structure, and patterns of living and working may be occurring, but, by and large, women feel their talents, expertise, and knowledge (grounded in their experience of caring and their beliefs about what matters in life) are not recognized by the social institutions in which they work. Under the present corporate model, caring has a long way to go before it's contextually interwoven and patterned in a fashion that relieves women of the conflict of caring on both sides.

According to Janeway (1971), women's roles are changing and even some of the mythology surrounding these roles has shifted and been replaced. Janeway believes the role of women provides an excellent laboratory for examining change "because it has been the scene of such a struggle long enough for us to note effects and not simply beginnings" (p. 133). Thus, women's changing roles are seen as having called into question the entire responsibility for caring—not only caretaking and caregiving, but accountability for caring in our society.

The effects of such role changes in regard to caring have probably contributed to massive confusion and discontent between men and women. Unfortunately, in women's experience, some men just don't get it.

Men Who Don't Get It

Margaret finds that the roles in a two-person career continue to be assigned in advance, particularly with men of her generation. She wants to share the "mechanics of living together" and finds this to be "a real bone of contention" in relationships with men. Creating career equity in intimate relationships has been "extremely difficult" for Margaret, to the point where she has "just given up."

For Naisbitt and Aburdene (1985), women's work patterns have metamorphosed. Love of work and the necessity of working are on an upswing. The recent history of two-career couples has also brought about a significant change in women's work patterns. But as women take on careers, women raise questions about the new patterns of women's work and women's need for support in order to have successful careers.

With the exception of Gerda, who describes her husband as someone who always shared in housework, the women in this study, all married with children or divorced, describe taking on a career while continuing the major role of caring at home. Extending beyond what Margaret calls the "mechanics of living together," for married and divorced women the role of caring at home includes much more. For Francene, Maxine, and Elena, who are married with children and have full-time careers, caring at home also encompasses what Francene says is "90 percent of the responsibility for my daughter," or the caring that occurs with raising children. Each women described her husband as responsible for "many things," but, as Francene states, "He's definitely not like the mother."

Janeway (1975) comments about the social construction of society reflected in a two-person career. She describes the phenomenon Freud referred to as "anatomy is destiny" in her book, *Between Myth and Morning: Women Awakening*. Comparatively, and at least when this book was published, Janeway finds that for women not much as changed:

> *The trouble with this situation is not really in the idea of a two-person career. We live in a very complicated world, and there are undoubtedly many areas of work which cannot be handled well by one individual without support from others. The trouble is that when the two are of different sex, the roles in career are assigned in advance. The man is the lead figure, and the woman is the chief of staff, along with being, quite often, the chief cook and bottle washer too. There's nothing wrong with dividing the work, but why is it always divided this way? And how are we going to get rid of this pattern? (Janeway, 1975, pp. 136–137)*

When I asked Elena what caring was like for her, her first response was "basically doing everything for everybody." Later, in relating how she cares for her children and what she experiences as distinct from men's caring for children, she told me that, for her, there is more stress involved than for a man. She feels a tremendous moral responsibility for caring, especially for her daughter. She illustrated what she meant:

If I take a child to the park, caring is keeping constant watch over that child, trying to avoid any other activity because I'm there to take care of the child. For a man, caring may be bringing a paper, reading it, and occasionally lifting his eyes to notice where there are sounds [coming from the child].

Francene reveals other ways in which caring is important to women and perhaps less widespread among men. She told me she needs to share her feelings, problems, and sorrow with her husband. Wanting his support and emotional presence, she says, "This is not the first time a man in my life . . . they just don't seem to care." She talks about other situations of sorrow, when she experienced the same reaction from her father. Knowing how to react or what to do in order to be helpful is perplexing to Francene. "How come women always know what to do? Or at least in my experience they do. My mother, grandmother, or girlfriend will always know what's wrong or try to calm me down."

Consoling, listening to, and participating in women's feelings may be challenging for men. Francene comments, "Men seem almost scared of a woman who's crying." Questioning where a man's empathy is, Francene's experience informs her: "It just doesn't exist for men like it does for women."

This is not to say men don't care; on the contrary, these women know men care. However, for some of these women, men's expressions of caring do not necessarily meet their need for support. What these women have said about their experiences with men, coupled with their changing roles at work, has raised for them questions about caring. What really constitutes caring? Do women care too much or not enough?

Caring Too Much or Caring Enough?

Dorothy says she has to watch very carefully that she doesn't care too much, particularly as a grandmother; for that matter, she has to be careful as a mother as well. "You know, so that you don't care too much to the point of wanting to rule. It's easy to want your children to do things the way you've done them."

Dorothy comments on the difficulty of separating her needs from the caring she gives. Keenly aware of her own needs to give care, Dorothy says, "Sometimes you care too much or you go too far." In retrospect, she wonders about a "real good kind of caring," the kind that truly helps another person, but doesn't allow selfish needs to get in the way. Presently caring for her mother, Dorothy "puts the caring" on her level, because her mother needs support and assurance in order to feel comfortable about what she can do.

Elena, on the other hand, says she doesn't believe there's such a thing as caring too much, but does think that there is caring too little. For her, caring has no boundaries: "You can never care too much." Interestingly, Elena distinguishes caring by action:

> *It's the action that accompanies the caring that could be suffocating to somebody else. Personally, I would have to control myself and make sure I was very subjective and very objective about what I was going to do. But from a mental, internal, emotional, psychological perspective, there isn't such a thing as caring too much. Unfortunately, there is caring too little.*

For Elena, the intensity of caring or the notion of caring too much is a misconception. For her, caring is eternal and should transcend time and space. It is the *action* that gives the caring its truth and character, or what Elena refers to as caring that is either suffocating and paralyzing, or educating and liberating.

According to Mayeroff (1971), caring may be considered as a matter of degree (in the sense of more or less, better or worse) and within limits. Yet caring is also compatible with a certain amount of blundering and lapse of interest and sensitivity to the other's needs, which brings in questions beyond that of degree.

Francene spoke of her grandmother's death, and the sorrow she now feels about her priorities at that time of her life: "I cared too much about my stupid job, friends, and social life to drop everything and go. I was too late." Explaining that her grandmother had died before her arrival, she regrets the ambivalence she felt that delayed her ultimate decision to leave. Reflecting now on her grandmother's death, Francene believes she cared too much about herself.

With caring a matter of degree, limits, and more, when is it time for women to care for themselves? Although being responsive to personal needs does involve taking responsibility for personal decisions, obviously such is not enough—conflict remains: women's needs are in conflict with others' needs.

Whether women care too much or not enough, the question certainly speaks to the reciprocation of need in caring, the kind of need for support and emotional availability found with other adults, particularly mothers.

Mothers Who Drive Us Crazy

The phenomenon of mothering and caring offers interesting insights about women's experiences of being daughters. Caring is uniquely portrayed in mother–daughter relationships. Dissected in women's literature, portrayed in psychological doctrine, and speculated about in popular culture, this extremely significant relationship conjures up profound emotion for women when it comes to describing the paradoxical nature of caring. Mothers tend to "drive us crazy" at times with their caring (or lack of it), yet women realize as adult daughters a need for compassion and sensitivity from their mothers.

Gerda, for example, was hurt one day when her mother remarked that Gerda's son had grown up to be quite a wonderful young man after being such a "horrible little boy." Privately admitting to me that, at the time, she probably did think he was horrible, Gerda remarked: "To have your mother say something like

that . . . you don't say things like that, even when your children
are as old as I am."

Gerda cares about her mother's opinion even in her adult life.
While intellectually she understands her mother's limitations, "it
still kills you to think your mother thought your child was horrible." Gerda told me she felt she understood this child; certainly,
she knew how his interactions could be interpreted as "horrible."
She also recognized the intent of her mother to offer a compliment
about her son; nevertheless, her good intention, for Gerda, was experienced as hurt.

When Margaret's mother visits, Margaret recognizes her mother's needs and mediates them with her own. Reflecting on her
perception that she and her mother are quite independent women
who are accustomed to living alone, Margaret realizes this tends to
create some conflicts. Yet she enjoys her mother's visits and appreciates the things her mother does that express caring.

Margaret realizes that, in spending time with her mother, reciprocation in caring occurs through a process of negotiation. Margaret is willing to negotiate in caring, but does experience times
with her mother that drive her crazy. She told me: "My mother re-
organizes my kitchen. When I open the cupboard, I expect to find
what I put there, but it's not there. She's moved it to where it's
more convenient for her."

Mother drive us crazy or hurt us not only by the little things they
do but also by telling us fairy tales about caring we received as
children and by neglecting to tell us or avoiding the truth about
caring as adults.

Childhood Fairy Tales and Lies We Were Told

Margaret, for one, feels she was lied to. Only as an adult did she
learn that women's reality is inconsistent with what existed in the
cultural and social norms of her formative years. The images she
experienced, the role modeling she was directed toward, and the
childhood fairy tales she was told all contributed to her having to
learn that caring develops and matures.

Adult life soon informs women of the lies they were told. Margaret did not want to put a career on hold or submit to the priority

of hearth and home. Living happily ever after did not happen for her and her trying came at great personal cost and feelings of betrayal. She said that she and her female co-workers have come to grips with childhood fairy tales and out-and-out lies about what caring is like in a woman's life.

This awakening to the disparity between women's experience and the social construction of reality is not new in women's awareness. Feminist writers have written at length about this phenomenon in both the popular and academic literature. But when it happens personally, the myths about caring in contemporary society become painful.

Today, Margaret has become much more easygoing about these discrepancies, and she has learned to accept life as she experiences it. She remembers having high expectations that now are dashed, tempered by the inherently conflicting nature of her attempt to achieve a woman's ideal of caring.

Women's socialization into caring, or learning what to care for and about, comes home to roost in adulthood. For some women, the realization that regardless of the extent to which they may go they will find themselves alone and contextually grounded in competition, reveals to them an ethic that reflects a different understanding of what constitutes caring.

Women learn, sometimes painfully, to let go of the myths, fairy tales, and unfulfilled dreams that are inappropriate to the realities they face. When they give up on adolescent expectations and operate from a core of experience, they gain a crisp lens from which to view the effect childhood messages had on their adult expectations of caring.

Messages from the Past

Messages received during the formative years ranged from clear blatant forbidding to subtler forms of advice on what a woman needs to do for herself. Francene told me that her mother always told her "to get into a field where you can earn a living because you can't expect a man to support you." The value of making a life as a single person and being economically self-sufficient was the message that many of these women received. Without the message, a few deliberately made it on their own anyway. For others, the same outcome happened by circumstance.

Francene, who wanted to be a dancer, didn't have the courage to take the risk: "I was too worried about how my going off and doing this risky thing would affect the family and I was also very afraid of failing. I cared more about being successful at whatever I did than I cared about doing what I really wanted to do."

Early in her young adulthood, Francene realized that caring about being a success had prevented her from trying. She states now that if she hadn't cared about her family and about what is best for her daughter and husband, she might have gotten an interesting position overseas. However, her choice to have a family and her responsibility to them mediate her decisions: "I have to think about what's best for them."

Some young women, who dream similar dreams, may lack the support of family, friends, and prospective partners, which deters their courage and ultimately their choice, or the reinforcement necessary to follow through. This lack of support must be viewed within the concept of intention and the desire, on the part of loved ones, to be helpful. But is it caring?

Gabrielle relates being told by her mom and dad that she shouldn't have to have somebody take care of her. "As a woman functioning in the world, you have to be able to take care of yourself, support yourself, and be independent. While you have to have other people in your life, you need to be a unit of your own." Stating that she has developed relationships of caring with friends, she feels "claustrophobic about being taken care of." She much prefers to be giving rather than on the receiving end of caring.

Typifying the ambiguous nature of expectations placed on women, Gabrielle remembers wanting to enter a male-dominated profession, medicine, and was instead steered into a predominantly female profession by her parents. Because the chosen field was not her "cup of tea," she has since selected another.

Messages from the past seem at best paradoxical for women in their formative years: Be independent, competent, and self-sufficient, yet have people in your life to care for and about. Gabrielle offered another vivid example of what appears to be an all-too-frequent twofold message to women. She said, when relating how her parents guided her to be independent, "I think they wish I hadn't taken it quite so seriously," referring to the fact that she is single with a career and desires to remain so.

Childhood myths, fairy tales, and other messages received during women's formative years can create misconceptions about women's experience of caring. When women recognize these illusions, let go of dreams that have been shattered, or recognize their self-deception, usually they get mad and find meaning in anger as caring. By so doing, the truth about caring in the lives of women can be encountered. As Heilbrun (1988) stated, "When there is an end to fantasy, adventure for women will begin" (p. 130).

FINDING OUT WHAT MATTERS IN LIFE: TAKING THE RISK

If I were given just one wish
I know what it would be for.
I'd simply wish that I could have
A hundred wishes more!

Helen Green Ansley (p. 33)

Lessons of Empowering Self: Getting Angry and Making Hard Decisions

Anger opens doors for women when they recognize it as their own. Freeing oneself of the burdensome conflicts inherent to caring, women begin to understand more their genuine experiences and express a willingness to make public the realities of their caring. Like Francene, who stated that she cared too much about being successful and not enough about doing what she wanted to do, caring becomes authentically present to women sometime in their lives.

For Sophia, caring starts with herself. "Helping me to help myself" is the "adventure of life" in caring. Sophia now says it's an adventure and not work—it had already taken a lot of work in the past for her to care for and about herself. That she didn't used to care for herself does not prevent her now from making a caring commitment to herself every morning.

Anger in caring is described as directed toward self and others. Recognizing that they don't have to live with the cards they were dealt, some women begin to free themselves of their preconceived destiny of caring. Realizing that opportunities come and must be taken with risk and effect, contextual compliance is not as attractive as it once was. As women recognize this newfound freedom, particularly later in life, they reject earlier ideas about women's role responsibilities for caring. Ansley captures this newfound freedom when she writes:

> *As the cells in my body renew*
> *And my purpose in life I review*
> *I find, growing older,*
> *I'm now growing bolder*
> *And increasingly hard to subdue! (p. 79)*

Helping women to realize that they create the meaning of caring in their lives—and for that matter, in the world—some women become politically active while others direct their energy locally and in their own communities. As Dorothy questioned earlier: Is caring something you develop yourself and fulfill for yourself? When women awaken to their anger, the answer becomes *yes.* While admitting she doesn't like to express or encounter anger, Dorothy also says, "I don't think caring has to be pleasant. I know anger is a form of caring." When anger is expressed, it is an expression of caring.

Some women, such as these women who told me about their experiences of caring, don't wait too long to get angry or grow bolder. When women tell about their experience, it takes on sense of purpose. Telling about a woman's life of caring helps women discern meaning unencumbered by gender, socialization, and culture.

Living a Life: Finding Meaning in Caring

Far into the night, while the other creatures slept, Charlotte worked on her web. First she ripped out a few of the orb lines near the center. She left the radial lines alone, as they

were needed for support. As she worked, her eight legs were
a great help to her. So were her teeth. She loved to weave,
and she was an expert at it. (White, 1952, p. 67)

When Lillian was young, she didn't know what caring was
about. Now she feels fortunate in all her endeavors: her present
work, her former work, and her family. She says, "I've nurtured
and loved and cared for them as well as I could." Today, without
caring as she understands it, Lillian would not be able to live her
life the way she's living it. Lillian echoes the meaning and form of
caring that she has constructed in her life. She told me, "When
you do something that you want to do, and this is your work as
well as your life, it's beautiful."

Elizabeth describes it as "getting out of yourself, and this is not
to say that it's a self-sacrificing venture, or that you neglect yourself." It's a commitment in caring for something larger than the
embodiment of one's life. "Speaking as a woman," Elizabeth is
grateful for the opportunity to do what she does best: volunteer
work. This is work she chooses to do. She told me that many facets
of caring have evolved for her as she has devoted herself to what
she now believes is the purpose of her life. But the service of her
purpose, like that of Lillian and others, has none of the flavor of a
self-centered, egotistical, or self-sacrificing endeavor.

Caring extends beyond the description of Elizabeth's life and
glimmers in the reflective thoughts she offered at the end of our
interview:

I think a woman has to analyze herself before she becomes
a caring person. Women have to analyze their motives, the
true nature of caring, and not be blinded by martyrdom.
This isn't the way a woman's role should be handled in this
day and age. Of course, women want to care for someone
else and want to be cared for by someone, but a woman
needs to get to know herself first and not pattern her life be-
cause it says so . . . .

For Elizabeth, like Lillian, caring is thoughtfully reflected in the
embodiment of good people: "There are a lot of caring people out

there and not the ones necessarily who beat on their chests and shout, 'Look at me.'"

INCREDIBLY GOOD PEOPLE: THE BREAD OF GOD

In Spanish we have a saying, "She was the bread of God," an incredibly good person.

Francene

Discovering Friends: Who Are They?

Friends are other women, men, mothers, siblings, daughters, lovers, and husbands. They are the people who know how to express caring in ways that these women found enjoyable and helpful. When they are vulnerable, women discover who their friends truly are.

Gabrielle found out who could offer her the kind of caring she needed once she made the decision to take care of her mother. Offering a unique description of her experience, she told me that when she decided to move home, she was pressured by her friends, who thought her decision was inappropriate and even "abnormal" for her.

Gabrielle said of her relationship with her parents: "They were always there for me, and I wanted to reciprocate in caring by being there for them." She found this experience tough enough, but some of her friends made it tougher for her by continually telling her that her decisions were inappropriate. However, for Gabrielle, only this "friendly" pressure was inappropriate. What she needed instead was support.

Gabrielle remembers having to pull away from her friends, who continually suggested she was ruining her life: "It was tough, and we were making lots of decisions. The toughest decision we had to make was whether or not to withdraw the care that was keeping her [mother] alive. They [her friends] didn't seem to understand."

Gabrielle remained connected to people in her life who offered her "a great deal of support"; the others, she "had to shut out."

Besides her longtime man friend, she maintained a friendship with a colleague with whom she worked. "She seemed to understand why I was doing what I was doing," she said. "I think there are positive ways of caring, relationships where caring is healthy, pleasant, and reinforcing," like the relationship Gabrielle has with her man friend. "He cares about me and, in that sense, caring isn't tough at all."

For Gabrielle, caring for her mother and then her father in illness was difficult. Yet her *caring* for them was also very satisfying to her. In addition, she found out through the experience with her mother who her friends were; good friends have a reciprocal, mutual *caring for and about* you. As she puts it, this is "a real integral part of being a whole person."

The Importance of Good Friends

My friends are little lamps to me,
*   Their radiance warms and cheers my ways.*
And all my pathway dark and lone
*   Is brightened by their rays.*

I try to keep them bright by faith,
*   And never let them dim with doubt,*
For every time I lose a friend
*   A little lamp goes out.*

*   (Whittemore, 1956, p. 380)*

Elizabeth Whittemore captures here the meaning of good friends. Each woman I interviewed also spoke of this essence in her experience of caring with friends. What is important about good friends is, as Gerda said, that they "relate to you as an individual and the caring extends to you as a whole person." After we had scheduled our interview appointment to talk about her experience of caring, she told me, she had given much thought to the question I had posed to her.

"I was thinking about friends and what caring is like with them." According to Gerda, caring is a regard for the whole person, at least between good friends. She says she has friends she shares different interests with, people she works with, and others outside her career. Good friends have a way of making her feel special. She mentioned that just the other night she was talking with a friend about what her children are doing, and she realized, "It's really nice that we have this larger framework of caring about each other and about other parts of our lives, not just the sides we share in common."

Sophia says listening plays a huge part in relationships of caring with friends. Friends listen and are there for one another with their whole being. Because they focus on loving and not on judging, friends give valuable support.

Margaret describes her relationships with good friends this way: "When they call, it feels like time just slips away." Being distant but never forgetting describes the connection that exists in spite of years and miles. A good friend is an "incredible source of support, a reality check, and the origin of ideas and alternatives," someone whose judgment is sought and trusted.

Over time, an emotional closeness develops with lifelong friends. Natalie talked of lifelong friends with whom she continues to enjoy a consistency of "showing each other that we are really concerned and care about one another." She told me these friendships started in college, years ago, and that over time these people have *always* been there for one another. Natalie feels lucky in having relationships with friends, particularly women friends, in many different spheres of her life.

Women Friends

"It's probably a universal phenomenon that you feel closer to some friends than to family." For Gerda, friendships with women have meant closely sharing some of life's events as adults. In fact, she feels much closer to some of her friends than she does to her original nuclear family.

The intensity that comes from experiencing together the ups and downs of life marks the nature of these deeply moving and profoundly affecting friendships as a source of caring for women. Comparable values contribute to having a similar sense of humor, and reveling in one another's accomplishments characterizes women's sharing as friends. Margaret, who refers to her women friends as "soulmates," suggests: "Our language is underdeveloped in this area, and overdeveloped in areas reflecting purely cognitive experiences." Margaret enjoys the emotional connection she feels with friends.

Lillian relates how she and her wonderful woman friend share "lovely words" and things they find on their travels or in books they read. Then, as she told me, they will have discussions about it. Although Lillian sees this friend every week, she receives cards from her "with the most beautiful thoughts about how she feels about our friendship." Lillian's friend sends cards more than Lillian does, but Lillian reciprocates by taking plants over to her friend, who has "a beautiful garden."

Women's capacity and desire for friendships are not limited to other women. Women seem to be able to create and maintain deeply loving relationships with men and with gay men.

Gay Men Friends and Men Friends

My friendships with men have always been good and I've seemed to have more men friends than women, but somehow getting to be friends with a heterosexual man is hard. Not so with gay men because there's not that sexual tension.

Gabrielle usually finds that friendships with straight men evolve toward other types of intimacies. With gay men, there is a very "unusual type of caring" that is satisfying and enjoyable, possibly because there isn't anything sexual attached to it.

Because the sexual tension that women describe in heterosexual friendships was absent, Gabrielle found a sense of comfort with gay men that she didn't feel with straight men. "With gay men I didn't have to worry." There was a felt freedom to be oneself as an individual and less tension to adhere to social expectations of pairing.

Margaret also speaks of the "male–female tension" in friendships with straight men. Describing heterosexual friendships, Margaret claims that they always have the potential to develop sexually. When this happens, she says, conflicts in caring may begin.

What Gabrielle enjoyed most with gay men friends was sharing the activities they had in common, "having a male best friend."

The friendships and the caring that I have had with gay men are very different from anything else I've experienced. The relationship is extremely positive."

Admitting that the caring in these friendships is distinct from friendships with women—less tension, less concern about being judged, liked, or accepted—Gabrielle found that most people were suspicious of her when they learned of these friendships. Unfortunately, this happens; but Gabrielle finds unconditional acceptance and real affection in her friendships with gay men. There are "no conditions on the caring and no preconceived notions."

Colleagues

With colleagues at work and with professional contacts, caring occurs for women. Natalie told me she makes time to go to lunch and takes breaks together with her colleagues. Frequently sharing ideas and collaborating on projects, Natalie finds ways to express caring with the people she considers her colleagues.

Some collegial relationships were considered friendships, usually when caring existed as affect and expression of concern. Caring exists in collegial relationships even when friendship is not the basis. Friendships, on the other hand, are characterized by the experience of caring as liberating. Friendships with colleagues, as Gerda described, extend beyond the immediate personal or professional interest or stake that colleagues have in common.

Husbands and Partners

Affirming each other and treating each other's feelings and needs seriously and with sensitivity are the characteristics of caring in women's marriages to men whom they experience as caring. Because her partner takes her "as who I am, no pretense, no female image, and no barriers of having to be the sweet, competent wife," Gerda feels free to be who she is.

Gerda describes the man she married as "generous with his time," a wonderful listener who possesses a sensitivity to her needs, and a companion both intellectually and emotionally. She told me that he's always "doing things for me that need to be done" or "picking up on stuff that needs to be done." Gerda says that the housework is an "equal split."

In this light, Peck (1978) believes: "Marriage as a truly cooperative institution requires great mutual contribution and care, time, and energy." Existing for the primary purpose of nurturing each of the participants for their individual journey toward spiritual growth, Peck states that both male and female "must tend the hearth and both must venture forth" (p. 167). Gibran's poetry is a fitting summary:

But let there be spaces in your togetherness,
And let the winds of the heavens dance between you.

Love one another, but make not a bond of love:
Let it rather be a moving sea between the shores
  of your souls.
Fill each other's cup but drink not from one cup.
Give one another of your bread but eat not from the
  same loaf.

Sing and dance together and be joyous, but let
  each one of you be alone,
Even as the strings of a lute are alone though they
  quiver with the same music.

Give your hearts, but not into each other's keeping.
For only the hand of Life can contain your hearts.
And stand together yet not too near together:
For the pillars of the temple stand apart,
And the oak tree and the cypress grow not in
  each other's shadow.

                                    (Gibran, 1951, pp. 15-16)

EMPOWERING CARING IN OUR LIVES: A MISSION

At the core of any new awakening is a jarring disjunction
between prevailing cultural norms and images and the daily

experience of large numbers of people. (Skolnick, 1991, p. 98)

Ownership–Leadership–Partnership

Sylvia clearly experiences caring in her life as matching Skolnick's depiction of America in transition. Sylvia is concerned about the lack of caring she perceives in American culture:

This is the interest that I have when I read that you are interviewing people for this type of research because this is what is lacking in most of the homes where I work. In the workplace, factories, corporations—a lack of caring. This is very necessary to improve the quality of the human being, the quality of the relationship—not only at home, but in the school and also in the community, in our society.

Based on women's experience of context and as a socially constructed phenomenon, we wonder about a lack of caring in our culture.

Skolnick (1991) reports that "cultural strain shows up first as trouble in the family." As the generation gaps grows wider, the confusion for parents who must guide their children becomes evident. Children rebel; husbands and wives quarrel; schools, churches, and social institutions provide conflicting guidelines; and the courts continue to punish mainstream behavior (pp. 98-99).

Sylvia said that when she owns what she cares for and about, she creates time to express caring for it. Francene told me that when she's the only one who cares for and about something, if she doesn't take the time to express caring, it doesn't get done. Both women here raise the questions of ownership (Who cares?) and leadership (Who is going to do it?). Sylvia and Francene state that, without ownership and leadership, partnerships or the ground for shared caring won't occur. Without communal caring, people don't get moving and feelings of being frustrated and burdened are the result.

Ownership of problems in Sylvia's life brings ownership of solutions. Placing blame, diverting attention, expressing massive denial, and other prevalent activities experienced contextually, highlight for Sylvia a misplaced sense of caring. Taking responsibility means owning the situation, and hope for "improving caring" illustrates what these women describe as the risk in caring. Sylvia says, "Take that risk and invite others to take it with you." Leadership is in the risk taking, and partnership is in the sharing of the ownership, risk, and change.

Skolnick (1991) describes "the next stage" of social transformation as the "private stresses that become public issues." Writing about America in transition, Skolnick attributes the 1960s as having irrevocably recast the "political landscape and transformed culture and private life" (p. 100). The social role of women and the relationships between women and men are where the origins of upheavals and change are found.

Sylvia vividly pointed this out to me in her experience within organizational systems and society. She said that caring does not exist on a massive scale in the greater context of her life, and she asks, Why not? Partnership, based in the freedom to choose what and how we want to care for and about each other, lies at the fundamental basis of community. Implicit to free partnership are choice and cooperation in caring.

When it came to translating caring to the larger social context, these women expressed their wishes for change in the future. They described how they were busy infusing caring contextually where they experienced it was needed.

A new pattern is emerging, according to leading scientists of our time. At the heart of a holistic approach, in science and in women's experience, are the notions of ownership, leadership, and partnership in caring.

Eisler (1987) points out that this theme underpins the future of science, referring to the examination of interconnectedness in science today. Eisler cites Jean Baker Miller (1976), who refers to interconnectedness as affiliation and what Jessie Bernard calls the "female ethos of love/duty." This new science, of which "chaos" theory and feminist scholarship are integral parts, focuses more on relationships than on hierarchies (Eisler, pp. 190–191). Perhaps caring will receive the attention that it so desperately needs.

CONCLUSION

Caring, for women, is multidimensional at best. Women's relationships to themselves, others, and their world are certainly characterized by caring. But the nature of the caring that these women describe in their lives suggests caring is an epistemological and moral matter for them. Moreover, the subtlety and variety of their narratives highlight the possibility that caring as ontology could very well be specifically gender-based ontology.

In the experience of these women, the social construction of caring and women's role to care, are clearly explicated. The value of women's caring seems to be a mixed bag. On the one hand, there exists widespread acceptance of caring to promote human growth and development. On the other hand, when translating caring into society, our institutions and ultimately the people making decisions lack the knowledge, the skill, and perhaps the desire needed to incorporate these constructs of caring. According to the women who have spoken here, there appears to be total disregard for their experience and for the values of caring in the roles they and women in general play in society.

Herein lie the seeds for conflicts in women's lives and for the risks that come with choices women make about the who, what, and when of caring. These conflicts and risks illustrate the array of choices women make in the course of a lifetime; they reflect how caring orders their lives. Sensitivity to the diverse and different choices these women have made is crucial to understanding their experience of caring. To this extent, the singularity of women's experience fades. What remain universal in every woman's description of caring are the conflict of caring and the risk in caring.

The gender of the experiencer shapes and constitutes the experience. We find between women and their friends the rich and diverse relationships from which women derive immense joy. Spelling out the features of good friendships, these women maintain continuity in caring throughout their lifetime.

Women's reflective stance and their wisdom about the past, present, and future of caring have generated for them a need to empower caring. Experience is always contextual, mediated by the location of the experiencer within a particular time, place, culture, and environment. Responsible reflection on experience assists in the development of and the shaping and reshaping of knowledge. Indeed, empowering caring in society is one essential theme that the women interviewed wove responsibly into their narratives. Vividly telling of the affective, cognitive, and moral experiences manifest in women's caring, these women know that both women and men must own, lead, and develop partnerships of caring that reflect changing roles, shifting responsibility, and collective accountability for constructing a culture where caring is empowered.

Women and Caring: What Can Be Learned?

Many of the women here described their experiences of caring in a way that emphasized what they learned throughout their lives. I have deliberately included this narrative and dialogue in the expression of themes because it is helpful to the reader. The knowledge generated from these women stands a good chance of retaining contact with women's experience. A supplementary consideration of what we can learn from these women, however, offers a useful complement to their narratives.

Many of the women shared information that exists in the literature about the effect of caring as support, comfort, and emotional connectedness to their sense of well-being. During the interview, Margaret, for example, shared her knowledge about the scientific literature bearing out the healing and therapeutic effects of women who receive support from other women. Breast cancer support groups seem to demonstrate this claim in particular, she said, confirming that women live longer or have extended periods of remission when they feel connected to a group of women who understand their experience.

The research Margaret cited is one example of the new literature and theories in nursing and in other disciplines that are concerned with caring and its relationship to well-being. Researchers are beginning to recognize and describe a link between caring and psychoimmunology. The benefits and outcomes of caring in terms of self-healing, remission, and prevention of illness and disease already exist in science.

My own research supports the connection of caring in nursing with patients' experiences of well-being. When nurses created deeply caring relationships with patients, patients experienced these nurses as truly helping them in ways that extend beyond what they imagined, a kind of help they described as liberating. Interestingly, patients who experienced caring with nurses believed these nurses offered the kind of help that extended beyond being just well-intentioned. Patients considered these relationships with nurses critically important and described them as friendships (Appleton, 1991, 1993).

Caring has been the focus of many philosophical ponderings. Perhaps caring in science will generate knowledge that will corroborate what philosophers have written about it for centuries. The emergence of women's experience only contributes to this shift in the focus of science. Caring's legitimate value to health, well-being, and survival not only is embraced in the public arena but is entering the forefront of knowledge development today.

As women, we have a critical responsibility at this point in history to tell our stories and to share them with one another, our children, our partners, and our co-workers, translating what we know into the social context of our times. We may find that the truth lies in theologian Van Bulow's last words, "Caring is the greatest thing in the world. Caring is all that matters."

APPENDIX

ABOUT THE STUDY

Phenomenological Inquiry and Method

In this study, I used the methodological structure of human science research, as explicated by van Manen (1990), to understand what caring is like for women. Van Manen asserts that hermeneutic phenomenological research is a dynamic interplay among six research activities:

1. Turning to a phenomenon of serious interest and commitment.

2. Investigating the phenomenon as it is lived, rather than as it is theorized or conceptualized.
3. Reflecting on the essential themes that characterize the phenomenon.
4. Writing and rewriting to describe the phenomenon as it is present in the lived experience.
5. Sustaining a pedagogical relation to the phenomenon.
6. Balancing the research context by considering parts and whole.

As methodology, phenomenology aims at the nature of the meaning of everyday experience. Consequently, phenomenological inquiry seeks a deeper understanding of a particular phenomenon by researching lived experience.

The phenomenon of this study is central to how women experience their lives. Personally as a woman and professionally as a nurse, caring has always been pivotal to my experience. As a researcher, I explored the meaning of the art of nursing and discovered that caring emerged as integral to the practice of nursing when it is art (Appleton, 1991, 1993). When I researched the experience of caring in nursing education, I found that the experience of caring for and about students on the part of the faculty is central to student competence and intellectual development (Appleton, 1990). Consequently, my commitment to know what caring is like for women comes from and is grounded in this personal-professional context.

In publicizing this study, I printed announcements and informed people by word of mouth. Twelve women responded and consented to participate in tape-recorded interviews. I asked each participant; What is caring like in your experience as a woman? The interviews lasted approximately 90–120 minutes and the tapes were transcribed into text.

Through reading and rereading the texts, and reflecting on these women's descriptions of caring, I analyzed and began to explicate what constitutes the nature of caring in women's experience. Thinking deeply about the individual and collective narrative descriptions given by all of these women assisted me to know essential, emerging themes; the work of helping; caring on both sides:

living the conflict; finding out what matters in life: taking the risk; incredibly good people: the bread of God; and empowering caring in our lives: a mission.

The chapter was organized thematically around the essentially themes of the phenomenon after initially interpreting the nature of the phenomenon. Context was provided by writing existential description or weaving the phenomenological description with existential themes of temporality, spatiality, corporeality, and communality.

"Bringing to speech" women's experience of caring occurred through writing and rewriting (van Manen, 1990, p. 32). By maintaining an orientation to the research question, I engaged in what van Manen (1984) refers to as a "dialectical going back and forth" among the levels of questioning (p. 68). This activity sensitizes the researcher to the language. In an effort to preserve the language of these women, I varied the examples throughout the chapter. In addition, I provided a transcendental form to women's experience of caring by offering literary expression of the phenomenon.

The study of human experience—what it means or the nature of experience as it is lived—is the concern of the phenomenologist, who as a researcher investigates experience as it is rather than as it is conceptualized. Van Manen (1990) suggests the following questions be asked of the entire phenomenological research study: "Is the study properly grounded in a laying open of the question? Are the current forms of knowledge examined for what they may contribute to the question? Are the current forms of knowledge examined for what they may contribute to the question? Has it been shown how some of these knowledge forms (theories, concepts) are glosses that overlay our understanding of the phenomenon?" (p. 34). I'll let you be the judge.

REFERENCES

Ansley, H. G. *Life's finishing school: What now?* Conscious Living/Conscious Dying: A Project of the Institute of Noetic Sciences.

Appleton, C. (1990). The meaning of human care and the experience of caring in a university school of nursing. In M. Leininger and M. J.

Watson (Ed.'s). *The caring imperative in education* (77–94). New York: National League for Nursing.

Appleton, C. (1991). The gift of self: The meaning of the art of nursing. *Dissertation Abstracts International, 52-12B*, No. 9215314.

Appleton, C. (1993). The art of nursing: The experience of patients and nurses. *Journal of Advanced Nursing, 18*(6), 892–899.

Dickinson, E. (1877). They may not need me—yet they might. In T. H. Johnson (Ed.), *The complete poems of Emily Dickinson* (p. 597). Boston: Little, Brown, 1960.

Eisler, R. (1987). *The chalice & the blade: Our history, our future.* San Francisco: Harper & Row.

Gibran, K. (1951). *The prophet.* New York: Knopf.

Heilbrun, C. G. (1988). *Writing a woman's life.* New York: Ballantine Books.

Janeway, E. (1971). *Man's world, woman's place: A study in social mythology.* New York: Dell.

Janeway, E. (1975). *Between myth and morning: Women awakening.* New York: Morrow.

Mayeroff, M. (1971). *On caring.* New York: Harper & Row.

Miller, J. B. (1976). *Toward a new psychology of women.* Boston: Beacon.

Naisbitt, J., & Aburdene, P. (1985). *Re-inventing the corporation: Transforming your job and your company for the new information society.* New York: Warner Books.

Peck, M. S. (1978). *The road less traveled: A new psychology of love, traditional values and spiritual growth.* New York: Simon & Schuster.

Skolnick, A. (1991). *Embattled paradise: The American family in an age of uncertainty.* New York: Basic Books.

Weedon, C. (1987). *Feminist practice & poststructuralist theory.* New York: Basil Blackwell.

White, E. B. (1952). *Charlotte's web.* New York: Harper & Row.

Whittemore, E. (1956). My friends are little lamps to me. In A. L. Alexander (Ed.), *Poems that touch the heart* (p. 380). New York: Doubleday.

van Manen, M. (1984). Practicing phenomenological writing. *Phenomeonology and Pedagogy, 5*(3), 230–241.

van Manen, M. (1990). *Researching lived experience: Human science for an action sensitive pedagogy.* New York: State University of New York Press.

Wedgefarth, D. W. (1956). In A. L. Alexander (Ed.), *Poems that touch the heart* (p. 49). New York: Doubleday.

ABOUT THE AUTHOR

I am the Interim Graduate Program Director at Florida Atlantic University. Since joining the faculty in 1981, I am one of the pioneering members of College of Nursing and integrally involved in the development of a curriculum that emphasizes the significant influence that nurses have when practicing nursing from a perspective of it as an art.

The majority of my research is an exploration of nursing as it is practiced and taught. My phenomenological research on the art of nursing explicated what constitutes nursing as art. The major implication of this work is that when nursing is an art it gives caring a new meaning of liberating help. The art of nursing goes beyond the notion of aesthetic practice. I regard the essence of the art of nursing as an ontology, epistemology, axiology and praxis gestalt. My research offers a paradigm for originating nursing.

Currently, I live in Delray Beach, Florida with my husband Bud Siddall. I grew up in Delanco, a small town situated in southern New Jersey and went on to receive my bachelor's degree in nursing from Trenton State College. My master's degree in nursing was from the University of California, Los Angeles and my doctorate from the University of Colorado Health Sciences Center.

In addition to my research and teaching at the university, I have broad based practice experiences in nursing. I am licensed as an advanced nurse practitioner and certified by the ANCC as a Clinical Nurse Specialist.

2

Power for Midlife Women: Written on the Breeze

Carolyn L. Brown

*In research, as in conversation, we meet ourselves . . . the
process of knowing involves a process of forming and transforming, and in knowing our world, we also form and
transform ourselves. (Morgan, 1983, p. 405)*

And so it is with my research. I research the things in my life that
I am trying to understand. I live in the land of my middle years—
somewhere in the center of my life's space, time, and being. I live
it in the middle of a world peopled by friends, family, co-workers
and many others; in the middle of a world that perplexes me. As I
experience my life, I stand apart from it yet squarely in it. I try to
capture its meaning—to understand it. For me, this means studying and coming to know power as a woman, in all its many dimensions. Power is the energizing life process that impels us all.

This journey of coming to know processes of power started in my own struggles and dissatisfactions with who I was as I tried to satisfy my soul's search for something I felt I did not have—something intangible that distressed me, something felt in subtle ways through my relationships with others. I am one person fragmented into many persons—wife, mother, nurse, teacher, student, researcher, woman—yet held together by the energic center that is me—a person in process, shaping and being shaped by the events and circumstances surrounding and permeating my life. In many ways, my life mirrors the stories of a host of other women who come to the middle of their lives and take stock of where they are, whether they are going anywhere, or whether there is anywhere to go. We are ordinary women living everyday lives that are a lush fertile ground for learning about the meanings we share. We are not top-level executives or celebrities; we are women living in resplendent ordinariness.

As I began to write this chapter, I was flying at 40,000 feet above the earth, looking down on an east coast area teeming with myriad groupings of houses and squared-off roads. I was suddenly struck by the speck in the universe that is *me,* trying to find and understand what shapes my life. Through relationships, I experience empowering or overpowering of self and other; my becoming is shaped by unfolding relationships. In my middle years (at least I hope they are middle), I find myself taking stock, as do most of us in the middle of any journey. We look at a map, trying to figure out where we have been, where we are, and where we are going. My circle of knowing starts with myself, reaches out to encompass the experiences of others, and comes back to myself. This chapter, then, is a composite of the stories of women channeled through my self. Please hear them, and join in the widening circle of our coming to know our experiences of power as women in the middle of our everyday lives.

DISCLAIMING OUR POWER

As women began to talk about their power, a comment like this was common: "I don't know why you asked me to talk about my power. I don't perceive myself as having power. When you asked me that, I wasn't sure you were asking the right person." Next came a suggestion about a person who might be a better choice, usually a person superior to the interviewee in a hierarchical work structure. For example, one response was: "You should talk to my principal . . . . She is really a very powerful person." Yet, as their stories unfolded, the women told stories of their power and related that they had come to know and understand their power more fully, a side benefit of participating in a phenomenological study. For these women, power was equated with power over someone or something. The women saw having potential power over another as negative, something to be avoided. I found myself wondering whether perceiving oneself as not powerful—and, in many cases, being in a position where someone else was wielding power over them—breeds a fear of the dominant side of such a power relationship. Having seen power played out in a negative way, women may be concerned about how they might use or misuse the immense potential in power over another. Power, as commonly defined in this culture, is *a big deal,* an enormous responsibility. It's *big* and it isn't seen as an everyday part of life. It's something "out there," not part of the self. Women, at the beginning of the interviews, disclaimed their power as something they did not have or desire, or something they should not have or desire because it's dangerous. With that sort of image, is it any wonder that women disclaimed their power?

MISSED OPPORTUNITIES

Women talked about how their lives were shaped as they were growing up, how their lives have changed, and the impact of the meaning of the context of their younger years on power in their everyday lives. Often, they spoke of diminished or missed opportunity, of shifting their goals and desires to fit societal stereotypes of what a woman's life should be. For example, Kathleen recalled, "Women of our generation were not socialized into being professionals, working and all that." She recounted that, of her college graduating class of 40 women, only three were not married within one year of graduation. College was something you did while you were in the process of selecting a mate; generally, you chose a profession to be an interim thing, before you quit work to settle down to the real women's work of marriage and children. The mores of the 1950s and 1960s included a back-to-the-hearth role for women; the role was expected of women who are now in their middle years. Reflecting on this time period, when the ideal role for a woman was super wife and mother, Kathleen said, "I was never going back to work and what was important was handicrafts, children, recipes, and volunteer organizations. We were mobile, we had money (our husbands') and time, so we could afford to go out and volunteer."

Stories about what it means to have limited opportunity originated from even younger years. Girls were cast into traditional roles for women—roles that subserved their own selves and subverted what they might become. For example, Lori chose to become a secretary:

I went through all the things that girls did. I went through nurse, and secretary, and teacher . . . [then wistfully, with a deprecating giggle] and astronaut. That was odd. Everybody just looked . . . odd. Yeah, [reflectively] I always wanted to be a secretary. If you wanted to have anything to do with space, you'd have to be really good with math, and I wasn't. So that kind of limited me.

This story reminded me of a time when I was asking the high school guidance counselor about dropping a physics course. I had not yet learned that knowledge comes with time, and understanding comes a little at a time. I was frustrated because I did not understand physics. I was doing well memorizing, but I was not understanding. The guidance counselor thought about it for a while and then predicted, "You are going to get married and have children and be a homemaker, so why would you need physics?" She signed me out of the course. When I took the pink slip to the teacher, he begged me to stay, promising that understanding would come. He informed me that I was his best student, doing better than anyone in the class. I left. Working that hour as a hall monitor, I read great novels to while away the time. Because that moment was a turning point in my life, I recall the story in vivid detail. I was assisted to diminish my own potential by well-meaning people who ascribed to the limited, societally and culturally defined role prescriptions of the times. My power was beginning to be constricted. I was not asked what my dreams were, but rather was assisted in finding ways to be happy with less than I dreamed of being. There was no effort to assist me to find a way to reach my dreams. Instead, I was encouraged to settle for less, and I participated willingly in choosing the easier path, which fitted into dominantly defined social prescriptions.

A story of diminished opportunity repeats in the lives of many women in their middle years. In an earlier study (Brown, 1987), several nurse executives told of dreams to become other than what they chose; they became nurses because their choices were limited to housewife, teacher, secretary, or nurse. They understood their choices as limited, and they chose nursing because it was practical and gave them job security. In effect, they had limited their power to choose with joy. That nursing as a profession would become richly fulfilling speaks well of themselves and nursing. Nonetheless, for them, nursing as a profession for women was diminished by societal definition. They chose to settle for a profession that, because it was defined as feminine, was seen as "less than." Thus, they harbor a question about what might have been and it surfaces through reflection on their power at midlife. For example, Lori related:

> *I did want to go to college, but I got the letter back and they said, you need to improve your math. That has been a nuisance for me. Math. I'd still like to understand algebra but I don't. [Reflecting on her life's work as a secretary] I really like the people part of it. And I like the telephone. And I love typing. It's been good.*

Within this statement is contentment with the choice made, but the choice was a settling for something less than what might have been. There lingers an undertone of regret for missed opportunity, for power lost. Power does not develop only through an act of will, but rather from daily choices shaped by the circumstances of everyday life. Gilligan (1982) states, "[W]e begin to notice how accustomed we have become to seeing life through men's eyes" (p. 6). Our society is still largely shaped by masculine values. The fullness of power develops from an array of choices unhampered by ascribed, contrived, undisclosed limitations. Somehow we, as individuals, take total responsibility for our choices and definitions even though much of the definition of roles for women is preordained by unconscious acceptance of societal meaning for women's lives and work. When women settle for less than, there is always regret and embarrassment for having chosen less than one's full potential. Society and individuals both define traditional women's roles as less than. Deprecation of role and person appears in such questions as: "Oh, are you just a secretary? [or just a nurse, just a teacher, just a woman?]" It echoes in the statements of women themselves: "I'm just a housewife [or just a nurse, just a teacher]." The definition remains diminished unless the person realizes that the self is always enough, and that societal valuing of role does not fulfill identity. The need to fit into roles and identities imposed by others limits the potential power of the person fitting in. In this sense, women are called to fulfill "a lesser life" (Hewlett, 1986). Ironically, the power potential for the dominant other is also limited because the partner in the relationship is less than he/she might be.

For women, however, development of their full self by coming to understand and live out the meaning of their lives within the limitations of imposed constraints increases their power in relationships and situations in ways perhaps less understood. Frankl (1984), a survivor of holocaust concentration camps, testifies to this ability. He found that people construct meaningful lives despite overwhelming assaults on their lives and personhood. He discusses three ways of arriving at meaning in life:

> *The first is by creating a work or by doing a deed. The second is by experiencing something or encountering someone . . . . Most important, however, is the third avenue to meaning in life: Even the helpless victim of a hopeless situation, facing a fate he cannot change, may rise above himself, and by so doing change himself. He may turn a personal tragedy into a triumph. (pp. 146-147)*

Although women's experiences of diminished opportunity are less dramatic than the concentration camp experiences related by Frankl, they are not less influential on how women construct their lives. They may be more insidiously dangerous to full development of selfhood: because they are so well-ingrained in society's fiber, neither men nor women are consciously aware of them. Women may experience only a vague discontent or unhappiness, an indeterminate energy drain. They sense a lessening of self, an indistinct feeling of discontent, but may not be able to voice these internal realities with any clarity.

The insidious nature of societal prescriptions is clearly stated in two recent books. Tavris (1992) speaks of women and men silently accommodating to gender-specific societal and cultural norms:

The prevalent inclination to regard masculinity and femininity as permanent personality traits has overshadowed the importance of the context in which men and women live . . . . By seeing the worlds of men and women as cultures that can be as different as Norwegian and Brazilian, we can identify the elements of those worlds that perpetuate or eliminate differences. These cultures, however, are not merely different and equal: they are vastly unequal in power, resources, and status. (pp. 293, 295)

Agonito (1993) talks about her recent book:

This book attempts to reach especially those women in the work force who are struggling day after day with assaults on their dignity, with barriers recognized and unrecognized, with burdens of children and work, with bread-and-butter issues, with survival itself . . . . The immediate problem, as I see it, lies in our inadvertent cooperation in our own oppression . . . . I hear story after story of passive nonresponses by women . . . . (p. 11)

Women in their middle years most often acquiesced to the tacit cultural expectations of their young adult years. Perhaps transcending the reality of what is given by societal cultural norms in their lives becomes a part of what women do as they live lives begun by settling for something less than. They rise above the limiting societal definition, finding value and meaning in the lives they have lived to date; they empower themselves, freeing energy for fuller engagement with life as they live out the second half of their existence.

POWER OVER

Power over something or someone—this, to most of us, is power. With power over, one has the prerogative to control something or someone, or other persons. Exerting power over, or overpowering, is characterized by asserting one's will over another against the will or desire of the other. In the present study, women spoke of the idea of power over as control of *others*. For example, in relation to children, Beth noted that, when children were young, they were under parental control.

> *When the children are younger you feel more powerful. At least you feel like you're more in control. You tell them what to do, you put them in the bed and they're going to be there until you take them out. The older they get, the less control you have over them—the less you can limit what they are doing.*

As their children moved into adolescence, the women's power over them diminished. Several women mentioned their frustration and feelings of powerlessness at their inability to influence their adolescent children. The heart of the matter—losing control over their children.

Power over also existed in the workplace, primarily as power over subordinates by someone in the hierarchical structure. Hierarchy is implied in the notion of power over. In order to have power over, one must be "more than," for example, stronger, smarter, earning more money, or having control over someone else by virtue of position or policy.

In their marital relationships, the women described their husbands as exerting power over them; in general, the women allowed it. Power over wives was expressed by men who controlled major decisions concerning money and the like. Those women who experienced being controlled by their husbands felt angry and diminished in the relationship unless they willingly allowed the husband to take charge. Is there a contradiction here? Not at all. The idea of power over involves consent. When a woman passively allows another to take charge but is silently unwilling, the woman experiences anger and a diminished sense of self. When a woman willingly gives over a task to her spouse or has a voice in making the decision and is secure within herself about the decision, then the resulting situation is not experienced as overpowering—the decision is mutual, respectful, and advantageous to both parties. For example, one woman stated:

Part of it is knowing what does and doesn't take your power away. My husband handles the checkbook. He's an accountant. To me, I don't feel any less powerful because he handles the checkbook. He's great with a checkbook . . . . Or, if someone wants to open a door for me, why not? Fine. For me, that isn't taking my power away.

Similar scenarios were played out in relationships with others—children, co-workers, persons in nonresponsive systems—and in the inescapable processes of aging. What differed was how the situations were defined and what was allowed to develop by the persons in the powering relationship.

Let us return to the children for a moment. With some entering adolescence and others beginning to move out of their parents' homes, several of the women I spoke with described a feeling of loss, a loss of control over them. This loss affected them in different ways. For some, it was difficult to let go of their preconceived notions of what it meant to be a parent, their image of what and who their child would become. Several women also told of disagreeing with their husbands over childrearing guidelines. The tension created by this disagreement worked to dilute their sense of power. Marital and child relationships took on conflictoral characteristics. Beth related:

With my husband it's a shared situation. When we have a disagreement and he comes back to apologize, it makes me feel more powerful. I really won that one . . . . Then there are times that I say things over and over again to him and nothing happens and I'm still not heard. One of our major problems is we both try to exert power as it concerns childrearing. It's an ongoing battle. It comes up almost weekly where one person feels like they have all the power and the other person doesn't. Where we disagree and he says "no" and nothing happens, it goes his way, that really bothers me.

Here, competition and hierarchical domination prevailed and anger and sadness grew, especially in full awareness of the situation. Lori talked of a friend whose marital situation had stayed pretty much the same over time. The husband was dominant and the woman did not seem to mind. The woman seemed unaware that anything was amiss.

I have a friend who did not go back to work. Her husband is still dominant. He is insistent on having his way. I would wonder, and ask myself, "Why is she taking that?" I'm above that now. And I see it. But it doesn't mean she is any unhappier than I am.

We talked further, likening the woman to a caged rabbit. If the rabbit has never known a different environment, it comes to accept the cage as its natural habitat and does not envision a life of freedom. A different way of being, where it would need to use its own power to seek food and shelter and to protect itself, would never enter the rabbit's consciousness. For a woman who had moved into a dependent marital relationship from a sheltered dependent childhood, there would be no conscious knowledge of anything different. Even "acceptance" is not the right word to describe her way of being in the relationship, because acceptance implies knowing the situation is less than it could be. When the dependent way of being simply *is* and is not questioned, anger may not be experienced. Lori's friend may feel as happy and content as Lori. In fact, Lori may experience more discontent because she is aware of the many possibilities in the situation.

POWER AND LIFE PARTNERS

Midlife provides an opportunity for women to reflect on the nature of power in relationships with life partners. Beth commented, "You trade parents for a husband to tell you what to do." When the nature of their partnership relationships changed over time, several women described experiencing upheaval and realignment of the nature of the relationship. These women no longer wanted to be told what to do; they wanted an equal voice in decisions and in the relationship. Karen reminisced:

As a high school student I went into nursing because I wanted a skill where I could support myself, and never have to depend on someone else. And I didn't come from a family where that was even an issue. I just wanted to be able to take care of myself.

For Karen, taking care of herself involved making decisions about her life, or at least having an equal voice in the marital partnership.

Several women spoke of going back to work primarily because they were bored in traditional homemaker roles. The secondary gain here was freedom in having a legitimate voice concerning money and how it was spent. None wanted to go back to a dependent role. Karen, who changed careers and, for a period of time, was economically dependent on her spouse, remembered her reactions:

I didn't like it when I worked part-time and had to ask for money. I don't like asking for money from my husband. I didn't ask when I worked full-time. We shared the bills and whatever money was left was yours. I went back to working

*full-time and that's the only way I like it. That's a measure
of power and control too, being able to make it on your
own. We [women] probably ought to feel good about that.
Right?*

There *is* freedom in being able to contribute economically. Jean
described what she liked:

*[T]he power of a full-time job. It gives an equality kind of
feeling. It gives me a sense of freedom where I can make
choices without having to consult on all of them. I like the
sense of responsibility.*

Kathleen joined in highlighting the sense of autonomy that comes
from economic contributions:

*Work gives me control. I don't like asking. We have one ac-
count and I like the feeling of dumping money into it. I don't
like not being able to contribute. I like being able to deal
from a position of equality.*

Kathleen went on to describe how the respect she had for her
mother increased when her mother went to work in the late 1950s
because she was more independent within the family.

Another way relationships with spouses changed over time was
in finding a voice and using it; a theme described more fully in a
later section of this chapter. For immediate purpose, however,
finding a voice in the partnership came through varied experiences—for example, engaging in family or individual counseling,
or reflecting on their lives with their partners. For some women,
the voice was just beginning as a whisper, the words perhaps
only creeping into their awareness. Finding a voice in the partnership relationship often came as the result of going to work and
feeling the greater sense of freedom that emerged through knowing "I can make it on my own" and contributing to the economic
welfare of the family unit. In partnerships, through a greater
sense of personal competence, a voice was a result of enhanced
awareness of individual value to the family and to society. Voice
makes visible that which is; in some cases, it makes a case for

change in the relationship. Midlife women in partnerships gave voice to a dawning awareness of full personhood, of making known the desire (demand) for full and equal stature. When there was no movement, or even recognition, by their partners in response, the women's anger was intense and deep, threatening the viability of the partnerships. Several women spoke of a possibility that their relationships might not survive because their partners demonstrated little willingness to change, denying the necessary space to thrive and to free the women's energy and, concomitantly, their own. Interestingly, such constriction of energy was expressed in little ways. Beth complained:

Last summer I got a scholarship to go to study. My husband had the hardest time because I was going. But he has always traveled. When I had to go, I had to make sure the house was running smoothly. He took no responsibility for these things.

Her resentment smoldered as she tried to understand.

Like Beth, Ellen spoke about the need to continue to fulfill the homemaker role while she worked full-time at a demanding job. When she went away, she felt the need to arrange everything for the kids—car pools, clothing, appointments, child care—and to put meals in the freezer. This was just taken on, with no voicing or recognition that the expectations might be excessive. Ellen just did it. When a man goes on a trip, he leaves; the woman maintains the home. For most women, reciprocation here is rare. Sarah observed:

In marriage, one of the two has to be more powerful. I leave that to my husband. He leaves the home to me. Sometimes we go head-to-head over things. We have both changed since we were first married. We were more carefree then; now we're more serious.

Jean spoke about a time of upheaval in her marital relationship, resulting in a period of chaotic change for all:

I had to be the solid foundation for everyone. My husband's reaction was so intense that I had to examine my

basic values and beliefs with a counselor's help. Once I re-
alized that my feelings about his behavior were valid and
started quietly speaking up, I found tremendous power. It
was a turning point . . . . I guess the most powerful les-
son of all of the turmoil was that I knew I could rely on
myself to find what I needed for my emotional security
and provide financial security. I didn't have to feel stuck
in an undesirable situation just for the sake of security.

Beth also spoke of turmoil in her relationship: "One time it [the relationship with her partner] was so bad I left for a few days. If it weren't for the kids, I might not have come back."

Partnership relationships also enabled women to grow and feel good about themselves. For example, Ellen spoke about a very supportive relationship with her partner. She had not felt very confident as a young woman. Her partner helped her to recognize her competence. "He convinced me I was successful."

For her part, Lori spoke about the change in her partnership relationship over time.

I've changed. I have more voice in decisions now. We share.
In making a decision, I normally agree with him, but if I
have doubts, I say so. We both realize you have your say.
Earlier it was my choice not to, to keep peace, or because I
didn't feel like I should. It was the way I was raised. But now
I do. We've made shifts and my husband is used to it. We're
on the same level. He's changed too.

Beth and her husband disagree about how to express affection. She would like more romantic emotional expression and he is content with practical expression, like washing the car for her. Neither is happy with the relationship and there is impasse. She related:

He says I don't respect him. I tell him I would respect him
more if he were more romantic. He says women value ro-
mance and men value respect. His respect, in my estima-
tion, is equivalent to letting him make all the decisions. And
I refuse to do that. That's the ongoing problem.

A significant part of women's power at midlife is their coming to terms with the changing nature of their partnerships. As a woman allows herself to feel and express her power, to free her energy, and to become and express herself, her partner must also shift and change. To be empowering, both must feel respect and value for the other, themselves, and the relationship. They must fit together like yin and yang, rather than feel subsumed into a relationship where individual identity suffers. Relationships work if neither partner is bound into a fixed way of being. There is power in the development of mutuality in a relationship, but mutuality is not easily achieved or preserved. Those women who spoke of counseling as a way of finding a voice in the partnership did so with a feeling of empowerment, of joy and pride in the outcome. Their collective exclamation can be stated as: "Look what we were able to accomplish!" They treasured the partnership relationships that developed. Perhaps this statement by Kathleen sums it up best:

With my husband, I don't worry about control. We have a good relationship. I trust him. He is my best friend. I don't like boredom and he is intelligent, respects my space. He is just what the doctor ordered. We love each other. Control doesn't enter into it. If I want to be alone, he respects that. I guess we have a mutual dependency.

LIVING IN AN UNPREDICTABLE BODY

Coming to terms with a changing body is another difficulty related to power development for women. Coping with menopause while continuing to fulfill their many responsibilities was a topic the women interviewed spoke about openly. For example:

My kids became teenagers when I was over 40 and I'm having to deal with the over-40 physical and emotional problems . . . and with the extra problems of my husband and I not agreeing. I have to cope with that and my own problems. Menopause and this other thing are overwhelming. Right now, I'm not feeling that powerful.

Karen spoke about her changing body with chagrin:

At midlife, it's really funny. I hated turning 50 this year. I didn't want the birthday recognized. I sort of resented the whole idea. Feeling old and saggy physically . . . angry at my body . . . . You take a look at yourself and you say, "This year I should not wear shorts!" I did make that proclamation, but then I've worn shorts anyway. OK, I guess the knees are saggy, but it's too hot to go around covered. People may think what they may if my knees sag, and my legs sag. Too bad!

Sarah also spoke about menopause looming on the horizon, heralded by greater premenstrual stress (PMS) symptoms and heavier bleeding: "That takes the power away because I'm irritable and difficult to be around."

In all these examples, women express feelings of loss of control of their bodies and diminishing power because of the energy drained in keeping up with their many roles and responsibilities while feeling less than wonderful. When the body no longer fits the societal prescription of attractive—young, firm, and vibrant—women experience a blow to their self-image. They settle for a diminished self-image based, in large part, in a youth-oriented definition of what it means to be attractive. Kathleen fought back. At midlife, she became an exercise enthusiast and worked herself into better shape now than she ever was. She gave up smoking and put on a few pounds, but she feels good about herself and her body. She described feeling good with a sense of joy, power, and energy.

POWER IN WORK

Women in their middle years found power in their relationships to work. They spoke of returning to the work force after having spent a number of years caring for their young children. As previously described in this chapter, work allowed women to envision themselves as autonomous and as making a significant contribution to the welfare of their families. Work was also a way of expressing their identities, of manifesting their competence. Power in work changed for these women over time. In their early years, they found their joy (and power) primarily in the work of creating a home. In their middle years, work outside the home provided an outlet for creating meaning in their lives, for developing fuller selfhood. Work sometimes substituted for unsatisfying partner or home relationships by providing an avenue where these women experienced control for self and a place to feel good about self.

Change in Power Over Time

Lori, a secretary, spoke about the change in her work situation over time. She had worked as a secretary right after high school, then married and had children. During those years, she stayed home. She reflected on the changes brought on by returning to work as a secretary:

> *Looking back, there is definitely more power in work [now] than there ever was. Now people rely more on my ideas to "make it better." I feel free to contribute. I have some input. They may not accept it, but I can say it, and I do have some power. I'm able to make decisions. In a lot of things, I don't have to check with somebody. I can give an answer—and I'm sure of what I'm saying, too.*

She went on to describe her job when she first returned to work:

> *I worked for a marketing department. In that area, secretaries were secretaries—there to do the work, looked down on. I hadn't thought about it being that way then, but when I look back it was: "Throw the work to them and they get it done." We rarely voiced an opinion there. It didn't bother me then, but when I look back, it does. You don't think about it, I guess, when nothing else is being said about it. It was just the way it was. A good place to work, good benefits.*

Change for Lori came as a dawning awareness of different ways of being: She no longer saw herself or accepted the image of herself as a machine to get the work done. She also became aware of power inequities and feeling denigrated. She was now able to decide about some aspects of her work and feels better about her job.

Karen, now a veterinarian, also highlighted changes in her power over time. She had been in a nursing education work role where she felt competent and powerful. Because she did not want to pursue her doctorate in nursing, however, this phase in her career was concluding. What to do? She had always loved animals, and one of her girlhood dreams that had not come to fruition was to be a vet. She explored the opportunities available in veterinary medicine. She found a nearby veterinary medicine school that would accept her application if she met the entry requirements. Then came the journey into feeling incompetent and powerless. She recalled:

> *It was hard to go from 15 years of good work, feeling good about myself and work, to the ignorant status of being a student. I was pretty low on the totem pole. At age 39, I was the oldest in my class . . . . As a student I had trouble knuckling down to memorization. Competency is a big one in self-esteem for me. I felt good when I graduated, and good about being an older person who had a lot to offer in the way you think and the way you handle people and the competencies in general, only to find that at the beginning you're absolutely incompetent again . . . going from classroom theory to the day-in, day-out ordinary practice. I felt pretty awful . . . kept thinking, I'll make this through . . . but* real anxiety provoking!

Karen went on to talk about the two jobs she'd held prior to opening her own clinic. Both were run by male veterinarians who had an entirely different management style than she did. Each in his own way was autocratic, demeaning, and neglectful in communicating respect for her. Her first employer paid her a low salary, telling her that even at the substandard pay, "You're not worth the money." She moved on to another veterinarian's office because, as she put it, "One thing I don't do anymore is choose to stay with things that I feel are damaging to me." About the second situation she related:

> *The boss says this is the way it's going to be. You are wrong even though you know you are not wrong, and you are forced to go along with it. I wondered if the change was going to work at all.* I was really depressed.

Then she moved on to a third situation:

> *I hired on with a guy who was a decent human being. He was OK. But I could not influence him. My opinion didn't matter. Even when situations were unsafe, I was unable to make him make the place safe.*

In this position, she made money as a percentage of what she produced. She did well and knew that she was competent, but was still unable to influence her colleague to make changes. Finally, she opened her own clinic as a way to get out from under the control of a parade of male veterinarians who overpowered her. Their overpowering was overt, brutal, and offensive, damaging the human spirit directly in the first two cases, and passive, obstructive, and insidious in the last case. In this last situation, the message was clear. Her opinion was devalued and, over time, her spirit suffered. To save her sense of self as worthwhile, she was forced to move out of the situation because there was nothing she could do to change it. Opening her own clinic was the solution.

Changes in power at work over time reflect changes in context and the necessary accommodations for self in interaction with such contextual changes. When changes allow greater freedom and self-control, energy is available to nurture self-development. When changes in contextual expectations diminish freedom and constrict self-control, energy is constricted and women expend their available energy in coping, rather than in creating health for self and others in work settings.

Caring for and Empowering Self and Others

All of the women in this study, as is common for many midlife women of this generation, chose work where they cared for others. These women experienced joy in work and felt empowered through successfully meeting others' needs. They found ways to increase their power to work on behalf of others.

Jean, a teacher, found power in greater education to enhance her knowledge of ways to serve others through her work. She had been a teacher for a number of years and chose to return to school to learn about educational administration in order to understand more fully why she had difficulties with the school system when she was teaching. She admitted: "I wanted more say over how educational environments are built." She had worked under an autocratic male administrator and was not able to make the changes she felt were needed to create a better learning environment. She also knew that things could be different. While working under a female principal, she had "blossomed." As she put it, "I actually *wanted* to go to work. I had her support. There was a sense of inclusion and participation." She went on to describe how, as a part of creating something, there was "buy in." She wanted to be involved; it offered excitement, joy, and a willingness to expend more energy. "Where there was disagreement, that was OK." There was give-and-take to figure out a solution. The vibrancy and joy in her voice as she described the difference were catching. I could feel it as she spoke. The energy was there.

Jean also found that education brought greater respect, enhancing her experience of power. When she was younger, she had been denied positions because she did not have higher degree credentials. Now, at midlife and midcareer, she has received a grant to pursue an administrative internship where she will be able to experiment with her ideas on flexible environments that empower teachers by creating freedom for them to explore new ways of teaching. One method is to allow the teachers free time from the classroom to reflect on their work life. Another approach is to be a role model by demonstrating different ways of teaching. Jean believes teachers are caught on a treadmill, doing things in old ways. Her strategy is straightforward: raise consciousness, allow the teachers to think through how they might work differently, but don't tell them how to do it. What she is looking for is enough space in a teacher's day to provide an opportunity for *thinking* work, rather than committing every minute to active *doing*. Creating a new, more flexible, and more responsive educational environment is, in her words, like "weaving a tapestry. Each person, each idea is one thread in the tapestry, and it is woven of people who have a whiff of what empowerment in education is and who support it." The tapestry Jean weaves will be more artful and beautiful through the appreciation of strengths and diversity. She will take her direction from the needs identified by the teachers and will provide the resources necessary for each teacher to make a meaningful contribution to the whole, the tapestry of shared vision. As she spoke more about this, her enthusiasm radiated from a deep inner strength. The feeling of energy was remarkable. Her commitment to creating opportunities for meaningful lives for all who are touched by educational systems, including herself and her family, is remarkable. Through empowering and caring for others, she expands her own power and is empowered.

Ellen, a media specialist for schools, told a similar story of empowering and caring for others as a source of power for self. She too regards knowledge as power but believes that most people define power as control over other people. For Ellen, knowledge provides the information to do what you need to do. She has a strong sense of responsibility and believes "my caring and sensitivity to others give me power. People seek me out." She went on to say that she doesn't like what happens to people "when systems lose touch with caring and sensitivity. It helps to have empathy for people." She has found that people in administrative positions, even in first-line teaching roles, can lose the human touch. They are removed from, or remove themselves from, the day-to-day situations of providing education. Ellen is motivated by positive feedback from others, by knowing she has made a difference. The joy in her work comes from serving others and from their pleasure in her contribution. This is where she experiences her power in her work situation.

Power that originates from empowering and caring for self and others through service work is experienced as feeling energized and joyful about work. Contexts are created to enhance selves through a network of dynamic energizing relationships.

Costs of Caring for and Empowering Others

Within stories of caring for and empowering others is the high cost to the one caring. For women, the experience of caring for and empowering others is often at the expense of self. Characteristics of this way of being are compassion and the wish to do good for the other, irrespective of cost to self. Perfectionism underlies the need to do everything possible to leave the other in a better state. Karen feels that she personifies this notion:

> *What traps me, too, is my unwillingness to do it [work] in a slipshod, uncaring way. I certainly know there are others who would do it differently, and probably protect themselves better. I don't protect myself well. I stay open to people and situations and continue to deal with them as I feel they should be dealt with, for the people's benefit rather than self-benefit. For example, after I get home, I am likely to call a client who is worried about her dog. I will get into a very longwinded call about the dog. For me, my self-esteem almost means handling things in such a way that people and the situations feel better after I've had contact with them . . . there really is a* do it right *attitude. You're not done till you're done. I don't tolerate it easily when I've walked out and know I haven't communicated with somebody . . . [or] walk out knowing I didn't call somebody back. I prioritize for the client's needs, not for my own.*

Karen recognized here a heavy cost to self; yet, because meeting the needs of others empowers her and helps her feel good about herself, she continues not protecting herself. This is where she feels joy: "I enjoy the people things and the animals." She admits, however, that she still gets tired—"stretched thin and stressed out," she terms it—because of the multiple competing demands on her time. Self takes a back seat.

Ellen, too, spoke about the toll of caring and empowering others at the expense of self:

*I have an incredible embedded sense of responsibility. . . .
I live as if I'm totally responsible and I allow myself to be
overwhelmed. I use my power to make change and benefit
others . . . but I don't know how to work smart. I don't
know how to delegate and just take on more and more. My
expectations for myself are out of reach. I don't expect the
same of others as I do for myself. It they are not at the level
they should be, or are overwhelmed by circumstances, then
I do it for them. I pick up the pieces.*

Ellen lives her life making it easier for others. She keeps a frenzied
pace, never quite coming up to her own expectations, never protecting herself. Both she and her family suffer. Her job creates
tremendous pressures for her. She works as a media specialist for
a school district with high expectations: to be first and best, to
succeed at all cost. She tries to live up to this image at a time when
more is expected and resources are diminishing. Trying to take on
the challenge to do it all costs her dearly. She related:

*There are big issues of legislation and the school board.
They are asking too much of people. And the needs of the
kids and families are also higher than ever. [As she tries to
meet them all] I feel squashed in the middle! What we need
is more bodies.*

Ellen indicated that increased salary and benefits are not what she
needs. Instead, she needs more people to share the heavy load of
kids and parents who increasingly need more caring educational
experiences. But *no one is listening!* Ellen is empowered by doing
a good job, by meeting the needs of parents, children, and co-
workers. She is overpowered by a system that demands too much
and by her own inability to set boundaries in the service of her
own well-being.

Sarah, who works in a special education program, told a similar
story: "My problem is, I'm a perfectionist. I have to get it all done,
and there is a right way to do it. That takes its toll. I need to learn
to let go. That's not easy."

Kathleen, on the other hand, who runs a large statewide program, takes pride in "doing it right" but sets limits on what she

will do. She has also traded-off moving up in the hierarchy for a life-style she considers more desirable:

> *I run a big program and I have never had a single grievance. Turnover has slowed. I solve my own problems. We've been named the program of the year for three years, and we're the third or fourth largest in the state.*

Her staff is happy, she cares fervently for the welfare of clients she serves, yet she maintains a good sense of balance. She talked about how she has set the boundaries for a healthier life-style, developing power for herself and her department at work, but not at the cost of her self:

> *I work 45 hours a week and I rarely bring work home. I like where I am. If I opted for a job with a bigger salary, I wouldn't have the control. I can set my own parameters. I give responsibility to others and have learned to compromise. I'm organized and meet my deadlines because I'm miserable being questioned.*

Contextual expectations of work environment, in concert with women's own expectations of self, shape their power. Their choices about whether to sacrifice self or create balance in their lives are, in large part, contextually determined. In our puritanically based society with its strong work ethic, perfectionism and self-denial are encouraged. Women are expected to serve perfectly, to keep things smooth, and to make others happy before they attend to their own needs. When demands become excessive, energy drains, power diminishes. When systems and individuals have more reasonable expectations, more energy remains for the system and the person.

CONTROL OR OUT OF CONTROL?

The essence of power for women in midlife is control—not in the sense of who or what they control, but in how much control they perceive they have over themselves and their own lives, whether in the context of work, family, or other relationships. Control provides a sense of not being constrained, bound, or defined by others, but rather of defining self. When women feel in control, they determine their own boundaries. Their personal space is not violated. They are able to have genuinely mutual definition of partnership relationships, with neither partner calling the shots, but both arriving at genuine consensus. Self-control is central to feeling powerful, to being empowered rather than overpowered in one's life situation. Descriptions of control varied among the study's participants. For example, Kathleen expounded:

I'm a control freak! And working gives me that control. I've arranged all through my working life to have that control. In my early jobs that meant, a lot of times, I was the only one there. So [I was] in control.

Kathleen went on about her current job:

I decide what's going to happen. If I don't want him [the boss] to know, I don't tell him. I want to be able to change my mind. I control a million-and-a-half-dollar budget. I make the decisions. He [the boss] signs off on it. I hire. I make the budget revisions. . . . I have been granted control but I make him look damn good. I don't cause him any embarrassment. They called me and offered me the job. When I agreed to take it, I set the parameters. I manage my own time. He leaves me alone.

All of this was communicated with a sense of satisfaction and feeling good about her work situation. *She likes it! It energizes her!* She feels in control, rather than being controlled.

Lori, too, described an ordered sense of existence with her life now in balance. She likes who she is, her husband and family, and her job. Similarly, Jean has her life more in balance. She has difficulty in dealing with unresponsive systems, but feels good about herself and her ability to make a difference in people's lives.

Karen, on the other hand, exemplified feeling out of control as she described shattered hopes for controlling her own life:

When you go into practice for yourself, you think you really have power and control. Right? No! *Labor and industry have you, the zoning board, the bank. I don't know who thinks they are in control of their lives. Does anybody? I do have a job.* I am my business. *But I'm not in control in that the business works me. My clients work me.* There is NO ONE ELSE! I am totally in control and I am totally controlled. *I'm at the whim of the people who work for me.*

Karen went on to describe how she ends up dealing with inter-office squabbles and "petty problems" of her staff while also being at the mercy of unpredictable animal illnesses. She is angry and resentful of the time spent dealing with staff squabbles, which reduces the time she might have for herself. She also talked about not being able to balance a feeling of being in control against the demands of her many roles:

It's like you get control of one area and lose control of another, like family. My kid sees it as me or the business. She hates the clinic: Feels she comes second. So you lose control and lose out in your relationship with your kid. For me that happened. My husband passively accepts it. I'm not home a lot so you lose the closeness of that relationship. . . . So why would you have your own business? Why did I become a vet? Beats me?!

For Karen, control is also being perceived as and *being* competent. Yet she lives a paradox, being seen and viewing self as competent while feeling at times anxious, insecure, and unsure. She said:

Feedback I get from my style at work is that I'm always competent in tough situations. That there is never a situation that I'm going to fold up on. . . . They [her staff] perceive me as very competent and strong.

What her staff doesn't see is how she worries, often about their relationship difficulties as well as about tough clinical situations. But she hides her insecurities, presenting an image of a woman in control.

Dealing with the staff squabbles eats away at what little time she might have for herself and at her self-perception of being able to manage competently. She stated: "Dealing with those kinds of things, and having little time of my own, I do begrudge giving another hour to deal with that kind of situation."

When she becomes annoyed, she does not voice it. It eats away at her, so she suffers. Karen's definition of power is feeling in control. She describes having sacrificed family relationships and her own sense of self-esteem, at least early on, in the pursuit of her dream. Now, much of her life feels out of control. She questions whether it was all worth it. It doesn't feel as good as she thought it would. Opening up the doors for greater autonomy and greater control netted less for her. She yearns for a simpler time, when life did not have so many pulls and she felt more in control.

For her part, Sarah defines power as people having control over themselves, yet she extends her definition to having control over others. However, she says she has learned that one has more power when one does not "take control over others." She went on to state:

> We all want to be in control sometimes. To stand back is difficult. I'm a take-charge type person. I've been lucky so far because I've been in jobs where I don't have to take charge.

What does not feel in control for Sarah is her life, with its many competing demands. She works full-time and has two daughters; one is approaching adolescence. She is active in their many activities, has family living near (with all of their demands), and is committed to finding time to spend with her husband. There is no "Sarah time":

> I feel like I'm on a merry-go-round and can't get off. The world is such a busy place there is no time for reflection. It's go, go, go! All of the time. It's busy, busy. Not much time for

me. I keep hoping for a light at the end of the tunnel but have not seen it yet.

Life feels out of control for Sarah. She does not believe men notice the extreme pull of many competing role demands in their lives. For one thing, they have far fewer home responsibilities than do women. Even when they share the work at home, their participation is not a societally ascribed expectation; it is viewed more as a gift than a duty. She looks toward a tumultuous time as her children enter adolescence. "It's heavy-duty responsibility. Lots of pressure and responsibility in a world you can't control . . . so there's a rough road ahead. They'll have the me-time until they are out the door." For Sarah, all of this, plus her changing body, diminishes her feeling of power and replaces it with a sense of being at the mercy of others.

Beth experiences her life as being out of control in many respects, even though her work situation provides a measure of feeling *something* is in control.

I feel in control at school. That is something! [amazed tone of voice] I do feel in control at school. [Her tone of voice has an Aha! quality of insight.] It's at home that I don't. . . . My life seems pulled in so many direction, I have to concentrate on my successes, and also my children's successes. . . . One has gone off to college and is struggling. I have to deal with what's going on with myself, and with what's going on with her, and it's major instead of minor, because it seems like until I can get her settled, I can't get settled. And I just want her to get settled so I can get on with my life.

Work becomes an escape, the one area that feels in control. Yet the future can seem uncertain. Beth sees herself as neither in control of her life nor powerful.

Ellen feels out of control most of the time. Multiple competing demands and her own inability to set boundaries often leave her feeling frenzied. As I heard Ellen's story, her priorities seemed to be work, family, partnership relationship, and self (taking last place). Her work situation feels out of control because of heavy demands on her to stretch diminishing resources and carry out increasing expectations.

The Expense of Living a Life That Is Out of Control

When they must live a life that often feels out of control, women feel a diminished sense of personal power. They feel stretched too thin, unable to stop the merry-go-round that whirls them through their days. In reaction, they describe a diminished sense of energy, a sense, at times, that their bodies have shut down. It is as if they are spinning in a centrifuge whose speed and pressure are intensifying. Their energy system—the self—is becoming more and more compressed with little freedom to grow and be. The costs to self here are great. When demands on self continue to intensify, women tend to move through their days just to "get through," rather than living a free, rich, healthy existence.

Ellen exemplifies this graphically when she talks about the increase in responsibility brought about in her district by attempts of her administrators to "empower employees" through greater participation in the work setting. She sees part of the impetus for demanding more participation as a way of cutting administrative costs. Upper-level administrators, she says, are out of touch with classroom interactions: "They just don't know." Her instructional responsibilities have become greater and are laced with a heavy dose of administrative responsibilities; her resources are fewer; and her commitment to doing a complete job for the benefit of children, parents, and school remains the same. The situation results in an incredible feeling of pressure with *no time for self-renewal!* In addition, she struggles with the mental and physical ravages of peri-menopausal, hormonal changes and returns home feeling drained:

> *Sometimes I think I am depressed. I come home so tired, I just go to bed and let my family do the "homework" for me. I suffer from headaches and know I should decrease the stress. My blood pressure fluctuates between high and low. It's all stress-related. I focus on getting the job accomplished and don't schedule time for me.*

She doesn't organize her day to include any "down time," so she is constantly racing to get her work done. Her plea is to have enough energy to do what needs to be done.

I operate by crisis with short-term goals. Get the project done! *It's all immediate with no thought for long term. I have learned I can't do two or three things at once [but she keeps on trying to do it all].*

Her constant level of intense stress results in a sense of feeling overwhelmed. Ellen described a number of frightening physical and mental health concerns:

A lot of times I can't come up with what I want to say. I am grasping for words, and they don't come. It's embarrassing to be talking to someone, and the words just won't come. I'm short of breath. I don't breathe. Sometimes I doze off in the car on the drive to and from school. I come home and crash. I am overweight, and I know I eat to satisfy the needs I'm not meeting. I have no control over anything. My life is in disorder and I can't bring order to anything. It's out of control. Outside, I try to maintain an image of being in control, but at home I allow myself to fall apart.

Underlying this, Ellen said, was her need to be perfect. Because her house is in disarray, she doesn't have people over. "Someone might see how it looks! I need to bring some order to my surroundings. I feel scrambled into a million pieces!" She reflected, "I know what to do. I just don't practice it. I need to take one day or one meal at a time and not get overwhelmed by the big picture." As I write this and recall the conversation I had with Ellen, I have a sense of rushing, whirling movement, and I catch myself holding my breath. Even after the fact, the sense of her anxiety and frenzied activity lingers.

Less dramatically, other women spoke of the costs of a life out of control. The most common complaint here was lack of time for self—the first thing to go, for busy women. Awareness of the need to create a balanced life did nothing to change a woman's frantic attempts to continue to meet multiple competing roles and self-expectations.

Finding a Way to Gain Control

Several women found ways to cope with a life out of control. Although each described a different solution, the sense of calm they radiated when they spoke of how they had "got a handle on things" was dramatic. For Sarah, getting away with her husband, in their camper, restores a sense of peace in her life. Lori takes the weekends to regroup, doing nothing related to work. She and her husband take time to have fun together. Exercise is another way Kathleen and Ellen cope with stress, although Ellen finds she exercises only sporadically. Other remedies were meditation, deep breathing, and distraction by focusing on another type of task. For some women trying to regain control, their solutions worked. For others, their efforts were only a finger in a dike; they were using temporary fixes for intractable situations. Continuing pressures from outside gave them little chance for a moment's respite to regain control.

As I reflected on their many stories and on how my own life feels out of control much of the time, I came to understand that women, to some degree, are *all* on an uncontrollable merry-go-round. Many of the stressors that deplete our energy and create in us feelings of being out of control, of diminished power and energy, are outside our control. Role expectations are often societally and culturally determined. The values undergirding role expectations are deeply ingrained in us, and, unless called to consciousness, operate outside our awareness. We are embedded in contexts that interact with our selves to create the fabric of our lives. We are created by, even as we create, the powering processes in our everyday lives. As we interact with others, the control perceived as the essence of powering relationships remains forever outside our grasp. It's a little like chasing the mythical unicorn, who remains free while in captivity (Lindbergh, 1984). The unicorn is a product of folklore and imagination, so in a sense is illusory. In Lindbergh's poem, the unicorn has been captured. Though he could free himself, he chooses to remain captive, and thus, paradoxically, remains free because he *chooses* bondage. We aspire to power and control, yet we must . . . we must remind ourselves that *control* is a cultural fantasy tied to the notion of an external world that we can control. Perhaps, just perhaps, power comes from relinquishing the idea that control is possible. Greater order in one's own life and peace with the idea that control is an unreal possibility are perhaps more in tune with what can be. At this point, I am musing, but I do wonder about the expectations I have lived with all of my life. Do they diminish and constrict the energy available to construct a meaningful life? How does one create a full and meaningful existence in a context that encourages insanity? I wonder.

REFLECTING ON POWER AT MIDLIFE

Midlife women related experiencing power in ways that are not unlike those identified by women at any point in their lives. The vantage point of midlife gave added depth to their narratives as they reflected on the meaning of power in their lives. Finding a voice was fundamental to their developing power and to their changing perceptions of power as they created meaning in their lives.

Finding a Voice

Why was finding a voice so basic to power development for these midlife women? When these women were young, they tended to keep silent rather than voice their needs and wishes. Their midlife vantage point revealed the significance of this experience. They described finding a voice that could speak to all of their relationships: work, family, and partnerships. Their ability to voice their thoughts freely was linked to experiencing greater power. As they spoke, I sensed a spirit that was alive, joyful, and proud. Lori put it this way:

> *Before, it just seemed that we didn't have any say-so in it. . . . When you're younger, you are more apt to not*

question things. Now I question everything! That comes with just growing up—both being a woman and the age factor. I think women have just progressed so much further . . . . More women are voicing an opinion. That makes it easier. I think we were maybe held back because of repercussions. The "Who does she think she is?" type of thing. I think we were intimidated. Especially secretaries. We were viewed as "We're there to serve," and [we weren't supposed to] question. That's how I always felt. Now I don't feel that way. I think that's part of the women's movement. It's made me more mouthy. And age does it too. You worry about what people think, to a point; but I don't worry about it so much as I used to. I don't have time for it.

Finding a voice comes with feeling more autonomous, or with mutually contributing, at an equal level, to the partnership relationship. When Karen went back to school and was economically dependent on her partner, her feeling that she didn't have an equal right to voice an opinion about how family resources were used diminished her sense of power and self-worth. Kathleen found a stronger voice in her partnership relationship when she began to put money into the family's joint account.

Finding a voice comes with self-esteem—a firm grounding in who you are, coupled with self-confidence. Ellen was a shy, quiet young woman without a lot of self-confidence. "At age 35," she said, "I opened my mouth, and I haven't closed it since." Her reluctance to speak out was linked to her low self-esteem, which she attributed to her very high self-expectations. "I was much more hesitant when I was younger. When I went to work and was successful at writing grants, I knew I could accomplish [something]. I *can* write grants." She credits her husband with helping her to gain self-confidence: "He convinced me I was successful." Now, Ellen has a greater sense of competence in her own right. As she described the experience of finding a voice, she also communicated her pleasure and her enhanced sense of power.

Greater *freedom* came when she found and used her voice. In the interview, I sensed the change: a lighter attitude, more exuberance. She had become more expansive.

The Changing Meaning of What's Important in Life

Women who reflected on power at midlife mused about the changes in their values over time. They talked about a downgrading of the importance of material things in their lives, and their greater emphasis now on relationships. For example, Beth stated:

> *I don't value clothes like I used to. I used to spend a lot on clothes. To be honest, I think I am becoming less materialistic. I always thought I wanted a fabulous house, fabulous furniture, a fabulous car. Now I just want a car and a house and it doesn't have to be fabulous. I think that's why I'm into the emotion and the romance because I'm devaluing all those other things.*

Sarah also described a shift in what mattered to her as she entered firmly into the midyears of her life:

> *I have a greater sense of what is truly important. I focus more on the real needs and don't waste my energy on little things. The important things I take control of, and I let the others slide. With the kids, I am more easygoing. I let the minor infractions go. I'm not as stringent because I know they are going to be OK as adults. My personal satisfactions are different now, too. When I was younger, my happiness was more superficial; I was more carefree. Now I have a harder time doing that. I'm more uptight. More serious.*

Midlife for women brings a greater sense of power through turning away from superficial, materialistic values. Relationships become more important. When a woman's focus on more meaningful values is not reciprocated in the contextual circumstances of her life, the cost is greater anxiety, frustration, and anger. Because a woman's values have changed does not mean that the values of others (systems or persons) in her world have also changed. A change of values reflects a fundamental shift in a person's identity, thus changing the ground rules for relationships with that person. Some acquaintances may deny or disbelieve that the woman means what she is communicating. For example, when Beth told her partner she wanted more focus on relationship and romance, her partner countered by telling her she was too materialistic to mean what she said. He persists in working hard to bring her *things,* and she continues to yearn to be valued in a different way.

Society and culture continue to pressure women to value superficiality in their lives—youth, physical beauty, possessions, disposable, throwaway new *things,* and individual ascendance over group well-being. As women turn toward more feminine relational values, they are out-of-step with the rest of their world. "The notion of the self-in-relation involves an important shift in emphasis from separation to relationship as the basis for self-experience and development" (Surrey, 1991, p. 53). This notion puts women at odds with strong societal values of individualism (Bellah, Madsen, Sullivan, Swidler, & Tipton, 1985). In many cases, it would be far easier to go along with the dominant values rather than persist in the direction of creating in one's life more meaning that is reflective of dissonant values.

Searching for the Self That Was

Another facet of reflecting on changes at midlife is a search for the self that was and a coming-to-terms with the self that is. Karen yearns for her earlier identity, a self that exists now only in fantasy. She stated:

> *You think of all the things you used to love to do. I used to love to cook. I don't do much of that. I used to knit, used to sew, I don't do that. All of those skills that I really enjoyed at the time—I don't do those.*

When she tried to recapture some of that lost self by making a prom dress for her daughter, she found the costs outweighed the pleasures: "It did feel good. But was it worth staying up huge late nights to do this? No, I think not! But there is a wistfulness, at least in me, for that old identity." Others also talked about missing those things that used to bring them pleasure and contributed to their power. Usually, they talked about things that reflected the dominant societal values. When they lived out societal values for a woman's life, they were rewarded but somehow knew their power was diminished. They felt some sense of the well-being they associated with their old selves, but it was accompanied by an uneasy knowledge that they could not recapture that self.

Musing on "The Way It Is": Power and Being a Woman at the Midpoint of Life

Control is lost as families, work, bodies, and life situations change. Midlife women also search for meaning in ways that differ from those of their younger years. They actively seek to identify what is important to them. As they begin to know and understand what is meaningful to them, their self-perceptions of their power change as well. Lori reflected:

> At this age, 50 or 51, you look back and think, Geez! What have I really done? . . . . I'm 50, and this is it? Midlife crisis. All I can do is be honest and try to improve that. It would be terrible to slide backward. Is any of that hormonal? I've had a lot of surgery, but a smooth transition through menopause. All I need is to make more money and I'd be happy. I don't make near what I'm worth. Secretaries are almost viewed like clerks, or clerk typists. I am not a clerk. "Oh, you are just a secretary?" in most people's minds. A stenographer sounds better. I want more! [She is laughing, using a joking-around tone of voice, but it has a serious undertone.] It makes a big difference in how you feel. Get me some coffee! And money!

Lori has a sense of peace in her life, but there are undercurrents of anger and sadness at not being afforded respect and not being esteemed by others because she is a secretary. She values herself, but knows that the work she does—and thus she, herself—is not valued highly in the societal context. At this point in her life, she no longer settles for a life of diminished value; rather, she is coming to terms with creating power in a life lived in the shadow of a societal definition of "less than." She is creating meaning for herself by accepting her life, despite society's conflicting messages that define her life as less valuable. Well-ingrained societal values are still patriarchal, discriminatory, hierarchical, and individualistic; their meanings are derived from materialism. A secretary serves without making much money—two negative, contextually derived blows to Lori's power, to her very being. At times, in musing on the way her life has gone, Lori sounded almost puzzled. Midlife is when a person tries to consolidate and integrate the many fragments of a life lived in context and to make some sense of it. The stated values and the values that do in fact so heavily influence the meaning of our lives as women are difficult to integrate. We have the promise of freedom, of equality, of having a voice; yet, even when we choose to live by or to conserve, the social fabric of our existence by expressing dominant values in our lives, we are disappointed by how we are treated. "Life ain't the way we were told it was," summarized one interviewee. At midlife, we are called to look squarely at where and how we are, and it isn't a pretty picture.

Karen, the veterinarian, contemplated her life, evaluating the changes that had evolved from following her dream:

> As you move to take care of your own dream, then you give up other things: family relationships and those things on which you have hung your self-esteem. I don't know if it's worth it, in the long scheme. I strictly don't know. You know, this whole process of getting more degrees, and more this and more that, I don't know . . . [her voice trails off, thoughtful]. When you look at the simpler ways of doing things, we probably were better off. But part of that is midlife, too. One task I've gone through is raising a kid—and feeling like I didn't do a very good job of it. That was a huge one I felt out of control with and had no power in. You deal with it, and that's that. I didn't do a great job, and that's part of me, too.

She had thought that, by this time in her life, she would be more comfortable:

*I would be traveling more, I would be doing more fun
things. And here I am,* working my ass off! I mean, what is
this? . . . *I thought 50 meant comfortable . . . . It seems
like I ought to be feeling in control and having some power
and I'm not sure where it is! The only positive thing about
being where I am is, I'm running my own business that's
flourishing. People think I'm good with people and a good
vet, and I guess that's something to be said about a life.*

Jean is committed to creating a meaningful life for herself and
others. While there is much she is unable to do in impacting systems, she trusts that a ripple effect will prevail. If she enacts her
own meaningful life and its power, the result will be change for the
better. In this respect, Jean is a leader. Wheatley (1992) described
leadership as being "*always* dependent on the context, but the
context is established by the *relationships* we value" (p. 144). Jean
knows how she chooses to relate to others in her world and what
she values; quietly, persistently, and gently, she lives the meaning
of her life. The energy of her power is radiant, reaching out to affect all those she touches. She empowers and is empowered.

WHAT IS THE MEANING OF POWER?

Power for women at midlife is created through the relationships
in their lives. At the same time, power in relationships creates the
meaning of the relationship. Women experience power as a sense
of energy, of vibrant well-being when they feel empowered. On the
other hand, when they feel overpowered, they feel a sense of energy shutdown and move to a self-survival mode. At midlife,
women experience a clearer sense of what empowers and over-
powers them than at earlier times of their lives. They courageously
empower themselves by creating meaningful lives, despite subtle,
pernicious contextual messages that their lives are less valued, em-
anating from the still dominant, patriarchically defined culture.
These messages are so deeply ingrained as to be almost invisible,
unless they are deliberately called to awareness. At midlife, women
see more clearly, often with great compassion for themselves, for

other women, and for men. Through awareness, they empower themselves to choose knowingly (rather than to live blindly) as they prepare to live the second half of their lives.

MAKING CONNECTIONS: NURSES, NURSING, AND WOMEN

I stated, at the beginning of this chapter, that my circle of knowing starts with myself, reaches out to encompass the experiences of others, and comes back to myself. I spent time reflecting on the stories of these women, filtering them through my own experience of power in midlife. As a result, I understand power in a deeper way. I have come to comprehend how integral power relationships are to our well-being, to our very selves as women and as nurses. As nurses, we can approach our dawning awareness of power for women from two differing standpoints: (1) to know and understand *ourselves* as women and nurses, thus beginning our own healing process and (2) to know our female clients who live, like us, in their many connections and often come to us in need of healing.

Awareness of Our Own Power

As I reflected on the experiences the women in this study so generously shared with me, I found myself in their stories. I also heard parallels to the stories of nurses who participated in two of my earlier phenomenological studies of power in the everyday work lives of practicing nurses (Brown, 1987, 1991). Reflecting on power from the perspective of women in their middle years added depth to my understanding, but, as I thought about it further, I realized that merely knowing and understanding, even though packed with potential for transforming selves, are not enough. Knowing in the sense of becoming aware is a first step because power for women is so directly linked to subtle cultural and societal messages about what composes a meaningful life for a woman. These messages have been constructed over years of definition and focused through a single exclusive lens. As Tavris

(1992) noted, our societal norms are built with the masculine as *the* standard. Only recently has the absence of women from our normative data in research, health, business, education, and other arenas been addressed. Normative data for evaluation of ourselves as women and nurses are based in tacit, hidden assumptions about the nature of our work and our very selves. As we move into the next decades, sure to be fraught with change, nurses must be alert to the meaning of change. Because standards are so often built on values derived from individualism, materialism, and masculine dominance, we need to be aware, to question, and to not fall blindly in line with expectations that do not feel right. As we evaluate ourselves and our work, we must be careful to preserve the core that is nursing—our humanistic, more femininely derived, loving center—and to think about the meaning of our central professional values as we work with one another to create nursing. These goals entail reflecting our core values as we live and work in all organizational contexts, including the health care delivery arena.

Awareness of Our Power in Organizational Context

As nurses, we are not known for being kind in our relationships with each other. When invited to take on upper-level positions in healthcare and academic organizations, women are often expected to mirror the competitive, individualistic, win–lose perspective of old-line bureaucracies. When granted positions at the top of these organizations, women are asked to live the dominant values or risk being excluded—literally, through loss of position, or figuratively, through being denied admission to the inner powerful circle. Women executives who have made it to the top of the organizations they work in might profit by searching their souls to see what values they are living. One way of getting to core values is by reflectively examining everyday practice. What is the basis of ordinary, minute-by-minute decisions? As we increase our awareness of everyday work situations, we come to understand our power and how we and others create it. Being open and vulnerable to the messages from others, and from our daily lives, will help us to increase our power—if we avoid defining power by a standard based in *power over.* Power is a life force, an energy, that is available to us all. It originates from choosing how we are with one another in dynamic interaction with the whole. Our choices either constrain or free energy for ourselves, groups, organizations, others. How we enact our power, and allow others to enact their power, creates the meaning of our work lives and our very selves.

Power comes from everyday, minute-by-minute choices based on lived values, rather than from any grand design. Nursing's campaign to change its image, born in the 1980s, was one such grand design that has been less than fully successful, perhaps because it started where it could only do less than succeed. It started "out there," trying to change the public image, rather than within each of us. We all live our choices day-by-day, moment-by-moment, creating power through the relationships in our everyday lives.

Awareness of Power in the Lives of Clients

As we experience our nursing lives, working with women clients who mirror our own circumstances, how can we be most helpful? Perhaps we should start by being fully aware of the context of a woman's life. To what degree is she responding to the subtle messages of what constitutes a meaningful life? How does she experience her power? Does she feel empowered or overpowered? How does her health status reflect her power? Is she so busy protecting her vital core that she has little energy left for anything else? Is she so angry about the circumstances of her life that she radiates angry energy in an effort to fend off attacks to her vital core, rather than directing her energy in creative ways? As we do traditional health assessments, how aware are we of the context of a woman's life? And with that awareness, how might we be most helpful?

First, let us not blame. When a woman has been trying to carve out a meaningful life, despite what seem overwhelming odds, heaping coals on her head—telling her what she *should* be doing—will reap little positive change. Change toward more healthful ways of being is far more likely when directed from an inner wisdom born of understanding. Such understanding comes when the nurse *listens to* and then *validates* a woman's experience. This is no easy task for a nurse, who lives a similar reality and is trying to understand herself and her own world, often postponing, sometimes actively denying, the dawning of unpleasant realities. When another woman's experiences call us to question our own fragilely constructed world, remaining open is difficult but inordinately necessary. Jones and Meleis (1993) proposed "[a new] model for health: empowerment. In this model, health is being empowered to define, seek and find conditions, resources, and processes to be an effective agent in meeting the significant need perceived by individuals" (p. 12). Such a definition takes into account the essential step of helping individuals explore the circumstances of their lives. It does not prescribe a treatment outside the context of a life, but rather brings the context of a person's life fully into the process. Nurses can help other women become aware of the full and holistic significance of their lives lived in context. For example, the cure for illness incurred by living a life too often experienced as out of control might be in bringing the contextual circumstances to awareness, rather than in tackling the illness symptom. Themes from the experiences of the women in this study provide a starting point for exploration. The meaning of the changes in a woman's life over time; the costs of caring deeply for and empowering oneself and others; the living of a life that feels out of control; the finding and using of a woman's voice; the definition, by a woman, of the power of her life; and the way a woman feels about the self that is, in relation to the self that was—all these are fraught with meaning and are interrelated with a woman's health and well-being.

REFLECTIONS ON THE WHOLE—UNITY OF MEANING
MESSAGES OF POWER FOR WOMEN IN MIDLIFE—
written on the breeze

Looking back on a woman's life
born into another time
half a lifetime ago
creating a self—
the fullness of potential.

And knowing now
a woman born to be all that she can be
in the land of freedom where
all men are created equal,
generally speaking, of course,
and all doors to the future are open,
more or less.

Small girl creating a future
with arms spread wide . . .
HERE I AM!
I want to fly!
and be a mommy.
I want to soar in a space ship!
and take care of the children, the sick.
I want to be president of this country!
and help other people.
HERE I AM, WORLD! I can be anything I want to be,
and you need me . . .
and messages are carried on the gentle breezes
Less than less than less than

School girl learning all she must know
to fly
to soar
to become!
HERE I AM, WORLD! I can be anything I want to be,
and you need me . . .
And messages come through the floorboards, the air, the
crackle of new textbook pages
Less than less than less than

Young woman popping with life born and to be born
caring for . . .

HERE I AM, WORLD! I can be anything I want to be
(when today's work is done)
and you need me . . .
And messages course through her veins
Less than less than less than

Woman in the middle of her years
wondering how she has come to this place in her life . . .
HERE I AM, WORLD! I can be anything I want to be
(in the time I have left)
and you need me . . .
And messages come from the places of her life,
creeping into her center
Less than less than *less than*
Because you squash the life force,
sap the energy you need,
because you are afraid
of the powerful energy
that comes from woman
giving.

And she moves into the second half of her life
with joy and anger
with tears and laughter
with pain and exuberance
with the possible yet to unfold . . .
and wonders

How will it???

ABOUT THE STUDY

Because I wished to understand power for women in midlife, as
lived in experience, I chose a hermeneutic phenomenological way

of coming to know (van Manen, 1990). "A good phenomenological description is collected by lived experience and recollects lived experience—[it] is validated by lived experience and it validates lived experience" (van Manen, 1990, p. 27). Thus, in doing this research, I have engaged in full partnership with those who chose to participate with me. Dialogue was characterized by full engagement of self and other. In doing this research, I followed the steps outlined by van Manen (1990). I turned to the nature of the lived experience by continuing my investigation of a phenomenon that continues to intrigue me, searching for full, rich, and deep description. I investigated the experience as lived by 7 women, incorporating, when appropriate, information from my earlier work. The women were asked to fully describe their experiences with power from the standpoint of being in their middle years. The 7 women in this study fulfill more traditional women's occupational roles and consider themselves to be ordinary, living lives similar to a host of other middle-aged women. Even though it is highly unlikely any would be recognized from their narratives, pseudonyms were used to protect their identities. After gathering data by way of in-depth, tape-recorded interviews, the data were transformed into script. I reflected on the whole and the parts of the data, generating themes, the foundation for the chapter's structure. When the description was clearly ongoing in the present, although told at an earlier time, the present tense verb form has been used. When the past is clearly indicated, the past tense verb form has been used. Writing and rewriting have produced the best description I am capable of at this point. The poetry at the end is a way of moving from pure description to an intuitive grasp of the unity of meaning (Ray, 1985, 1990) for the whole of the study. Often, poetry serves me well as a way of expressing the essence of the whole of a study.

I ask readers to engage with my work and to share responses to it. Does it ring true in terms of your own experience?

REFERENCES

Agonito, R. (1993). *No more "nice girl": Power, sexuality and success in the workplace.* Holbrook, MA: Bob Adams, Inc.

Bellah, R. N., Madsen, R., Sullivan, W. M., Swidler, A., & Tipton, S. M. (1985). *Habits of the heart: Individualism and commitment in American life.* New York: Harper & Row.

Brown, C. L. (1987). *Power and images of nursing in the lived worlds of nurse administrators.* Doctoral dissertation, University of Colorado, 1987. Dissertation Abstracts International, *48,* 3247-B.

Brown, C. L. (1991). *Empowerment and nursing care delivery systems outcome variables.* Unpublished data.

Frankl, V. E. (1984). *Man's search for meaning: An introduction to logotherapy.* New York: Simon & Schuster.

Gilligan, C. (1982). *In a different voice: Psychological theory and women's development.* Cambridge, MA: Harvard University Press.

Hewlett, S. A. (1986). *A lesser life: The myth of women's liberation in America.* New York: Warner Books.

Jones, P. S., & Meleis, A. I. (1993). Health is empowerment. *Advances in Nursing Science, 15*(3), 1-14.

Lindbergh, A. M. (1984). *The unicorn and other poems 1935-1955.* New York: Pantheon.

Morgan, G. (1983). In research, as in conversation, we meet ourselves. In G. Morgan (Ed.), *Beyond method* (pp. 405-407). Beverly Hills, CA: Sage.

Ray, M. A. (1985). A philosophical method to study nursing phenomena. In M. Leininger (Ed.), *Qualitative research methods in nursing* (pp. 81-92). New York: Grune & Stratton.

Ray, M. A. (1990). Phenomenological method for nursing research. In N. L. Chaska (Ed.), *The nursing profession: Turning points* (pp. 165-172). St. Louis: Mosby.

Surrey, J. L. (1991). The self-in-relation: A theory of women's development. In J. V. Jordan, A. G. Kaplan, J. B. Miller, I. P. Stiver, & J. L. Surrey, *Women's growth in connection: Writings from the Stone Center* (pp. 51-66). New York: Guilford.

Tavris, C. (1992). *The mismeasure of woman.* New York: Simon & Schuster.

van Manen, M. (1990). *Researching lived experience: Human science for an action-sensitive pedagogy.* New York: SUNY Press.

Wheatley, M. J. (1992). *Leadership and the new science: Learning about organization from an orderly universe.* San Francisco: Berrett-Koehler.

ABOUT THE AUTHOR

I believe I have been engaged in trying to sort out power for myself as a woman all of my life. In my attempts to understand it, I have been through a variety of stages, from denial that power was a concern at all, to angry fighting against the concept, to disclaiming, to asserting, to an active curiosity fulfilled through research. I am in the middle of my years and I am still trying to figure it out. As a small girl, I wanted to be a nurse, because it seemed a wonderful, caring thing to do (I had been ill and seen nurses in action), and because society reinforced it as a worthy goal for a woman. In my teens, through an English course, I explored career options and learned that nurses had little power—that, in fact, the doctor, administrators, and others directed nurses' activities. So I gave up the idea of being a nurse, thinking I would be a pediatrician. The goal of physician was still in mind as I entered nursing school at the University of Arizona. I vehemently informed the faculty of this aim, indicating that nursing was my stepping stone to medicine. No one informed me that it didn't work that way. When I searched my soul, the truth was I loved what nurses did but did not like the way I, as a nurse and a woman, was treated. I stuck with nursing, but have had ups and downs, at times deciding to leave the profession. Finally, as a doctoral student at the University of Colorado, I came to recognize that what I was struggling with was my power as a nurse and as a woman and that I shared this struggle with many nurses and with other women in traditional women's roles. Since that time, I have been engaged in phenomenological study of power. Questions of power for women continue to engage my interest. Daily, through reflection in both formal and informal ways, I am deepening my understanding.

3

Surviving

Diane Cope

You Can Survive

The doctor says, "It's cancer," and so begins the dread,
The endlessness of sleepless nights—of what will lie ahead.
At first you're feeling numb, then there's anger, fear, and
doubt . . .
You're not sure if you want to cry—or if you want to
shout.
"Why did this have to happen, Lord, and why did you
choose me?"
Of course there are no answers to the why's that have
to be.
You know that fear's the culprit you must beat to get you
through;
The only thing to conquer fear is faith inside of you.
And so begins the treatment; what can you expect?

Will you be sick, will you be bald, and what will happen next?

You're pleasantly surprised to find the treatments aren't so bad.

Your family is supportive, but they're frightened and they're scared . . .

The very thought of losing you is more than they can stand.

Sometimes no words are spoken, they just want to hold your hand.

They need to share their feelings—they feel helplessness, it's true.

They wait and watch and try to take their every cue from you.

You hear about support groups where you share just how you feel.

You take the risk—try reaching out—and think that you can heal.

These groups consist of people going through things just like you.

These people understand you even better than you do.

As you listen, as you learn, the fog begins to clear . . .

You get things in perspective and you know what you hold dear.

You're ready for the battle; you take charge and you can cope.

The cancer doesn't have you, and there's reason now to hope.

You can survive this cancer; be the best that you can be.

You exercise, eat right, and rest and soon begin to see.

You learn to take things day by day—and take some time to play.

And soon you start to realize how many times you pray.

They say that out of every pain there comes some good for sure.

Disguised, perhaps, in cancer, is the blessing to endure.

There is a peace that fills your heart, you won't leave things unsaid . . .

*For life and time are precious—no one knows what lies
ahead.*
*The chance to say "I Love You" to all those you care
about.*
You've got the time to wipe away all areas of doubt.
*Your life has purpose and you strive to go on with your
plans.*
*Your comfort lies in knowing you are nestled in His
Hands.*

Del Coccia

SURVIVING

The journey through breast cancer is a road that women do not
choose to travel but suddenly their bodies force them to walk the
frightening path. In the beginning, the path is very dark and lonely.
It is impossible to see any light at the end of the path, but there is no
turning back. Each step is guided by a shred of inner hope that the
living nightmare of medical tests, therapy decisions, surgery, and
treatment will soon end. After an eternity of darkness, light begins
to appear and the living nightmare ends, free of cancer. However,
the women now assume a new identity in a new place—they are
breast cancer survivors in the Land of the Unknown.

Recognizing the Challenges of Life as a Survivor

What is it like to be a breast cancer survivor, to live in the Land of
the Unknown? As a group leader for two breast cancer support
groups, I have had intensive contact with women diagnosed with
breast cancer. Through these meetings, I have had an opportunity
to observe women enduring the various stages of breast cancer:
diagnosis, therapy decisions, chemotherapy, and radiation. During
these stages, some women have a great need to attend support
groups, to be with other women who have breast cancer and receive information, support, and guidance. Among the women, being there and reaching out to help each other encourages close
friendships. As a result, many women have continued to attend

the group even after completing treatment—a rather new phenomenon. As I sat and listened during the support meetings, I became intrigued by the comments expressed by the survivors in the
group. At first I thought, "It's great, you are free of cancer." Then
I listened and saw the anxiety. The women who had completed
treatment appeared to be struggling with life as *survivors*. Issues
surrounding life as a survivor included changes in family relationships, reprioritized values and personal goals, fear of cancer recurrence, and feelings that vacillated from a positive attitude to
depression. Some comments made by women in the group were
especially unforgettable. For example, "One day I feel fine; and the
next day, I feel like I could shoot myself. Right now I feel like I am
just so crazy." Or, "Now I get—it's like I am off chemo—like walking into the unknown." Another survivor said, "I questioned my
doctor after my last visit of chemotherapy. I said, 'O.K., now
what?' He said, 'Well, you go home and do what you want. You live
your life.'" The women also discussed the lack of understanding by
family, friends, and health care professionals. They knew that their
family and friends were very loving and supportive, but these
other persons could not truly understand because they had not
gone through the same experience.

Coming to Know the Experience

The women's statements started to sink in. A woman cannot go
through the living nightmare of breast cancer and then resume
life-as-usual the next day. I saw that women were in great need,
but what were their specific problems? How could health care
professionals, family, and friends help more than they already had?
For instance, although I am familiar with helping women who
have just had surgery and are now in outpatient chemotherapy and
radiation, *survival* is something else—a completely new area. In
order to help survivors, I knew I had to learn more about life as a
survivor. Although the limited literature on cancer survival provided some information, substantive descriptions of the everyday
experiences of women who survived breast cancer were lacking. I
thus set out to learn from those who really knew.

Through the American Cancer Society and the Y-Me Breast Cancer Support Program, I found women who were more than willing

to talk to me about their lives as survivors. Looking back on this experience, I recognize that when I started out I did so systematically. I thought I would be able to produce a concise list of topics that described life as a survivor. How wrong I was! In addition to providing a wealth of knowledge about life as breast cancer survivors, the women revealed something about the true meaning of life itself—of what it meant to them and what it can mean to and for others. I hope to share this with you as I uncover the Land of the Unknown through the words of women who know this terrain as their own.

The Vast Unknown

As I sat and asked Barb, a 40-year-old woman who had been diagnosed the previous year, in her fifth month of marriage, what it was like to be a breast cancer survivor, I had no idea that the Unknown was so vast. Barb's initial response was, "Well, that is such a loaded question." Now I know that even that response is an understatement. As all of the women told stories of their experiences, it was apparent that this question opened up a Pandora's box of ups and downs, pleasures and horrors, and radical life changes. It is an experience that women surviving breast cancer learn about moment by moment, on their own. No one tells them; I am not sure that it is frequently talked about or written about. Delores, a 63-year-old who plays tennis every day, teaches bridge, and volunteers for Y-Me, described her feelings about living in the Unknown:

Everything you read about breast cancer is about going for mammograms, checking your breasts, monthly self-examinations, and not eating fat. It is telling you how to avoid it. But once you have it, what can you expect? Nowhere, nowhere *do you ever see that. There is an abyss.*

The Ever-Present Fear of Cancer Recurrence. Breast cancer survivors are plagued by fear of cancer recurrence. Distressing thoughts of recurrence assume permanent residence in the recesses of the survivors' minds. As the women described their thoughts and fears, I reflected on my personal experiences with fear. Although I have experienced fear before, in each situation that fear has subsided. Such brief encounters with fear do not begin to resemble the thoughts and degree of fear experienced by women surviving breast cancer. Fear for their life, for their very existence, never leaves them. I am not sure that anyone free of that fear can truly imagine what it is like to live each day under constant threat that cancer will return. Delores, despite her active life, admitted: "I am petrified of a recurrence. That is the biggest fear that is nagging in the back of my head."

Alison, a 42-year-old, was diagnosed three years ago. Despite having a mastectomy and being free of cancer, she experienced fear similar to Delores's. She described her vacillating reactions to living with fear every day and yet knowing that the cancer experience was over. "It is frightening to live with the fear of your own body," she stated, "and that is exactly what a breast cancer survivor has to do." Alison is experiencing another concern that faces persons who have been diagnosed with cancer—health insurance. The insurance industry and the laws that regulate its practice promote discrimination against those who are ill or who have a history of illness or high health care usage. Cancer is one of many conditions designated by the insurance industry as financially risky; barriers are created to reduce access to benefits. It is not uncommon for persons with cancer histories to face insurance barriers such as refusal of new applications, policy cancellations or reductions, higher premiums, excluded preexisting conditions, and extended waiting periods before eligibility. Alison's first devastation came when her insurance company went bankrupt shortly after her surgery. I asked her what this meant for her. She explained:

Well, I had been trying to get through to them because they hadn't paid any of my claims and my doctors were calling me. When I finally got through to them, the lady said they were in liquidation and that none of my claims were covered. I was at work and I just literally started screaming. My boss didn't know what happened.

Alison's cancer history now prevents her from getting health insurance. As she still tries to pay off her previous medical expenses, a recurrence at this time would be mentally, physically, and financially devastating.

Other women struggle greatly to force such thoughts of cancer recurrence from their minds. Sandy was enjoying her retirement in Florida with her husband when she was diagnosed. She had heart problems but never had to face this type of fear before. Sandy stated:

> *I push it out of my mind. I just don't allow myself to think about it. Truly it's almost like there's a curtain. I'm just not allowing myself to go beyond that curtain, beyond that barrier. You have a way of burying that fright so that you really don't realize that you are scared. It is so deep. You have this façade that you think is how you feel and you don't know that you are scared.*

Although Sandy's approach is effective for some women, others soon learn that their efforts are in vain. It is impossible to escape the ever-present thoughts of cancer recurrence. After a constant struggle to escape thoughts of cancer recurrence, Nancy, a survivor who facilitates a Y-Me breast cancer support group, has reached this conclusion:

> *I can't live my life like that. I don't dwell on it but it is a fact of life. I just learn to put up with it.*

Coping with Fear in Everyday Life.   How do thoughts of cancer recurrence enter into the women's daily lives? Is it possible to think or do other things? Elaine, a breast cancer survivor for two years, is a nurse who works full-time in the emergency medicine department. She is involved in cancer support groups, is very active in the National Coalition for Cancer Survivors, and is a wife, mother, and grandmother. Elaine described it this way:

> *I heard this expression, "I would like to stop thinking about cancer one minute before I wake up," which means to me it's just always there, it's always there. Every time I say I've had enough of this and I just want to forget about it, it*

comes right back to me. Like last night at work we had a lung cancer patient come in. So it's always there for me.

Getting back into the "mainstream of life" has helped Elaine confine the plaguing thoughts to her subconscious mind and think about recurrence less and less:

In the beginning, it sort of monopolizes your every thought. You just have to learn to deal with it. I am personally a very busy person. I try to keep myself busy and that doesn't allow me to think, but when I'm left alone, it's usually there in some shape or form. I also try to deal with it on a day-to-day basis as opposed to worrying about what's going to happen next week, next month, or next year.

Barb, who more recently completed treatment, is still trying to deal with her thoughts of cancer recurrence:

I think the psychological aspects of it will always be with me. Hopefully, they will wane as time goes by, when the years or numbers are higher and higher, but it is still frightening. I must say that it is always in the recesses of my mind.

Barb, explaining that she and her husband are both retired, went on to say:

It hasn't prevented me from doing all the things that I did before. As a matter of fact, I think I am doing more now than I did before I became ill. We both volunteer and I think we are much busier now than when we were in business.

Eventually, each woman has found a unique way to live with her plaguing thoughts of cancer recurrence, but the process takes much learning and effort. Alison described her long learning process: "As time goes on you learn to deal with it better. It does take time. It was three years last week that I had my surgery and I am still dealing with it." Length of time as a survivor helps not only in learning ways to alleviate plaguing thoughts but also in gaining more confidence. Elaine described it as "getting more recovery under your belt."

The Five-Year Anniversary.   The passing days turn into a passing year, and the women move closer to the five-year cure mark. Historically, surviving five years without a recurrence has been designated as a cure marker. This marker, arising from a medical perspective, encompasses the scientific rationale for the diagnosis and treatment of cancer. The five-year parameter indicates that a patient who has no evidence of disease at that date possesses the same life expectancy as a person who never had cancer (American Cancer Society, 1992). However, the women whom I talked to stated that this has not been true for all survivors they have known. Many of the women talked about friends who had had a metastasis after five years. Despite their awareness that it can return after five years, the women count the days until their fifth anniversary, in an attempt to lessen their plaguing thoughts of cancer recurrence. Alison, for one, explained how she wrote "third anniversary" on her calendar at work:

One of my co-workers asked me about it and I said I had an operation and I am going to have a party on the fifth anniversary. That's supposedly a milestone. I don't know if it is or isn't, but it is getting a little easier.

Mind over Body.   During the past decade, alternative healing methods have emerged as popular means for treatment. Patients with various life-threatening diseases have sought controversial pharmacological and nonmedical treatments in hopes of a cure. The controversy over use of these treatments arises when a person chooses to discontinue standard medical protocols and use alternative methods as the sole treatment. More recently, a less controversial method has emerged that does not negate medical treatment. Instead, this supplemental healing method uses the power of the mind. Bernie Siegel, in his 1986 book, *Love, Medicine, and Miracles,* discusses self-healing through mind–body connections. A practicing surgeon, Siegel observed that patients who had the courage to love (turning outward and giving to others) and the courage to work with their doctors (becoming actively involved in planning and implementing their treatment program) influenced their own recovery. For Siegel and his patients, the mind became a powerful entity in healing.

The breast cancer survivors who spoke with me have utilized their mental powers to lessen their fear of cancer recurrence. Mental closure, which shuts out any negative information the women do not wish to hear, is an especially effective technique. Negative information includes breast cancer statistics, breast cancer deaths, and news of friends with breast cancer who are not doing well. Jane, an upbeat school counselor in a middle school, told me about being at a breast cancer support meeting and hearing some "horror stories." Jane said, "I have been to other meetings and it has been fine. If I don't want to hear something, I will walk away if I have to."

Conversely, positive mental thoughts and a positive attitude can ease the plaguing thoughts of cancer recurrence. Jane want on to say:

> *I have always believed in a positive mental attitude. It is not always easy to do but I believe that it does make a difference. Think negative and you will be down, and I don't want to be down, I want to be up. I feel good about me.*

Barb also indicated a strong belief in a positive mental attitude as she described her recovery:

> *I really believe that positive energy is very powerful. Your faith and a positive attitude are major factors in your recovery rate. I have read Dr. Siegel's books and a lot of books on cancer and treatment. A lot of what I have read has proven to me over and over again with case histories that your faith and your positive attitude bring you a long way on the road to recovery. There are so many positive things to dwell on, it's not that difficult.*

Relief through Sharing.   Talking and being with other breast cancer survivors provides women the greatest relief from their fear. When they share their emotions, their fear of cancer recurrence, and their terror, the women find that others experience similar feelings. They are consoled by knowing that they are not alone and that others share their reactions. Alison, who didn't talk to any support persons for a long time, thought she was "going crazy." Then she started talking to other breast cancer survivors and found comfort. "Talking about it helps," she said. "It is good to hear other people in my situation say the same thing. That makes me feel good because I know I am not crazy."

Accentuated Fear. For much of the time, the women deal quite well with the specter of cancer recurrence. By keeping busy and maintaining a positive outlook, they keep fearful or distressing thoughts under control. Yet there are times when fear of cancer recurrence becomes overwhelming and blanketing. Events associated with breast cancer—bodily aches and pains, follow-up mammograms and blood tests, friends' cancer recurrence or death from breast cancer—temporarily invade the women's lives and evoke immense apprehension and distress.

The experience of little body aches and pains is a nerve-wracking event. What might previously have been dismissed as a sore muscle or a common cold now stimulates intense, questioning panic. Thoughts of cancer recurrence leap to the forefront and suddenly trigger vivid anxiety. Phyllis, an elderly woman, recovered quickly from her surgery with the loving support of her husband of 52 years. She told me about her one experience with pain and how she worried that it might be cancer again:

A year has gone by and I feel like a queen. Suddenly I am getting pain in my left breast. I was afraid to tell the doctor because I was afraid that I might have to go through the same thing. Finally I said I have to go whether I like it or not. It is getting me nervous and it is affecting me. I am frightened thinking maybe cancer has gone through my system. . . . Well, I had to have another mammogram and it was nothing. But I was so nervous.

Alison also told me about an experience she had when she found a lump under her arm. She said it can just drive you "crazy."

"Tell me about that experience," I said.

She replied:

If you get that little ache or get that little pain, you are concerned. And if it goes away, you are still concerned. I mean you don't know which way to turn. Are you happy that it's gone or should you go to the doctor? One time I felt a little something under my arm and I right away called the doctor. It was nothing.

The Anxiety of Follow-Up Tests. Follow-up mammograms and blood tests can be another trigger of overwhelming fear. The actual tests aren't difficult; the women perceive them as a security measure to check that cancer has not returned. When asked how she felt about the tests, Cheryl, a 45-year-old woman diagnosed with early-stage breast cancer, replied: "When I go for my checkup, I always feel very good because I feel good physically. I think everything is going to be fine and it is just a reassurance."

The difficult part of checkups is the l-o-n-g w-a-i-t for results. Delores told me how she felt: "You wait to hear everything is OK; you are just hanging on those words." During the wait, the women's minds are flooded with fears about cancer recurrence. The anxiety is so great that physical symptoms can appear. Terri, a successful real estate agent, told me what happens when she goes for her checkups. She laughed and said: "When I go for my mammography I am nervous. The funny thing is that the first one [malignancy] never showed up on mammography." I asked her to discuss her nervousness further. "I am not nervous when I first come in and . . . while they are doing it," she replied. "But then . . . you sit and wait to see the doctor and talk about it. When she calls me in, my heart is always racing just a little bit faster than normal."

"Heart racing?" I observed; "I am sure your palms are drenched!"

"Yes," Terri replied. "That is when I am nervous."

Jane had an even more terrifying story. She had her follow-up mammogram in the same room in which the original problem had been found! She told me:

When I went for my follow-up blood work and mammogram, I was nervous. When I went in for the mammogram, I was concerned because I went back into the same room I had gone into the first time. I told them that I didn't know if I liked being in this room again because the last time I was there I walked out without a breast basically. When I went in, I said to the nurse that as soon as possible I would like the results because the last time I was here it was not a pleasant experience. They must have developed them immediately and came right out and told me everything was fine.

What a flashback that must have been.

For Delores, who did not receive the same compassion as Jane, the experience was more terrifying. "How they don't tell you, how you must call your doctor and how you must wait, especially with mammograms," Delores exclaimed. "Women getting routine mammograms are one thing, but after you have had a problem they should tell you." I definitely agreed with her. "I beg them," she said, "'Can't you just tell me something?' They always say, 'You have to call your doctor.' It is so cold and totally uncaring."

The Doctor, a film released in 1991, made an excellent point. Actor William Hirt, the doctor in the movie, was diagnosed with cancer and suddenly saw health care from the patient's perspective. When he returned to practice, he was more compassionate toward his patients and even had his students become patients for a day! The experience is truly a good learning exercise. It should be mandatory that all health care workers become patients for a day!

The Community of Survivors. Women with breast cancer create their own tight-knit communities. They appear to have the ability to locate one another, whether at their jobs, in their neighborhoods, through other friends, or even in a store's lingerie department. When Cheryl told me about an experience she had in a lingerie department, I was truly amazed. Cheryl had had a modified radical mastectomy with immediate reconstruction. Then she "met a lady in the bra store." Cheryl laughed as she narrated:

This sounds ridiculous but I was going for a bra, a strapless bra, the year after this happened. The lady noticed my scars and asked me who my doctor was because she thought [the scars were] better than anybody's she had seen. . . . It turned out she was just a customer in the store. She had not had reconstruction although her surgery was seven years ago. She was debating about going to Atlanta for her surgery. So I gave her my name and the name of my doctor. She went to see the doctor and then she called me. We have become very close friends.

The friendships among women with breast cancer come about partly because they have shared the same experience. Each woman was clear on this last point: Others who don't have breast cancer can't understand because they haven't gone through the same thing. When Barb told me how she felt about his, it affected me. When I went to talk to Barb, I met her husband, John. In less than five minutes, I saw how close and loving they were with each other. Yet, despite their close bond, as Barb explained:

You really can't expect anybody to understand what this feels like. John can be empathetic. He really can't sympathize because he hasn't gone through it. Nor did my family members ever go through anything like that. Yes, they were there for me, but you are really very much alone when you have cancer. Nobody can understand what it feels like unless they have gone through it. Sometimes it is even difficult to put it down in words that truly describe how devastating it is to a person, especially a young person.

The Loss of a Community Member.   Although the community of women with breast cancer is a necessary and supportive one, cancer recurrence or the loss of a member is devastating; it is the most difficult of all fear-provoking experiences for breast cancer survivors. The women grieve for a lost friend and are petrified that they could be next. As Nancy showed me pictures of her friends, she explained:

Unfortunately, every other month someone has been pass-
ing away. These are people that I've gotten close to because
of our illness but also we've made friends. I've gone to a lot
of funerals and it bothers me every time. I am not only
grieving for this friend that I met and their pain and suffer-
ing, but knowing that I could be next.

The women try to rationalize that their situation is different
from their friends', but the harsh reality is that, without a known
cause and a known cure, this disease doesn't make sense. "You
just can't predict," Nancy said, "and you can't help thinking sometimes, 'Why isn't that me?'" The terror that runs through the
women is insurmountable.

Some women have found their reactions to other women's outcomes totally unbearable and have taken steps to alleviate their
overwhelming fear. Barb realized that she couldn't handle the fear
anymore and sought professional help. She told me about knowing
other women with breast cancer and what it did to her:

I have a cousin who died last year on Mother's Day. She was
56 and a year prior to that she was diagnosed with breast
cancer. A year later, she was gone. Then there were three
other people I know very well that went through it, two of
whom have had recurrences to the point that it will take
their lives. I think that is when I started to get professional
help because it was just blowing my mind. I was just con-
vinced that it was going to happen to me.

Sandy has also found her terror so unbearable that she must run
away from women who aren't doing well. She exclaimed:

I don't want to hear about women or anybody who had
breast cancer and then had other cancers come up. I don't
want to hear any of that because that's frightening. There
was one woman I couldn't talk to. She had cancer about five
years ago and then it came back in her bones. And she was
talking to me. She wanted to talk to me. I couldn't talk to her.

I could see the terror building in Sandy's eyes but she continued:

I saw her the other day; she was walking with her husband and I stopped and said hello and I put my arm around her and we embraced. We both wished each other luck and asked how each of us feels and so forth. But I found it very difficult.

The Role of Family and Friends. These situations within the community of women with breast cancer are extremely difficult. However, the community offers a great deal of comfort to each of its members. There is a bond of *really knowing* one another. I have observed the same bond in support groups. One woman might express her fear or emotions and, although the other women in the group don't immediately respond verbally, I see them all nodding their heads in agreement. They *know;* they have been there. I also see what powerful comfort and strength this sharing can bring to those in distress. This is exactly what Barb had said about her husband, John; he is there for her but he can't really understand because he hasn't gone through it.

As a result of the women's cancer experiences, family relationships change. Family members can become loving and supportive, their relationships growing stronger because of their giving. Terri, describing her family, said:

Actually, I would like to stay sick forever. It wasn't that I just wanted attention or anything. I liked the fact that it glued the family together. I liked how wonderful my family reacted, how beautifully they pulled together, how wonderful they were. My husband is wonderful and he is there.

Yet, with time, life for family members returns to the way it was before breast cancer. Family members cannot truly understand the breast cancer experience in the same way as another breast cancer survivor can. Terri continued:

Slowly but surely everything slips back. It is easier for everybody else to slip back. I don't know why, maybe because it didn't affect them directly; but in a way—sometimes, honestly, I resent it. I guess those are the realities and life goes on.

Elaine told me of her similar situation:

My family relationships are good but I would have to say right now that things are pretty much back to normal for my children. They don't always understand when I come home from a support meeting and I'm upset, because they see Mom back to doing whatever she was doing, looking pretty much the same as she looked before the surgery. After surgery, they were of course more supportive, more attentive, and more considerate.

I asked Elaine how she felt about that. She replied:

Sometimes I would like them to have more—oh, I don't want to throw everything back on the disease—but sometimes I expect them to understand without my telling them. They can't be mind readers, but I just feel like they don't think about it like I think about it.

Family and friends sometimes become uneasy when the women attempt to discuss breast cancer and their fear of cancer recurrence. Jane told me how much stronger her marriage has become, but she has noticed that discussion of breast cancer is forbidden. Explaining her conversations with her husband, she said:

I think he just wants this all in the past. If I talk about different things I have heard on the radio or something about my surgeon, I don't get a give-and-take conversation with him. I really think he wants this all in the past. Maybe there are some fears on his part. You know, talk about it and it will appear again. I don't know why but it is something I have picked up on.

Friends have similar reactions. Sandy maintains her positive attitude, in part, because she knows that people don't want to see her depressed. She told me:

You know, if you cry, you cry alone. If you smile, the whole world smiles with you. It's so true. If you have this attitude of feeling so sorry for yourself, people really don't know how to react. They really don't know what to say to you. They run away from you, not because they don't care, but because they don't know what to do.

Being with other women with breast cancer is not like that, though. The women really know and understand each other and they can express freely all of their emotions.

Breast cancer survivors understand that thoughts of cancer recurrence and an uncertain future have assumed permanent residence within their minds. Fear waxes at times, and blankets them until, just at the point of near-suffocation, the fear wanes.

Strong and loving relationships with family members help, but the more important relationship is with those who really know: other women diagnosed with breast cancer.

The Courage to Survive. For women who have not had breast cancer, the women's strength in getting through their survival seems amazing. As the women told me their stories, their strength as individuals became clear. Yet they did not see themselves in this way. Terri said:

People said to me, "You are so courageous." I don't think it is courage; I think it is doing what I had to do. I never felt courageous. I think I have a good attitude because I am so determined to do everything I must do. Courage is when you have a choice. I have had courage when I had a choice; but [here] I didn't have a choice. If I did [laughing], believe me, I wouldn't have done this. I don't know how much I did it for my family but I must be around for my youngest son, to nag him to go to college and to take his exams.

For Terri, the mother role had surfaced again, but even the women who did not have children stated that they just did what they had to do. As I sat and listened, my mind disagreed. These are strong, courageous women whom I admire greatly.

A New Outlook on Life. What has thus far been presented about life as a breast cancer survivor may give the impression that each day is frightening and unpleasant. However, at the beginning of this chapter, I stated that the women had given me a wealth of knowledge about the true meaning of life. Being a breast cancer survivor does not exclude contentment and a true appreciation of beauty and life. The women are happy and grateful *to be alive.* There is a sudden awakening to what is really important in life.

Terri couldn't believe how quickly and radically her life priorities changed. She explained to me, as her favorite cat slept curled in her lap:

Every little thing became so important, especially after being in the hospital for surgery. When I came home the following day, the grass was so much greener and I was so happy to see my pets and my children and everyone. I think I became so appreciative of little things. My priorities changed so radically—and so fast. I just decided right then what was important.

I asked her how she felt now. Terri replied:

Once in a while, I let the little things get me down, and then I stop and think about it. Was this really important four years ago and will it be important 100 years from now? I don't think so.

Elaine had a unique way of maintaining her new life-philosophy. She and her husband started collecting chiming clocks. As we sat and talked, we were suddenly interrupted by their noise, but Elaine explained:

The great clang of clocks you just heard is something my husband and I started collecting. We decided to do it as our way of reminding us that time is very precious and should not be wasted. They remind us each time they go off. As time goes on and your life gets busy or you have a flat tire, you sometimes forget. Even my children are now part of it because my son recently bought us a cuckoo clock.

Time *is* now precious, and the women want to live each moment to the fullest. Their lives are focused on meaning and pleasure, on time spent with family, and on the beauty of nature. They refuse to let daily hassles and pressures, pettiness, money, and a quest for constant perfection govern their lives. Nancy told me her life had changed for the better:

I am not pushing myself to have a spotless house every day. I have taken some pressures off myself. I take time to smell the roses, time to relax, time to read, just time to do things for myself. I like to live my life now in peace and love and I don't have patience or time for pettiness. Life is too short for those kinds of things.

Barb changed her outlook on life and said she was making a conscious decision not to worry anymore:

My husband is so disciplined and so regimented, like I used to be. Now it's not that important. If something needs to get done, I will get it done, but I don't kill myself worrying about getting it done. I do it in my own time, in my own pace. I have become much more mellow and not so frantic. I have a whole different frame of mind and I find myself working slower and smaller.

The Importance of Self.   In addition to the change in life priorities and the greater appreciation for each moment, the women place greater value on self. Choices in life are now guided by self-interest. Terri told me that she needs to please herself but she grapples with the word "selfish." "Somehow," she said, "this gave me permission to be a little more selfish—if that's the word. I used to think it was selfish, but there has to be a better word. To reach personal goals, to do the things that really give me pleasure." There should be a better word, because "selfish" doesn't sound appropriate. On the other hand, why can't the women be selfish after what they have experienced?

Barb went through the same debate on selfishness, but knows it is OK. She described how enlightening breast cancer was for her:

I learned a lot about myself. They were profound things. I think one of the main things that I learned about myself is to put myself first because I was . . . always so worried about helping everybody else and doing for everybody else. The most important thing that I learned is that I really did have to concentrate fully on myself and my own needs, desires, and happiness. This is something I have never ever done before. [The cancer] helped me do a great deal of soul-searching and determine what is it now that I can do to make my own life better, more purposeful, and more meaningful for me. I just do whatever I want, whenever I want. Sometimes I feel really selfish in doing that, but it only takes me about a second to get in check and say it's OK.

I smiled at what Terri and Barb had said. Because of their roles as mothers, women often try to do for and please others. As they were talking, I could see myself exactly in their shoes, doing for others, and feeling uncomfortable with the word "selfish." So I ask you to take a few moments here to consider this question: When was the last time you said "No" without feeling guilty? When was the last time you did something for yourself, took an afternoon for you? (I couldn't remember.) Time *is* precious and life *is* short. Life should be happy, pleasurable, and lived to the fullest. Would the world be more loving if we all faced death and then had a second chance to live?

The Need to Reach Out to Others.   Although the women may believe that they think only of themselves now, they have all reached out unselfishly to help other women with breast cancer. They want to share their experiences and provide guidance and support. More than interesting is the message the women want to tell others who are newly diagnosed: You *can* cope.

Nancy receives calls from women with breast cancer through a hotline phone number. Explaining how she tries to make the women feel better, Nancy told me:

> *Some women will call and be crying because they just got a diagnosis of breast cancer. You talk to them and toward the end I always try to make some kind of joke so they will laugh. I want them to laugh. Maybe then they will say this isn't going to be so bad after all.*

Cheryl described the same thing with her calls: "I find that I feel very good when I can talk to other people who are newly diagnosed."

"What do you say to them?" I asked.

"Well," Cheryl replied, "I guess when you hear about cancer, you keep waiting to feel awful and you hear how bad it is going to be. I think that somebody has to say that you can go through it without the problems." With this type of message and with more people surviving cancer today, societal pessimism about the disease may change toward the better.

FACING TOMORROW AS A SURVIVOR: A SUMMARY

What is it really like to be a breast cancer survivor? Surviving breast cancer arouses plaguing thoughts and emotions about life. The possibility of cancer recurrence, an uncertain future, and death are components of everyday life that can contribute to overwhelming fear when confronted with breast cancer information, personal physical changes, follow-up tests, and hearing about metastases or breast cancer deaths in friends. Personal coping strategies, such as mental closure to negative information, positive thoughts and attitude, increased faith, lengthening survival time, and sharing emotions with other breast cancer survivors lessen the fear.

Surviving breast cancer changes relationships. A new pattern of attachment develops as family and friends respond uniquely to the breast cancer experience. Open expressions of deep concern and support are conveyed to the loved one, although discussion of breast cancer and of the fear of cancer recurrence makes family and friends uneasy and is often discouraged.

Surviving breast cancer changes women's perspectives on life. The realization that time is precious inspires a new way of living each moment to the fullest, guided by self-interest. A change in priorities increases the valuing of family, nature, and self. A greater sense of self and of personal growth stimulates engaging in life activities that are personally pleasurable and valuable.

Surviving breast cancer and breast cancer treatment is associated with a physical recovery process. Gradually, strength and vitality return, and life activities are resumed with immense feelings of happiness and gratitude for being alive.

Surviving breast cancer also provokes a commitment to help other women who have breast cancer. Reaching out consists of being available to share experiences, to provide guidance and support, and to say, simply and clearly: "You will be able to cope."

ABOUT THE STUDY

The collection and analysis of material for this study were guided by the descriptive phenomenological research methodology developed by Colaizzi (1978). The first step in this process was returning to the phenomenon—in this case, being with women who were breast cancer survivors and who could articulate that experience. After gathering the material, analysis involved the following steps:

1. All the participants' oral descriptions were read in order to obtain a feel for them. Reading the descriptions in this manner attempts to determine an overall sense of the data.
2. From each description or protocol, significant statements and phrases that directly pertained to breast cancer survivorship were extracted. This process is known as extracting significant statements.

3. Meanings were formulated from these significant statements and phrases. Creative insight was utilized in order to leap from the descriptions to the formulated meanings. The formulations must discover and illuminate those meanings hidden in the written descriptions.

4. The formulated meanings were organized into clusters of themes. Again, creative insight was used to allow for the emergence of themes.

5. The clusters of themes thus far were integrated into an exhaustive description of the study phenomenon.

6. Final validation was achieved by returning to the participants with the clusters of themes and the exhaustive description. Any new relevant data that were obtained from the participants were incorporated into the fundamental structure of the experience.

REFERENCES

American Cancer Society. (1992). *Cancer facts and figures—1992.* New York: The Society.

Colaizzi, P. E. (1978). Psychological research as the phenomenologist views it. In R. Volle & M. King (Eds.), *Existential phenomenological alternative for psychology* (pp. 48-71). New York: Oxford University Press.

Siegel, B. S. (1986). *Love, medicine & miracles.* New York: Harper & Row.

ABOUT THE AUTHOR

Seven years ago, I began my personal journey with women who were diagnosed with breast cancer. Working in a surgical area in a hospital in Ohio, I saw the anguish in women's eyes as they suffered through the diagnosis and treatment of breast cancer. At that time, I became involved in support groups because I wanted to assist in alleviating this pain. Through these groups, I was able to reach out, listen to, and provide support to these women.

Knowing these women and learning about their life with breast cancer made me want to stop this from ever happening to any other woman. As a result, I became actively involved in educating women in the community about breast screening techniques, specifically mammography, breast self-examination, and clinical breast examination.

Four years ago, my husband and I moved to Florida with our two "sons" (dogs), Nicki and Bernie. Upon arrival, I immediately contacted the American Cancer Society and I have continued my involvement with breast cancer support groups and with breast health education programs in the community since that time. My direct involvement in these areas has generated numerous research questions and subsequently has been my focus of research. Although I am drawn to women with breast cancer and to this area of research, I hope someday that I will be forced to change my focus because breast cancer will no longer exist. I believe in my heart that such a day will come, because, seven years ago, I did not believe that I would be able to share beautiful stories about breast cancer survivors.

4

Fifty-Something: A Phenomenological Study of the Experience of Menopause

Geri L. Dickson

*I don't know how to be fifty. I'm not going to be fifty like my
mother, and there haven't really been any models.*
(West Coast woman, cited in Sheehy, 1993, p. 38)

---

*Of one thing I am sure. And that is that my experience of
menopause is more than the machinations of my hormones.
It is longer and wider and much, much deeper than the happenings in my physical self.*
(McCain, 1991, p. 19)

*I*n the summer of 1993, the headlines reported an intense heat
wave along the east coast. Temperatures reached record-breaking

highs of over 100 degrees for several consecutive days. The humidity nearly matched the temperature. Deaths in Philadelphia and New York were attributed to the heat. One group that was acutely aware of the heat was women who were experiencing the menopausal transition.

The hot flash that announces that transition is the trademark of menopause for over 50 percent of midlife women, according to research reports from primarily Euro-American women (McKinlay, Brambilla, & Posner, 1992). Irregular menstrual bleeding, sometimes heavy, sometimes light, also signals the change. Each woman is different: Menopause comes in many varieties. Women in my research reported a multiplicity of experiences when their periods and reproduction ended (Dickson, 1990; in press). Some women experienced intense reminders of menopause, others had some evidence of it, and still others just stopped menstruating. All wondered about hot flashes—why they got them or why they were spared. Sheehy (1993) likens the vagaries of menopause to the thumb print: Each is unique to the DNA of the individual woman.

PERSPECTIVES ON MENOPAUSE

Different perspectives have evolved about menopause. In American society, however, one perspective is dominant: Menopause is seen as a hormone deficiency disease. This perspective is the result of extant "scientific" research modes in which experience is studied through analysis of evermore discrete "variables." Such analysis is based on a causal, linear model that promotes cause-effect explanations. But is it possible to understand the menopause experience in this way?

The Traditional Perspective

In American society, indeed in the Western world as a whole, a stereotypic picture has evolved of the menopausal woman as in a state of crisis that is personally catastrophic and generally renders the woman inferior and incapable of rational functioning (Voda &

George, 1986). Scientific literature as well as social practices have contributed to this picture. Here is a perfect example of stereotypic thought about menopausal women, quoted from a peer-reviewed, nationally recognized medical journal:

> *The unpalatable truth must be faced that all postmenopausal women are castrates. . . . our streets abound with them—walking stiffly in twos and threes, seeing little and observing less. It is not unusual to find an erect man of 75 vigorously striding along on a golf course, but never a woman of this age. (Wilson & Wilson, 1963, p. 360)*

At first reading, this description may appear to embody an outdated view of women; nonetheless, the male continues as the norm in the aging process. Although perspectives are changing, the male as norm can still be seen in the exclusion of women from many medical clinical trials and in the need for medical science to restore and "tinker with" the hormonal steady-state brought on by the appearance of menopause (Wilbush, 1993).

Despite scientific advancement, stereotypes of menopausal women persist. Traditional research, based on a causal, linear model, reduces the experience of menopause to one of measurable variables. Thus, menopause can be identified using biological or sociocultural variables. Although the "symptoms" of menopause are described in glaring detail, only the cause varies as being biological or sociocultural. It is the *normalcy* of menopause that remains undocumented (Voda & George, 1986).

Current biomedical literature views menopause as a breakdown in the reproductive system that causes a cluster of symptoms characterized by hot flashes and a dry vagina, often with diffuse, psychological problems. This conceptual basis of menopause allows for the identification of menopause as a hormone deficiency disease—a disease similar to diabetes (a deficiency of the hormone insulin) or hypothyroidism (a deficiency of the thyroid hormones). Menopause biomedical research, which arises from a model with a focus on the biological, has revolved primarily around the relationship of hormones to symptoms.

Research originating from a sociocultural focus has sociocultural, rather than biological, variables as the cause of menopausal problems. In these studies, it appears that menopausal symptomatology is a behavioral phenomenon of Western culture. In cultures where diets may differ or where the role of older women is valued, "symptoms" as expressed in North America are not known (Beyene, 1986; Lock, 1986). From such cross-national studies a challenge arises: the hot flash as a universal menopausal experience can no longer be assumed.

One day, in the newspaper cartoon, "Ziggy," Ziggy is peering into the front window of "Mom's Diner," which appears to be closed. There is a makeshift sign posted in the window, "Closed for Hot Flashes." Usually, "Mom" is caring for others by providing home cooking in her diner. But when the symptoms of menopause overwhelm her, she retires to her bedroom, unable to deal with her obligations. Stereotypical examples like this one create limiting images in the minds of women and men. Humorously here, not so humorously in "the real world," women's capabilities are negatively equated with supposed limitations of their unique reproductive systems and hormones.

Carol, a 49-year-old, attractive, and very active divorcee, expressed these beliefs about how people, including her grown children, view her:

You're sort of over the hill or pretty close to it, and yet, I feel like I could almost start over. You know, a whole new life. But it's that age in your life when you're just really supposed to—I shouldn't say you're supposed to, but I have the impression that—you're supposed to be very settled. It's what people expect of you. (Dickson, 1989, p. 183)

The message to midlife women in our society seems to be that we should become and remain invisible. As more and more mature women become accustomed to being assertive and career-oriented, things will change. Gail Sheehy (1993) predicts that, over the next few years, the boardrooms of America are going to light up with the heat of hot flashes.

The Women's Perspectives

I have designed this research narrative to counter the biomedical discourses of menopause by giving voice to women's experiences of menopause. Descriptions of the lived experiences of menopause follow, as told to a woman by midlife women. I have based this research on van Manen's (1990) assumption that "human beings express their experience of the world through art, science, law, medicine, architecture, etc. and especially through language" (p. 14). Yes, this is phenomenology. In this chapter, then, I will weave a tapestry of the experiences of menopause from the "stories" of ten midlife women living the menopause transition and the themes I have identified in this analysis. By understanding or beginning to understand the meaning of this highly complex and individualized experience of women from the women themselves, nurses may discover ways to enhance quality of life for midlife women.

The Women's Voices

Let me introduce the women themselves as they tell their stories about menopause. There are various images of menopause. The experience is lived differently for each woman.

Hanna is a 54-year-old, single, Euro-American woman who works as a teacher in a community college. She was eager to tell of her experience:

I want to tell you about my menopause. It was wonderful, just WONDERFUL. For a long time I had very heavy bleeding and cramping with my periods. It would be awful. I had fibroids so I was really glad to see the periods go. I never had hot flashes or any changes in my periods. It seemed like one day I just happened to think, "When was the last time I had a period?" I actually could not remember. They just stopped. I was just through it and I didn't even realize it. I was just glad that it was over. I feel good, now, without periods and without hormones.

For Hanna, menopause was over before she knew it and it was wonderful to have it behind her.

On the other hand, women like Sara experience myriad problems that make their lives miserable. Sara is a Euro-American woman, married, with two grown children. Now 53, she experienced her last natural period when she was almost 51. Life became unbearable for her because of her frequent and intense hot flashes. In her full-time work as a nurse, her clients looked at her uneasily as she broke out in sweat every 30 minutes or so. Her sleep was constantly disturbed. Sex was unpleasant and undesired. However, she believed that she should have been able to cope with the changes she experienced:

> *I felt really bad about starting on Premarin. On one hand, feeling I had really copped out and that I wasn't strong enough to overcome this business. I thought I was aware of all of the social conditions, and so forth, that I was dealing with that. I had a good sense of myself, but it didn't make any difference. I couldn't control it and it was interfering with my life. And so I started on Premarin.*

Sara was as acutely aware of her menopause as Hanna was unaware of hers. Sara found the uncontrollable nature of the vagaries of menopause more than she could handle and sought medical help.

Barbara, Gwen, Bette, and Alice all expressed a great relief and joy in no longer having periods. Barbara is a 52-year-old, single, African-American woman who recently experienced a surgical menopause. She is not taking hormones and has some "warm flashes" occasionally. They are not particularly troublesome. She believes menopause isn't so bad:

> *My perceptions of menopause were very negative. Most of my age group are starting, or have had a surgical menopause, and they share the same feelings that I have. I'm so glad it's over! But I don't know if it's only hormonal change; your feelings change, your perceptions. Like, I really never thought that I would still be single and not have any*

children. But it's not so bad. Part of my experience was having a lot of bleeding; I had fibroids, and much bleeding. It was totally annoying. I was very anemic and very short-tempered. I don't really miss having children. I don't miss having a period.

Barbara was just glad to have it all over.

Gwen spoke rather matter-of-factly: Menopause meant no more periods. A 51-year-old, married, Euro-American woman with four children, Gwen had her last period more than a year ago. She described her experience:

I had a few periods of feeling warm, mostly at night. They were not bad, they weren't uncomfortable. In fact, I rather liked the warm feeling. They also weren't that often, just once in a while, once a day or so. Menopause means no more periods and I don't want to change that. I never had any particular problems with my periods, but they are messy. But I am still the same, I am the same person. Life goes on, no particular change. But sometimes I wonder about my bones. All in all, menopause is about changing periods. Before I stopped, my periods were irregular and then they just stopped. I believe the mind and the body are connected, but I didn't notice any other changes; otherwise I am the same person.

Gwen did not want to take hormones because they would reinstate her periods.

Bette also was glad not have periods because she had had cramping and heavy bleeding. Because of fibroid tumors, Bette also could not take hormones. A childless, 52-year-old white divorcee, Bette is now restructuring her career by attending college full-time. In her words:

I'm a 52-year-old woman who hasn't had a period in 3½ months, thank God. I've had so much pain and heavy bleeding with my period that the doctors couldn't do anything about. Menopause is a blessing! But what bothers me now is my forgetfulness. It's very strange; because it's almost as if I have Alzheimer's. I used to have a very keen memory and now I lose things, I'm losing things. I have so many thoughts in my head at once and they go right out of my head. So I get very frustrated. I've gone to school for the past two years and I have had difficulty concentrating. I'm thrilled that I am able to absorb as much as I am and I'm getting all As. Sometimes I wake up with joint pains that disappear once I get going. I have difficulty sleeping at night. What bothers me lately is that I get angry—so angry. Things can anger me so much easier than in the past. I don't know if it's menopause or just age or whatever; it's just all combined in one person. I'm having a lousy time of it.

Although Bette did not dwell on her bleeding or pain through the rest of her interview, she was still frustrated by experiences of forgetfulness and joint pain.

Alice is a 44-year-old African-American woman who had her uterus removed five years ago. She has a grown daughter. Her ovaries were left intact and she began last summer to experience some changes that she attributed to menopause:

Every now and then my whole waistline breaks out in perspiration. I've discussed this with a few other ladies and they told me that this is what happened to them in menopause. And it's just that mine attacked me around the waist. Theirs attacked down their backs, and some people told me that their chests perspired. I had such heavy bleeding with my period that I feel that not having a period is the most wonderful thing that ever happened to me in my whole life. Life is actually getting better. When you are young, you think that 40 is old. Now that I'm in my 40s, I really do not want to be 20 again. And I don't want to be in the 30s either. I don't feel old, I don't feel sick, and I'm not tired. I think, and I know, the value of what I want.

Menopause, without heavy bleeding, was wonderful for Alice.

Cecilia, a 45-year-old white woman, has not had a period in a year. She has two children, is divorcing, and is attending college full-time.

I'm 45 years old and in the middle of a messy divorce. I've had endometriosis and fibroids. I was told that the best thing for me was to go into the change of life. So actually my mind said to go into a change-of-life mode. My periods stopped. I've had like five or six in the last two years and I haven't had one in at least a year now. Most of my friends think I'm too young. My contemporaries don't want to hear about the change of life. I'm coming to terms with who I am as a person first, rather than as a woman. I feel much more comfortable with that. I'm just coming of age now. I would like to be healthy and be the best I can be, but I know I can never be 35 again. And that's all right. I don't like wasting anymore time, but it's still all right. It's knowledge that changes the dread of the menopause: knowledge of menopause and knowledge of myself as a person.

For Cecilia, the knowledge she has gained of herself and the knowledge that came from learning about the experience of menopause took the dread out of facing menopause.

Some women in their 50s are still menstruating. Irene is a white, married woman with four children in their 20s, two of whom live at home. She has experienced menstrual changes, but no other indicators of menopause. She says:

I'm 52 years old and still having periods, but I know that I no longer ovulate. I can tell the difference in my periods. They also are irregular. I've had only one friend that I have ever had discussions with, relative to menopause. [Our talk] dealt with hot flashes and those things. I always felt sorry for her because she constantly talked about her hot flashes. It seems that's all she could talk about, they were so all-consuming. I've never had anything like that. I haven't had any hot flashes. I've heard some bad things about hormones.

I'm very mixed up on the estrogen versus the hormones versus this or that, whatever. So I don't know at what point I would be forced to get involved with that. I guess my doctor and I will have to meet that issue when it happens.

Irene was concerned that she had not experienced the all-consuming hot flashes and worried that she may still experience them or, if not, wondered why she had been spared.

Some women, such as Anne, if they suddenly become menopausal through surgery, may have the choice of whether to have children taken away. Anne had a Dalkon Shield in place, which caused massive pelvic inflammatory disease. Consequently, she had a hysterectomy and oophorectomy at age 39. She described her experience:

I'm 42 years old and have had a surgical menopause. I don't take hormones because they do not agree with my gall bladder and I don't have much in the way of symptoms. I also don't have the money to pay for hormones. Because of my always drinking milk and the size of my bones, I'm not concerned with getting osteoporosis. However, I don't seem to have the same resiliency, I don't tolerate heat and cold very well, either one, as well as I did. I also don't have the capacity to ignore my blood sugar. It's like if I don't eat, I notice it. Menopause wasn't something I really had thought about, but the thing I really resent is having the choice of having children taken away from me. It closed down possibilities for me. Even though I thought it was probable that I would never have children, there's a difference between "I'm not going to do that yet" and "You can't do it." A little thing that bothers me is that my memory is not as good as what it was. I don't know if it has anything to do with menopause or not, but I find myself forgetting little things. One of the good things about this time of life is the evening out of my hormones. I don't have a problem at all in living without the hormonal wang-a-wang kinds of things. Living without that and not having periods is just fine.

The most disturbing factor about this unexpected menopause for Anne was having taken from her the choice of whether to have children.

Faye, a white, married woman with one college-age child, described how this time of her menstrual life reminded her of beginning menstruation. She described this as another phase of life:

> *I just turned 50 and I'm menopausal. For the past year I've noticed changes in my periods. They seem almost like the ones I had when I began menstruating. I spot a little and flow for a while and then some more spotting. I occasionally get some warm spells at night; I can't really call them hot flashes. I've always been so cold that I go to bed with two layers of nightclothes and socks to keep warm. Now I can take off the socks and the extra layers. I rather like that. The doctor said because I smoke I absolutely can't take estrogen. Menopause means to me the end of reproduction, just like starting menstruation was the beginning. I don't feel bad about ending menstruation, although I didn't mind my periods. It's just another phase of life.*

According to Faye, her experiences from the beginning to the ending are all part of being a woman.

THE LIVED EXPERIENCES OF MENOPAUSE

> *Menopause, the end of one's menstrual cycle, is an equal-opportunity employer. It happens to all women. It's a sure thing, like death and taxes. There is nothing exclusive or exotic about it. This isn't a ride on the space shuttle or a cruise to Tahiti. This is a trip every woman gets to experience. For some it will be smooth sailing, for others it will be scary as a jump on a bungee cord. Whether you live in Beverly Hills or Belgrade, Manhattan or Marrakesh, sooner or later you'll be riding the Menopause Express. (Sand, 1993, p. xiii)*

Part of my professional experience has been as an Independent Generalist Nurse in private practice. I cared for women clients who were experiencing or approaching menopause. At the time, I began searching the literature for helpful information about menopause. I found little. Ten or so years ago, few studies were conducted and self-help books were limited. Since then, research has grown, particularly regarding hormones; new popular-press books are published regularly. Some, such as Sheehy's *Menopause: The Silent Passage* (1993), have become best-sellers.

As the women of the Baby Boom generation approach midlife, the numbers of women entering menopause are increasing dramatically. Estimates of midlife women in the United States range from 39 million to 43 million (National Center for Health Statistics, 1985). Today, as more information is gathered about menopause, women have choices as to how they want to live the last third of their life. Quality of life thus becomes an important issue for women growing older, as well as for nurses who can assist women in making choices about life after menopause.

Although a woman's childbearing years are limited, being a woman continues far beyond and until death. As women age, the hormones that promote the menstrual cycle and fertility gradually diminish until all periods stop—usually around a woman's fiftieth birthday. However, this cessation can occur at any time in life if the ovaries are removed surgically. If the uterus is removed with ovarian tissue left intact, the natural process of diminishing hormone supply will continue, although periods and childbearing become impossible. Hormone therapy can ameliorate the unpleasant experiences associated with a surgically-induced menopause by replacing the normal hormones supplied by the ovaries. As we see, there are many facets of menopause; a surgical/medical menopause adds yet another experience to the range of naturally occurring menopause.

PUTTING THE WOMEN'S STORIES TOGETHER

From the women's stories, we can get a sense of what their experiences were. However, it is possible to put the stories together in order to discover common themes describing this time of life. All of the women viewed it as a time that would pass. Just as other periods in their life, "this too shall pass." Yet, it reminds them that they are getting older, that they are a certain age.

Just as there are common themes of the experiences, each woman's story varies a little from the other. But it is the themes that give us the "knots in the webs of our experiences, around which certain lived experiences are spun and thus lived as meaningful wholes" (van Manen, 1990, p. 90). The themes allow us to describe an experience and compare our own to it. They are a means of presenting a different view of menopause than that found in the biomedical or sociocultural literature. The themes describing the menopause experience are: "Hot Flashes and Other Annoying Things," "Periods or Period—All Part of Being a Woman," "Hormone Therapy—Friend or Foe?", "Getting Older or Getting Better?", "Overcoming the Silence of the Last Taboo."

Hot Flashes and Other Annoying Things

It starts as an intense heat deep inside my chest and burns its way out the top of my head. As it does, small rivers of sweat form on my forehead and around my hair line. It is a flash of short duration, but it steals my concentration and runs its own course.

The women's perceptions of their experiences of menopause represent a wide range. Hot flashes, forgetfulness, sexual disturbances, and sleep problems all give rise to frustrating and embarrassing episodes—the varying images of menopause. All but one woman interviewed, Hanna, experienced a changed sensation of heat/cold tolerance. However, the sensation ranged from a welcomed feeling of warmth at night to intense and frequent hot flashes that disrupted though and concentration. Nonetheless, embarrassment, frustration, and annoyance characterized some of the unpredictable events associated with the menopausal transition.

Our society's concern about keeping secret the effects of menstruation has been satisfied here (Delaney, Lupton, & Toth, 1988): Menopausal hot flashes often are viewed as something to hide, however difficult it is to do. One midlife woman put it this way:

I'd be sitting there happy as a lark, yapping away and all of a sudden you're dripping wet and sweat is running off your chin and your whole body is soaking wet, your clothes are all clammy. It would last a few minutes and then it would go away (Dickson, 1989, p. 185)

Sara described her feelings of embarrassment when she was having lunch with a male colleague and had a hot flash:

He looked at me strangely and said something like, "Are you warm?" I said, "Oh, yes, I am." And he said, "Gee, I was just thinking of putting on my sweater" or something to that effect.

Sara felt, and the implication was, that something was wrong with her. Although a friend of the man, she did not feel comfortable disclosing that she had had a hot flash. She continues to find hot flashes frustrating, especially since she takes hormones:

Though the flashes are much less severe, they still are there inside—a little less frustrating. But the disturbance of sleep and just the general annoyance during the day is not pleasant. That's how I look at it now, as just a little annoyance; it's not that bad. It has been almost four years since they started. How long will they last?

Weideger (1976) considered hot flashes a sign that menopause exists, and any sign that menopause exists can be as much a source of shame for a mature woman as the signs of menstruation can be for a younger woman.

The traditional view of the hot flash is met with concern and displeasure by Cecilia. She says:

Hot flashes are not bad. I'm sitting here now and I'm hot, but I'm going to cool off. . . . It's like you shouldn't be a prisoner in your body or to anybody. I don't think you should feel bad if you are sweating because you are having a hot flash. I think it is terrible what women do to each other. I find the competitiveness, about why is it you and not me, disturbing.

Some women flushed—that is, turned red— during the flash of heat and others didn't. The hot flashes started before the periods ended, although periods had become irregular. One woman's hot flashes were short-lived and she was able to conquer them with vitamins. She described the flushes this way:

There is no hiding when you have a hot flash. If you are in a very serious conversation with a mixed group and you turn beet-red, people tend to stop and say, Are you all right? You know, I found that very distracting. Or, when [the hot flashes] came and you couldn't concentrate on what it was you were supposed to be concentrating [on]. But, yet, it wasn't a sick kind of thing. (Dickson, 1989, p. 186)

Other women described changes related to temperature that were neither intense nor upsetting. Anne noticed some changes in temperature shortly after her surgery. She described them as:

Ambiguous. Which means I would be sitting in a room and suddenly I would think, "Gee, it's warm in here, isn't it? Is anyone else warm?" So the thing that made the most sense to me actually was something I read, because I also find that I do not tolerate cold/heat very well, either one, as well as I did. And I read somewhere that it's more like the thermostat is out of whack. That's what made sense to me, like my thermostat is out of whack.

She had read about flushes and flashes but said her experience wasn't anything like that; it was just a change in perception of hot and cold. Cecilia also experiences feelings of being warm: "They come up my chest into my neck and I ask people if it's hot and they say no. I don't get soaking wet, but I get damp."

Barbara had minor occasional feelings of being warm, which she described as "warm flashes." Gwen and Faye also experienced occasional feelings of warmth, often at night. They felt good rather than uncomfortable. Alice talked about earlier episodes, which have now stopped:

I had these episodes of a fast breakout into perspiration [and] I'd assumed that it was menopause. Every now and then, although it hasn't happened for a while, my whole complete waistline breaks out into perspiration. Mine just attacked me around the waist.

Forgetfulness was disturbing and annoying to some of the women, particularly those who had had exceptional memories. Anne described the change:

I still have a very good memory, but I used to have a photographic memory. And it's just gone now. I just don't know what happened to it. So I don't know if it has anything to do with menopause or not.

Although Anne's change in memory was annoying, Bette found her problems with memory most upsetting. Bette compared her forgetfulness to having Alzheimer's disease:

It's not a normal thought thinking. I get very confused, I often get confused. It's not like me, for example, to go into a room five times for something. When bills come, I pay them immediately so nobody—God forbid—should say you haven't paid your bill. But you see, it's problematic because it worries me and the more I worry the more confused you can get. So it feeds upon itself.

Despite her feelings of frustration at forgetting things and her confusion in thinking, Anne has maintained all A's in her college classes.

Sleep disturbances also act as annoyances. Most often, the women were awakened by hot flashes, but Bette described falling asleep when she'd like to be awake:

There's another thing that's embarrassing me to death. I fall asleep. I never fell asleep before. It started before these three months. Last winter I took an art course at the Museum. I was interested in it, I couldn't wait to get there. I got there, I sat down, and I fell asleep! I hear it, but I'm sleeping. That's very, very embarrassing to me. I can't do anything about it right now.

Four of the ten women who shared their experiences were not sexually active, primarily because they did not have interested partners. Bette mentioned feeling a little sore after sexual intercourse. Sara had problems with vaginal dryness that she did not find easy to relieve:

They say things like just add a little lubrication or stuff like that. I didn't find that to be real satisfactory and I wasn't real interested in having sex nor did I find it particularly enjoyable, which I had in the past.

In a recent book that gives a humorous twist to the experiences of menopause, Sand (1993) describes her sexual experiences:

Lately, my sex drive has gone from neutral to reverse, and with good reason. My vagina is dry, my clothes are wet, my hormones are low, and sex hurts. When my husband and I make love it feels like a root canal. I moan like Monica Seles, but it is out of agony, not ecstasy. (p. 45)

Concerns like these may be somewhat relieved by hormones, but, as both Sara and Sands discovered, it's not quite the same.

Changes in temperature perception, bouts of forgetfulness, sleep disturbances, and changes in sexual activity are annoyances of this time of life. Not having control over when hot flashes or other changes may occur remains frustrating. Some of the frustration revolves around not knowing how long an annoyance will last, but it is comforting to know it will pass. Bette says: "What I try to say to myself, because it frightens me, is that it will pass." Cecilia also expressed optimism that this time will pass. Bette reminds us that all the experiences are in the context of being a woman and that it is difficult to separate the physical from the emotional or the sociocultural—or, in fact, menopause from aging. "I don't know if it's menopause, or just age, or whatever; it's just all combined in one person."

Periods or Period—All Part of Being a Woman

Ruby-colored friend,
for forty years
you visited me.

then fled like the flasher
who shames young women
by spreading his raincoat
blackly open

and I don't miss you
nor think of you
except once in a blue moon
when the sun defers
to the power of night

leaving me nothing
to howl about.
(Seltzer, 1991, p. 25)

Today, in our society, women have choices in planning their families. Women can decide how many children to have and when to have them. The decision to have the last child may be made long before periods end and the ability to reproduce ceases. Women no longer expect to spend many of their adult years pregnant; they now menstruate for much of their adult lives. Because of these available choices, the closure of reproductive life may not have the same consequences as it has had in the past. However, menopause may have other meanings, revealed as the women in the study shared their experiences and feelings about the beginning and the end of menstruation.

The irregularities of periods that most women experienced at this time of life led to some ambiguity about the cycling's end. Irene complained, "It's been like every other month I skip and sometimes I have it every month and sometimes I think, I've finally finished this time, but no, it shows up again. Fine (1991) reports taking refuge in the reality of being menopausal and looking forward to joining an ancient sisterhood; however, approaching menopause is not without ambiguous feelings:

> *And this bloody bleeding. An end to that. The mess. The clocking and calculating. The worry and wondering. The cramping and irritability. The stained underwear and sheets. The mountains of paper products/forests sacrificed to absorb blood. Would I miss this? MAYBE. (p. 12)*

Faye described menopause as meaning the end of periods and the end of reproduction:

> *Menopause means the end of reproduction just like starting menstruation was the beginning. This is the ending. It means a fact, and doesn't seem to hold any greater meaning. I don't feel bad about ending menstruation, although I don't mind my periods. It's just another phase of life.*

Faye has noticed changes in her periods during the past year and reminisced as to how her periods now are like her early periods in the nature and consistency of the flow.

Gwen echoed Faye's matter-of-fact description: "All menopause means is no more periods and I don't want to change that. Otherwise, life goes on, no particular change." Having periods is all part of a woman's life, which can, and does, go on without the cycling of the menstrual cycle. Womanhood is important; it is not defined by menstruation or menopause.

Alice remembers that time in her life when she was awaiting her periods and the beginning of cycling:

> *I was twelve when I started having my period. We couldn't wait to have it because that means you're a woman. But we didn't know what trouble you could get. So this [no more periods] has been the . . . happiest time so far as*

that is concerned. Sex is wonderful, you don't have to worry about getting pregnant. That's always very stressful.

Cecilia expressed similar feelings: "I honestly feel better not getting my periods. I feel, when I had it, I had cramps and crying, and if you yelled at me I would melt. And I don't have that now. Part of it is, I am older, but it is also not the same."

Barbara, a childless woman, described how her feelings and perceptions changed over time. She really hadn't anticipated being unmarried and childless at age 52. She continued: "But it's not so bad. . . . I don't really miss having children. Maybe in another life." She was extremely relieved to be rid of her very heavy and annoying periods.

Anne, who had had an early surgically induced menopause said:

I don't have any children. And I think so much happened that I kind of pushed that all off to the side, rather than deal with it. And also, because I think it was too, too painful to think about and so much was going on.

Menopause, then, may come as part of a major life-event—in Anne's case, a life-threatening infection requiring surgery—or as a result of medical treatment such as chemotherapy or radiation therapy for cancer. Anne continued:

Circumstances in my life have changed, and changed in such a way that if it was something I could have chosen, I would have chosen to have children. But my life is what it is. Things happen and you lead the life you have. But that whole kind of life crisis, that was the hardest part, and years passing in coming to terms with the regret did not make a difference. Nothing makes a difference. I have the life that I had and this is it.

Sara, who has two grown children, described how she had her family as a young person:

I had my family before I knew it. I had my children as a teenager and spent the rest of my life avoiding pregnancy. I had my last child a long time ago and decided not have any more. In an almost romantic sense, I wouldn't mind another child, but in reality, I really didn't consider that an option. In fact, I often think that had I to do it over again, I would remain childless.

Although she enjoys her children and her two grandchildren, Sara's decision not to have more children was made years ago.

Some childless women, such as Hanna and Barbara, did not express any particular feelings about not having children or ascribe to menopause any greater meaning than the end of cycles. Bette was so upset by the periods of forgetfulness, the joint pains, and the anxiety of anticipating another heavy bleeding episode, that she didn't think about any greater significance. Some of that preoccupation also was expressed by Anne when she talked about menopause being buried in an avalanche of all the other "stuff" surrounding her surgery.

The experience of cycling has been part of a woman's life for 35 or so years by the time she reaches menopause. Periods and cycling are experiences of the "lived body": the beginning and the ending of periods have particular significance to women. Although the official end of cycling, menopause, has been defined by researchers as 12 months past the last menstrual period, this medically derived definition carries with it a context about women and menstruation that does not necessarily fit with women's accounts of their own experiences. Many women identify themselves as experiencing menopause when they are having irregular periods, hot flashes, and other annoyances, even though by the "official" definition they are still menstruating and not menopausal. Medically, this time has been identified as perimenopausal, but women do not seem to recognize that term.

Hormone Therapy—Friend or Foe?

*To estrogen or not to estrogen: That is the question
It would be great to get a good night's sleep and a good
     night's sex
and skin that looks younger and to feel better*

and not to worry about heart disease and osteoporosis.
But is estrogen safe? (Sand, 1993, p. 58)

Although only Sara was currently taking hormones, all of the women interviewed were aware of hormone therapy. Anne and Barbara took hormones immediately after their surgeries, but no longer take them. Several factors played a role in their decisions on whether to take hormones. Physical conditions such as fibroid tumors or gall bladder disease were deterrents to taking hormones. If the women were smokers, they were advised not to take hormones. But, overall, the women were facing problems that they believed they could handle, and they preferred to be without hormones.

Some women, such as Irene, expressed some confusion over hormone use. Irene felt that she would consult her doctor if she believed that hormones could help her. Although the oral regimen is most popular, several different dosages and prescriptions are possible. Greer (1992) pointed out the variations:

[Hormone] treatment may be long-term, or short-term, or even for the term of one's (un)natural life. The hormones may be taken by mouth, by injection, as a subdermal implant, as a topical application, or absorbed through the skin from a cream, gel or patch. (p. 174)

The current generation of midlife women is familiar with the use of hormones. With the introduction of oral contraceptives in the 1960s, many used the high doses of estrogen pills available in the first oral contraceptives. Others remember the use of diethylstilbestrol (DES) for the maintenance of problem pregnancies during the 1940s, 1950s, and 1960s, and the dire consequences suffered by children born from these pregnancies. They also remember the increased incidence of endometrial cancer associated with the use of estrogen therapy, publicized in the 1970s. Generally, they are aware of the current debate about the incidence of breast cancer and hormone use. These factors, along with currently "feeling good," contribute to many women's decisions that they do not need hormones. Cost also was considered a factor by one woman.

Menopause has often been used to explain away or "dismiss unacceptable thoughts, feelings, or behavior of women" (Perlmutter & Bart, 1982, p. 187). Stereotypes continue to put forward the view that menopause is catastrophic. A recent example of this view appeared in an episode of a popular weekly television series, "Picket Fences." A middle-aged woman was accused of killing her husband during a menopausal "frenzy." Found guilty, she was released on probation by the court, but ordered to remain on hormone replacement therapy. In the last decade of the 20th century, this TV court action seems preposterous. Equally silly was the first mention of menopause in a television show in the 1960s, when "All in the Family's" Archie Bunker, in traditional Archie fashion, ordered his wife Edith to hurry up and complete her "change."

The belief that hormones can cure menopause builds on an assumption held over from the 19th century—that women's reproductive systems are inherently pathological and every phase of women's life cycle is viewed as potentially pathological (Ford, 1986). The politics of pharmaceuticals have thus resulted in big business in which physicians act as the medium for the administration of menopausal drugs.

Admittedly, hormones do ameliorate some of the annoying aspects of menopause, especially for women who have had a surgical/medical menopause. Yet some women, like Anne, choose not to take hormones. She described her reasons:

My decision not to take hormones is partly because I can't afford it . . . but partly because they didn't agree with my gall bladder, and partly because I really don't have much in the way of symptoms. Other than possibly preventing osteoporosis, they didn't have any immediate effect on anything.

Although a hysterectomy was a possibility for Bette, she was relieved to avoid surgery to control her heavy bleeding. She said:

I was praying, it's time [for menopause], and I thought "I'm better off without the surgery." I can't take the estrogen, and I don't think I'm able to take the progesterone. I got hepatitis once from the birth control pills.

Cecilia also expressed concern about taking hormone therapy because she developed blood clots after taking birth control pills for only three months. She also feels fine: "I honestly feel better not getting my periods."

Most of the women spoke about hormones for relief of the current discomforts of the transition, rather than for the possible long-term benefits. Because Gwen had a family history of osteoporosis, she expressed concern about taking hormone therapy:

I called the university and talked with a nurse and she explained to me about the hormones. She said if she were me she would take the estrogen/progesterone because of the possible buildup of the lining of the uterus. Otherwise, she convinced me that they were safe, but I don't want to get my periods again. I don't want to mess with that.

Hanna felt good at reaching menopause. Although she was familiar with hormone therapy and had discussions with her friends about hormones, she decided not to take hormone therapy. She said, "I never had a problem, I never got hot flashes, I never needed hormones, and I haven't been back to the doctor since." Anne expressed a similar reaction; she felt better without the "hormonal wang-a-wang kinds of things" and without periods.

Sara, on the other hand, was miserable with intense hot flashes and sleepless nights. Her colleagues, clients, and others, noticing her hot flashes, asked whether she was OK. The annoyances of menopause were making her life unbearable. Despite feeling she should have been able to control these "symptoms," she sought medical help and started taking Premarin. She admitted:

That was one of the biggest disappointments of my life. From what I had read, I thought estrogen would take away the symptoms and I would feel the same as before I turned 49½. But that didn't happen. I still had hot flashes. I still woke up frequently and I still found sexual activity difficult.

She continued to take the Premarin and gradually her hot flashes became tolerable, but they never completely went away.

Faye asked about hormones when she had her annual visit to the gynecologist. As she described it, "I went in for a pap [test] about four months ago and I asked about hormones. They said absolutely no estrogen because I smoke. End of discussion."

Alice did not take hormones nor feel the need to consider them, even though she had episodes of sweating around the waist. Her ovaries were left intact and, therefore, she "was not experiencing these mood swings and these other things that most women experience when they have a hysterectomy complete." Based on what she was experiencing, she saw no need for hormones.

Although there have been full-page advertisements for hormone replacement therapy in papers such as the *New York Times,* as well as women's magazines, the women's stories here do not reveal a real movement toward taking hormones. Despite the advertisements and the news reports regarding hormone therapy, these women are not interested in hormone therapy until they perceive that they have a problem that hormones may help. They may make life-style changes such as adding exercise, giving up alcohol, reducing stress in their lives, and trying vitamins or minerals to feel better. Many of the women are concerned about their bones and are aware of the risk factors for osteoporosis. However, many remain skeptical about the long-range effects of hormone use. It is estimated that about 20 to 25 percent of eligible females in the United States take hormone therapy (Oddens, Boulet, Lehert, & Visser, 1992).

Getting Older or Getting Better?

At menopause as never before, a woman comes face-to-face with her own mortality. A part of her is dying. If she has been encouraged all her life to think of her reproductive faculty as her most important contribution, the death of her ovaries will afflict her deeply. Nothing she can do will bring her ovaries back to life. . . . At the turning point the descent into night is felt as rapid; only when the stress of the climacteric is over can the aging woman realize that

autumn can be long, golden, milder, and warmer than
summer and is the most productive season of the year.
(Greer, 1992, p. 124)

Some women clearly identify the menopausal transition as a
marker of aging and a time of coming to grips with getting older.
Others view it as an opportunity of time "for me," time for enjoying a new and different kind of life. Delaney et al. (1988) suggest
that the symbolic importance of menopause gives greater weight
to the occasional physiological or psychological disturbances.
Although throughout our menstrual lives there were times when
we felt depressed, unable to sleep, or noticed wrinkles under
the eyes, "the actual changing of the cycle, the expectation that
soon there will be no blood, brings into focus other common
signs of aging, labeled 'menopause,' that had simply been ignored" (p. 235).

Sara seemed to bear this out when she said, "Menopause means
getting old. I think it is a real low blow to come as you turn 50. I
think that, in and of itself, is enough to cope with, without adding
menopause." In a similar vein, Irene expressed concern about getting old, "Menopause means like getting old and wrinkled. That
kind of bothers me and gray hair bothers me." Yet, growing old
with gray hair and wrinkles happens to all of us, men and women
alike, and is not linked to menopause.

Bette expressed a variety of feelings about getting older, as she
began talking about age:

Some women have a problem saying what their age is. I
never had it. I couldn't wait to be 40, or in the 40s or 50s. I
should not have the period. I was proud; anybody could ask
how old I was, and I'd say, "I'm 44, I'm 45." On a conscious
level, I'm not aware of an age problem.

Later in the interview, she described how thrilled she was to have
been without a period for the past 3½ months:

[Y]et this aging is creeping up and there's so much we want
to do as people. We want so much to achieve more, to do

more. We look at our time, we wake up (not all of us, some are lucky) with aches and pains and [we] say what's going to be a little bit down the road. Hopefully, it will be better and if it isn't, why we have to live with it. I never was age-conscious, now I am. . . . And I think that's where my anger comes from.

Although no more periods was a blessing, other reminders of aging were disturbing.

Cecilia also expressed some ambiguous feelings about aging. On one hand, she said: "I don't mind saying I'm 45 because I know I can't be 44 next year. It's something I've always understood about age. I would like to be healthy and be the best I can be, but I know I'm never going to be 35 again. And that's all right." On the other hand, she expressed a desire to deny the whole thing because she was 45, instead of 50:

I don't know if I would stand outside and say "I'm going through menopause," but I won't say I haven't gone through it if someone asked me. . . . I think years ago I might have said "I'm not going to talk about it." You know, I'll wait until I'm in my 50s. Even if it happened at 30, I would like to deny the whole thing. And I just do remember this second, keeping a box of Tampax somewhere. If I am going through menopause I'll keep a box of Tampax in the bathroom, you know, after I'm through with it. For ten years I'll have this dusty box of Tampax sitting on the shelf, like [I'm] a real woman.

Anne's mother died at age 46. Anne assumed that the same thing would happen to her. Yet, Anne had a serious illness and didn't die. She had to come to grips with not dying. It helped her to realize, "I have to be a grown-up." She began to take life more seriously as she aged, and she seized the opportunity to start a business.

Barbara talked about her experiences of menopause and how different they were from her expectations. She had very negative perceptions of menopause. When she was younger, she thought menopause showed that women were getting older, but now she is glad it's over. Along the same lines, Alice said:

Things are OK; it seems that I felt like I was trying to cram a lot into improving myself. After I got to be 30, I wasn't like that.

Not only is it OK to be in the 40s, according to Alice:

I think it's like that old saying: The older you get, the better you get as a woman. That's actually true. I really feel that way. And I feel that I look pretty good, I feel OK, and I really feel that I still have things to look forward to. I feel that life is getting better, so life is actually getting better.

Returning to school, starting new careers or enhancing old ones, and starting a business are just some of the ways in which these women are renewing their lives. These actions are consistent with what Delaney et al. (1988) have identified as a common theme today "of menopause as 'rebirth,' a time when a woman is freed from childbearing and childrearing, freed to a new enjoyment of sex and a renewed dedication to her work" (p. 222).

Cecilia described how she is coming of age now and viewing herself as a person first and then a woman:

I think [I'm] coming in tune with personhood (it's not my favorite word) . . . feeling my identity, getting an identity, rather than being a female vector for having children, and giving up the idea that if something is wrong with me, I could just be tossed aside.

From Cecilia's experiences, in the context of her life, being female meant being unblemished. In her marriage she knew that, "If I lost a breast, he would divorce me. I didn't even do that and he divorced me." However, now that she has gained a new perspective on herself and her life, she is able to return to school and pursue her new interests.

The varied and fluctuating patterns of a woman's body are somewhat foreign to men's experiences. Thus, a male "norm" has been applied to the female aging process.

The normal, natural, harmonious aging rate with respect to lifespan is found in the example of a healthy man. A man remains male as long as he lives. . . . No abrupt crisis has to be faced. A man's life proceeds in smooth continuity. His feeling of self remains unbroken. (Wilson, 1966, p. 51)

Such thoughts about aging, from Wilson's popular book, *Feminine Forever,* have left their mark on women. In her study of midlife women, Cohen (1984) concluded:

In our society, women are deemed "medically old" at 40. The "disease" to which all women succumb, according to the vast majority of members of the medical profession, is menopause. Considering that 40-year-old women can anticipate approximately 40 more years of life, it is difficult to accept that we have been stereotyped as "aging" when 40-year-old men are perceived to be at their vigorous best. (p. 53)

The female experience is biologically different from the male experience, but is it pathological?

Menopause remains a marker of the female aging process, but the women's perceptions of menopause were colored by society's generalized negative view of getting old. Yet, some women can accept aging and move into a life that has more time for them, more money for them, and more opportunity to do as they please. In a poem entitled "Warning," Joseph (1991) advocates practicing for old age and writes about what she will do:

When I am an old woman I shall wear purple
With a red hat which doesn't go, and doesn't suit me . . .
I shall go out in my slippers in the rain
And pick the flowers in other people's gardens
And learn to spit (p. 1)

Can we look forward to growing old gracefully and learning "to spit," whatever that metaphor may signify for us?

Overcoming the Silence of the Last Taboo

Recently women have begun to talk to each other about their personal experiences and to look for guiding images from antiquity, when women had community rituals to help them through life's changes. Rites of passage are needed to integrate the personal and the transpersonal, to make social our individual crises, and to find validation for our experience. (Strahan, 1990, p. 189)

Partners don't always know what is going on. Sara told me: "I was concerned about my husband and I didn't really feel able or willing to share with him what I was experiencing. I really didn't want him to know about it." To open the closed door on the taboo subjects of menstruation and menopause, Delaney, et al. first published their book, *The Curse: A Cultural History of Menstruation*, in 1976. They described the purpose of their book as breaking the silence about menstrual taboos and showing men and women how their bodies have defined them. To accomplish this, they wrote, "Flippancy was the tool we used to shock women out of their embarrassment into an acceptance of this natural process and an understanding of how negative attitudes about menstruation led to the devaluation of women, by themselves and others" (Delaney et al., 1988, p. xii). Weideger (1976) also had observed the silence surrounding both menstruation and menopause. Although the anticipated hot flashes of menopause are not viewed as pleasurable experiences, "not many of us have talked about them, thought about them, or questioned our assumptions about them" (p. 225).

New books on menopause are coming out regularly now and are covering a wide range of perspectives. The traditional biomedical books that advocate medical treatment are still with us, but new ones are also appearing. For example, *Women of the Fourteenth Moon* (1991) is an edited collection of firsthand experiences of menopause by midlife women writers. These books tend to bring menopause into general conversation, which may help to debunk myths about menopause. Eventually, the silence surrounding menopause can be broken and the unspoken fears and myths associated with it will fade.

Yet, many women find it difficult to talk about their experiences with people close to them, let alone to announce to the world that they are menopausal. Irene expressed trepidation when she said, 'I think I had part of the idea that when you go through your change, you're getting old. You know, that type of thing. And I . . . didn't care to talk about it to anybody" (p. 13). Other women have noted a loosening of the cloak of silence surrounding menopause. Barbara believes, "People are more relaxed now. People are more open and talk about it; they know what to expect. The unknown is always very frightening." Perhaps the influx of books and publicity is helping to educate people and, in turn, exposing some of the previous taboos.

Most of the women in this study did not talk with their mothers or daughters about menopause. Some had memories of their mothers going through the menopausal transition, but it was not discussed. Cecilia, for example, remembered:

My youngest brother is 26 and mother was 39 when she had him. And shortly thereafter, she could have been 40 or 44 or 42, but I don't remember her being old, she probably barely mentioned symptoms, it was something we didn't talk about.

Other women, such as Barbara, recalled discussing experiences with relatives:

My family is very close. African-American families are extended. We would talk about our menstrual experiences. They didn't know anything about going to the doctor and getting hormones. My mother went through menopause and I never knew it. It was a very smooth thing. My grandmother went through the change and thought she was dying. She had palpitations and hot flashes and never went out by herself. She only would go out when someone took her out in a car.

A variety of experiences of menopause are apparent in the family history of Barbara.

Alice, also an African-American woman, did not discuss menopause with her mother, but has very clear memories of her mother's experience. She expected a similar pattern, but that didn't happen.

> *I watched my mother go through menopause. I guess I was expecting something like what I saw her going through, with hot flashes and ripping the window open and then all of a sudden she'd be cold and slamming the window closed. She had mood swings. I though she was going to go crazy!*

For herself, Alice thinks that "I'm pretty much the same person, I haven't acted like that."

Other women, such as sisters and friends, are good sources with whom to discuss menopause and learn about others' experiences. Faye has a sister slightly older than she is, and they have talked about each other's experiences. Faye has also talked with friends: "One friend in particular is having a very rough time of it. She took hormones for a while but had many problems and now has stopped. She feels much better." Irene, on the other hand, has had few discussions with friends. She had just one friend who talked on and on about her hot flashes; Irene really felt sorry for her. Sara talked about sharing hot flash stories with her friend. They could laugh over them as they shared their "sweating" over coffee.

When menopause is early, as in Anne's case, friends may not be experiencing the same things. A friend of her sister sent Anne a copy of an article to read, and she bought Anne a book that she had found helpful. For the most part, the women did not find talking to their doctors helpful. Anne's comments represented this general sentiment: "And I don't recall that my doctors were very helpful. [laughing] No, not very helpful at all."

This study of the women's stories supports the idea that it is helpful to discuss menopausal experiences with others who are encountering this time of life. Even though experiences vary, talking and being listened to do help. Sara said, "We need someone to seriously listen to us and that usually isn't the physician." Talking with each other and sharing stories will help to bring menopause out from the pages of biomedical research and into the "reality" of menopause among women living the experience. The numbers of books and the media attention given to menopause, along with more open discussion among women and men, will help to change the outdated stereotypic picture of the menopausal woman.

Cecilia, a 45-year-old member of the Baby Boom generation, talked about how women had changed during the 1960s. "My aunt is 50 and she is still getting her periods. I've talked to her about it but she is from a different generation. She's not quite part of the 1960s when you were liberated, or I thought I was." Cecilia felt a real connection in being able to talk with me about the topic of menopause. "I was happy about your sign [recruiting women] because it was a connection: from me to you personally and with the subject matter." From her liberation and her feelings of connection with other women, Cecilia expressed her frustration with the current definition of menopause, which originates from the male model of biomedical research:

> *If menopause is life, so be it. And I'll be damned if some _____ man is going to tell me that I have to have this image. I don't want it. You know, so I want to be able to sweat. I want the right, so I'm sweating. It's part of life and I like it.*

Although other women may not put it so forcefully, thoughts about becoming "the woman I always wanted to be" are resonating. It is a time of life, when "I have time for me; a time to please me." Greer (1992) identifies it as a time that marks the end of apologizing. With a loosening of the grip of stereotypes, the menopausal transition can be viewed from a woman's perspective as having a positive aspect, in spite of annoyances, that leads to a new place in life where, perhaps, older is better and wiser. It can be, as Sheehy (1993) writes, a time that invites meditation and spiritual exploration. "A wise woman will make time to contemplate things eternal and appreciate the life she has" (p. 218).

KNOWLEDGE OF THE LIVED EXPERIENCE
OF MENOPAUSE FOR NURSES

*Nursing has advanced a philosophy that embraces the whole
of the human condition. It professes values that include respect for each individual and their cultural interpretation of
meaning in experience and events. Following from this is an
emphasis on self-determination and autonomy. A qualitative perspective then becomes essential from the philosophical perspective of nursing not only as a research design but
also for actual implementation of a holistic, empathic, individualized delivery of nursing care. (Munhall, 1989, p. 27)*

This research study was undertaken in an attempt to understand the meaningful whole of the experience of menopause.
From the process of phenomenological reflection, five essential
themes were identified and explored as aspects of living the experience of menopause. These themes can be viewed as the
knots in the web of the lived experience of menopause and as
new directions from which to understand the living experience
of menopause. However, the formulation of themes is at best a
simplification of the phenomenon. Although the research is from
the perspective of the persons living the experience, it falls
somewhat short of picturing the whole experience (van Manen,
1990). Yet, the description and themes of phenomenological
reflection and writing present a picture much closer to the
"meaningful whole" than do other kinds of research.

This research, which is a process of coming to understand
rather than one of identifying and evaluating outcomes of the
"treatment" of the event, is consistent with the philosophical values inherent in the practice of nursing. This represents new
knowledge that is not based on a linear, causal model of research
that supports the current medical view of menopause as a breakdown in the reproductive system—a hormone deficiency disease. The rich description of the menopause stories and the
essential themes identified can be used as a basis to provide
knowledge for nurses in helping to understand the experience.

Women want someone to seriously listen to them and to acknowledge their individual experiences. Women have unique stories to tell; indeed, their stories are as individual as their DNA (Sheehy, 1993). Although the essential themes identified in this study describe certain fundamental aspects of the experience of menopause, each woman will live the themes in her own way. Nurses may have general knowledge to share with a woman regarding the physiological changes taking place during this transition. But, as McCain (1991) has identified, menopause is more than the machinations of hormones, "it is longer and wider and much, much deeper than the happenings in my physical self" (p. 19). The meaning of the experience for each individual woman is what nurses may help women to understand and to grow with.

Building on the first theme, hot flashes and other annoyances, nurses can recognize the individual differences among women by listening seriously to each woman's menopause story. What annoyances are being experienced? What are the meanings of these annoyances to a woman? How can the nurse affirm and support these experiences as within the normalcy of the menopausal transition? Here is an opportunity to give holistic, empathic, and individualized nursing care.

In approaching the second theme, periods or period—all part of being a woman—nurses can help women to grow into nonmenstruating women, to accept this inevitability. Although periods may be messy and inconvenient, there are times when most women will miss the whole experience of having a period, will miss the ebb and flow of hormones. The context changes along with the experience, and nurses can teach, counsel, and support a woman as the context of her life changes. Change is continuous and dynamic, but it also can be frightening. From the stories of the women presented here, an assurance emerges that this too shall pass and that womanhood is more than a matter of hormones.

The use of hormone therapy is an important issue to women in the menopausal transition. Nurses, being knowledgeable about research in this area, can share research findings with women. As evidenced in the third theme, hormones—friend or foe, to eliminate confusion, nurses can teach women about the various hormone regimens available and what they mean for individual women. Through nurses' general knowledge of menopause, they can help women make decisions that will enhance the quality of the rest of their lives.

The time remaining in their lives is important to midlife women, as borne out in the fourth theme, getting older or getting better. Is there a special satisfaction with life when a woman feels good and knows what she values in life? How can women, as Greer (1992) suggests, learn to recognize the autumn of their lives as their most productive season? Joseph (1991) suggests they should "learn to spit." Nurses may hold the key to possible answers to these questions because of their ability to listen to women and their menopause stories.

Beyond the individual, nurses may help to teach others to gain and maintain a healthy attitude toward growing old. Aging and old age are awaiting all of us unless we reach a final stage of life first. Health care and economic policies do not support our current generation of long-living women. Becoming activist by reaching out and advocating for our older sisters will help all of us to fulfill our later years as best we can.

To help women and men to understand better the living experience of menopause, nurses can help overcome the silence surrounding menopause and lift its taboos. Building on the fifth theme, overcoming the silence of the last taboo, nurses can help women to connect with each other by encouraging group dialogues that will validate their menopausal experiences. Women are hungry to talk with other women and to exchange stories. The recent influx (and popularity) of books about personal experiences of menopause supports the need for dialogue among menopausal women. Nurses are ideal health care providers who can offer support groups counseling from a woman's perspective rather than from a medical perspective. That does not mean that women may not seek medical help at this time of life, but neither does it assume that all menopausal women need medical care. Nurses can provide information and help women to decide on a course of action.

Lastly, nurses can help women "put it all together," recognizing that the "all together" is not a static state. Life is always changing. Today's knowledge about menopause is a moment in history; the discourses and meaning of menopause are already changing.

Their [women's] need to know was beginning to overcome their fear of knowing. It convinced me that the pacesetting women of this generation will shift the boundaries as well as the meaning of menopause: They will redefine it, and live it, *as a mid-life experience of minor importance in the scheme of a long and lushly various life. (Sheehy, 1993, p. 85)*

ABOUT THE STUDY

The Sample.   The ten midlife women interviewed regarding their experiences of menopause raged in age from 42 to 53. The participants responded to a flyer asking for help from women who were experiencing changes they attributed to menopause. The women were recruited from church or community groups, not from among patients, and were purposively sampled in order to present as diverse a picture of the menopausal transition as possible. Five women had stopped menstruating naturally and were not taking hormones. One woman, with an intact uterus, was taking hormone therapy and was experiencing hormone-induced withdrawal bleeding. Two women had experienced a surgical menopause and were not taking hormones now, although they had taken them briefly at the time of their surgeries. Two women were still menstruating, albeit irregularly. They were not taking hormones. Before beginning this research, permission to conduct this study was obtained from the New York University Human Subjects Committee.

Two of the women were of African American extraction and the rest were Euro-American. Four of the women were married, one was in the process of a divorce, two had been divorced previously, and three were never married. Seven had children ranging in age from 8 to 35 years. They were all in the middle-income category ($40,000+); however, two were in the lower strata ($25,000–35,000) of that category's range. Six of the women were nonsmokers; six were slender, four were slightly overweight. One of the overweight women believed that her weight helped produce estrogen and therefore she experienced fewer problems. However, one woman, who had many problems and was taking hormones, was about 20 pounds overweight.

All of the women were involved in full-time work outside the home; two of them were full-time students. Their education levels ranged from high school to graduate school. Besides the two attending school full-time, others were involved in taking classes. Their occupations included teaching, nursing, clerical work, and business entrepreneurship.

Data Collection. The research questions for this study was: What are the experiences of menopause as perceived by menopausal women? The original interview with each woman was about one hour in length and was tape-recorded. Each audiotape was then transcribed. From the written text, I completed a phenomenological writeup of the woman's experience, using the woman's words as much as possible. The "stories" of the women in this chapter are abridged versions. Each woman was contacted again to read her story to confirm that it described her experience. Points were clarified or added, if necessary.

Data Analysis. The audiotaped interviews were transcribed to a written text for analysis. The researcher's field notes and personal log also were analyzed as data. Hermeneutic phenomenological reflection, van Manen's approach, was used to analyze the data. Each woman's interview was written as a phenomenological story with a major theme that tried to capture her experience. In addition, five essential themes, each representing an aspect of the structure of lived experience of menopause, were identified across the interviews. Although the themes cannot "unlock the deep meaning" (van Manen, 1990), they have touched on the essential core of the experiences of menopause.

REFERENCES

Beyene, Y. (1986). Cultural significance and physiological manifestation of menopause: A biocultural analysis. *Culture, medicine, and psychiatry, 10,* 47-71.

End note. Because we speak differently from the way we write, the language in the stories of the women was edited at times to make the narrative flow better. The names and some other identifying characteristics were changed in order to protect the confidentiality of the participants. None of the enhancements altered the meaning of the text.

Cohen, L. (1984). *Small expectations: Society's betrayal of older women.* Toronto: McClellan & Stewart, Ltd.

Delaney, J., Lupton, M. J., & Toth, E. (1988). *The curse: A cultural history of menstruation* (rev. ed.). Chicago: University of Illinois Press.

Dickson, G. L. (1989). *The knowledge of menopause: An analysis of scientific and everyday discourses.* Unpublished doctoral dissertation, University of Wisconsin–Madison.

Dickson, G. L. (1990). A feminist poststructuralist analysis of the knowledge of menopause. *Advances in Nursing Science, 12*(3), 15–31.

Dickson, G. L. (in press). Fifty-something: A phenomenological study of the experience of menopause. In P. Munhall (Ed.), *Composing meaning: Women's experience in context.* New York: National League for Nursing.

Fine, M. (1991). Split second of denial. In D. Taylor & S. C. Sumrall (Eds.), *Women of the 14th moon: Writing on menopause.* Freedom, CA: The Crossing Press.

Ford, A. R. (1986). Hormones: Getting out of hand. In K. McDonnell (Ed.), *Adverse effects: Women and the pharmaceutical industry* (pp. 27–40). Toronto: The Women's Press.

Greer, G. (1992). *The change: Women, aging and menopause.* New York: Knopf.

Joseph, J. (1991). Warning. In S. Martz (Ed.), *When I am an old woman I shall wear purple* (p. 1). Watsonville, CA: Papier-Maché Press.

Lock, M. (1986). Ambiguities of aging: Japanese experience and perceptions of menopause. *Culture, medicine, and psychiatry, 10*, 23–46.

McCain, M. V. E. (1991). *Transformation through menopause.* New York: Bergin & Garvey.

McKinlay, S. M., Brambilla, D. J., & Posner, J. G. (1992). The normal menopause transition. *Maturita, 14,* 103–115.

Munhall, P. L. (1989). Philosophical ponderings on qualitative research methods in nursing. *Nursing Science Quarterly,* 20–28.

National Center for Health Statistics. (1985). *Current estimates from the National Health Interview Survey, United States, 1982* (DHSS Publication No. 85-1578). Washington, DC: U.S. Government Printing Office.

Oddens, B. J., Boulet, M. J., Lehert, P., & Visser, A. P. (1992). Has the climacteric been medicalized? A study on the use of medication for climacteric complaints in four countries. *Maturitas, 15,* 171–181.

Perlmutter, R., & Bart, P. B. (1982). Changing view of 'The Change': A critical review and suggestions for an attributional approach. In A. M. Voda, M. Dinnerstein, & S. R. O'Donnell (Eds.), *Changing perspectives on menopause* (pp. 187–199). Austin: University of Texas Press.

Sand, G. (1993). *Is it hot in here or is it me?* New York: HarperCollins.

Seltzer, J. (1991). No more Xs on my calendar, no more PMS. In D. Taylor & A. C. Sumrall (Eds.), *Women of the 14th moon: Writings on menopause* (p. 25). Freedom, CA: The Crossing Press.

Sheehy, G. (1993). *Menopause: The silent passage.* New York: Simon & Schuster.

Strahan E. S. (1990). Beyond blood: Women of that certain age. In C. Zweig (Ed.), *To be a woman: The birth of the conscious feminine* (pp. 181–195). Los Angeles: Jeremy P. Tarcher, Inc.

van Manen, M. (1990). *Researching lived experience.* New York: SUNY Press.

Voda, A. M., & George, T. (1986). Menopause. In H. H. Werley & J. J. Fitzpatrick (Eds.), *Annual review of nursing research* (vol. 4, pp. 55–75). New York: Springer.

Weideger, P. (1976). *Menstruation and menopause.* New York: Knopf.

Wilbush, J. (1993). The kaleidoscope of menopause. *Maturita, 16*(3), 157–162.

Wilson, R. A. (1966). *Feminine forever.* Philadelphia: Lippincott.

Wilson, R., & Wilson, T. (1963). The fate of nontreated post-menopausal women: A plea for the maintenance of adequate estrogen from puberty to the grave. *Journal of the American Geriatrics Society, 11,* 347–362.

ABOUT THE AUTHOR

As my life moves on, I've come to think of myself as a "recycled" woman. I spent a major portion of my life fulfilling the dream of 1950s women by getting married early and moving to the suburbs. I devoted my time to creating and raising children and all the associated tasks. The work was important, demanding and never-ending. Somehow, my growth and development seemed to have been arrested in the process.

But a book written in 1966 by Bette Friedan helped me to identify the veiled unhappiness I felt with my life-style. Reading that book and realizing that others felt the same way opened a whole new world of possibilities for me.

Gradually, I began to venture outside the home as my three children entered school. I took nonacademic classes, socialized with other women, and became active in volunteer work. After a time of hospital volunteer work, I decided to learn more seriously by taking academic courses. That decision led to an educational path of almost 20 years' duration. Requirements for an A.D.N., B.S.N., M.S.N., and Ph.D., along with a work history of professional nursing, filled those years. My children grew up and left home. My marriage ended in divorce.

Now, I have a new and different kind of marriage with a loving partner. I am a faculty member caught up in the stresses and standards of academic life. My passion is twofold: to develop new ways to generate nursing knowledge and to change societal discourses depicting aging women. This work, hopefully, will contribute to the movement to humanize society and enhance the quality of life for long-living women. On a personal level, I continue to nurture my children and their families.

5

Mothercare

Ellen Goldschmidt Ehrlich

I wasn't aware of exactly when the topic of conversation at the tables (boardroom, kitchen, or bridge) switched from care of children to the care of our mothers, but suddenly mothercare became a fervent topic among my middle-aged group. I realized then, I was not alone in my concern for my mother's care (Ehrlich, 1992).

E llen Goodman (1985) spoke about this topic in "Family Secrets" in her book, *Keeping in Touch:*

In middle-age, most of us are flanked by adolescent children and aging parents. We are the fulcrum of this family seesaw, expected to keep the balance. As one set of burdens is lifted gradually by independence, another is descending, sometimes slowly, sometimes abruptly, pulled by the gravity of old age or illness.

In the past year, a neighbor of mine has helped her son choose a college and her mother choose a retirement home. A friend who has just stopped accompanying her children to their doctor's appointments has begun driving her father to his. A colleague who filled her thirties with guilt about being a working mother is entering her fifties with guilt about being a working daughter. It's her parents who need her now.

Like most Americans, my friends were raised to believe that independence was the norm. We learned to value it, nurture it, respect it, and demand it of ourselves and others. Today we "stand on our own two feet." It was hard for some of us to have that independence challenged by the helplessness of our children. It is much harder to see our parents become needful. (p. 282)

My own concern about the experience of mothercare began when my mother first went into a nursing home. Placing my mother in a nursing home was an extremely stressful occasion for both my mother and me. My mother and I wanted her to continue to live in my home. However, she had become very depressed and isolated, and was unable to walk. Even with outside help, her needs did not seem to be met; finally, she agreed that going into a nursing home would be best.

I was not a stranger to caregiving. I had cared for my children's great-grandmother for more than six years. Yet, I began to wonder how other daughters continue to cope and keep their mothers at home when I no longer felt that I was able to do so. What was their experience like? Was there meaning in their caring for their mothers? What helped them sustain the care of their mothers at home? Was there something lacking in me? As a mother caring now for a mother, I wondered how nursing and other health professions could assist them. From this beginning, I began to explore the phenomenon of caregiving as a researcher.

My mother was, at that time, an 84-year-old woman who had lost her husband while residing in Florida. She was not able to cope alone in Florida, and she agreed with my brother and me that a move back to New Jersey, closer to both of us, would be best.

In the following year, my mother underwent major abdominal surgery and moved to my home. During the next year, she became increasingly forgetful and confused. In an attempt to discover what was causing the changes, she was seen by numerous physicians and underwent neurological and psychiatric evaluation. A medical diagnosis of early-stage senile dementia was presented by the neurologist.

Because it was no longer safe to leave my mother home alone, a home health aide was hired. My mother expressed feelings of isolation when she was at home during the day with just an aide, but she was unable or unwilling to go to a day care center or a similar alternative.

While I was at work, my mother fell and fractured her hip in the presence of the home health aide. After the fracture, my mother was unable to walk again despite both aggressive and long-term physical therapy. I was then faced with the dilemma of how to best care for my mother while also coping with two teenage children, a job, and a commitment to finish a college degree. It was, literally, overwhelming. My mother became increasingly confused, could no longer ambulate, required almost total assistance with the activities of daily living and expressed frustration and resentment with her situation. I voiced my own concern: I felt overburdened with the responsibility of the care of my mother, my children, our home, my job, and school. My husband stated that it was fine with him if my mother lived with us and that we should build an addition onto our home, to make living conditions easier. This was all the assistance he provided. I found (to my surprise, because I was a health care professional) that I needed more help in planning care for my aged mother (Ehrlich, 1992).

According to Ebersole and Hess (1990), "It is estimated that over 5 million people are involved in parent care and the number is increasing rapidly. They provide support of many kinds, concern, affection and socialization." In 1988, the U.S. Bureau of Census reported that women, on average, spend 17 years caring for their children and 18 years caring for elderly relatives.

I began to realize what an enormous task this was and how little attention was given to it. I wanted to know what life was like for other women who cared for their mothers. I then began to talk at length with 12 women from my nursing practice who had mothered their mothers for more than six months. In fact, six of these women had taken care of their mothers for more than ten years!!

Hundreds of themes appeared in the women's narratives. The 23 most common themes will be shared in this chapter, each will be discussed individually. Specific sources of assistance for mothers and daughters are also offered. Here is a list of the themes:

1. Constancy of care.	12. Families.
2. Obligation.	13. Family support.
3. Change in roles.	14. Family bonding.
4. Gender issues.	15. Significance to the family.
5. Anger.	16. Confinement.
6. Not knowing.	17. Loss of time.
7. Self-recognition.	18. Emotional stress.
8. Significant changes.	19. Moral dilemmas.
9. Abuse.	20. Sources of assistance.
10. Fear.	21. Relief from confinement.
11. Maintenance of independence.	22. Interventions.
	23. Meaning in mothercare.

The most prevalent theme that occurred in all of the daughters' talks (interviews) was the constancy of the mothercare responsibility.

CONSTANCY OF CARE

Daughters talked first about the daily commitments. Then, days turned into weeks and the weeks became years of constant responsibility. Ten years of care was not unusual. After months and years of mothercare, most daughters sought some form of relief.

Lorraine is a 59-year-old Catholic who has never married. She has a significant other in her life. However, until this year, when her friend retired, she lived alone with her mother. For several years, she gave up work and devoted herself to her mother.

Recently, she has returned to her own business, which has somewhat flexible hours and can accommodate the mothercare and relief schedules.

Lorraine said, heavyheartedly:

> You know, doing it 24 hours the whole year, it's a long time and a lot of emotions and a lot of energy through the year. *You're using up a lot of energy, both physically and mentally, but I made it a point to reinforce myself. Because otherwise you can't do it.*

She went on further:

> *You just don't expect an 80-year-old woman who has had a massive stroke, who is paralyzed on one side, who is weak to begin with—*you're not thinking in terms of 12 years at that particular time. *You're thinking a year, a year and a half, two years, two and a half years—that's a long time; at that time. And you adjust to that, and every year that goes beyond that, you're adjusting to that year.*

Helena is 58 years old, a Protestant, and divorced. She has four children; her son and youngest daughter still live with her. She works as a secretary in a radiologist's office close to her home. Mothercare began when Helena's father died four years ago and her severely arthritic mother could not manage to live alone. Helena spoke sadly:

> *You know what it is,* it's a constant responsibility; I think—I think it's never off your head, *that you—you are responsible for somebody else and you have to concern yourself with that person, you know, and your children grow up [but there is no end in sight].*

After many years, the daughters aged. A person 49 years old became 59; a 59-year-old became 69. The daughter was not able to function at the same level. Moreover, the mother's needs frequently became increasingly more complex and demanding.

Another caregiving daughter, Kathleen, is a 56-year-old Catholic widow whose husband died of cancer. Kathleen cares for her 90-year-old mother, who has diabetes and severely debilitating congestive heart failure. Mothercare began ten years ago when the landlord raised her mother's rent three times in three months and economically forced her to give up her home. Kathleen said:

> *It's like forever going downhill. And it's like it's never going to get b-e-t-t-e-r and it's going to get progressively worse.*

Caregiving continues without intermission and seemingly without end. Despite their monumental sense of frustration, daughters felt a sense of obligation to care for their mothers.

OBLIGATION

Several daughters used the same word: they felt an *obligation* to care for their parents. One daughter termed this obligation "Love." This theme was dominant in the talks. Some daughters stated it directly; other daughters implied an obligation in subtler ways.

Vivian is a 59-year-old Black woman, a Baptist, whose mother is from North Carolina. She came to live with Vivian when her dementia no longer made it possible for her to live alone. Vivian works at two jobs, cares for her mother, and, until he died last October, cared for her partially paralyzed husband as well. Vivian spoke tenderly:

> *Well,* it's something that I really want to do because it's my mother *and I love her very dearly, and I would give my life for her. I [might] get fired from the job because of taking care of my mother taking too much time [from] work.*

Helena expressed concern:

> *I don't think the younger people really realize what a job it is and what a responsibility it is; you know, as I said, it's my parents. I would always do it . . .* because they are my

parents. I felt that was my obligation *to them. . . . I would have liked to [have] stayed home with her more, you know; I felt that I myself couldn't give that much time, but my evenings were always hers.*

The feelings of love and obligation and the realities of real-life situations (work, children, care of the home) introduce dilemmas that daughters need to resolve in order to function. Most daughters talked about how they feel that it is their obligation to care for their mothers and that not doing this would be inconceivable. Several women described the love they feel for their mother and how this is a chance to express their devotion.

Much as Goodman (1985) talks about independence and the relationships with other generations, Marilyn French (1987) expounds on the same subjects in *Her Mother's Daughter:*

I don't remember the sullen baby I was, although I know the sullen child; I recall the sense of being unwanted and unloved, and always, always unsafe. All I wanted, when I was a child, was not to be a child, to be grown up so I wouldn't be dependent upon those who didn't want me dependent upon them, to be free and out and away. This would surprise my mother, I imagine. She was so careful to give me those things she had painfully lacked in her own childhood that she can't imagine that the thing she really lacked wasn't attention or education, but that lap "moja kochanie," that close embrace. [A] baby rat taken from its mother at the moment of birth, before the mother has time to lick it clean, will in her turn, not lick her infant clean when she gives birth. And so on, down the generations. Even to the edge of doom, . . . and this is doom: unless there is some way to break it. The truth is it is not the sins of the fathers that descend unto the third generation, but the sorrows of the mothers. But when I was a young woman, I believed that I could break the chain. (p. 171)

When I reflect on *Her Mother's Daughter,* I am struck by the bonds of suffering, the giving up of one's own needs so that the next generation can have what the previous generation did not have. Mothers find it very important to give things such as an education, a warm and loving home, or simply combing or brushing hair. Yet children do not want—they even reject—these things when they are offered. Why is the offering not appreciated? Why is it such a struggle to be a mother and then to mother one's mother? Mothers give so much, yet one may not see their struggle until one experiences it for oneself or reads a perceptive book. This wisdom can help daughters appreciate their mothers more, knowing how hard it was for them, and realizing that they may have a hard time dealing with a lack of overt affection. When no overt affection has been presented, it may be difficult for the person not to reciprocate in kind—a daughter may find it harder to become a caregiver for an undemonstrative mother. At the very least, the mothercare situation may become arduous for all who are involved.

Some daughters question: Did my mother do this for me? Did my mother give up her life for her children? (The daughter may have done this for her own children.) The daughter wonders whether she is willing to do this for her mother. Care of self becomes a second question. How do the two questions converge? How does one best care for one's mother when caring for one's mother often involves a dramatic change in role?

CHANGE IN ROLES

Daughters frequently specified the change in roles that accompanied taking on their new responsibilities. Often, a return to a previous role was required. Primarily, the daughters took on the mothercare role, becoming daughters again, members of the "sandwich generation."

Kathleen spoke with exasperation:

> *I was aware of giving up a lot of my freedom. I mean, not so much my freedom, but my privacy and the same things, when you settle down with someone when you've been free a while.* Having to be a daughter again, after you're an adult.

Having to account for your time, and so forth, *like, I'm going here and I'm going there, you know. Before that, I'd just G-O-O-O.*

Frustrated, Helena noted:

I have to work; I'm divorced and I have four kids. My kids are all married, but this youngest one. I'm still paying tuitions for her as well as . . . a loan . . . , and I had a home equity loan out and I had my house sided and all that, and I have obligations that I have to meet and there is the responsibility of caregiving as well.

These women already have many different roles. Mothercare adds more, and life becomes more complex. The issue of the constant responsibility remains. Loss of personal freedom is reported, and anger surfaces. Although the roles are different, many roles relate to gender issues.

GENDER ISSUES

Gender issues are linked to role definition. This linkage appeared in the first theme, constancy of responsibility, when one woman asked her brother to relieve her and was told, "It's YOUR JOB; you are the one appointed." Another daughter related this experience:

My brother did nothing. My brother was 20 minutes from here and had all the time in the world to help and didn't. Well, that's always the case and I see it all of the time. The women get stuck and the males in the family are just—you can see that they're dust. *And that's the way it was with my brother. He was—he had more time than I did to do this because he's not married, has no dependents. And could have come out and stayed with my mother. You know, at night, while I went to the shore, took a vacation, got a break, and he did NOTHING.*

It is quite apparent that society frequently assigns the mother-care role to women based on gender, and women accept the assignment, often without a fight. In the home, the role of the woman in today's society has changed little. Although women are involved in work outside of the home, they continue to be the primary source of care within. Mothercare places added pressures on anyone—particularly on the working woman who now has another role. It is little wonder that the next theme, anger, is frequently felt and voiced.

ANGER

What I remember most about the time my mother lived with me, after she was no longer able to care for herself, was my constant worry about being able to keep her safe and feeling cared for while I continued going to work and caring for my own family. I never knew when the help that I had so carefully and laboriously organized would not show up. The home health aide personnel changed quite frequently. Mother could be quite verbally abusive and, at that time, rarely had a good or kind word for anyone. I wondered how frightened and angry she must have been at being so incapacitated. I too was very frustrated and constantly anxious. Today, I am grateful when my mother, now in a nursing home, has a day when she is responsive and knows me.

When we had a 24-hour live-in home health aide, our privacy was deeply invaded. It seemed that there was always someone looking over our shoulders and offering unsolicited advice (often well meant). I think back on the strange parade of individuals who lived in my home while my mother was with me. On one day, an emaciated-looking young man with shabby, torn clothing and a wild hairdo came to take care of my mother. The aides had such a varied assortment of life-styles and backgrounds that, under other circumstances, I am not sure I would have welcomed them into my home.

My children were wonderfully caring and supportive. My youngest daughter volunteered to take care of her "Nana" when she was not at school. My brother felt that he was doing his part by taking care of my mother's finances. I felt the weight of a never-ending 24-hour commitment to care. I was furious at the injustice of this division of labor and at my brother for not helping more!

I remember being tuned into all the little noises in the house, just as I was when my children were infants. At times, I noticed a great deal of resentment and enormous anger in myself. Yet I had many resources and strengths, and I knew the caregiving system; I wondered how others cared for their loved ones without all of these to call on.

I felt anger that, despite my nursing background and all of my knowledge, I was unable to care for my mother in a way that allowed us all to be comfortable. I often felt alone and angry because the burden of care was primarily my responsibility and because I was not able to cope with this responsibility in the way that I would have liked to. I felt enormously frustrated. After several years, I wrote this poem:

Deep trouble
turmoil lie

within my soul
A churning that
knows no end

A search for
meaning
in this life

Thrashing about
in my head
the thoughts
come—

What for?
What's this about!
Why?
I want to scream

I know no peace
  especially from within
I feel a torment
  from within
A rage that knows
  no end
A burning that has
  yet to express itself
A fire that is leaping
  and creeping up the walls
  but cannot get past the
  concrete barriers of my
  mind

A rage, that smoulders
  squashed by I know
  not what
  it screams to be let out.

Mothercare can be a lonely experience. Often, no one was around to whom I could express my anger and frustration. For me, writing about my feelings liberated me and brought relief. Other daughters share their anger in different ways.

Anger was expressed both overtly and covertly in the monologues of the daughters I studied. Anger was not generally directed at the mothers, but at the situations and the frustrations involved in attempting to resolve them.

Kathleen displayed her frustration:

. . . I get impatient sometimes with—with my mother, and I get frustrated, and I get, I get angry at her for being sick. *That sounds terrible, that comes out once in a while; I get—I realize that I'm really angry because she's sick. Well, who do you get angry with?*

Different things would surface at different times. This is what I get angry about, I guess, or get ambivalent feelings— in most diseases or most sicknesses, you know, like my

*husband had cancer, and you know, we went through that,
and he died, after about nine months, but there's a beginning and an end.*

Another mothercaring daughter was Carolyn, a 59-year-old
Catholic who lived in a small bungalow with her husband, college-age son, and mother. Her mother had lived with them for
most of the 30 years of Carolyn's married life. About four years
ago, her mother suffered a stroke, which complicated matters
even more:

*I get very angry—I feel like, you know, if my husband is
away on business or if he were involved in a Scouting Weekend, I used to be free to do what I wanted to do.*

Anger is expressed toward life events that are beyond the
daughters' control, occasionally toward the mothers, toward family members who do not contribute and yet maintain unchanged
expectations, and toward loss of freedom. Frequently, the condition of the mother deteriorates right before the daughters' eyes.
Family members sometimes are a source of resentment and distress. The loss of freedom once again is a dominant theme throughout the daughters' narratives.

For most of the daughters, anger is not present continuously.
One daughter noted: "Different things would surface at different
times." There are good days and bad ones, and descriptions of
caregiving at times relate to the most recent events.

With few exceptions, one daughter is placed in charge of mothercare. Therefore, it is imperative to seek family support at the onset for either daily or weekly respite time and for vacation time
each year. Contingent plans must be made so that other family
members will assist if the backup member is unable to cover the
respite time. It is not unusual for a family member to back out of a
commitment or for circumstances to change after several years,
leaving the mothercaring daughter as the sole source of the care.
Contingent plans for another family member to assist are essential
and should be established at the inception of mothercare and

revised periodically. An added source of relief for daughters is the elimination of problems that are caused by a lack of knowledge.

NOT KNOWING

Several daughters expressed a desire for more knowledge that would assist them in caregiving. Not knowing has caused problems for some daughters. One daughter agonized:

> *I felt very guilty about her having those bedsores. I felt bad about that, yeah, because I should have picked up on it sooner, but I didn't know what a bedsore was. I had no idea what a bedsore was, never saw one in my life. Didn't even know what it looked like; I didn't know how you get them, why you get them, ...*
>
> *But . . . I felt guilty at that time, I don't feel guilty now because I can understand, I JUST DIDN'T KNOW.*

It becomes apparent that if appropriate information is supplied, the daughters can be helped. Knowledge assists in relieving some of the stress for the daughter and prevents complications in the mother. In the case of the decubitus, prior knowledge could have prevented the bedsore and, equally important, prevented the guilt. Implicit in this knowledge deficit is a self-questioning and, at times, a guilt about what is done. Daughters wonder whether they are doing the right thing. However, in one area, daughters know that they make a difference: They are doing something important for their mother. This self-recognition is significant.

SELF-RECOGNITION

The daughters interviewed validated the fact that they made a difference. Their self-recognition was important, particularly in the way the daughters viewed themselves and their personal outlooks. Positive remarks were frequently noted during our talks. These daughters made a major difference in the lives of their mothers.

As an example, Lorraine ardently related:

I was the only person that she accepted and allowed to do anything. *NOBODY could do anything for her unless I was there, or I had to do it. That was HER. And I allowed them to do that; . . . but I had no choice because we were alone—I mean, I was here all by myself with her. ALL day long. It's only normal for her to turn to me. I can understand that from her side of it. She's incapable of doing anything. I'm her security. So I understand that.*

But I do notice that when I get her up in the morning, I tend to her, she's in a better mood. *When other people tend to her, she'll go to sleep and she won't start drinking until maybe two o'clock in the afternoon. Or she'll be just nasty, or she'll just be throwing stuff at you, kicking around, looking away.*

These daughters are faced with numerous problems and situations in which the mother is both physically and verbally aggressive. Yet these daughters continue to care and recognize their own importance.

The daughters talked about themselves and their personal reactions to their own situations. They also talked about their mothers—now, and then. They described their mothers' condition and the changes in their lives and in those of the people around them. They probed the significance of those changes.

SIGNIFICANT CHANGES

Descriptions of the mothers and of the changes in their lives and in those of the people around them were revealed. Some daughters talked about the major changes they observed in their mothers. For many women, the normal pattern of aging and of changes in body systems is hastened by acute or chronic illness. The daughters reported significant degeneration and deterioration in their mothers. These changes are particularly difficult and painful to watch and live through helplessly.

Helena, who works as a secretary for a radiologist, unhappily observed:

You go from a walker to a bedridden state in a couple of years—totally bedridden, and totally unable to do for herself.

Many of the changes in aged mothers are physical and lead to the need for someone else to take over most of the mothers' activities of daily living (ADLs). However, changes in mental status are also quite prevalent in many aged mothers. Individuals who managed the care of entire families often are now unable to cope with their own basic needs. This change places an enormous burden on others, especially the primary caregiver, and it is devastating to both the mother and the family.

Personality changes most often are reported as exaggerations of the mother's basic personality traits. Daughters have a difficult time sorting out the variations. Frequently, the mother is remembered as she was ten or 20 years ago. This image makes it extremely difficult to deal with the behavioral changes that the mother manifests because the daughter at first relates to the individual who existed at that earlier time and not to the individual who is now present. These behavioral changes often lead to abuse.

ABUSE

Because of the changes in their mothers, many daughters suffer both physical and mental abuse. Changes in the mother directly impact on daughter; for example: "She'll be just nasty, or she'll just be throwing stuff at you, kicking around, looking away."

Lorraine's tone showed frustration:

She'll love you one minute and she knows you're her daughter one minute and the next minute, she'll call you a bum and get the hell out. But you have to accept that and you have to accept the fact that she says you're no good or you're a bum, but she certainly has never said that in her life, nor

*ever said that to you in her life; so, you know you have to
take it from where it is.*

Several of the daughters reported changes in their mothers that
produced outbursts of mental and physical abuse directed toward
the daughters and others. Generally, the daughters reacted by trying to understand the behavior and dealing with the immediacy of
the situation in a manner that protected both the mother and
daughter. Physical restraint was used by one daughter; more frequently, the daughters attempted to discover the precipitating factors and eliminate or modify them. For example, one daughter is
present for early morning care each day because her absence creates a situation where the mother is abusive to everyone throughout the rest of the day. Regardless of the daughters' attempts to
deal with certain situations, one area that often defies control is
fear in both the mothers and daughters.

FEAR

It is not uncommon to hear talk about the mothers' fear of being
alone. Feelings of isolation and loneliness are expressed by both
the mothers and the daughters. Several mothers have problems
with episodes of choking—one cause of their fear of being left
alone. Helena, whose severely arthritic mother has had episodes of
choking, tensely commented:

*In the beginning we only had [the home health aide] two
hours but she [mother] wasn't doing that well and we tried
for more time and the doctors said we needed [it] because of
choking. I had to have someone here for lunch time. I'm
home for the dinner time, but that long span in between was
just too long of a span, for sure, and toward the end she was
getting frightened to be alone. She really didn't want to
be . . . by herself and I thought, what could I do? I couldn't
afford nursing in the house.*

This fear could relate to a fear of death; episodic choking while
alone could intensify it. Loneliness and confinement are major

issues for the mothers. Moreover, because the mothers often cannot be left alone safely, for either physical or psychological reasons, this need becomes an issue for the daughter, who often is forced to remain at home. One notes immediately how the changes in the mother impact on the daughter. One way to mitigate some of the mother's fear is to try to allow everyone to have as much independence as possible.

MAINTENANCE OF INDEPENDENCE

Maintenance of independence is quite important to both mother and daughter. Even when the mother moves in with the daughter, both try to maintain as much independence as possible for the mother. Mothers want to maintain their independence but, at times, that goal is quite difficult because of issues such as safety, health, and finances. Kathleen remembered with frustration:

You know she was, she was 80 then, but probably, if she could have afforded to, maybe could have stayed another two years on her own. With that arrangement—that would have been OK. And she would have wanted to, but at that point, it really was more financial.

Kathleen's mother's apartment rent had been raised to a level where she could no longer afford to live alone.

Daughters try to maintain the independence of the mothers, sometimes searching for ways to maintain the appearances of independence. These ways may seem small, but they prove to be significant to all involved. Helena said encouragingly:

She couldn't do anything for herself *except if you gave her the cup of coffee. She spilled a lot of it on herself. We would make her put a bib on her, but, you know, she didn't see real well either, so when she'd go in with a spoon, she'd spill it too,* but that she could manage to do.

The small act of drinking a cup of coffee by oneself served as a way of maintaining independence and a sense of self-worth. It is extremely important to preserve this sense of self-worth. When daughters talk specifically about their mothers, maintenance of independence is a prevalent topic. Some other key topics relate to family members and how they impact on the mother and daughter.

FAMILIES

Family legacies, family bonding, and establishing the significance of caregiving within the family are some of the themes that caregivers mention when they talk about valuing the caregiving situation for the family and themselves.

Families play many important roles in mothercare. Often, family members are involved in the decision of who becomes the caregiver. At times, family members are quite supportive to the mother and daughter, but the contrary is true on numerous occasions as well.

Lorraine experienced both attitudes:

The first four years, I had a good support system as far as my family was concerned—when we talked about it, this was something I wanted to do. *This was something that none of them could do, none of them were in the position to do this.*

After ten years, Lorraine began to question her role:

. . . sometimes I say, gee, I'm one of seven, why am I doing this? And then I think how can they (my brothers and sisters) go about their life and not say, Hey, I should be doing something for my mother.

Caregivers often feel that they are better prepared to provide care than other family members are. For example, Lorraine noted with vigor:

My sister, by nature, could not have done it. I hate to say it, but I think I'm a stronger person than my sister.

Even when family members initially support the caregiving daughter, after many years this *support declines* or fades away.

Nonetheless, daughters find value in the family support system and particularly note how the caregiving experience impacts positively on the individual family members and on family traditions.

Society's assignment of the role of caregiver to women has been noted. It follows that family members often expect a woman to accept or volunteer for the role of caregiver. Generally, daughters accept the role without much question initially, but, over a period of time, they begin to question "Why me?" and report anger at being immured in this role.

In relation to the gender issue, it is interesting to note that Lorraine, who lives alone and was involved in a business, emphatically states: "My other brother is out in Michigan, he's a professor at the university; he certainly couldn't do it. He's alone."

One of Lorraine's brothers, quoted earlier, made a statement about the caretaking role that deserves repeating here: "In every family, there's one person who has to take care of [family], and it's YOUR JOB, you are the one appointed." There is a great deal of talk about how some family members do support the daughter and the mother and how this support changes over time.

FAMILY SUPPORT

Some family members help by giving up a weekend or a Sunday. Here are two heartwarming examples, from Helena and from Lorraine:

You know I just have one sister and, well, a few months before my mother died—[my sister's] husband has a bad heart; he's had two heart attacks and he's not operable, and he's had an aneurysm and all that, and she worked, but still in all my sister came on a Sunday and did a little help.

For the first four years, my sister came out, every other weekend, to give me relief.

Lorraine's sister took a bus and a train from New York to New Jersey to spend the weekend with her mother and her sister. This visit allowed Lorraine to do some of her errands and gave everyone involved another person to converse with. Lorraine expresses great comfort and a feeling of closeness with her mother and her sister.

Carolyn's family members provide relief by staying home so that she can have time away. "If he's [her husband] home, he'll say to me, OK, go and do what you want to do."

Sometimes even the dog assists: "If mother calls, the dog barks and my husband hears the dog and then he comes in to do whatever she wants."

The passage of time and changes in the mother often affect family members and the support they provide. Children are involved in caregiving as well and can provide support for both the mother and daughter. When *other* family members, usually siblings of the mother or daughter, are confronted with distressing changes in the mother, they frequently tend to distance themselves from caregiving.

Despondent, Lorraine commented:

> *She [her sister] wouldn't do it [come on weekends] anymore because my mother turned on her. And she couldn't take it emotionally. Mom turned on me but it doesn't bother me. I mean, my sister couldn't take that.*

Family reaction has a major impact on mothercare. Daughters reflect on why they are the family members best suited for caregiving. Initially, the family may start out assisting with caregiving, but as the years pass the assistance declines significantly. Often, family members distance themselves because the caregiving situation is upsetting to them. When help is given, the daughters still perceive it as quite limited. This rationing of help and other forms of nonsupport generate resentment and anger toward family members; the daughters feel they are "being taken for granted." Nonetheless, they find much value in the family and whatever family support is given. Occasionally, caregiving enhances children's relationships with their grandparents. Grandchildren frequently are able to accomplish what others cannot. A "laidback" or relaxed spouse facilitates caregiving. An added dividend for all involved in caregiving is the forging of closer family bonds among them.

FAMILY BONDING

For Kathleen, a widow, her mother has become the focal person around whom other family members congregate. This benefits Kathleen as well, because she is able to develop relationships with her nieces and nephews that would not have been possible if her mother had been placed in a nursing home.

> *They come to see her, and that's a joy. That's another plus that I wouldn't have—I wouldn't have had all of that if my mother wasn't with me. Because they come to see her, . . . I get to see them.*

Kathleen's mother is a great storyteller when her grandchildren come to visit. The stories told to her grandchildren are repeated and have become family legends. For example, when one of the grandchildren was in college:

> *She had to get up and talk about something that was close to her and she got up in front of the classroom and talked about her grandmother:*
> *"Grandmother talked about how she was born on the farm, and how she went to England when she was twelve years old, and how she left England, and came over here, and came into Ellis Island. She came steerage and she had to pay back her aunt for her fare over."*

Another daughter told how supportive her immediate family is, and how her little girl has a major role in caring. She continued to describe the family bonding:

> *So, . . . we told them [the children] that, when she died, you know, that they helped make her happy. I think that they will look back and feel that that was a good experience. That they were supportive, that they were able to help like that.*
> *My own personal immediate family, I think we built ties and bonds that will last for lots and lots, lots of years, and feel very good about what we all did.*

This collective contribution and other matters connected with the caregiving have great significance to the family.

SIGNIFICANCE TO THE FAMILY

One daughter talked about how she remembers her grandmother, who lived in her home when she was a child. "It was a very vivid memory of grandmother living there for years, her last years, with my parents." Family members may be carrying on a tradition of caring for parents that has been established in their families in past generations. The legacy of caring for parents is passed on from one generation to the next as a tradition of family honor:

> . . . it just was the thing that goes on in the family. I guess it started with caring for my grandmother; that, you know, that was the accepted thing.

Caregiving members of the family form valuable bonds with one another, and relationships are either developed or maintained among family members. When grandchildren have the opportunity to develop a deeper relationship with their grandparents, a resultant familial cohesiveness is sustained. Family traditions and history are preserved and transmitted to future generations. The mother continues to be the focal person or central figure around whom the family congregates, and this centering strengthens the preservation of the family unit. In contrast, there are many sources of discontent in mothercare. The theme most pervasive throughout the interviews was confinement.

CONFINEMENT

Confinement leads to loneliness and isolation. Although all but one of the daughters interviewed work outside the home, confinement became important. Within the constraints of the mothercare situation, the daughters are unable to function optimally or take care of their own needs: they do not have free time. Often, their time is divided among work, chores, and caregiving. Vacations, time for shopping, time to attend family or work functions, or just the chance to visit with friends are commonly unavailable. Confinement and loneliness, as noted earlier, begin with the confinement of the mother and extend inevitably to the daughter when the mother can no longer be left alone or demands constant attention. Feelings of isolation in the daughter often relate to having the full caregiving responsibility, with no one else available to take over the 24-hour commitment.

Because the mother might choke or fall, the daughter feels unable to leave even for a short time. This is when some daughters feel "the walls are closing in." Other sources of frustration relate to not being free. "I feel like—I'm in jail. Closed in, I don't get a chance to do the things that I want to do."

Any freedom to adjust the caregiving time or to attend to personal wants and desires is lost. Resentment is sometimes displaced to the mother's condition.

Kathleen admitted:

I do get very frustrated when sometimes it's just a nice day and I just want to jump in the car and go out. Just take off and do "whatever." And that's really impossible for me to do, so, those are the times that I get frustrated. And I get impatient sometimes with my mother, and I get frustrated; and I get, I get angry at her for being sick.

Confinement also involves time constraints and loss of time.

LOSS OF TIME

Typically, some daughters do not feel comfortable leaving their mothers alone for any extended period of time. They feel rushed even when grocery shopping, because they are worried about the mother's being home alone. Daughters complain of *always* feeling rushed. "I'm always rushing" and "When I go someplace now, I'm looking at my watch and I know my time is limited" are two frequent statements of caregivers. Agencies and/or other resources provide respite only for short periods of a few hours, so the daughters never have adequate time to complete everyday tasks before they must rush home.

Lorraine found grocery shopping trips frustrating:

I would no sooner get in the A&P, and I'd be in line, and I'd look at the time and . . . get a nervous stomach because I would have to get back. Two hours didn't DO IT!"

Helena agreed:

Now that she can't be left alone at all, things have changed. Well, even going to the supermarket now, when I go, I "zip" through the supermarket so fast.

Daughters continue to try to cope with the loss of personal freedom. Some daughters recognize that it is not the person whom they are annoyed with; it is the fact that their mothers are ill and respite or relief services are unavailable. One daughter summed up their typical reactions:

I'm annoyed with [the fact] that I can't do it. But it has nothing to do with her. It's I don't have the people. *Now who do you get mad at, the people? That's right. I don't have* anybody *here.*

Loss of time to spend with children and grandchildren is a prevalent subject. Daughters say: "I have children and grandchildren, and I'd like them to know me too." Or, "I would like to be alone with my children and the grandchildren, just to have 48 hours, without anybody, and I feel badly."

Daughters also note their divided allegiance in some situations. They want to devote more time to their mothers but have to meet their own personal needs and those of their work.

The juggling act that daughters face is clear: They try to give as much time as possible to their mothers, to work, and to other necessities of life. As a consequence, daughters frequently can give little, if any, time to their own children and grandchildren. Mothercare is the priority, and other areas of the daughters' lives are often neglected because of a lack of time. With mothercare as the priority, it is not unusual for the daughters to fear leaving their mothers alone when they need to attend to other obligations.

Emotional Stress

Kathleen was afraid to go to work, an emotion that was not unusual:

> *But there were mornings when I'd be afraid, you know, to leave the house because she'd be having a bad spell. Like should I go, should I stay? But you know, so, that's very hard. You know you're torn between your job. And you know that's when I would feel the most stress.*

Anger and resentment surface again because of the confinement—a quite natural outcome, in view of the constraints and demands placed on the daughters. Daughters forfeit a great deal of their personal freedom in order to care for their elderly mothers. The daughters relate how they made the choice to give up their personal freedom so they could care for their loved ones. The constancy of the mothercare responsibility is inherent in their talk.

"The walls are closing in" reflects the daughters' thoughts. There is no "peace of mind," for either the mothers or the daughters, when the mothers are left alone.

Daughters recognize they need time away, yet this time is quite limited. Social outings need to be restructured because of the mothercare. The availability of other people who can relieve the daughters directly impacts on issues of confinement. The daughter has to restructure her life around the availability of others so that her loved one will not be left alone. Frequently, respite services are available for only limited amounts of time. The daughters find themselves rushing to get back home so that their mothers will not be alone for any length of time. The demands of work interfere with mothercare, and mothercare interferes with job performance. Once again, the daughters place their own needs in the background. Their capacity for patience, understanding, and endurance is surprising. After many years (12, in one case) of mothercare, the daughters continue to give loving care to their mothers.

Anger and resentment do surface, however, in response to the constraints and demands placed on the daughters. Inevitably, predicaments arise as to what they should or should not do to care for their elderly mothers. Their dilemmas range from whether they should supply cigarettes to issues of facilitating a comatose mother's death. Each situation becomes intensely emotional for the daughters.

MORAL DILEMMAS

Thoughts about the mother's death and when this might occur form another theme. "It's almost like waiting for a shoe to drop." Daughters have conflicting feelings about their mothers' dying. They desire to see their mothers at peace, yet they wonder how they would function without their mothers. Kathleen solemnly pondered:

I can't even think beyond the times when I won't have her. And other times, I'm thinking, it would be better if it just happens, you know, if it just would end.

Part of the frustration of this situation is that the caregivers feel quite helpless. The daughters wish they could find a better way of relieving their mothers' discomfort. Even the small things that they do—giving a backrub, putting warmed clothes on, or trying to divert the mothers' attention—seem insignificant to the daughters. The overriding lament is that they can do nothing significant to reverse the progressively downward trend of the mother's health. It is difficult to see the discomfort of their mothers and know that there is little they can do to stem their mothers' deterioration. Situations in which there are choices of different actions often produce conflict and moral dilemmas for the daughters.

Moral dilemmas extend from simply being an enabler to questioning one's thoughts about a parent's death. Daughters question their beliefs, agonize over "the right thing to do," and then worry about doing it. Great concern for their mothers' thoughts and wishes is expressed. Daughters wonder whether anything can be accomplished more effectively. Feelings of guilt surface, and the emotional drain on the daughter may become evident. Some stress arises from being caught between two or more important needs. The spirituality of these daughters is apparent in their concern with giving good care to their mothers. This element of spirituality comes into the thinking, motivation, and feelings of these women when they encounter situations that involve intense reflection.

In Toni Morrison's *Beloved* (1987), Denver takes care of her mother and psychotic sister:

> *Denver served them both. Washing, cooking, forcing, cajoling her mother to eat a little now and then, providing things for Beloved [her sister] as often as she could to calm her down. . . .*
>
> *Denver decided to do the necessary. Decided to stop relying on kindness to leave something on the stump. She would hire herself out somewhere, and although she was afraid to leave Sethe [her mother] and Beloved alone all day not knowing what calamity either one of them would create, she came to realize that her presence in that house had no influence on what either woman did. Growled when they chose; sulked; explained, demanded, strutted, cowered, cried and provoked each other to the edge of violence, then over. . . .*
>
> *Somebody had to be saved, but unless Denver got work, there would be no one to save, no one to come home to, and no Denver either. It was a new thought, having a self to look out for and preserve. . . . Weeding the garden, pulling vegetables, cooking, washing, she plotted what to do and how. The Bodwins were most likely to help since they had done it twice. Once for Baby Suggs [Denver's Grandmother] and once for her mother. Why not the third generation as well? (pp. 250-252)*

This passage reflects the dilemmas many daughters revealed in their conversations about mothercare. Themes such as the fear of leaving mothers alone, the conflict between the necessity of going to work and the need to stay home, the verbal abuse that occurs, and the realization of the need for self-preservation, are all present. Outside sources of assistance are essential, for both mothers and daughters.

SOURCES OF ASSISTANCE

Daughters readily identify sources of assistance when they talk about mothercare. Knowledge of the fact that family legacies and traditions are being maintained also helps. Self-acknowledgment— making a difference—is very important. One daughter discerned: "You HAVE TO WANT TO DO IT and you have to be comfortable with the decision that you've made."

Multiple examples of what helps during mothercare were cited by the daughters studied. Primarily, the daughter must be comfortable with her decision to become a caregiver. Hugs or other simple signs of acceptance or affection from family members are important. Children often provide valuable support. Laughter and humor serve to relieve tension, as does acknowledgment that what the daughters are doing is significant. These aids are important but probably offer insufficient support, given the enormity of the problem. A key factor is the daughter's own self-recognition.

Self-Recognition

Any serenity found in mothercare has an element of understanding of self and of the changes in personal life cycles that occur as a person ages. The daughter recognizes that she also has changed and is aging, and she is ready to change her life-style as needed for the mothercare.

With resignation, Kathleen explained:

I've done all the things. I've had a lot of trips. I've had a lot of going out over the years, and, of course, I'm getting to an age where my life would quiet down a little bit; so, it's sort of coinciding with what has to be, anyhow.

Even though the changes are recognized, the need for relief from confinement des not diminish.

RELIEF FROM CONFINEMENT

Having a break in their confinement and some free time to themselves was quite important to the daughters interviewed. Being able to leave their mothers in competent hands and enjoy sufficient time without worry provided necessary renewal and support. Lorraine's family gave her scheduled relief during the first four years, then she spent two years without a break. She was unaware of community resources, and it took a crisis in her mental health to move her to look for help. She remembered being overwhelmed:

> *It was those two years, praying for a day of relief, after about six years or so. I was ready for Graystone [the local psychiatric hospital], and I knew it. I knew I had to do something, because I couldn't go on that way anymore. So, what I did was, I just got somebody in to help me.*

When she finally found help, however limited, it offered great relief:

> *At that time, that was a tremendous help. To know that somebody was going to be here for two hours a day, three days a week.*

Even a few hours of reliable relief is appreciated. Time away or being able to work outside of the home is almost a luxury. Knowledge that there are reinforcements or that someone can assist is treasured.

Sources of Support.   In some communities, sources of relief include organized external supports such as a nursing service, a respite house or hospice, and self-help support groups. Lorraine described how her mother's catheter became clogged at three in the morning. She was able to contact a nurse immediately to explain the situation, and the nurse told her what to do. Lorraine took care of the catheter, and the nurse arrived to check it at 8 A.M. Lorraine was encouraged by the professional availability:

I call any hour of the night. Get through to them, to talk to them, for them to advise me. For them to listen, for them to tell you what to do, or just talk to you, or to get you through the night. I won't leave it [the nursing service] because the support system there is tremendous.

This particular home health service provides only limited home health aide coverage, but, because of the 24-hour access to a nurse, Lorraine chooses to remain a client. Teaching given by the health professional is also treasured by daughters, and meeting the educational needs of these daughters can be very significant for the mothers' care. Nurses in one nursing service taught Lorraine how to care for her mother's bedsores.

What the daughters learn is reflected in the mothers' care. Lorraine now knows how to prevent bedsores in her mother. As a result, both she and her mother are more comfortable. Bolstered, Lorraine commented:

She taught me how to do them. She did them in the morning, and I did them before Mom went to bed.
This nurse was TERRIFIC!—with bed sores—TERRIFIC! and she knew skin, and the treatment was a lot of work, but it worked. [Now], I know what to do and what not to do and to spot anything.

Daughters value access to a nurse or a doctor when there is a problem or a question. A 24-hour hot line to a nurse provides significant relief. Nurses and doctors also help by informing caregivers of what to expect and instructing them on how to deal with anticipated problems. Other sources of assistance include being able to compare their own situations with others' via a support group, and working off stress via busyness around the house.

Diversion activities, both at home and at work, are a ready source of support for caregivers. Gardening or even chores such as scrubbing the kitchen floor can provide relief. Kathleen talked serenely about her diversions:

> *I get out to go to work, and I work in the garden. My job is really very fulfilling. I'd burn up some of my energy out in the yard. You know, mowing the lawn, or planting tomato plants, or whatever.*
>
> *I work off a lot of frustration that way, too. I'm a person who gets physically active when I'm upset.*

Vivian also resorted to gardening:

> *That's my special thing—my vegetable garden and my flowers—and people ask me why do you do it if you don't have to and I say that's the only enjoyment I get, that's my therapy. That's my pleasure, because I can't go out now.*

Sources of support relate to general areas such as acknowledgment from family, relief from confinement, assistance from nursing and other resources, and diversional activities. In summary, mothercare includes the mother, the daughter, and the family, primarily. Issues such as confinement, moral dilemmas, and sources of support impact on the participants involved in caregiving and the nature of the mothercare experience. When the daughters in this research were shown this phenomenological writing about the nature of mothercare, they validated that this indeed was their experience. The next step is to take care of a most valuable resource: the women who mothercare.

INTERVENTIONS: TAKING CARE OF WOMEN WHO MOTHERCARE

What do hot lines, hugs, laughter, humor, gardening, and a breather have in common?

After six months—or ten years—of mothercare, a caregiver who did not learn to use some (and preferably all) of these as outlets for the tensions produced in day-to-day interactions with her mother and family would be in a frustrated state.

The mothercaring daughters interviewed reported that these are some of the resources that make it possible for them to carry on. A 24-hour hot line to a nurse or a service provides help and a sense of security. Family members who provide hugs, laughter, and jokes make long days bearable. Getting out into a garden or just getting away for a few hours allows time for care of self. An important concern for an individual taking care of her mother is that she must take care of herself, in order to be better able to give the continuing care. It becomes critical for the caregiver to find ways to take care of herself.

Finding reliable support services and respite can be a chore, but, if undertaken in the initial stages of mothercare, much distress for everyone can be avoided. Two areas need to be explored for possible help: (1) the family, which we have already discussed, and (2) community resources.

Community Resources

Community resources can provide a wealth of services. Nurses, social workers, and national hot lines (such as the Denville (NJ) National Hot Line for Support Groups; the Home Care Hot Line sponsored by the National League for Nursing (NY); and the respite service for people with dementias, sponsored by the Brookdale Center on Aging, Hunter College (NY)) can provide access to these resources. Other sources of information are newsletters such as: *Caregiving,* National Council on Aging, 600 Maryland Avenue, SW, Washington, DC 20024; and *Parent Care: Resources to Assist Family Caregivers,* Gerontology Center, 316 Strong Hall, The University of Kansas, Lawrence KS 66045. Examples of some specific services and organizations available are: Retired Senior Volunteer Program, Family Caregivers of the Aging, National Council on the Aging (Washington, DC); National Association for Families Caring for their Elders Inc. (Silver Spring, MD); National Association of Private Geriatric Care Managers (NY). Individual communities may offer some of the following resources: rehabilitation centers for the handicapped, day care centers for the aged, senior centers, noontime meals for the elderly both at home and at specific centers, community health and mental health services, pastoral counseling sources, vocational rehabilitation services, commission for the blind and visually impaired, glasses for the elderly, dental care for the elderly, Medicare and Medicaid services, transportation assistance, county board on aging, abuse protection, housing rehabilitation programs, weatherization programs, legal information and referral for the elderly, home health agencies, social clubs, support groups, and hospice services.

Health Professionals

Health professionals and nurses can assist daughters by eliminating their *not knowing*. Teaching about caregiving, by nurses or health professionals, is exceedingly important; it is a significant part of home care as well as of other aspects of professional practice. Timing is a factor: the new mothercarer can be overwhelmed by uncertainty, and health care professionals can assist by teaching about prevention.

A new mothercaring daughter can be connected early with services and support groups that will help her navigate this difficult course. However, this can only be accomplished if the health care professional is aware of the caregiver and the needs of the situation. For best results, the health care professional must involve the mother, the daughter, and the family. One can often find health care providers at geriatric assessment services associated with local hospitals, social services departments in hospitals and nursing homes, and departments of the aging in city and county governments. Peer support groups can be located through local newspapers, through a telephone hot line such as the Denville (NJ) National Hot Line for Support Groups, and from computer bulletin boards.

Health professionals can also assist caregiving daughters by helping them to define their role: teaching them what to expect and how to deal with the problems when they do arise. Preparation for the possibilities can make the difference between a panic reaction to a crisis and a calm resolution of an anticipated occurrence. Daughters have stated that instruction in what to expect is one of their primary considerations when they consider the difference between adequate and good nursing care.

Nurses, especially community health nurses, can provide service to mothercaring daughters by developing courses on caregiving (given at times that are convenient), organizing associated resources so that daughters may comfortably leave their mothers, or providing on-site care services during the sessions. Local divisions of departments for the aging, and visiting nurse services, both community- and hospital-based, may offer these resources. Courses may be given at local night-schools, YW- or YM-CAs, or churches. If the daughter works, her corporation may provide facilities for lunchtime programs. If the daughter is restricted to the home, either on-site or in-the-home attendants can be made available so that the daughter and the mother can be comfortable during the educational programs. A personal computer can be another source of contact. Bulletin boards and networks have been established so that one caregiving daughter can "talk" to another from the privacy of her own home. Many intimate friendships and valuable information have been shared via this medium. It is also important for daughters to develop personal resources to deal with the changing landscape.

Personal Resources

Mothercarers often have to face moral dilemmas. For example: Is it OK to give morphine? Should I buy those cigarettes? What do I do about the family member who is stealing my mother's medication? Another important area is coping with the changes that occur over time.

A caregiver must know that changes are inevitable and that the person she sees today is not—and can never be—the person remembered from ten, 20, or 40 years ago, even though some of the same characteristics keep reappearing. It is hard to accept the reality that the mother who cared for her entire family is now unable to care for herself. Personality changes also occur; often, the person's basic personality traits are exaggerated (for better or worse).

Fear and isolation often affect mothers. Fear of being alone is a major concern. The reasons are unending; the fear induced is the same. The mothercarer feels she must find a way to provide a sense of well-being for her mother; community and family resources can help.

The ability for the mother to maintain her independence, even in small ways, is of prime importance. If the only action a mother can accomplish independently is to hold a cup, then she should be encouraged to drink her beverages from the cup and without help. Ways that mothers can walk without another person's assistance—by using walkers or quadcanes—offer another source of maintaining independence. Use of the telephone can be enhanced through dial-panel numerals, amplifiers, or preprogrammed dialing. When mother and daughter meet the challenge of finding ways to maintain independence, the result is an increased sense of self-worth.

Daughters also need to recognize their own self-worth and to acknowledge their anger, which is a normal part of caregiving and of life. Finding a safe way of expressing this anger is important for them and their mothers. Family members, counselors, nurses, peers, and support groups are meaningful resources.

Finally, there must be recognition that the caregiving daughter is providing a valuable and important contribution to her mother, her family, and herself. This contribution should not be minimized by others, and it should be rewarded by the caregiver's taking care of herself—doing small things that make her happy; taking some time for herself, perhaps to take an uninterrupted bubblebath; buying flowers, perfume, or a new outfit; taking a walk alone or with a friend; reading a chapter in a good book; listening to a favorite tape or CD; watching an absorbing or relaxing videotape. Each caregiver must find her own personal meaning in mothercare.

MEANING IN MOTHERCARE

What's it like to mother one's own mother? It's like mining a rough-cut diamond and carrying it out from a deep mine shaft. It has many facets; a few shine or glimmer with fire in the light, but most are dark. Yet, the owner hopes that skillful cutting (caring) will bring light to all facets, creating a gem that could last into eternity. Such is the care that a daughter provides for her mother—often dark and foreboding, but containing the hope of light, strength, and a meaningful life for those involved. At times, the fire from mothercare can be quite scaring—something a daughter fears and wants to avoid. Nevertheless, the firelights in the diamond can be very beautiful and may well be cherished for the rest of one's life.

Elizabeth Bennett's (1987) poem, "The Trouble Was Meals," in the collection entitled *When I Am Old I Shall Wear Purple* (Martz, 1991), reflects mothercare:

Dad was the head of the family, for sure.
When he got us all together
it meant either a baby was on the way
or we were moving. So when the question was put,
How would it be if Grandma came to live with us?
I thought, no big deal.
I was glad we weren't moving.
   I found a picture of Grandma,
a young dancer in a dress, sequins and feathers.
She had me tape it onto the mirror
over the dresser where she kept Grandpa's remains,
his gold cufflinks, glass eye.
   It was all right,
Grandma the dancer in residence,
all right for me, hard for Mother.
Dad would come home, pour a glass of Old Crow Bourbon,
one for Mother, drink them both.
   The trouble was meals.
Dad was used to holding forth,
and the first night, halfway through Chicken Cacciatore
Grandma turned and said, "Rest your gums, dear."
She called everyone dear, all of us, the mailman,
even the exterminator.
She took to humming in a loud voice
and dropping her knife and fork on the floor.
   One night she shouted, "Leftovers, leftovers,
where's the original?" and shoved her plate
on the floor. Baby threw his bottle
on top of the broken china. The plate crash
became a regular occurrence.
   Fridays at school our teacher read us poetry,
"Poitry," she called it. . . .

I didn't like poetry. What I liked was Shop.
I made a wooden bowl, sanded the rim smooth,
carved my initials on the bottom.
I brought it home to Grandma
and we served her dinner in it every night.
She still shoved it on the floor
but nothing broke.
    When I was at the orthodontist's one afternoon,
Grandma took a nap and never woke up.
We cleaned out her room. I helped Mother.
She was in a mood to throw everything out,
flannel sheets that smelled of urine, everything.
She only kept the picture. That night after dinner
I found the bowl in the trash.
Dad said, we won't need that *anymore,*
but I washed and dried it
and put it on the shelf next to Old Crow
so I could find it when Mother got old.

In this poem, Bennett shows the teaching of mothercare. What do we teach our young? As a society, we need to show more concern and care for our elders and our caregivers.

Mothercare is so prevalent and so important for our elders. Mothercare can also be extremely demanding and frustrating. Thus, it is extremely important to support those who care for our elderly—in most cases, the mothercaring daughters. Many means of support are available, and mothers and daughters need to utilize both internal and external resources. Sharing the experiences of others in the same circumstances can be a continuing source of help and reassurance.

ADDITIONAL INFORMATION ABOUT THE CARE OF THE AGED

The number of aged persons in our country increases daily. Life spans are lengthening, and it is not uncommon to live to be 80 or

90. In 1900, the aged (those over 65) numbered 3 million, or 4 percent of the total population. Today, the aged number over 30 million and comprise 12.6 percent of the population (Ebersole & Hess, 1990). As an individual ages, he or she is more likely to need nursing and the health care system. Of particular concern are the increasing numbers of frail elderly who require some form of assistance to continue to live in a home setting.

Traditionally, women have cared for the elderly, and, despite the fact that many women are now employed outside the home, they continue to be the chief caregivers. The average American woman will spend 17 years raising her children and 18 years helping her aged parents, according to a 1988 U.S. House of Representatives report.

The majority of the literature on caregiving has been primarily quantitative and has listed stressors such as emotional stress, nocturnal disturbances, aggression and agitation, and incontinence (Brody, 1981, 1985; Cantor, 1983; Danis, 1978; Gurland, Dean, Gurland, & Cook, 1978; Hoenig, 1966; Kleban, Brody, & Hoffman, 1984; Lang & Brody, 1983; Lopata & Norr, 1980; Soldo & Myllyluoma, 1983). These same researchers have cited demographic changes that will significantly increase the amount of parent care in coming decades (Brotman, 1980; Ebersole & Hess, 1990; Lechner, 1993; Townsend & Poulshock, 1981) and describe caregivers, most of whom are women (Bowers, 1987; Brody, 1981; Horowitz, 1985; Kleban et al., 1984).

ABOUT THE STUDY

Caregiving to mothers involves experiences of health, illness, suffering, and rewards for the participants. A descriptive study utilizing a phenomenological approach was chosen so that the nature of the experience of caring for elderly mothers could be revealed in a wholistic manner.

The prerequisite for any data was that they had to have some relevance to the nature of the experience of women who were caregivers for their elderly mothers. The narratives and other sources of data were rich with themes. Themes that consistently appeared in the data and gave a meaningful description of the phenomenon were highlighted.

Once themes had been discovered and organized from among the multiple sources, the final step in the van Manen (1984) caveats was the phenomenological writing. In this chapter, the writing has described the nature of the experience of women who cared for their elderly mothers. This writing was shared with the caregivers for validation.

Sample and Setting. A convenience sample of 12 women caregivers of elderly mothers living within the community setting was employed; for this study, the community encompassed Morris County, New Jersey, and Rockland County, New York. The convenience sample of caregivers was obtained primarily from the researcher's nursing practice as a Nurse Supervisor and as Director of Professional Services for a community health agency in northern New Jersey. It was believed that, because of an established rapport with the caregivers, they were more likely to be open, comfortable, and willing to divulge material that they might not discuss with a stranger. Nurses must begin to utilize their nursing practice situations as sources of research so that the research will be more relevant and applicable and so that nurses can be encouraged to utilize published research in their practice.

Other criteria for participation in the research were: the caregivers had to have aged mothers, living within the same community setting, who required assistance from the caregiver in order to continue to live (as determined by both mother and daughter) in their present setting. Eleven of the daughters studied lived with their aged mothers; one mother lived in a boarding home nearby. (Many of the same themes occurred in this daughter's talk as in that of the other 11, whose mothers were living in their homes.)

Daughters were primarily in the middle-income category, and ranged in aged from 42 to 59. One was Black; the rest were white. The Baptist, Catholic, Episcopalian, Jewish, and Protestant faiths were represented in the sample.

Daughters who participated in this study were caregivers for at least six months' duration and were available for at least two one- to three-hour interviews. Conversations were conducted in seven of the caregivers' homes, and the remainder took place in my home or office.

Gaining Access. Once the participants were contacted and appointments were made, the research was explained and human subject considerations were outlined with each person. The women were informed that they could leave the study at any time.

My experience with my mother was shared as a starting point for our conversations. My interest in caregiving as a nurse, particularly in the public health sector, was also shared.

Data Collection and Storage. Conversations were taped with the consent of those involved. I took written field notes (a detailed description of the events, actions, interactions, and feelings as they presented themselves in the natural setting). These notes were written immediately after the tape-recorded sessions. Additionally, I kept a personal journal for the entire period of the data collection and analysis. All thoughts and ideas pertaining to my personal reactions and experiences and relating to the nature of the caregiving were included. This involved my continuing interactions with my own mother and with a support group for caregivers, which I attended; conferences; visits to seniors' residences in California, while on vacation; literature and visits to art exhibitions; and so on.

After the interviews, van Manen's (1984) suggestions were followed, to transform the understanding of the personal experience related by the caregiver into conceptual categories that I believed to be the essence of that original experience.

REFERENCES

Bowers, B. J. (1987). Intergenerational caregiving: Adult caregivers and their aging parents. *Advances in Nursing Science, 9*(2), 20–31.

Brody, E. M. (1981). "Woman in the middle" and family help to older people. *The Gerontologist, 21*(5), 471–480.

Brody, E. M. (1985). Parent care as a normative stress. *The Gerontologist, 25*(1), 19–29.

Brotman, H. B. (1980). Every ninth American. In U.S. Senate Special Committee on Aging, *Developments in aging: 1979, part 1.* Washington, DC: U.S. Government Printing Office.

Cantor, M. H. (1983). Strain among caregivers: A study of experience in the United States. *The Gerontologist, 6*(23), 597-604.

Danis, B. G. (1978). *Stress in individuals caring for ill elderly relatives.* Paper presented at 31st Annual Meeting of the Gerontological Society, Dallas, TX.

Ebersole, P., & Hess, P. (1990). *Toward healthy aging: Human needs and nursing response.* St. Louis: Mosby.

French, M. (1987). *Her mother's daughter.* New York: Summit.

Goodman, E. (1985). *Keeping in touch.* New York: Summit.

Gurland, B., Dean, L., Gurland, R., & Cook, D. (1978). Personal time dependency in the elderly of New York City: Findings from the U.S.-U.K. cross-national geriatric community study. In *Dependency in the elderly of New York City* (pp. 9-45). New York: New York Council of Greater New York.

Hoenig, J., & Hamilton, M. (1966). Elderly patients and the burden on the household. *Psychiatra et Neurologia,* Basil *152,* 281-293.

Horowitz, A. (1985). Family caregivers of the frail elderly. *Annual Review of Gerontology and Geriatrics, 5,* 194-246.

Kleban, M. H., Brody, E. M., & Hoffman, C. (1984, November). *Parent care and depression: Differences between working and nonworking adult daughters.* Paper presented at the 37th Annual Meeting of The Gerontological Society of America, San Antonio, TX.

Lang, A. M., & Brody, E. M. (1983). Characteristics of middle-aged daughters and help to their elderly mothers. *Journal of Marriage and the Family,* 45, 193-202.

Lechner, V. M. (1993). Racial group responses to work and parent care. *Families in Society: The Journal of Contemporary Human Services,* (2), 93-103.

Lopata, H. Z., & Norr, K. F. (1980, June). Changing commitments of American woman to work and family roles. *Social Security Bulletin,* (43), 3-14.

Martz, S. (Ed.) (1991). *When I am an old woman I shall wear purple.* Watsonville, CA: Papier-Maché Press.

Morrison, T. (1987). *Beloved.* Markham, Ontario: New American Library.

Soldo, B. J., & Myllyluoma, J. (1983). Caregivers who live with dependent elderly. *The Gerontologist, 23*(6), 605-611.

Townsend, A. L., & Poulshock, S. W. (1981). Intergenerational perspectives on impaired elders support networks. *Journal of Gerontology, 36,* 92-99.

U.S. Bureau of the Census (1988). *Statistical Abstract of the United States* (108th ed.). Washington, DC: U.S. Government Printing Office.

van Manen, M. (1984). Practicing phenomenological writing. *Phenomenology & Pedagogy, 2*(1), 36-69.

ABOUT THE AUTHOR

I am Ellen Goldschmidt Ehrlich, Ed.D., RN. I live in northern New Jersey, pursue work as a qualitative phenomenological researcher and as an Assistant Professor of Nursing at the College of Mount Saint Vincent, Riverdale, NY. I am the mother of two young women, Beth and Janice. My education includes a diploma from Johns Hopkins Hospital School of Nursing, a BSN from Kean College of New Jersey, and Master's and Doctoral degrees from Teachers College, Columbia University.

My favorite pastimes are visiting art museums, working with water colors, going to concerts, traveling, and sitting down with a good book while listening to music (almost any kind except hard rock). I have lived in several different states: Michigan, New Jersey, New York, Connecticut, and Louisiana.

In nursing, my career has included three major areas: education, administration, and clinical practice. A few of my positions were: teaching at the Hospital of the University of Pennsylvania School of Nursing; directing the professional staff at a community health agency; teaching natural childbirth; helping to establish the EMT-Ambulance Program in New Jersey; being assistant supervisor at Mount Sinai Medical Center in New York City; staff nursing in adult, geriatric, and psychiatric health; and President of Sigma Theta Tau, Lambda Iota Chapter. I was honored to be listed in *Who's Who in Professional Nursing* and have enjoyed presenting my research at several conferences.

6

See My Abuse—The Shelter
Transition of Battered Women

Carol P. Germain

INTRODUCTION

I would see this sort of glassy-eyed stare, and his foot would start tapping and his hand trembling and I knew it was coming. I know this time it was about due but I got out the day before, I think. He would always get me in a corner where I couldn't escape and would always choke me. The last two times everything went black and I just figured one of these times I'd go into laryngospasm and that would be the end. I had enough. [Angela]

Angela became a resident in a shelter for abused women.[1] Our paths crossed when I was doing a study of the health needs and related health issues in the shelter. One of many women who volunteered to talk with me about their transition from abuse, Angela and I shared several conversations and experiences during her transition. But more of Angela later.

THE PERSONAL DOCUMENTS OF
SHELTERED ABUSED WOMEN

Near the end of my field work in the shelter, a staff member made reference to a notebook that contained the writings of some of the women. Curious, I asked some questions about it, and because no written sources of information were off-limits to me, one day I perused the ledger. I became fascinated with the entries, which I considered then to be contextual data but later realized were phenomenological sources in the form of brief personal documents (Ruffing-Rahal, 1986) that displayed the women's attempts to make sense of their own experiences. As I reread the collection, I was impressed that, even though each individual's experience and contribution were unique, there were patterns throughout. I moved from a kind of playfulness with the texts to a systematic analysis[2] directed at answering the question: What do battered women living in a shelter find meaningful to share about their lived experiences in unsolicited written personal documents?

Residents, at the time of their admission, were invited by the staff to write whenever and whatever they wished on the blank pages of a plain, bound ledger that was readily accessible to anyone in the shelter who wanted to read it. When I read it, there were 23 handwritten or handprinted one- or two-page entries from 18 women. One woman provided five entries, four of them very brief. Most entries were narrative, but four were poetic in style and one was an allegory. The presentations ranged from large handwriting with clear penmanship and fine composition to rudimentary printing and a partially illiterate text. In most instances, the author did not use her own name. Some entries were unsigned; others were signed by "Me" or "Your family member." The specific times of four of the entries were at 7 days, 9 days, 5 weeks, and 3 months of a length of stay usually limited to 2 months if no housing was available.

The authors chose to address different phases of their transition from their violent situations, but the text as a whole provided a mosaic of the women's collective experience. The phases, roughly chronologic, were overlapping and did not follow an invariant sequence. They were: the flight for life, bearing and dealing with psychic wounds, acclimation and interdependence in communal living, finding and healing the self, and departure with hope and concern for others. Themes that persisted through all stages were the centrality of the self concept and the value of peace, including peace of mind.

The Flight for Life

The women had to have documented physical abuse (battering) in order to be admitted to the shelter, but no one directly identified or addressed physical injuries in the ledger. Only one alluded to physical abuse: "Most of the time males ask themselves are females only punching bags?" Another referred to the abuse still more indirectly: "I keep think about how I was abused and how I ever made it out alive."

The more common descriptors of the spouse or partner abuse, however, were being controlled, trapped, jailed, or locked up. One woman wrote: "The worst thing . . . was being trapped in that house, with the doors locked and my husband pacing by my side, not letting me get the help I needed." Another stated, "I was granted a pardon from jail when I left our home."

The women referred to their abusive situations as "a horrible life," a "nightmare," a "violent environment," a "hell hole," and "a lonely fear time in my life." Another wrote, "I was never at peace in my past home."

References to the length of the abusive situation included 21 years, 16 years, and "5 years of hell." The decision to enter the shelter was, for some, a thoughtful one over time; for others, it was abrupt. One woman wrote, "I finally decided on my 40th birthday, I won't be abused any longer." The decision to leave home was marked by ambivalence and courage. "A few months ago I looked the number up but was too scared to dial the number," wrote one woman.

Many indicated that their feelings about themselves prompted the decision to leave. Three women wrote: "I had lost self-respect"; "I had this great sense of worthlessness about myself"; "I lost all my sense of happiness . . . and who and what I am all about."

Women explained their hesitancy to leave in such statements as "I thought I couldn't make it with no plans for myself and my two children," and "I was constantly telling myself it [the marriage] will work, it will work . . . I was only kidding myself."

This first phase, the abused woman's flight for life and escape from submission to violence, can be interpreted using Sarbin's (1984) life-event transition theory. The flight involves a breach of cultural norms for the woman that has ramifications for other abused women in her community who are ascribed the culture's role expectations for wife or partner. By fleeing and entering a shelter, the woman enters an abrupt role transition without the usual supportive rituals or rites of passage that accompany a community's positively sanctioned life events, such as marriages or graduations. Fortunately, by fleeing, the abused woman becomes unavailable for any community ritual of degradation imposed for cultural deviance. In the case of abused women, the deviance is failure to maintain a submissive role and failure in their prescribed status to present an image of a unified home to the world (Boyanowsky 1984).

Bearing and Dealing with Psychic Wounds

Cultural values are deeply ingrained. Leaving an abusive home, even though a protective move for the woman and her children, is interpreted by many women as an admission of failure, if the role of wife or partner is the major component of their self-identity. Thus, many women entered the shelter not only degraded by the physical and psychological abuse but self-degraded by perceived role failure.

After entering the shelter, most women were unable to engage quickly in shelter activities such as networking with community agencies, even though this was a constant activity in the shelter. They needed time to bear and deal with a variety of raw emotions. With counseling, they had the opportunity to reflect on their past lives. This evoked such written responses as "I must have had some sickness that led me to acceptance of a horrible life." A resident described her abusive situation as "so unreal like I was in a movie." The work of dealing with losses and building a new life from different starting points compelled a range of descriptions, from a simple and plaintive "I am sad" to a not-so-simple "I'm gladly alone rather than have the life sucked out of me by the violent needs of other minds and bodies." The emotional struggle is evident in one woman's statement: "I hope I can find my self again and stop dying inside. I want to cry all the time but it doesn't help." Still another wrote: "I have nobody to turn to . . . all I have is my three boys. I know my life is hopeless to me."

One resident used an allegory to relate her profound depression. She described a woman walking alone through desolate streets, searching but lost, rebuffed by several men when she asked directions. After finding a poor beast of a dog in a gutter, the woman covered them both with her coat and, with a smile on her face, holding the dog in a loose hug, settled down for the night. She decided that "a dog is a much better bedfellow than a man who will not aid another." In the morning, she did not awaken to the kicks of children. A dog was her companion in death. Another entry by this woman was a poem that also had a theme of death.

Length of time in the throes of depression and despair varied. One woman wrote: "Time knows no meaning of how long it takes to find peace of mind and forget your mistakes." But another described her own course as being "like a baby taking his first step," adding, "the rest of the way gets easier for me."

In addition to degradation, depression, and despair, the women suffered from: continuing fear that their abusers would come after them, loss of valued expectations in the relationship, loss of home and belongings, loss of familiar roles and patterns of activity of daily living, and a concomitant loss of self-identity and self-esteem.

The safe shelter and the staff served to protect each woman from her abuser and provided her with exigencies such as food and other basic requirements while she grieved her losses and began a healing process. Mothers were expected to provide the care for their children.

Acclimation and Interdependence in Communal Living

Despite the staff's efforts, the wear and tear of the continuous turnover of 7 or 8 adults and 17 or 18 children took its toll on the renovated but very old farmhouse, as did the personal hygiene habits of some residents and the inconsistency with which some completed their agreed-on household chores. However, most of the women did not write about the deprivations or inconveniences of the abrupt change to living in a shelter. Rather, they related their amazement that they were not alone and had found others with whom to share the hidden shame and humiliation of their abusive situations.

The shelter was one resident's "lifeline to sanity, peace, love, understanding, learning, and growing." Women wrote that they were "grateful," "thankful," "appreciative." The shelter was "great" as a "place to help women and children who are in trouble;" and "it was just wonderful being with people who believed in me no matter how insecure I felt." Another added: "The shelter was the best thing for me . . . the right choice . . . I seen I was not the only one . . . I never had it better."

The metaphor of family and home was evident. One resident wrote: "I'm so grateful for this place that feels like home." Another described the situation as "a family away from family." In some entries, residents were addressed as "sisters" or "family."

On the other hand, three residents' comments indicated that the course of shelter life didn't always run smoothly. The anger of some of the women was sometimes displaced on other residents and staff, or was acted out in the deliberate breaking of rules that they had agreed, on admission, to observe. One woman, who lived in the shelter for three months, wrote as she was preparing to leave:

The only real problem is the women who come here that are in the same boat as the rest of us but try to be better. Some women that have come here are down to earth but some are bitches.

Two residents expressed their disagreement with certain shelter policies or procedures, such as those related to safety for the household, curfews, signing in and out, and the prohibition against the disciplining of children by physical means. One wrote:

I like most of the people here but you really don't get freedom. If you want to go somewhere be back at a certain time they say. . . . You can't beat or smack your child if they are bad, most of them act bad because they know they can't get hit.

The degree of communality varied with the mix of women and children. One woman, who had experienced difficulty getting back into the shelter after a brief hospitalization, found the shelter to be ". . . just like jail . . . I just fed up with this whole damn place. Fuck the shelter. P.S. I wouldn't recommend it to my dog."

Contrasted with this last message, and considering the fact that the ledger was not intended as an evaluation tool, the vast majority of comments about the staff were positive. "With the help of the counselors," one resident wrote, "I made it." Another added: "The workers here are great and never hesitate to listen to your problems"; still another wrote: "I like you all for helping me so much."

During this third phase of the transition from violence, the abused woman forms attachments to her new reference group, defines her position in the new social structure, and uses the shelter's services to facilitate and maintain self-identity change and to access other community resources. A few women, however, do not adapt to some of the perceived constraints of shelter life.

Finding and Healing the Self

Although no specific shelter program component was cited by any of the women, messages indicative of gains in self-esteem, self-identity, and self-confidence were evident in the majority of entries. Here are some examples:

What I've learned about myself and how I really can make it amazes me.

I've learned what it means to be and feel human again.

I've regained my love for myself.

It's about time to put myself first.

When you come to terms with your own self you are able to reach out to others.

I know now the only way for me to start being me is not to run away from anyone.

Others added the notion of freedom:

I've been set free to live and I want to live. To be whatever I can be.

Today I know what Dr. Martin Luther King meant by "Free at last" . . . I feel delivered. I feel born again. Free to be me. . . . Here I found peace and found myself.

During the field-work year, only one woman was observed in overt religious practice. She knelt and prayed silently twice a day on a playroom cot or in her bedroom. Yet more than one-third of the women exhibited a spiritual dimension by referring to "God," "Jesus," or "my Creator" in their entries. Some extended thanks, such as, "I thank God I am alive to tell my story to others like myself," or petitioned, "God please help me. Let me find happiness again," or made a promise "to my Creator that I will devote my life to helping other women to realize the dangers of living in a violent environment and try to help them along the way as the staff and women helped me."

In this fourth phase, healing is evident with gains in self-identity and self-esteem. There is acknowledgment of interdependence with peers, shelter staff, community agencies, and, for some, God.

Readiness for Departure

Readiness for departure from their transitional home (a more apt term than "shelter") was indicated in many parting messages to remaining and future residents and staff. General messages included: "Love and peace to you all," or "Best of luck," or "Have fun . . . and don't go back to the hell hole."

Two women who planned to return to the abusive home gave explanations for their decisions. One wrote:

Six years to me is not that easy to throw away . . . if I don't give him the chance my conscience would bother me . . . if I ever have to leave him again, I will be free and have peace of mind. I believe in the principle of marriage which is why this man is getting a second chance.

Another woman perceived her imminent return home as a "victory and not a defeat. I had to go back for myself." She added: ". . . if I had left my past unresolved I would have been haunted by what if's for the rest of my life. Now I have the chance to resolve my past and at the same time get with my future."

The women left advice and encouragement for newcomers to the shelter: "Give yourself time to gain wisdom and insight into yourself and your situation and from there . . . you can reach your inner peace." Another advised: "Thank yourself for having enough courage to get out of a bad situation that only gets worse. . . . Don't say you can't make it on your own because you already did. You left."

Some women were able to formulate and share general goals:

I will grow each day into whatever dreams and hopes I have for myself.

I will go on now with my life doing what is best for me and the children next.

Even though it won't be easy all the time I will be able to have peace of mind.

The women's hopes included: ". . . that the problem of abuse of women can be wiped out completely so women can once again enjoy what we are all about"; ". . . that the friends I have meet still keep in touch with me"; ". . . that I can find a nice place and be happy with it."

The women who wrote of this final stage of shelter transition indicated readiness to leave the shelter and move on with their own and their children's lives. This readiness was evident in their written messages to peers, staff, and newcomers, in which they demonstrated goal formulation, hope, and concern for others.

The optimism of the writers was evident among those who were and those who were not returning to the abusive home, even though the future posed formidable challenges for each group. For example, for mothers who wanted to be self-sufficient, it was almost impossible to find an affordable and suitable combination of job, apartment, school, public transportation, and part-time child care. Advocacy and options counseling helped the women to link with community resources such as welfare, food stamps, Medicaid, legal services for custody and support, and General Educational Development high school equivalency programs.

Although various hypotheses in the literature have suggested that return of a woman to the abusive situation is prompted by economic reasons, hopelessness, helplessness, or lack of exposure to acceptable alternative female role models, different reasons were given by the two women who wrote about their deliberate choices to return. Their reasons supported Campbell's (1989) conjecture of the possibility of purposeful return to a formerly abusive situation. Nevertheless, although the two women's psychosocial and cultural perspectives may have changed to incorporate new resources and problem-solving strategies, the possibility of successful return is limited unless there is change in the abuser, and, in some cases, in the home community as well.

Theory Generation

Analysis of this relatively brief but dense set of personal documents has yielded a rudimentary life-event transition theory of women who flee abusive situations and enter a shelter. The theory is different from other life-event transition theories such as those of Sarbin (1984) and Boyanowsky (1984). As Sokol and Lewis (1984) have pointed out, transition theories in the career transition literature and the life-event transition literature, in general, provide a view of role transition as being a normal occurrence in life that is enhanced by rituals of communal support. Flight for one's life, from a male abuser to an abrupt role transition in a safe shelter, is, thankfully, not a normal life occurrence. Thus, these existing transition theories do not account for the phenomenon of abused women who leave the abuser and the community as well.

This emergent theory of transition from abuse during the shelter phase of rehabilitation needs continuing development based on the analysis of multiple sources of information, particularly since the participants for this personal documents analysis were self-selected and the full range of sheltered women did not choose to communicate the meaning of their experiences in written personal documents.

The larger issue of theory here, however, is theory to what end? The emphasis is not on building empirical theory for ultimate testing but on van Manen's (1990) notion of theory that is developed from the analysis of lived experiences:

> *So phenomenology does not offer us the possibility of effective theory with which we can now explain and/or control the world, but rather it offers us the possibility of plausible insights that bring us in more direct contact with the world.* (p. 9)

The emergent transition theory can help us to organize and focus on certain aspects of the voluminous phenomenological material that seems to pour out of so many abused women when they are asked the single, simple question: What was the experience like for you? Let us return to Angela and listen to what she found meaningful to share about her transition from abuse and violence.

ANGELA'S STORY

Introduction

Angela's story is used as an exemplar, not because she was typical—she believed she was stronger than most of the women in the shelter at the time—but because her story captures, in an articulate, evocative, and powerful way, the uniqueness and the essence of the experience of being abused and battered, and in transition. Her story also adds credence to the transition theory developed from the personal documents analysis.

Angela had been a respiratory therapist in a hospital, but lost her job because of frequent lateness and absence. She left amicably; she was given the option to resign and was told she would receive a good recommendation. She told her employer that she was resigning because of "domestic problems." Angela had appeared at work nine times in the previous two years with visible bruises around her eyes, face, neck, or arms, and had a pattern of lateness and absence, yet no one ever asked her whether she was being abused. How was she abused? "I can count the ways," Angela remarked. For example, Fred, her cohabiting partner, was supposed to leave her the car on Saturdays so that she could get to work, but he often didn't and the bus service was very poor on Saturdays. She was also late on weekends, when he was supposed to mind the two children; he took off and she had to find a baby sitter. Some mornings, when he was supposed to drop her off at work, he would wait until the departure time and then take off in the car, leaving her to find public transportation. "He was so inconsiderate. You can't run a hospital like that," Angela said.

Angela had a relationship with Fred for 12 years but had actually shared a house with him and their two children, a girl age seven and a boy of 19 months, for only the previous three years. She took Fred's last name when she became pregnant with the first child: "No one [then] worked in a hospital and had a baby without being married." The cohabiting arrangement was all right with Angela, who said:

> *I never married him . . . something always held me back, and you know, he always wanted to get married. I wasn't overjoyed at having two children [both unplanned; contraception was her responsibility] and not married but they're my children and I had them and I knew that I could take care of them no matter what . . . but if I had married him, and left, he would follow me to the ends of the earth. He always wanted me to have more than one child, more than*

two, because he felt that I would be bound to him then. Three years ago I decided my daughter should be with her father. I figured . . . maybe he's grown up and he appeared to have grown up. I'd try it with him. He saw her twice, three times when she was growing up. When I got pregnant with her he said that she wasn't his child and it upset me a great deal because I didn't have any other boyfriend. And any time he wants to upset me he would say that, and she looks just like him.

After high school and respiratory therapy school, Angela went to college for several semesters. Fred didn't like this. Angela said:

He didn't want me to go to college because he was afraid I was going to meet someone. He would pick me up and if I was a few minutes late he'd ask who I was with. He would get upset if I was reading a book, he was that insecure. I didn't know that he couldn't read. He's a truck driver and he needs to read maps and signs. He would look at the front page of a newspaper or the cover of a magazine and make believe he was reading.

Woven through Angela's story is a litany of types of abuse. Instead of "growing up," Angela said that Fred fell back into his old ways and habits after "my son" was born even though the sun rose and set on the baby. Angela recalled:

He'd curse all the time and be vulgar; he didn't know how to talk to me and the kids. With everyone else he'd be a perfect gentleman, but when he got home anything goes. He did a lot of running around . . . he used to say it's better to be with someone else than harassing you . . . that was salvation for me, but then I was getting further and further away from him. He didn't see the rent was paid on time, he didn't care to see that there was food in the house. All these things were left to me. I'd fly down the highway coming from work, almost having an accident, hurrying to get the kids and get home and get dinner for this man who'll say,

'You're five minutes late.' He resented the fact that I can read. He'd time me when I was in the bathroom, asking me if I had a book in there. He promised me he was going to get these things for the kids for Easter and he didn't do any of it. Instead, he bought himself an outfit from head to toe and hid it. He was one of those people who would go out and buy clothes and then hide them 'cause he knew he was wrong. Then he'd dress real quick and dash out the door. When he was around his friends I was always 'his wife' . . . it just used to get under my skin . . . he had all the comforts and I paid the price.

Added to the psychological abuse were the increasingly violent episodes of battering that ultimately prompted Angela's flight to the shelter. "He's beaten me up about nine times," said Angela, "and there wasn't one time that he didn't leave marks on me." She continued:

It wasn't just a slap; it was being choked, being held on the floor with his knee in my chest because I wouldn't sign papers to buy the house; it was my head being banged on the floor, then I was kicked across the floor. He'd knock me around, push me around. And always someone from his family was witnessing . . . someone was always living with us. Only once were we alone and that time wasn't as bad as some of the other times. Once he had me on the floor kicking me and I said to his cousin, "Why don't you call the cops?" and his cousin said, "Hey, man, don't do that." And he [the abuser] said, "Don't tell me, if I want to kill her in a passion, that's between me and her . . . she's my woman, and if I want to beat her up, I'll do it."

Angela continued with this scenario:

He abused me the whole night. He got me in the room, he put his knee in my face. He would do things off and on. Every time he would think of my telling his cousin to call the police, he would say, "Bitch!" Then he would grab me and abuse me more.

Angela explained that sometimes "I did fight back with him," continuing:

Once I had him on the floor on top of his chest with my hands at his throat and I could have really killed him but I figured why should I go to jail. He ain't worth it. Each day after a beating I would still be sore and then the next day I got a little better and the next day a little better and he's going out of his way . . . he'll spend his whole paycheck to buy you something to try to make up for it. He'll pick up his clothes or do other things to show that he's trying but that doesn't take the memory away.

I asked Angela if she had ever pressed charges and she replied, "No, I never pressed charges because if I did and he caught up with me 100 years from now, he would kill me on the spot, because he's the kind of person who harbored that kind of malice."

Angela's Flight for Life

After the last choking episode and her real fear of death from laryngospasm, Angela decided that she'd had enough. She explained:

I can't jeopardize my kids. They're my responsibility. All they saw was their father fighting, getting dressed to go out, not coming home at night, coming in early in the morning causing a commotion, telling everyone what to do and how to do it. I had thought of leaving before but I kept putting stumbling blocks in my own way . . . I have two kids . . . how am I going to get to work? . . . I don't have a car . . . I don't have this, I don't have that. I didn't know about a shelter then.

But then Angela did find out about a local shelter. "Not everyone was as fortunate as I was," she said, adding, "The counselor started talking to me by phone long before I came to the shelter and she explained to me a lot of things that I didn't believe at the time." Angela made plans to flee the house during the time she knew her partner wouldn't be home. She described other plans as well:

This last pay before I left, I didn't pay any bills and I took that money to get the furniture out and put it in storage for when I can get an apartment because all that furniture and stuff was mine, that I worked for, that I sweated for. I was determined that I wouldn't leave it for him. Why should he have the comforts and why should my kids and I sleep on a bare floor?

Bearing and Dealing with Psychic Wounds

Each battered woman who entered the shelter had a unique experience and individual responses to it. Angela's response was different from those the women shared in the ledger. She described her state on entering the shelter as mental exhaustion:

You see . . . when you're living with a person that doesn't understand you, you start thinking for two people and that's a lot of wear-and-tear on your brain after a while and so in the last year or so, I was two people. I had to think if I say this, will he say that, or if I do this, will he do that. You have to second-guess every move and every action.

Retrospectively, Angela was able to identify her major emotional response as shame. She explained:

I think abuse of women is common; women just don't talk about it . . . I was ashamed to tell anyone that I was abused. Women are really ashamed and I think that is something that has to be dispelled because there is no reason for a woman to have to be ashamed if she's been beaten. In the public eye, if her man beats her, then he doesn't love her. And no woman wants anybody to think that her man doesn't love her so that's why they keep that to themselves. I kept it to myself . . . I should have been gone from the first blow.

Angela continued her explanation of women's reluctance to tell others that they are being abused or battered:

Women don't tell because people don't sympathize with you.
The first thing they say is "Well, you should have been gone
a long time ago . . . why are you still there, he's going to
hurt you, he's going to kill you." They don't know what your
circumstances are. They might not even take that advice
themselves if it were them.

Acclimation and Interdependence in Shelter Life

When Angela arrived at the shelter, the only available sleeping
place was in a large dormitory that held a combination of about
16 beds, cots, and cribs. She had a difficult time adjusting to
communal living. "You know," she said, "when you just walk into
a room . . . and you know that everybody is sleeping in this
one room and you kind of think, 'Well, I don't know. I don't
know if I can deal with this or not.' And for me, I couldn't." Angela added:

For so long, sleep was my only escape. I used to rush to get in
bed every night at a certain time before he came home be-
cause I knew there would probably be an argument or some
sort of aggravation and the main thing I wanted was a good
night's sleep.

Other aspects of the environment bothered Angela also. She
explained:

You do need privacy and you do need time to sit and think.
There are so many people here, even outdoors, that if you
are not a real strong person, you'll get very confused. And I
think the people themselves need intensive therapy; they do
counseling here but it's not that intensive. I'm not as con-
fused as I might have been because I was lucky and got the
same counselor I talked to on the phone. When I came in she
got me on the right track right away. This place to me is
a godsend. Where else can you turn? The thing about the
women who've been enduring it for ten years and 15 years
. . . they didn't have anywhere to go.

Eventually, Angela would have gotten a small room for herself and the children but, unlike a lot of the women, she moved quickly to find an apartment. She did not relish communal living; more importantly, her abusive home was in the same community as the shelter and she thought it would be a matter of time before her abuser would find out where she was staying and come after her. Because her resignation from her position made her ineligible for unemployment compensation, the staff took her to apply for welfare and other benefits and to hunt for an apartment. Angela appreciated these efforts but also noted:

I think the shelter is the best thing that ever happened to me as a woman, although after being here a while, you can see that problems do exist. You come from one traumatic experience to another . . . you've been under some kind of control and you need a little leeway but the idea of some people having to share a room and having to deal with other people's habits and problems makes you a little shaky, too. You start off being grateful and you end up being grateful but you undergo some kind of transition while you're here. Little things start to agitate you because all you have on your mind is freedom, being on your own, being independent and you kind of want to, you know, break loose. That's the way I feel. I can't speak for anyone else. As far as I'm concerned, a shelter is a place where you're safe. Once you get outside that door you don't know whether you're safe or not. Some of the women can't deal with a curfew and things like that. A shelter is a beginning, but you have to be ready for it to accept the rules. I feel I live here and I say "live" because after a while you begin to think of this as home. The best they can do is see the shelter is run properly, and there is so much with ordering of food, and making up the menus, and seeing the kids are in bed at nine o'clock and doing this and that . . . there's no way they can help that much with therapy. And these women need intensive therapy, and they need it badly.

When I first spoke with Angela, she expressed annoyance with the house rule that children cannot be disciplined by physical means:

My son [19 months] has the full range of the house and he needs his fingers slapped. He's starting to have temper tantrums when I correct him. He's constantly messing with the push buttons on the TV set and it has to be reprogrammed every time he touches it. This place is really messing up his behavior. He knows that I won't hit him on the fingers here and he just deliberately laughs at me when I correct him.

A week or so later, a staff person, Angela, her toddler Michael, and I went by car to look at an apartment. On the way back, the staff person stopped the car outside a shop to do a brief errand. Angela was in the front passenger seat holding the boy. It was a very hot day and the afternoon sun was coming directly through the windshield. Angela was struggling to hold the restless, tired Michael while looking backward, talking with me. Becoming distressed herself, she said, "It's so hard to deal with him when I'm feeling this way myself. Now I understand why they don't let you hit your children in the shelter . . . it would be easy to take out your feelings on them." Michael and I took a little walk to give Angela a break.

Angela acknowledged that she benefited from interactions with the other women. "We compare our stories," she said, and added a comment that showed recognition of commonalities, "and it's like we're all married to the same man."

Finding and Healing the Self

"Since I've been here," Angela said, "I've had a chance to sit down and think about the relationship and what kind of relationship it was, what was wrong with it." She shared some of the results of her introspection:

He'd say, "Honey, when I'm like that [becoming violent], all you have to do is put your arms around me and kiss me, and tell me you love me and hug me and I won't fight." A lot of times he would show that he was becoming violent and there was no way I could walk up to him and put my arms around him and tell him that I loved him because it just wasn't there. So what I would have to do is talk him out of it and he didn't like me to talk to him at those times because he just figured I was smarter than he and that I would try to talk him out of things like that. So that was a mental strain.

Angela had some theories about the origins of Fred's abusive behaviors. She said, "He's so insecure in himself . . . that he hasn't enough worth . . . that somebody could care for him." I asked if that pertained to all abuse. "Insecurity, yeah," Angela said, adding, "I don't see abuse has anything to do with cultural, racial, or anything. It's the men who are born with some kind of problem. I think it's an inborn problem." But Angela thought it was also more than insecurity. She continued:

The ones who are abusing can't share equally. They have some problem, probably deep-rooted. In my case, his mother didn't raise him. He wasn't around his father. He didn't see any abuse when he was growing up. All he got was an overdose of love with too many people loving him. But he never had a responsible family unit; he was the one everyone showered everything on and he thought that's the way his life should be all of his life. And that's where the abuse came in. Because he saw me as a person who shared . . . not a selfish person . . . that I would take all my responsibilities and carry them out well. He couldn't deal with that. And that's the problem with a lot of these men. They can't deal with the idea that they have a good woman and they are not doing what they are supposed to be doing. Even if they're paying the bills on time . . . they either don't know how to talk to their women or how to treat them. A lot of them are into physical abuse as well as verbal abuse. I think a lot of women are subjected to sexual abuse. A lot of women don't even understand "abused sexually." They think what these guys do is the norm. I don't know what the norm is but I know what it is for me. If anybody asked me to do something weird, I'd call it sexual abuse if you don't want to do it and they do it anyway. One girl here referred to "my abuser." I asked her, When did you start using that word, "abuser?" Did you use that word before you came here? No, she said. I said, See that, all of us being abused and didn't even know it. These women being abused, they have to find out what "abused" means in the dictionary and then figure out, Is this happening in my life? It is, to a lot of women, like the woman from the foreign country, something you take; it comes along with marriage, for better or worse. All right, maybe he might accidentally kill you, that's just the chance you have to take. But you don't leave your husband. You know, what would people say? That's what women have to get out of. I don't care how smart a man is, they try to raise a woman and that's what the majority of them are doing.

Angela continued with further thoughts and feelings about Fred, her relationship with him, and herself:

Like I had compassion for him when I first left, but as I sat down and talked with these other women, I realized, boy, was I abused. He must have been crazy but I must have been crazy, too, for staying as long as I did. What kept me there for a long time was, What's my family going to think? Like I never had a lasting relationship with a man. I know what the problem is . . . I'm a loner. I don't like anyone who does things differently from me so I should never attempt to get into a relationship. I know that I'm not going to change . . . it's just useless to make someone else miserable and make myself miserable. That might make somebody abuse me.

This last comment indicated that Angela, at this point, didn't seem to have gotten the shelter's major message: *No one deserves to be beaten.*

Turning her eyes down and looking away, Angela said:

I want to tell you something. This is the second man that abused me. I never even talk about the first one. The first one I didn't even live with. He visited and abused me . . . I left my own apartment so he wouldn't find me anymore. I just didn't want anything to do with him. This man sent me to the hospital. Here, I've started noticing what kind of men I had been involved with . . . they are people that are insecure.

Angela continued her reflective summary:

There must be something that I'm lacking. I must be attracted to people who are not as intelligent as I am or something like that. But it's an unconscious thing. So, I have to sit down and think, Well, if this is what I'm doing, I have to reverse that. From now on, I'm only going to try to deal with people, as far as a relationship, that are higher than I am, who can teach me something. I can't be with people who can't teach me anything. It took me a long time to realize that, so maybe I show my frustration and I cause these feelings of insecurity and inadequacy in a person that it wouldn't take much for them to be an abuser. [There's the self-blame again.] So I've got to change my whole life around. But I would have felt better if there was someone here for intensive therapy.

I asked Angela if she would be able to get some psychotherapy after she left the shelter. "Probably not," she responded, "because I don't have transportation, but I can work on myself." She added:

All I need is time to sit down and think . . . you know, peace and quiet, all night now. Before I was rushing, always driven, rushing to get home, trying to do everything. Now I

*can sit down, take my time. I would probably have left a
long time ago if I had time to sit down and think. If I had
the Yellow Pages out, I'd have to hurry up and put them
away 'cause he'd say, "What are you looking for, a moving
company? Or a psychiatrist for me?" or something like that.
I know I can get myself together with time and I'm going to
take that time.*

My question about what she projected as the next phase with
her partner brought this response:

*I want him to cool down and realize that I'm not coming
back 'cause then he'll go on his merry way. He's the kind of
person that doesn't want somebody that doesn't want him.
Too much pride for that. So, after six or seven months, he'll
realize that I'm gone for good, he won't bother me, then I'll
feel safer about everything.*

"Will Fred be concerned about the children?", I asked.
"Package deal," Angela replied. "When I saw him last week with
the children, he told me that if I'm not coming back then he is leaving and not coming back. If he feels that some other man is going
to take his place, then he can't play second fiddle." (Angela used
the term "father" in relation to Fred and the children but never
spoke of Fred as a parent, or as having parenting responsibilities.
Angela's children were "my" children, never "our" children.)

Readiness for Departure

The day before she left the shelter, Angela rented a car, which she
said she really couldn't afford. She went to her new apartment in a
town about 20 miles away, had her stored furniture delivered, and
set up the apartment because she didn't want to bring the children
there with the place in disarray. When they saw their beds, the living room, the stereo, the children started spinning around in cir-
cles with delight, according to Angela.

As she was preparing to leave the shelter, Angela was still frightened that her abuser would come after her, although he was not

familiar with the area where she would live. While she had the car, she went grocery shopping. She said, "I went to the store today and I bought enough food for a month . . . and I'm going to stay inside . . . I don't feel safe enough. I might take the kids to the pool in the complex. It will be a long time before I become safe and secure." Angela thought she would take the summer off to be with the children and look for a job in the Fall. She didn't expect any difficulty in finding a job but wanted "to get myself together."

Angela had changed as a result of the shelter transition. Although the shelter was not a formal educational setting, Angela's statements and the women's written personal documents indicated that the shelter provided opportunities for a transformative learning experience. In this sense, it supported the perspective transformation theory of Mezirow (1978) and extended it to non-formalized learning systems. Mezirow stated:

> *A woman becomes a transformative learner when she realizes how the culture and her own attitudes have conspired to define and delimit her self-conception, her life-style, and her options in terms of a set of prescribed stereotypic roles. As a result of recognizing these taken-for-granted cultural expectations and how they have shaped the way she thinks and feels about herself and her relationships, the transformative learner comes to identify her personal problem as a common one and a public issue. . . . Bringing these unexamined cultural assumptions and attitudes into critical consciousness makes a woman aware that she is trapped in her own history, and this insight precipitates a concerted effort to extricate herself. (p. 15)*

One's personal history also limits access to resources for change as well as the desire and ability to seize transforming opportunities. Angela's transformation included hopes for a different future for herself and concern about others. She explained:

> *Since I've been involved with it, this is what I want to work at. I've made up my mind that I'm going back to school and get a degree and this is the kind of work I'm going to do.*

*Maybe my conclusions aren't the right conclusions but I
know how I feel. And I've been abused. And I started listening to other people. And the pieces started falling together for
me. I just found my calling right here. If I had stayed where
I was I would never have the chance to go back to school.
Maybe you don't believe in God telling you things but He
just descended this on me: "This is what I want you to do—
go and do it." I've made up my mind!*[3]

CONCLUSIONS

To paraphrase van Manen (1990), the question of the value of this
phenomenological research is not "Can we do something with this
phenomenology?" but "Can this phenomenology, if we concern
ourselves deeply with it, do something with us?" (p. 45). Angela's
story raises many unanswered questions, and the women's writings left many blank spaces that are beyond the scope of this chapter to answer or try to complete. They are for the reader to ponder.
The texts offer many opportunities for coming to understand the
lived experiences of battered women. The voluminous multidisci-
plinary professional literature on aspects of the abuse of women
and considerable lay literature of high quality can further en-
lighten the reader in interpretation and understanding. For example, Campbell and Parker (1992) have provided a summary review
of significant research. There is considerable empirical research
on the problems and issues raised by the women related to their
abusers, such as jealousy, dependence on the woman's dependency, insecurity, self-absorption, power, control, the cyclic pattern of battery, and ownership of the woman. There is also a body
of research on abused women's depression, despair, degradation,
hopelessness, fear, terror, ambivalence, retaliation, anger, isolation, guilt, self-blame, and low self-esteem. But abused women do
not live life in such isolated variables; they experience the interplay of all of them as part of a life-threatening daily pattern.

One value of this work is an increase in personal knowledge—
knowing the self and being able to see and understand events from
the perspective and experiences of others (Carper, 1978). To the

extent that the women's own written documents and Angela's story may have evoked in the reader a feeling for and understanding of what it is like, in part, to be an abused or battered woman, or to be in transition, then this research contributes to personal knowledge as well as to more holistic empirical knowledge. This knowledge, used wisely, can promote more insightful care of women fleeing from abusive homes.

Personal knowledge increases personal responsibility. Someone who suspects a woman is being abused should ask a direct question, such as: "Is someone hitting you?" If yes, can you give her a shelter number or domestic violence hotline number so that she can get some advice? What are the laws regarding abuse and battery in the woman's state? Is the woman aware of them? Although not absolutely guaranteeing safety, recent changes in some states permit the woman to remain in the home and the abuser to be removed and, by a restraining order, kept from harassing or abusing her. In some states, police can arrest the abuser if there is evidence of battery even if the woman is too frightened to press charges. These changes in the law have reduced the need for lengthy shelter stays; thus, more women can be admitted to shelters for short, intensive help. A short stay affords safety, respite, counseling, education, referrals, and "think time" that can give the woman new strengths to deal with the abuse and the abuser. Know the location of shelters in your region. Support shelters with funds and volunteer efforts. Are there programs in your area that help abusers? If not, can you help to get one started? Learn more about domestic violence. Use your public library, if not your professional literature.

The blank writing ledger in the shelter gave a voice to the women's personal experiences and enabled them to tell meaningful parts of their own abuse-related stories. This technique can be useful as one vehicle for expression for persons in other crisis situations—at centers for rape victims, in diagnostic waiting rooms, or at temporary residences for parents of hospitalized, critically ill children.

I am indebted to the 18 anonymous co-authors who wrote personal documents and to my other co-author, Angela, for their provision of the text and the face and content validity for this research. Listen to them. See their abuse. Help them.

ABOUT THE STUDY

This background information has been keyed to the text in the manner of footnotes, for added relevance to particular sections.

1. The 25-bed shelter, staffed mainly by social workers, was sponsored by a private, nonprofit community service agency and the government of the large suburban municipality where the shelter was located. For further detail, see Germain (1984). The research proposal was approved by the above two agencies and the institutional review board of the University of Pennsylvania.

2. The methodology combines aspects of the phenomenological approach of van Manen (1990) with aspects of Ruffing-Rahal's (1986) personal documents analysis. Personal documents are firsthand descriptions of human experience that focus on the individual's definition of meaning and reality. They give the cultural point of view of an insider, "devoid of investigator-imposed interpretation" (p. 51), and thus reflect the "elemental context of all health and illness experience" (p. 51). Comparing and contrasting several persons' accounts of their shared life experiences within a similar sociohistorical and cultural context is believed by Ruffing-Rahal to be the most advantageous use of personal documents because the similarities and diversity of common human experiences can be exemplified.
The textual analysis proceeded from line-by-line coding to categorizing, clustering, and identification of commonalities or patterns.

3. Unfortunately, the shelter staff was unable to conduct any formal follow-up of the women's post-shelter transition. For a study that includes the post-shelter transition of several women, see Hoff (1990).

REFERENCES

Boyanowsky, E. (1984). Self-identity change and the role transition process. In V. Allen & E. van de Vliert (Eds.), *Role transitions: Explorations and explanations* (pp. 53-61). New York: Plenum Press.

Campbell, J. (1989). A test of two explanatory models of women's responses to battering. *Nursing Research, 38,* 18-24.

Campbell, J., & Parker, B. (1992). Battered women and their children. *Annual Review of Nursing Research, 10,* 77-94.

Carper, B. (1978). Fundamental patterns of knowing in nursing. *Advances in Nursing Science, 1*(1), 13-23.

Germain, C. (1984). Sheltering abused women: A nursing perspective. *Journal of Psychosocial Nursing and Mental Health Issues, 22*(9), 22-31.

Hoff, L. A. (1990). *Battered women as survivors.* New York: Routledge.

Mezirow, J. (1978). The transformation process. In *Education for perspective transformation: Women's re-entry programs in community colleges* (pp. 11-17). New York: Center for Adult Education, Teachers College, Columbia University.

Ruffing-Rahal, M. A. (1986). Personal documents and nursing theory development. *Advances in Nursing Science, 8*(3), 50-57.

Sarbin, T. (1984). Role transitions as social drama. In *Role transitions: Explorations and explanations.* In V. Allen & E. van de Vliert (Eds.), *Role transitions: Explorations and explanations* (pp. 21-37). New York: Plenum Press.

Sokol, M., & Lewis, M. (1984). Career transitions and life event adaptation: Integrating alternative perspectives on role transition. In V. Allen & E. van de Vliert (Eds.), *Role transitions: Explorations and explanations* (pp. 81-94). New York: Plenum Press.

van Manen, M. (1990). *Researching lived experience: Human science for an action-sensitive pedagogy.* Buffalo, NY: SUNY Press.

ABOUT THE AUTHOR

My very first clinical nursing experience was to care for a woman who had been attacked by her male partner with an ax. The attack left lacerations from her brain to her ankle on one side. She ran into the emergency room bleeding profusely and, after surgery, was admitted to a private room. The brain damage left her mute and also must have propelled her to walk constantly around the periphery of her mattress. She seemed larger than life as I stood looking up at her, trying to reach her, aware of my own fright, and appalled that one human being could do this to another. That lasting impression influenced me, years later, to become a volunteer in a new shelter for abused women. I found little in the nursing literature to guide me on the subject of domestic violence, and that led to a study of the health care needs and related issues in the shelter.

I am Associate Professor and Chairperson of the Science and Role Development Division of the School of Nursing, University of Pennsylvania. Here, I have taught undergraduate, master's, and doctoral students, and have been a chairperson or member of dissertation committees. I have also held faculty positions at two other universities, and clinical nursing positions as a hospital staff nurse, occupational health nurse, and nurse clinician in an urban health center. My other research includes an ethnographic study of a community hospital cancer unit, and survey research on diabetes self-management and hospitalization. In addition to research reports, I have published on research methods and ethics of field work, as well as clinical articles and textbooks on adult health and illness, monographs, and poetry.

My goal in publishing "See My Abuse . . ." is to promote understanding of what it is like to be an abused or battered woman, so that greater enlightenment may promote prevention.

7

In Another World: "Essences" of Mothers' Mourning Experience

Sarah Steen Lauterbach

Baby

Where did you come from, baby dear?
Out of the everywhere into the here.

Where did you get those eyes so blue?
Out of the sky as I came through.

What makes the light in them sparkle and spin?
Some of the starry skies left in.

Where did you get that little tear?
I found it waiting when I got here.

What makes your forehead so smooth and high?
A soft hand stroked it as I went by.

What makes your cheek like a warm white rose?
I saw something better than any one knows.

Whence that three-cornered smile of bliss?
Three angels gave me at once a kiss.

Where did you get this pearly ear?
God spoke, and it came out to hear.

Where did you get those arms and hands?
Love made itself into bonds and bands.

Feet, where did you come, you darling things?
From the same box as the cherubs' wings.

How did they all just come to be you?
God thought about me, and so I grew.

But how did you come to us, you dear?
God thought about, and so I am here.

George Macdonald (1824–1905), from
"At the Back of the North Wind"

Endnotes. This chapter contains original writing of the author's personal experience, interpreted and narrated in the language of the findings and discussion of the doctoral nursing dissertation completed by Lauterbach (1992) in partial fulfillment of the degree of Doctor of Education, Department of Nursing Education, Teachers College, Columbia University, New York. A chapter based on the dissertation is in P. Munhall & C. Oiler, *Nursing Research: A Qualitative Perspective* (New York: National League for Nursing, in press).

This chapter, like the dissertation, is dedicated to the memory of Amy Liv Lauterbach and to the babies about whom the mothers studied shared experiences and stories of loss.

I. PERSONAL RETROSPECTIVE

This was one of two poems that I read aloud at my baby's funeral nearly 12 years ago. On a cold day in February, while going through reference books in our branch library for an appropriate poem for Amy's burial, I came across these lines, which described some of my feelings and thoughts about what I had lost when Amy died.

Amy was a twin baby girl who died nine days after her birth, as a result of a birth emergency. At the time of her death, in July, we had decided to have her cremated. We were new parents to a new baby girl and two small children. Our very young children also experienced the baby's death in a personal way, and much of our energy was spent trying to cope with and maneuver through the activities of daily life while caring for and protecting the living children as much as we humanly could under the circumstances.

We involved the children in activities and rituals that both celebrated our fortune in having Alexandra and mourned our loss of Amy. Jared, who, at age three, was very affectionate and verbal, snuggled with Alexandra. He loved holding her and smelling her newborn smell, gently touching her hair and cheek with his face. He told me he missed his "yucky baby," a baby whom he envisioned covered with vernix. Before the delivery, he and I had spent hours talking and looking at pictures of babies in utero, and he often referred to the babies as "one for me and one for Mommy." He assumed that the baby who had died was his baby. I tried my best to reassure him and to answer his questions. I said that Alexandra was *our* baby, that we all belonged to each other, and that, although Amy was not with us, she was still our baby girl and he was her big brother.

That next February, six months later, we thought we were in good enough shape to make a trip to bury Amy in Florida. Philadelphia was our present family's home; however, I had spent most of my childhood in the backwoods of northern Florida, and thought of that sandy farmland where my ancestors had settled and reared generations of Hendrys and Millinors as providing the taproot of my life. We had gone through the birth tragedy without the comfort of physically being "with" family, except for my mother, who stayed with us for about three weeks.

In Philadelphia, we lived in a close-knit urban university community, among people who were, to me, much like an extended family. After the death of Amy, I felt that our experience set us apart. Our family, with three young children and a necessary preoccupation with activities of daily living, required that we maintain the appearance of normality.

We had decided to bury Amy in Florida, because eventually, I thought, I would again return there to live, most likely as an elderly single woman. We hadn't know what to do about Amy's body at the time of the tragedy. In retrospect, and from comments shared by other mothers who had a similar experience, we could have used some help in making decisions. We needed to have someone suggest that arrangements and decisions all be slowed down. This is one of the direct practice implications that is a reason for my writing about my experience and about the research that resulted from it.

As newlyweds from England, we had moved to urban Philadelphia eights years earlier. Marlow, our first child, a daughter, was born two years later; she bears the name of the village in England where we had lived and married. Jared was conceived when Marlow was 18 months old; we were in North Carolina, during a postdoctoral year for my husband. The conception occurred in a setting similar to the one where my husband and I had first met and fallen in love. The pregnancy and our son's birth were therefore very special to me.

My pregnancy with my daughters was unplanned but very much wanted, by me especially. In February, at 17 weeks, we discovered I was carrying twins.

We came to view the twin pregnancy as having very special meaning. It represented a commitment to our life together as a family. It was, simply, a gift. Our house was small for four children, but we planned to stay in the community for a while because of our wonderful family of friends.

Like many other mothers, I have learned that, after a child dies, there is a need to be intimately involved with a personal memorial service. That cold February day, leaving beautiful, six-month-old

Alexandra with a babysitter, I turned to the comfort of literature and poetry as I planned the burial service. The next week, we were to take the trip to Florida.

The following poem touched me particularly. The twin pregnancy had made me feel that my body was hosting a phenomenon of great importance to my life as a mother and person.

Unborn

Little body I would hold,
Little feet my hands enfold.
Little head my tears have blessed,
Little mouth that seeks my breast,
Little shining soul that cries
From the worship of his eyes,
I must wait that I may be
Great enough to mother thee.

Irene Rutherford McLeod

Amy was buried later in February, in the Shady Grove Hendry cemetery. Her grave was located very near where my grandfather was born. My mother picked out a spot, somewhat distant from much older graves, and near where my brother's baby had been buried. Amy's was the third infant death experienced by me and my siblings. My mother planned to have all five of her children—me, my three brothers and my sister, and our families—buried together. The family's mortician dug Amy's grave and provided a temporary marker. For years, that marker sat above my stove in my urban Philadelphia townhouse. A photograph of her headstone remained on our refrigerator for nine years, often taking the breath of the unsuspecting person.

For years, I have kept and displayed memorabilia of my child's grave. It was important to have these memories around me as I continued to mother my living children and to make a firm commitment to living as fully as possible. As years have passed, the need to have constant reminders has been less than in the beginning, but how does one go about removing pictures? When my husband removed the temporary marker from above the stove and

put it in a drawer, I would put it back again. The memorabilia and artifacts of loss have disappeared from the refrigerator within the past few years and I have not replaced them.

In this small but significant way, I kept the experience of the baby with me. I mothered my dead child in my mourning; I kept close to me, alive in my heart and mind and spirit, the memory of what she meant to me and my family. I mothered and nurtured my own spirit and healed as I mourned my loss, continuing all the while to nurture and care for my three young, living children. I felt very fortunate to have children, especially Alexandra, to guide me back to life. My husband supported me and didn't obstruct my mourning too much. I felt as if part of me had died with Amy, and my body physically ached with loss.

Having a baby die is very difficult for mothers, families, and friends. I have learned, in my conversations with mothers, that the significance of the particular baby for the mother makes the death a personal assault. My own experience validates this finding.

A baby's death in late pregnancy is especially difficult and differs from early pregnancy loss. The death of a baby whom the mother has experienced outside of her body, particularly a sudden and unexpected death, is different from an infant's death in late pregnancy or shortly after birth. In perinatal loss (in late pregnancy or up to one month after delivery), the mothers commonly express the experience as "part of me died with the baby." This finding was validated by my own experience with perinatal loss.

During my pregnancy, caring for my two young children and having them become involved in our midwifery weekly visits, became my primary occupation as a mother. I was euphoric with Alexandra's uncomplicated delivery, an apt end to a pregnancy in which I had sensed every moment that my body was hosting an event larger than myself. I have a picture of me that was taken at that moment, right before I knew something was wrong.

Then the doctor came in and took over and, in the mirror arranged for me, I saw the baby's cord and arm prolapse. Immediately, the room was silent, and I, along with everyone there, knew that a race against time had begun. In the next 32 minutes, I endured a very painful, physically invasive, and personally devastating attempt to turn the baby. I requested that a cesarean section (C-section) be done, not knowing that an anesthesiologist wasn't present. Eventually, the doctor turned Amy and delivered her with the use of high forceps. Her heartbeat was recovered easily by the pediatric resident who had come in during the ordeal, but we all knew what her seizures indicated. The doctor had been warning me from about 15 minutes on, suggesting that I not wish for the baby to be born alive.

One minute I had been euphoric; the next, the bottom dropped out from under me, and I was coached by my doctor to hope for the worst. About 20 minutes into the attempt to turn and deliver

Amy, I began to fear for my own life. I remember thinking that I was a mother of a newborn baby, a three-year-old, and a five-year-old, in addition to being the mother of this baby who I knew was not all right.

I captured the delivery on audio cassette tape, and when I listened to that tape, which I did many times in the weeks and months that followed, I was always impressed with the silence, except for my moans as my vagina was invaded by the doctor's hand and arm and my abdomen was pressed on by the nurse, in their efforts to force the turning of the baby. Even though a valiant attempt was made, it just didn't work. Worse still, there was no medical or surgical backup plan in place. In listening to the tape in the months that followed, I learned to identify the times when the pediatric resident came in and when the anesthesiologist arrived (25 minutes too late), a fact that later became the central issue in a legal suit.

The last few weeks of my pregnancy had been very difficult. The institution had not followed protocol set up for high-risk pregnancy, and I kept attempting to get them to address my concerns. Verbally, I was assured that they were capable of handling the twins' delivery. Finally, at my insistence, X-rays were taken. They revealed two babies in head-down position, one lower than the other, and ample pelvic room. I was somewhat relieved, and was told that an anesthesiologist and pediatrician would be "in the house" during my delivery. I felt as if I was being treated as an overly anxious mother.

After the delivery that late July morning, my husband went home to sleep and I was taken back to my room. I felt as if I had been run over by a truck; I could not raise my arms or care for myself. I was returned to a shared room. My roommate was refusing to have an X-ray done; her baby was in breech position. (Marlow had been a breech delivery.) This incident, on the heels of a tragedy, was very disturbing.

More importantly, no one cared for me in this critical postpartum period. The obstetrician came in several hours later to discover I was bleeding too much and had not been checked by a nurse. It was then about 9:00 A.M. The babies had been born between 4:18 and 4:50 A.M. I asked the doctor if he had given me anesthesia, because I could not lift my arms. He said, "No." He said he would send a nurse in, and some time later a nurse appeared. She wanted to know if I wanted an early discharge. In my experience with mothers in my research and in general conversations, I learned that this formality is very common, but to suggest early discharge at such a time is insensitive and borders on inhuman! It had happened with three of the mothers in my study. A fourth mother discharged herself about two hours after delivery because her baby was transferred to a children's hospital. She received no postpartum care during her baby's two weeks in the intensive care unit (ICU).

Later in that morning of my delivery, a team of people who were involved in transferring Amy to an institution that had a neonatal intensive care unit (NICU) came in to my room. This was my first viewing of my baby up close. I still could not raise my arms and was devastated when I saw her constant seizure activity. She required breathing assistance and was in an isolette. Looking back, this would have been the time to have someone help me touch and hold Amy while being held myself. All they wanted to know was whether I needed any information. I was at a loss for words or questions, even though I was a nurse and the mother of the distressed baby.

Within hours after Amy's transfer, I was on the phone to the NICU, which had had the only available bed in the area. In my need to make contact with the baby, I was able to use my arms for the first time since the delivery. From then on, I recovered from the feeling that I had been drugged or overpowered by the experience. I knew the point when Amy's seizures would come under control with medication, and talked with the nurses often. I began the process of requesting a second transfer, to a large urban NICU, so that we could have more control over the decisions to be made in the next few days and weeks.

Later that morning, I took a shower by myself, called and talked and cried with my mother, who was caring for Marlow and Jared, talked with them, and only then asked for Alexandra from the nursery. My husband had held her for a long time after she was born, but I had been physically unable to lift my arms. I desperately needed to nurse my new baby and tried not to beat myself up about the fact that I had not done so. I had nursed my other babies immediately, on the delivery table. I was still overcome with a physical feeling of heaviness, and finally asked the nurse to take Alexandra back to the nursery. I talked with nurses at the NIC unit off and on all afternoon. When my husband came in to visit after dinner for a short time, I was really struggling with being optimistic. We had Alexandra with us during the visit and we were overcome with the inability to hold both babies as we had envisioned. In the months to come, there would be many such connections to what would have been. Finally, exhausted, he left to return home. I requested a room change.

I was moved to a terrible room—a single room with a very noisy air conditioner. I nursed Alexandra almost constantly and just held her sleeping to my breast. I finally became so tired, I thought I might drop Alexandra or go to sleep and not hear her, so I called for a nurse to take her to the nursery. Then I fell into a deep sleep, and awoke at about 4:00 A.M. with a feeling that I was in a war zone after a very bad dream. I had forgotten where Alexandra was, did not know where I was, and was frantic and totally disoriented for a few minutes. I ran from the room to the nurses' station; when I found the midwife who had delivered Alexandra, I became very upset for a very long time. Reality finally hit me and my feelings poured out.

In looking back over my experience when my research was completed 11 years later, I arrived at this interpretation concerning the central role of this midwife. The midwife's being in the delivery room provided the connection and shared experience necessary for me to involve her in my pain and my resolution of the experience. She was the only nurse, in the 24 hours since the delivery, who seemed to have any clue as to the significance of what had happened. I felt as if I had been abandoned by the nurses because one of my babies was ill; I had received no personal care or help with the other new baby. This midwife continued to be available to me until she left Philadelphia to return to school a year later. Because of her understanding, I believe, I was able to take a proactive stance in mourning. Her compassion and presence during and after the delivery and in the months that followed facilitated my healing.

In my study, the mothers discussed in detail their experiences with nurses. Some were helpful, many were unhelpful. Sadly, the mothers in the study validated my own experience. In general, mothers got very little personal postpartum care and almost no help in making decisions about what to do with their babies. Mothers were moved from the delivery suite and separated from other mothers and babies, which they were glad for; but they were also separated from their nurses. They had no continuing contact with the nurses involved in the delivery. Instead, they were asked about early discharge.

Amy was transferred early the next day, and we left the hospital on pass to see her. This was just one day after she was born. On the way to Amy's hospital, I experienced such shortness of breath that I felt I would suffocate unless the tight band was removed from my chest. After seeing beautiful Amy, perfectly shaped, fair-haired, blue-eyed, I thought I would simply die. She weighed seven pounds and eight ounces, about a pound heavier than Alexandra, and her coloring was fairer than dark-haired Alexandra's. She was wonderfully pink and absolutely beautiful. What more could a mother want?

Amy was very critically ill from having suffered tremendous anoxia. At the time, I felt that I could not survive the loss, which had already occurred, even though Amy was technically alive. The seizure activity had been controlled, but she made no voluntary movements. I never nursed her, even though, in the days that followed, I expressed milk for her and other babies. I held her, knowing that things were very bad, cried, and went back to my hospital and spent another night in another wardlike room, all alone except for Alexandra, who slept in a bassinet beside me. I nursed her off and on during the night and slept quite well.

The next morning I prepared for going home. Before I left, I requested my chart. I talked with the doctor about Amy and what had happened, and I still did not understand why the C-section had not been done. This question continued to plague me. I kept calling the doctor, saw him at the postpartum visit, and continued to ask the question, still unsatisfied with his answer. Not until I was told, quite by accident six months later, that the C-section wasn't done because of the anesthesiologist's not being there, did

I really understand. From then on, in the midst of mourning, I pursued another course. I was committed to collecting as much information as I could about the experience.

As I read the chart that morning, I was shocked by the nurses' notes: "Shows no interest in the baby," "Hasn't asked about the baby." Which baby? How could they know? The nurses did not come into my room, except to ask me whether I wanted early discharge or had any questions about Amy before she was transferred later in the morning of the delivery. Angry, I confronted the nurses and asked, "Who was the person who wrote the notes?" I know they were glad to get rid of me; frankly, had I had a better place to stay, I would not have remained there after the delivery. But I did need the privacy the hospital provided, to care for myself and to keep informed of Amy's condition. I had help with Alexandra from the nursery and my mother was taking care of my other children at home. The hospital provided me with space, which I knew I would not have after I returned home. Jared had a new cold, and I thought a couple of days would protect me and Alexandra a little. I had managed to get on top of some of my feelings and cope with what had to be done. It would have made a tremendous qualitative difference if I had had help with it all.

Later, I was glad I had read the chart. It included the doctor's delivery note, which I discovered was missing from the record months later, when I requested a copy. It was not until I discovered that the chart had been altered that I understood why the doctor had not been able to answer my questions. I then began to think about taking legal action; almost two years later, I finally decided that I *must* take legal action. The doctor was still delivering babies in high-risk pregnancies without anesthesiology backup. Once I decided to bring suit, I was able to put my experience aside and move back to my primary commitment to mothering my children and my mourning.

The doctor died with cancer at about the time the suit was filed. He had been involved with each of our pregnancies and deliveries and, each time, I had said, "Thank you, Dr. _____." His death was like a loss of a member of our family and, although I was angry with him for his mistake and the outcome, I was very sad because he had been so intimately involved with us as a growing family. His philosophy had provided the hospital with its family-centered program and had helped us bring our babies into the world in the manner that we had wanted. We were very much a part of a community of families who believed in family-centered maternity care. The suit was settled out of court a few months later. As soon as the suit was filed, the institution stopped high-risk deliveries without medical backup.

After I went home from the hospital, the days until Amy died were filled with nursing Alexandra and being with Marlow and Jared, going to the NICU, rushing home to nurse the baby and see the children again, going back to be with Amy, hurrying home to nurse and have dinner, and returning with my husband to be with Amy. I slept very poorly; I nursed Alexandra several times during the night and often called the NICU then to see how Amy was doing. Almost every night, I awoke from a nightmare that involved losing or misplacing a baby. I often dreamed that I was pregnant again with both babies, then awakened with leaden awareness of what had happened. The pregnancy dream continued until Amy died. I felt the loss acutely when the dream stopped.

The course in the NICU was rocky. In spite of the miracle-baby stories we were told by varying doctors, the EEG and objective tests were very discouraging. Amy died during her ninth day of life, in the arms of a nurse while I was on my way to the hospital.

I had spent most of the afternoon before her death, holding Amy, who, took a turn for the worse. Her breathing became very irregular and her heart rate slowed. Finally, I had to return home to nurse Alexandra. I had hardly arrived home when the nurse from the NICU called. We had talked and I had asked her to hold Amy, especially if she was dying, until I returned. I rushed back; Amy's heart rate had picked up. I spent the next several hours holding her, watching the monitor, cuddling her and talking softly into her ear, reassuring her that she would always be with me because of my love for her, and that it was all right for her to die. It was a very difficult time. I held her more during those hours than I had before. I prayed for death to come gently and quickly, while she was in my arms. By late evening, I was very exhausted and the nurse encouraged me to return home. I really needed to nurse Alexandra. The nurse agreed to stand in for me if Amy's condition worsened. I went home, went to sleep with Alexandra at my breast, and was awakened by the NICU nurse's call stating that

Amy was worse. Again, I said, "Please hold her for me until I arrive." I told my mother and my husband about the call and he and I left. Amy died in the arms of the nurse. We were left alone with Amy. From the pink baby we had grown to know and love, she had changed to a graying baby who felt very different to hold after death. I held her to my chest and cried. I arranged to continue to bring frozen breast milk in for other babies, and I thanked the nurse who had been my surrogate.

We finally left and returned to our home. My mother was holding Marlow and Jared as she watched the royal wedding of Britain's Prince Charles and Lady Diana Spencer on television. It was July 29, the early morning of the day after my maternal grandfather's birthday. Our ordeal was finally over, but I embarked on a mourning course that had only just begun. Later that morning, I told a friend, who became upset with the news, that at this point we were relieved that it was over. A young adolescent boy, a neighbor, came by to find out how Amy was and became very sad when I told him. Years earlier, he had babysat for Jared and had become our son's very special friend and mentor. His father had died recently.

In those days right after the delivery and tragedy, my attachment to Alexandra, her responsiveness, and her need for me helped affirm my mothering and validated the loss that was invalidated by those close to me. My friends knew but generally did not acknowledge to me in person the significance of what had happened. One person visited me and offered what she thought was an answer to why Amy had died: "God wanted babies with him too." Although well-meaning, these words were of little comfort. Our close friends mourned and suffered, were supportive, but had a hard time with conversation. I think they feared for me, for what the death would do to my relationship with my husband, and for our young family.

Recently, someone asked me how many children I have, and I said, four children: three living, and a twin baby who died as a result of a birth accident. I went on to say that my dead child had required as much, if not more, from me as my living children. This woman told me that her four-year-old daughter had drowned in their backyard pool, and she talked about her long mourning period.

Over the years, I have continued to see effects of the experience—my choice of topic for my nursing doctoral dissertation

(Lauterbach, 1992); my printing of the final copy of the dissertation one day after my father died; my insisting that my father's funeral be planned and done by me and my siblings; my taking many pictures of the funeral and of my father postmortem, and videotaping the funeral for my mother and us; my continuing interest in the human experience of loss; my continuing to make space for my mourning; my ongoing discussions with my children about life and death; and my awareness of the effects of the experience on each child's view of the world.

The only pictures I have are of the ultrasound image, late in my pregnancy; the delivery of Alexandra; myself just before I knew that there was a problem; and Amy's headstone and grave. My husband had not wanted me to take pictures of Amy in the NICU, and we had jointly decided not to take our little children to see her—decisions I have regretted many times in the years that have passed. I needed pictures that I did not have after Amy's death. The children often share their disappointment at not having seen Amy and not having pictures of her. After 12 years, I need visual reminders of Amy. I embroidered a cross-stitched heart with Amy's name, and hung it near my husband's and my bed, but it got misplaced in our move three years ago. I wear close to my heart a small gold heart engraved with Amy's name. Each time I defended the research proposal or the completed dissertation and whenever I have presented the findings of the dissertation, I have worn the heart. For years, I took my children's pictures and the gravesite pictures with me as I began to carve out a return to the academic nursing profession and a new life for myself. In conducting my research, I discovered the rich world of mourning art and mourning jewelry, validating a theme in my own and other mothers' experience of mourning.

At Amy's burial, my mother and I read the selected poetry and the Lord's Prayer, and I closed with a parenting prayer I had written. Jared and Marlow threw pink carnations into the little grave with the urn, before it was covered with earth. My husband held beautiful Alexandra, in a dress hand-made by a friend in Philadelphia. Two dresses had been made for our baby girls, but only one was given to me at the time. I had bought two of everything before the delivery. Alexandra, as a baby, always had twice as many clothes as she needed.

In addition to my husband and me, and our children, my brother, parents, sister, and the funeral home attendants were at the funeral. At the end of the ceremony, as the urn was covered and the grave was filled with earth, Jared pointed to the urn and cried, "I want my pinkest flower." We comforted and held him, comforting ourselves by helping him with his sadness. The ceremony was sweet, personal, and very sad.

The experience of having my baby die after I, as a mother, had bonded with it and began to experience it as a special person inside me, fulfilled the worst fear I had had as a mother nearing the end of my pregnancy. When I was pregnant with Jared, our friends' four-year-old daughter died with epiglottitis during a severe snowstorm. One morning when Jared was two months old, while nursing in bed with me, he developed respiratory distress. We rushed him to the children's hospital near where we lived; the physician treating him prepared us for his likely death. Jared is the only child I know who survived epiglottitis, and I felt fortunate that he was spared. After Amy died, I thought back on that threatened loss, and realized that there was a connection between the two experiences. I had dealt with that early experience as a loss, even though Jared miraculously recovered and was discharged from the ICU in two days.

I had viewed each of my pregnancies as very special, very different, and each baby I delivered was very much wanted, even if unplanned. The twin pregnancy had special meaning within the context of continuity for our family. To have the ultrasound discover a second baby was a joy.

Preparing for twins had been a wonderful, impressive, and joyous experience even though there was much discomfort and some physical compromise. I was able to focus on the physical nurturance of motherhood.

In the weeks and months that followed Amy's death, as I cared for her wonderful twin, the attachment made my loss more acute. As I fell in love with the little person of Alexandra, I mourned the loss of Amy more. I continued to experience the euphoria of being a mother to Alexandra, and the devastation of losing the mothering of Amy. I had too much milk, so I expressed some for other babies in the hospital nursery. It seemed as if I had excess mothering available: my older daughter had a little girlfriend over for dinner and baths very often; there were always many children at our house for dinner and play; I often made pizza with another mother and fed the children in the courtyard of the Mews where we lived.

The midwife who delivered Alexandra made a couple of visits to our home, and I gave her a set of pictures of the delivery of Alexandra. My husband had stopped taking pictures when it was evident that an emergency situation was present. However, in the months that followed, I tried to find out whether any of the hospitals involved had taken pictures. I requested records, got the X-rays, and continued to pursue any avenue, hoping for someone's forethought.

When my mother left, one week after Amy died, I was well on my way to coping with the three children. Neighbors were wonderful; they rotated in bringing dinner, prepared Chinese stir-fry meals, invited Marlow and Jared over. Our community helped out, even though conversation was difficult. My anger—evidenced in confrontation, in not letting anything pass my acknowledging, and in constantly correcting the perception of reality—made casual conversation difficult. I was not very silent and retiring.

Immediately, we began the work of establishing new routines in our house for napping, making dinner when the baby was fussy, and continuing to do "special" things like going to the zoo. All of my energy was spent on living day-to-day. Alexandra was a wonderful sleeper by the time she was three months old. Later, as a toddler, I called her the "perfect" baby for me as a mourning mother. She was very social and pulled me into arranging regular contact with other toddlers in our community. I laugh when I remember her hitting our front door running, as she went out to the courtyard to play with her little friends. I cautioned neighbors and drivers about her not waiting to stop, look, and listen.

At her eight weeks' pediatric visit, a significant heart murmur was discovered. Initially, I saw this as a loss, but with cardiac evaluation, her wonderful appearance of health, and her normal growth, the ventricular septal defect (VSD) improved significantly. For Alexandra to have a heart defect, on the heels of Amy's survival depending solely on her heart's strength and health, was an irony and another loss. At the end of two years, it was pretty clear that surgery would not be required.

When Alexandra was 18 months old, Marlow dropped her after being bitten on the finger, and Alexandra's front two incisors were pushed out of sight, requiring surgical removal by the dentist. It was initially very painful to have my baby without front teeth. In time, I came to love that look, and I missed it when her permanent teeth came in. Other events and health issues with all three children were often interpreted as losses during those first few years after Amy died.

That Fall, just weeks after the tragedy in July, Marlow was to begin kindergarten. There was a Philadelphia school strike, so, along with a cooperative parents' group, we participated in organizing an alternative program. With Marlow and Jared in kindergarten and nursery school, I experienced a powerful feeling of separation and temporary discontinuity, which was repeated every September for many years. I still have problems with the back-to-school transition after having my children home during the summer. The discovery, during that next Spring, of a learning disability in our oldest child was seen as another loss. Her placement in a special school, which required her to learn to go daily, by train, to a school in a distant suburb was experienced by me as another separation. We spent the next several years organizing our life around learning needs for her. We involved the other two children as best we could, and continued to plan for their separate needs.

Life goes on after a tragedy. Together, my husband and I attended a grieving support group for two years after Amy died. We were the longest tenured parents who attended the group sessions regularly. Until my decision to bring legal action, I could not terminate with the institution where Amy was born. After such a tragedy, if one is a mother, there is the comfort of caring for family, even though, at the time, it felt as if I could "give" to no one. I gave to myself in caring for my young children. I mourned and was sad as needed, and tried to not be too down. My spirits always recovered, and I have been filled with hope and appreciation for my continuing calling to mothering, and for having a husband who is not too obstreperous. I worried about his consuming too much wine in the evenings, but I tried not to feel responsible, trusting and knowing he would be all right. It must have been hard for him to see me determined to feel as I felt and to do it as I felt it had to be done.

After the funeral and our return to Philadelphia, I felt that having Amy buried in Florida was not the right decision: she was too far away. At times, I needed to be near her, so I called my mother and asked her to get flowers and visit my baby's grave for me. She was perhaps the only person who indicated to me that she truly understood. She provided unconditional support, allowing me to carve my mourning in any way I saw fit. My husband understood and was also supportive, but he needed more from me, so his love and support were given with conditions. As I mourned, I needed my own mother to love me unconditionally; fortunately, she reciprocated. This, along with the midwife's commitment and relationship, and my therapy later, were critical components in the healing that followed. Four years after Amy's death, I sought the assistance of an analytically oriented psychotherapist, and she helped me tremendously in understanding my life and my loss in the context of a larger picture. I am deeply indebted to these women who helped me integrate my loss into a way of living and being that reflects their learnings and experience.

My experience of having a wished-for baby die, like the findings in my research, connected me with the women of my family in very powerful ways. My paternal grandmother had experienced the death of a twin daughter, her tenth child, and had two more babies afterward. My maternal grandmother had experienced the death of a 19-year-old son from pneumonia. My former mother-in-law had experienced the death of a daughter at age 14. My sister had had a baby die in utero in the last month of a pregnancy. My brother's wife had experienced a late pregnancy loss just three months before my twins were due. The older women among my family continued to mourn for many years. I had not been very involved with my sister's experience because I was living in England at the time, but the death of my brother's baby touched me greatly.

Years later, in conversations with people close to mothers, comments and statements about mothers "not ever getting over it" are common. At the present time, after completing my doctoral research and reflecting on my own personal experience, I think I understand the special difficulty mothers have in mourning. Mothers are often too sad for conventions of ordinary social discourse. They are isolated and they isolate themselves to find space and solace in mourning. Or, they are completely silenced and are unable to move "through" and "away from" the mourning experience. People don't say, "She never got over being a mother," even though many mothers feel that once they become mothers, it is for life. But they say a mother "never got over" losing a child.

Infant death in late pregnancy is a phenomenon that possesses special features and meanings, the significance of which is often not understood fully, even by mothers themselves. My understanding of my own experience, as narrated here, reflects a reconceptualization of personal experience within the language and findings of the phenomenological research.

When Alexandra was six, she dictated a poem written about her lived experience of having her twin sister die. She used to say to me as we walked around the neighborhood, "You know, Amy is everywhere. She's in the air and you bump into her all of the time." At another time, she said, "She's everywhere, just all around." I said, "Who?" "God," she said. In the words of Alexandra, at age six years and eight months:

> *Amy is my best friend.*
> *She is dead.*
> *She was only ten days old.*
> *I will see her when I get up there.*
> *We will talk and love each other.*
> *She will be an old lady, too.*
> *We will dive into the ocean of clouds.*
>
> *(Alexandra Ashley Lauterbach)*

From the personal experience of helping my children deal with and understand the death of a very much wished-for baby and the ways it colored and was colored by our lives, my conceptualizations and beliefs about the pivotal role of the mother in guiding her family and friends through mourning were both validated and shaped. Family, friends, and care providers, especially nurses, all share, to varying degrees, the existential experience of being abandoned in another world following death. Nurses' staffing and protocols for managing "infant demise," as it is called, are done by sensitive caring people but indicate a need for greater human understanding. It was for this purpose, to create greater human understanding of the phenomenon, that an investigation with mothers was undertaken.

What does it mean to have a wished-for baby die? What does it mean to experience being-a-mother when there is no opportunity to experience being-a-mother to the newborn baby, or to have any continuing relationship with one's child and with that child's children over several generations in the life span? What do the brief life and the death of one's baby mean in the bigger picture of life? What does it mean to experience being-a-mother to the dead child? What does one do with the disappointment and loss that death evokes? What does it mean to be fully human, to be fully mothering within the world, when the relationship with one's child is over almost before it even began? What are common shared meanings and experiences among mothers who experience the death of a baby in late pregnancy or deliver a stillborn baby? What features are unique to the particular mother and child? These questions provided the interest for an investigation of women's experiences with having a wished-for baby die. What follows is a narrative about the findings of the nursing qualitative research that was an outgrowth of the personal experience. The remainder of the chapter reports on the findings and their significance for mothers, caregivers, and mourners.

II. INVESTIGATIVE RESEARCH

The investigation into the phenomenon of late pregnancy death of a wished-for baby and its meaning to mothers discovered meanings and "essences" of experience. The purpose was to create greater depth and breadth of understanding of the phenomenon for all who experience it, but especially to use the understanding to transform care.

Mothers who experience their wished-for baby's death usually find that their experience is more common than they had thought. Only after they live through their own experience do they become aware of the relative frequency of infant deaths. This was certainly true for me; I was shocked at the number of people who had had similar experiences. Also surprising was the fact that few of the people I knew from social contacts were able to help. Mostly, their efforts were to continue to silence me. I, like the mothers in my research, turned to a support group network to find human help. Among the women who participated in the research, family, friends, and work associates invalidated their experiences, by inability to comprehend the magnitude of the loss or accept the mother's preoccupation with the baby's death. Many people just withdrew in silence.

The investigation described this phenomenon as representing a "shroud of silence surrounding death of a baby," which is seen as the ultimate tragedy in this era of advanced medical technology. Exploring the experience, making mothers' experiences explicit through articulation in their own voices and stories, helped in uncovering the silence. The aims of the investigation into mothers' experiences were: to increase human understanding of the death's effects and, in doing so, to transform nursing and other human caring activities for mothers and families who experience this ultimate tragedy. As a nurse educator, I was particularly interested in direct practice implications that might emerge from the discovery.

To understand the meaning of the death for the mother, it is important to understand what the baby's life—being-a-mother, the mothering experience—means to the mother. Mothers' stories and descriptions of their lived experiences conveyed the meaning of the particular pregnancy, the imagined baby and child, motherhood, the transition that becoming a mother has required at this particular junction, the timing of motherhood, the complex web of relationships into which the mother enters, and the multiple contexts of a mother's life. My own thoughts about being-a-mother, "the babies dancing under my heart," found in my personal journal about my own experience, were expressed by mothers who participated in writings, poetry, and personal journals.

The investigation into mothers' experiences followed a phenomenological perspective. Phenomenology as a research method begins in silence. The study of mothers' experiences with mourning began in silence. A gap between what was known about the phenomenon as determined through professional literature and research and what was known about the phenomenon through discussions with mothers, focusing on their experiences and their care at the time, was determined to exist. This gap, interpreted to be a discrepancy between knowing and understanding, was discovered through listening to mothers' stories of loss. Once identified, the phenomenon and its surrounding silence were explored, using the phenomenological perspective provided by van Manen (1984, 1990). The phenomenological method is described in detail in Figure 7-1. The inquiry was also guided by nurse-researcher Patricia Munhall's (1992) model (Figure 7-2), which places the researcher's personal experience within the existential investigation.

Figure 7–1   van Manen's Method of Phenomenology (1984, p. 5).

Four Concurrent Procedural Activities Involving 11 Steps

TURNING TO THE NATURE OF LIVED EXPERIENCE	1. Orienting to the phenomenon 2. Formulating the phenomenological question 3. Explicating assumptions and preunderstandings

THE EXISTENTIAL INVESTIGATION	4. Exploring the phenomenon: generating "data"
	  4.1 Using personal experience
	  4.2 Tracing etymological sources
	  4.3 Searching idiomatic phrases
	  4.4 Obtaining experiential descriptions from subjects
	  4.5 Locating experiential descriptions in literature, arts, etc.
	5. Consulting phenomenological literature

PHENOMENOLOGICAL REFLECTION	6. Conducting thematic analysis
	  6.1 Uncovering thematic aspects
	  6.2 Isolating thematic statements
	  6.3 Composing linguistic transformations
	  6.4 Gleaning thematic description from artistic sources
	7. Determining essential themes

PHENOMENOLOGICAL WRITING	8. Attending to the speaking of language 9. Varying the examples 10. Writing 11. Rewriting, etc.

Figure 7–2   Munhall's (1992) Model of Existential Investigation

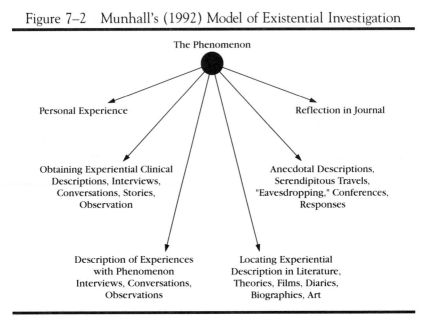

Van Manen's (1990) method for conducting human science research uses the phenomenological perspective, investigating the phenomenon within the context of human "lived" experience. In the current work, it included exploring the phenomenon through in-depth conversations with mothers in their homes, sharing memorabilia of the experience, reflecting on mothers' writings and journals, and investigating how mothers memorialized their babies through memorial services and funerals.

Multiple conversations with mothers were audiotaped over a period of eight months: three conversations with each of four mothers; two conversations with one mother; and two conversations with the mother with whom the phenomenological interview was piloted. In general, the conversations lasted from one and one-half to three hours. Conversations were taped, transcribed, and stored on floppy computer discs.

I also was guided by the phenomenological perspective to investigate human experience with the phenomenon within contexts of art-mourning and memorial art, painting, music, creative literature, and poetry. Professional literature, phenomenological literature, creative writings, and poetry were explored; all provided insight or examples of "lived" experiences with having a baby die. Figure 7-3 details the investigative avenues that were followed, and Figure 7-4 gives the phenomenon of interest a central focus for reflecting on meanings.

As each example of the lived experience was contributed, I returned to the phenomenon with increased understanding. This reflective process, which is part of existential investigation,

Figure 7–3   Model of Phenomenological Perspective of Inquiry

Four Concurrent Steps

#1	Turning to Phenomenon of Interest: Mothers' Experiences of Perinatal Death of a Wished-for Baby

#2	Existential Investigation of Phenomenon:
	    Researcher's Personal Experience
	    Professional Clinical Experiences of Researcher
	    Reflection Recorded in Researcher Journal
	    Mothers' Descriptions of Experience:
	        Interviews
	        Stories
	        Journals
	        Writings
	    Sharing Mothers' Memorabilia of Experience:
	        Tapes
	        Copies of Memorial Services
	    Inquiry into Creative and Artistic Sources:
	        Art and Painting
	        Observation of Memorial Art in Cemeteries
	        Mourning Art
	        Mourning Photography
	        Literature, Autobiography, Poetry
	        Historical Literature
	        Music
	    Professional Literature
	    Consultation of Phenomenology Literature

#3	Phenomenological Reflection on Phenomenon
#4	Phenomenological Writing and Rewriting of Discovery

Figure 7–4   The Existential Investigation of Phenomenon: Mothers'
Experience with Death of a Wished-For Baby

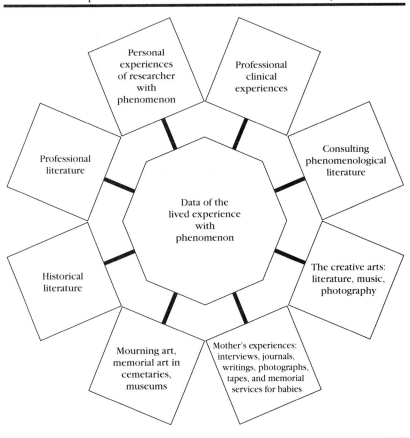

included exploring the historical context of mourning and
memorials relating to the phenomenon; the researcher's experiential contexts with the phenomenon; and the body of literature
in existential philosophy, particularly the phenomenological
writings of Merleau Ponty and Heidegger. Because the purpose of
this chapter is to detail the findings rather than the research process per se, the reader is referred to the original dissertation
(Lauterbach, 1992) for greater detail.

Being-a-Mother in Another World

I found that mothers who experience perinatal death find themselves existentially "in another world," abandoned first by the baby in its death, and then by society in its refusal to acknowledge the significance and magnitude of the death. "You can have another baby," a recurrent message to mothers from the helping and social world, is intended to soften the reality of the baby's death but only heightens the mother's isolation. The mother had begun to bond with that particular baby. When being-a-mother to that particular baby was lost, no softening of reality from the outside was welcomed, necessary, or effective. The worst thing imaginable had happened to the mother when the baby died. My own experience validated this finding.

Mothers' experience of mourning their babies is a very physical one. It embodies loss, feelings akin to having experienced their own death, and symptoms of acute grief that continue to be exacerbated for months, with each remembering. The mothers experienced the babies' deaths as requiring that they abandon concern for everyone but themselves and concentrate on what they, in their role as primary mourners, interpret to be the "social" thing to do. They experienced a need and an empowering ability that projected and actually required them to carve out their own course of mourning, regardless of responses of those around them, once "the worst thing possible" had happened to them. (This mother elected to mourn her baby "any damn way I choose.") Mothers found that mourning was the closest thing to having the baby still with them. Again, my personal experience validated this finding. In one mother's words, "It was so bad, there was no way out, but through it."

Heidegger (1962) described death and dying from the perspectives of the one who died and of those left behind:

In Being-with the dead [dem Toten], *the deceased himself is no longer factually "there." However, when we speak of "Being-with," we always have in view Being with one another in the same world. The deceased has abandoned our "world" and left it behind. (p. 282)*

Mothers' experience of mourning, beginning with the first knowledge that "something was wrong," propelled mothers to another place where they were free to "be with" their babies through their mourning. Mothers gradually gave up being in that other place, as the reality and acceptance of what had happened and of being in that world only as a mourning mother were fully experienced. Several mothers were very aware of their need for their working and social worlds to pull them back into functional relationships, but they were equally aware of how their own needs were put on hold to assist their friends by reassuring them and telling them, "I'm OK," regardless of whether the mothers felt that they were. One mother narrated:

> *I remember standing outside a baby store, on the second level of the mall. My tears were falling down to the first level. It was so hard trying to find something. I mean, just the idea of going and looking for something to bury your child in. But, we did. . . . We found a very pretty dress. . . .*

> *I don't know how I did it, but I went out to dinner with friends, on two different occasions . . . two, three, days after I buried my child. Here I am sitting in a waiting room, a bar on one side and a restaurant on the other, waiting for a table. And I think back later . . . I know I was in shock. I mean . . . this was just impossible to believe that I was doing it. But, I did it two nights in a row . . . one, with one girlfriend, and one, with another. It's almost ridiculous now. I think my friends didn't know what to do or what to say. They thought that being company for me was helpful, but at the same time they weren't helpful. Whenever I mentioned anything, I would be quieted and not allowed to talk about it.*

Joseph Campbell (1973) stated:

> *[We] do know that burials always involve the idea of the continued life beyond the visible one, of a plane of being*

that is behind the visible plane, and that is somehow supportive of the visible one to which we have to relate. (p. 90)

This explanation and a statement that death supports life were recurrent themes in the mothers' experiences. For the duration of the research, my own experiences were bracketed, or put aside, so as not to color or bias what I found. I have since interpreted my experiences in the language and conceptualizations gained from the study, so that my experiences, along with the experiences of the mothers studied, validate and are validated by the findings.

In my own experiences, as in the research, there was an intimate connection between life and death. While I was mourning my baby, my continuing to mother my newborn baby and two small children helped me turn to the necessities of living. I was thankful for the small routines established with my children before Amy's death. The routines helped me to mother not only in spite of, but because of the death. In caring for Alexandra, I understood poignantly what I had lost. Regardless of efforts to have my loss minimized by those who understood it but tried to convince me otherwise, in that space allowed for mourning, my nurturing/ mothering, healing, and recovery were facilitated. My mother helped with my mothering of Amy and my mourning her loss after her burial, when I was too far away. In doing so, my mother mothered me so that I could continue with my life.

In a poem, written close to the anniversary of my father's death, my original loss was intimately connected with his death; both events occurred near the completion of my doctoral research. The experience of perinatal death of my child continues to be intimately connected to life and death in my own existence.

Mothers in the investigation found that the experience of having a wished-for baby die greatly affected their ways of being in the world—in relationships, in the multiple contexts of their lifeworld, and in their world views. Mothers found that they could not continue to move within their worlds in the same way. Their changed perspectives had enduring effects on their ways of being—privately within their intimate relationships, and publicly within relationships and connections with others. "I will never be the same again," one mother stated as she described the changes in her life; she no longer behaved as "a cheerleader." She found more enthusiasm for her work when she was actively dealing with issues and relationships. A little more impatient, taking greater chances, and assuming a more active role with her clients, she found she couldn't tolerate what she called "wasting time."

In addition to being deprived of the public and longed-for role as mothers to their babies, mothers found that their babies' deaths left them with a dilemma of *being*. They were suspended in a transition between being in a mothers' world and being in a nonmothers' world. Each mother became pregnant again. Four mothers experienced subsequent live births and two mothers each experienced another pregnancy loss. Mothers found themselves, even after delivering subsequent babies, continuing to mourn the dead child. One mother stated:

I am really the mother of three girls, not just one baby girl. And I find myself saying, "All right, girls, we're going to do so and so."

Mothers shared what it was like to live through the experience that produced the "essence" of loss in their lives. One mother described going home "with only flowers; I think that was the worst time." The time following her stillbirth was, she said, "a time of loss," a time when she needed pictures of her pregnancy and her dead baby boy within arm's reach. The nine months that followed the stillbirth were like a "cocoon":

It was very protective. The things that had always bothered me didn't bother me. It had a niceness to it. . . . That's where you go. There's nowhere else to go.

The silence surrounding babies' deaths and the mothers' experience of being in another world may be interpreted to be related to denial, a healthy mental mechanism used by humans to protect and ensure a gradual awareness of reality and its consequences. The denial that assists and protects mothers during pregnancy seems to be present also within those around them, including health care professionals. However well-intentioned, silence and isolation serve to compound and invalidate the mothers' mourning. They further isolate the mothers of the dead children from the social world that would have been available had their babies survived.

Three central dimensions of meaning were found within the mothers' experience: (1) temporality, (2) connection, and (3) context. Each is discussed here in turn.

TEMPORALITY

The experience of mourning the death of a wished-for baby, with the resultant and consequent abandonment of the mother by the baby and the social world, is an experience in temporality. Temporality was a central dimension that permeated the discovery of meaning in the experience. It was present from the beginning material shared with mothers, and it continued throughout the process of the mothers' sharing of material.

In reflecting on the concept of temporality in existential philosophy, Heidegger's (1962) work and writings on *being* and time were especially informative. Time was experienced by the mothers as a collapsing concept: present, past, and future being was all integrally connected. The experience was temporal in that it was bound in time by the nature of the loss, the meaning of the loss for the mother, the mourning process, and the sense the mother made of the loss over time.

Within writings of T. S. Eliot (1963) is immersed the concept of temporality. Interestingly, during the 1930s in Europe, Bergson's philosophy of intuition was dominating French thought. Written around the same time, Eliot's poem "Burnt Norton," in *Four Quartets,* stated that time present and past are present in future time, and the future is contained in the past. The author has found Eliot's poetry particularly helpful in understanding temporality as a phenomenological mourning concept.

Temporality is integrally related to the other two dimensions found in the study: connection and context. As a concept, temporality is constantly evolving and changing, with exacerbations in connections and contexts within the mother's life-world. One mother stated poignantly: "No one understood that when Mary died, part of my future was gone forever." Another mother felt "as if part of me died, too." And finally, a mother said that she had "lost something that was going to be with you, not just for the moment, but over the years."

CONNECTION

The mothers' experience of being abandoned in another world following the death of a wished-for baby is a connected experience, one that is shared with only a few who dare to "be there" with presencing concern. Mothers shared how their close relationships with their family and friends and with their partners or husbands, or the fathers of the babies, supported them in "living through" the experience. They also described how maternal mourning differed from paternal mourning.

Robert Frost's poem "Home Burial" (Untermeyer, 1962) describes the lived experience of a mother and father whose child has died. The poem also speaks about the social world's inability to comprehend death, and the retreat back to the living world by friends and family surrounding mourning mothers:

> *. . . God, what a woman? And it's come to this,*
> *A Man can't speak of his own child that's dead."*
>
> *"You can't because you don't know how to*
> *speak. If you had any feeling, you that dug*
> *With your own hand—how could you?—his*
> *little grave;*
> *I saw you from that very window there,*
> *Making the gravel leap and leap in the air,*
> *Leap up, like that, like that, and land so*
> *lightly*
> *And roll back down the mound beside the hole.*
> *I thought. Who is that man? I didn't know you.*

And I crept down the stairs and up the stairs
To look again, and still your spade kept
lifting.
Then you came in. I heard your rumbling voice
Out in the kitchen, and I don't know why,
But I went near to see with my own eyes.
You could sit there with the stains on your shoes
And talk about your everyday concerns.
You had stood the spade up against the wall
Outside there in the entry, for I saw it."

"I shall laugh the worst laugh I ever laughed.
I'm cursed, God, if I don't believe I'm cursed."
"I can repeat the words you were saying.
'Three foggy mornings and one rainy day
Will rot the best birch fence a man can build.'
Think of it, talk like that at such a time!
What had how long it takes a birch to rot
To do with what was in the darkened parlor.
You couldn't care! The nearest friends can go
With anyone to death, comes so far short
They might as well not try to go at all.
No, from the time when one is sick to death, One is
alone, and he dies more alone,
Friends make pretence of following to the grave,
But before one is at it, their minds are turned
And making the best of their way back to life
And living people, and things they understand.
But the world's evil. I won't have grief so
If I can change it. Oh, I won't, I won't. (pp. 28-31)

Relationships with professionals, particularly nurses, were important but often "not available." Mothers described how their physical needs were left unattended. One mother described how a friend had to help her after she had had a large and painful episiotomy. This mother had a "wonderful" nurse who stayed with her during delivery and took pictures of the baby. However, she had no continuing contact with the nurse. Mothers described their nurses as "just gone." They "missed" their nurses after being transferred out of the maternity units; they could have used help in making decisions about funerals, mothering the dead baby, holding and "being with" their babies as much or as little as needed; they needed help in dealing with the painful physical responses to the death. "After all," one mother said, "I had never experienced having a baby die before."

Mothers described in great detail their bodies' mourning responses—physical aching, empty and heavy arms, painful episiotomies that received little or no care. Their bodies continued on an unknowing motherly course punctuated with their "milk coming in." They described how they yearned to mother the baby, long after the death, funeral, and "appropriate" time for acute grief had passed.

Mothers could find only a few people who were able to "be there," supportive of their mourning needs. New relationships formed during the mourning experience were especially helpful. The support group network was particularly valuable for three mothers. One told why:

We met a lot of couples who had lost children . . . and they were very helpful, both before the baby died and afterward. They rallied around us when we were back home. They phoned, they visited if we wanted them to visit. Most of the time we didn't want anybody to visit, but they phoned. Sometimes I answered the phone, sometimes I didn't. Sometimes I unplugged it so I wouldn't even hear it ringing. And that was all helpful. We continued to go to the support group and that's how we got through it.

From reflection on the mothers' stories, it appears that the working and casual social world around the mother is less supportive than people who have experienced having a baby die. One mother stated, "It was a rare person who asked me how I was doing, and really wanted to know. There's only one person at work who came up to me and put her arms around me and said, 'I'm so sorry about what happened.'"

Another mother stated:

I started to work gradually. It was very hard to go back to work. Everyone had seen me come along in my pregnancy . . . and nobody called. One clinician said to me that he was very concerned. It was like living in a twilight zone. It was horrible. I literally snuck in and out, trying to avoid everybody for weeks.

One mother described how the funeral was the only public way she was able to be-a-mother. The ritual was important in that it was validating her public role as a mother, however brief.

CONTEXT

The meaning of the experience of being-a-mother in another world was found to be related to the context of mothers' lives. This context included connections and relationships within life and work, and intimate relationships with the father of the baby, with family and friends, and with the larger social world to which the mother relates. The contexts of circumstances, connections, and temporality surrounding the pregnancy and the expected baby were found to be related to multiple, complex meanings of experience. Intimate relationships with partners and husbands were supportive following the deaths; they enabled mothers to carve out their own private cognitive and behavioral mourning responses.

Of particular interest was the context of work in mothers' lives. For three of five mothers, important changes in the conduct and meaning of work followed the loss of their children. These mothers all work within the support group network for grieving families. Two mothers have written professionally on issues of pregnancy loss, and these writings were consulted as further material of the lived experience of mothers.

One mother wrote:

. . . I have the great pleasure of being present with clients as change happens. Sometimes it comes in flashes of insight.

*Sometimes a new behavior springs into being, seemingly out
of nowhere. At other times, change comes as a subtle shift in
the colors of a person's life. Change can come with profound
feelings of relief or heightened anxiety or acute sadness. But,
it always has a familiarity about it—a stillness.* *

Of particular interest was the context of being-a-mother again
after the loss experience. Mothers experienced an almost reflexive
focusing on beginning another pregnancy. Each mother experienced another pregnancy; one mother experienced another loss
and will probably not have the being-a-mother experience again.
One mother experienced another death, a stillbirth; the baby experienced a genetic problem similar to that of the first baby she
lost. Continuing her quest for a child, the woman delivered a
healthy baby girl who was two months old at the time of the interviews. Each of the other three mothers has gone on to have another baby; one mother has had two babies since her stillbirth.
They described these new mothering experiences with a heightened and enhanced valuing of the opportunities and risks of motherhood, and a greater awareness of what had been forever lost to
them in the deaths of their wished-for babies.

Mothers discussed in great detail their continuing mourning after the new pregnancies and births, and how issues concerning
mourning the dead child continued to be present in mothering
again. Mourning, over time, loses some of the intensity—it becomes less of a general, pervasive experience—but it escalates in
intensity at the birth anniversary and other particularly significant
times. Again, mothers talked about how difficult it became for others during the exacerbations of mourning. Family and friends
were worried that the mourning would be all-consuming again.
The mothers experienced a continuing existential existence—
being in another world where mourning became again a private,
personal experience.

The context of mourning while caring for new babies and older
children, and while being involved in the everyday activities of
family life, presented mothers with particular challenges. Finding

---

* Reprinted by permission from participant mother.

the time to continue to think about and work on issues related to the dead child was hard for mothers with young children. Mothers with new babies found themselves often thrown back into remembering and mourning the previous loss or losses. In total, this inquiry uncovered 13 pregnancy loss experiences from within the participants, the pilot mother, and the researcher. Mothers with young babies were more welcoming of the opportunity to participate in the research because it provided an opportunity to reflect on and revisit issues that were unresolved. One mother said, "I have her, but I still cry."

Mothers were also concerned about how to continue mourning in the presence of their other young children. One couple scattered their baby's ashes along a particularly beautiful river, somewhat isolated from urban surroundings, but then found that, after a subsequent baby was born, it became difficult to walk there, so they were unable to visit the site as often as they wanted. At the time of the interviews, this mother was uncertain about how much she should allow her two-year-old daughter to be aware of her continuing sadness, especially at ordinarily happy times such as Mother's Day, which was the anniversary of her stillborn baby son's birth. The following poem, "Mother's Day," was written by this mother, who experienced two pregnancies after her son's death:

Mother's Day

On Sunday I was a mother for a little while.
With one final push the baby was out.
And everyone said how beautiful he was,
Perfectly shaped little fingers and toes.
They let me hold him, and he really was beautiful.
He lay there motionless, dark hair like his father's,
One eye opened slightly as I shifted his position,
And closed again.
They weighed him and finger-printed him and took his
  picture.
They let me hold him again.
He seemed to be growing older and more wizened.

His arms and legs no longer felt warm to the touch.
They left us alone with him for a long time, and we sat
and gazed at him.
Then they took him away.
Now I'm a mother no longer, left only with a brief
moment, and an emptiness where I had felt full before.

Figure 7–5 is a graphic model of the dimensions of temporality, connection, and context throughout mothers' mourning experiences. From these dimensions, shared thematic groupings yielded nine shared themes that were found in the material from

Figure 7–5   Conceptual Model of Meaning in Mothers' Experience with Perinatal Death of a Wished-For Baby

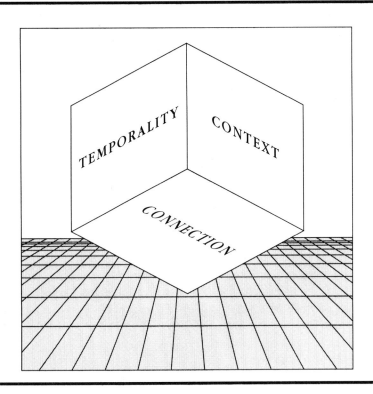

the beginning to the present. Data and material from the creative, artistic investigation validated the discovery as a credible description of the "essences" of the phenomenon.

SHARED THEMES DEPICTED IN MOTHERS' LIVED EXPERIENCES

Figure 7-6 identifies the shared themes present in dimensions of mothers' experiences as determined by a hermeneutic, interpretive analysis of material generated in the investigation. The interpretation discovered and uncovered both hidden and explicit meanings or "essences" of mothers' experiences.

A theme is defined by van Manen as a description of the structure of the lived experience:

[T]hemes are more like knots in the webs of our experiences, around which certain lived experiences are spun and thus experienced as meaningful wholes. (p. 20)

Figure 7–6   Findings of Study

IN ANOTHER WORLD:
Discovery of Meaning in Mothers' Experience
of Perinatal Death of a Baby

Temporality • Connection • Context

Essential Themes:

- The Essence of Perinatal Loss
- Reflective Pulling Back, Recovering, Reentering
- Embodiment of Mourning Loss
- The Narcissistic Injury
- The Finality of Death of the Baby
- Living through and "with" Death
- Death Overlaid with Life
- Failing and Trying Again

Themes uncovered by reviewing the material carefully, repeatedly using phenomenological and interpretive literature, were isolated from descriptions of mothers' mourning and were found to be embedded with meanings or "essences" in experiences. In writings and responses to presentations of the work, the findings continue to be validated, not only as representative of the mothers' experiences from the study, but as having relevance to the larger world of mothering mourning experiences. Care must be taken, however, to not overgeneralize from the findings; instead, the interpretive process must be used to further elicit, from others with experience of the phenomenon, material about differences as well as similarities, about unique as well as common mourning experiences. The written presentation of findings continues to generate material for analysis of mothers' experiences.

"ESSENCES" OF LOSS

At the time of writing the dissertation, the first central theme was identified as "essence of perinatal loss." In retrospect, when attention to the language of lived experience was accomplished at a greater distance from the requirements of the dissertation manuscript, this theme was reworded to be "essences" of loss. Writing and rewriting have guided understanding of the linguistics of loss and have helped to clarify meanings within the language surrounding the phenomenon.

The theme of loss was ever-present in mothers' descriptions of their lived experiences with perinatal death. Losses took many forms: loss of a dream; loss of unfulfilled dreams; loss of many missed opportunities. The particular perinatal loss was further colored by multiple and recurrent losses. As shared earlier, one mother described the nine months following her stillborn baby's birth as a "time of loss" spent within a "cocoon," "a place where no one goes." She needed to be within arm's reach of the pictures of her stillborn baby for weeks on end. "There was no way out, but through it."

The theme of loss was persistent, consistent, and recurrent in the mothers' lives. Each mother, in describing experiences of living through loss, gave poignant examples depicting how loss had colored and had been colored in her life.

One mother described the period of time following her still-birth:

> *I think that's why I didn't get depressed. It took me a long time to get depressed. I was in a cocoon that lasted a good nine, ten, eleven months. It was during that period that I was grief-stricken and angry, but I was not depressed. It was as if I were in this holding place; that was very vital. There was nothing dead about it, and the work I did during that period was really in the journal. It was very vivid, but I was not depressed. It was a "loss time." When that period ended, I really missed that cocoon. The reentering is really the critical part that nobody looks at and I think that that's the point where the trouble comes. . . .*
>
> *During the early time, I couldn't understand what was wrong with me. I knew I had grieved. I had done everything by the book. I knew I wasn't crazy. I felt the loss as a blow.*

PULLING BACK, RECOVERING, AND REENTERING THE SOCIAL WORLD

Mothers unanimously described their withdrawal from the larger social world following the first indication that "something was wrong." Only those most intimately connected to the mother were allowed into the "other" world. The mothers were assisted by husbands or partners and by families to pull back from the larger social world; its subsequent abandonment of the mothers actually assisted them in creating a boundary for themselves within which they privately grieved in the manner they chose. The mourning experience was a narcissistic personal commitment of the mother to herself, which validated her mourning, her loss, her separating herself by "being with" her baby in death. Mothers were adamant about how, in the immediate period following the baby's death, they grieved "any damn way I chose."

In addition to their withdrawal from the larger social world, mothers were selective in withdrawal from intimate relationships following the babies' deaths. The withdrawal from connections and relationships was both preceded and followed by periods of feeling isolated and fearing that no one would know the extent of their suffering and disappointment. During the acute phase of the mourning, many mothers made new connections with people who had personal experience of the phenomenon. The "old" social and intimate world of the mother often invalidated the loss and became impatient for the mother to move "on" or "away from" the death and her experience of mourning. The isolation and experience of loss are interpreted as having propelled the mother into initiating and forming new connections, reflecting her altering views of the world based on her new experience of being in the world.

Eventually, all of the mothers became reinvolved with their "old" social world and the larger world, but, in many cases, the changes in world views dictated changes in personal behavior within the world. One mother described her withdrawal from her social world in the months that followed the death, and her gradual reentry into that world:

> *I couldn't open my front door. I just sat here looking out the window at what I would never have . . . a little girl across the street, who was just learning to walk. I couldn't get the mail. I didn't have the strength to open the door, to face anybody, or see anybody. I called a person the support group had recommended, and she made me promise to go out. And for a while if I saw anybody, I would automatically move to the other side of the street.*

This mother's first child had a genetic problem and died shortly after birth. Immediately afterward, she spent time with her parents. Her husband returned to their home alone in order to keep his job. The couple had relocated from another party of the country during the pregnancy, and had bought a row house in a neighborhood where they were just beginning to get to know people. This mother recounted details of her activities of daily life and the agony with which she experienced acute grief. She had been appreciative of the fact that the adjoining house was unoccupied; it provided her greater privacy for behavioral expressions of her feelings, which were sometimes audible and verbal. She described throwing pillows, taking care to miss her prized collection of ceramic angels. She gradually ventured down the street, crossing to avoid children and people; she timed her daily outing to avoid children coming home from school and trolley stops delivering people to the neighborhood.

This mother connected with a support group facilitator, who guided her gradual reentry to the world in her neighborhood. After her first loss, this mother experienced a perinatal death, during delivery, of another baby girl with the same genetic problem. She was in the third trimester of pregnancy when she consented to participate in this study. A healthy baby girl was born and was two months old at the time of the first interview. The mother is currently a support group facilitator for a grieving group.

EMBODIMENT OF MOURNING

This theme, clarified since the writing of the dissertation manuscript, is now simply "embodiment of mourning." Embodiment is a phenomenological concept that refers to the experiencing of the world through one's body. Each mother described similar bodily experiences of acute grief that included intense physiological, emotional, cognitive, and behavioral symptoms. The data of the immediate period following the death are interpreted as meaning being-a-mother in mourning, or the embodiment of mourning. Mothers described in detail their lived experience: the agony of the physical experience of acute grief; the ache of empty arms; vivid memories and images of the time surrounding the first awareness that something was wrong; thoughts and feelings relating to the idealized baby; emotional and mental pain; the gradual realization and consequences of the experience of loss of the particular baby; and the gradual return of interest in daily life during the months that followed:

My husband was at work, and I was here. Me, and the four walls, and my pictures, and my memory. We had taken a lot of pictures in the delivery room in the hospital. . . . Going through those, crying, then eventually putting them into a little book.

So, some days I didn't get out of bed at all. I tried to. It was winter, and days were very short, and nights were very long. There were times that I wouldn't get out of bed until it was dark. I tried to get out of my nightgown by the time my husband walked in the door. Sometimes I succeeded, sometimes I didn't. It took me a long time before I felt like there was something to do in the day. I'd try to do a load of dishes, and it would take me all day to do the glasses. I'd start the water, start things soaking, and get back to it about three hours later.

I cried, I screamed, and cried. I had a white bear that my sister had given to me as a birthday present a number of years ago. Well, that was my child, after she died. I had aching arms, empty arms. They were like weights. They hurt so much. At the time no one lived next door. It made it easier.

Mothers described how, as time passed, they realized the impact of the experience on their subsequent life and its value; gradually, they moved to another level of mourning. They described their subsequent preoccupation at times, their suddenly being pulled back into feelings of acute loss because of reminders in the world around them, their reactions to anniversaries and opportunity for remembrances. They described a process of gradually incorporating the experience as part of their changed world view and family history.

For all of the mothers, who were aware of unfulfilled and lost dreams, missed and ended opportunities, the essence of loss was felt and experienced as losing the child forever. It was described variously as losing a part of the future, losing a relationship with the child in the future, losing the personal and social role of mother to the baby, losing forever the context of being-a-mother to the child. The brief, but intense, experience of being-a-mother to the dead child was captured in thoughts, memories, and life experiences since the death.

Mothers lost their feelings of invulnerability and of the denial that helps pregnant mothers deal with the anxiety connected to being-a-mother. Instead, they realized that bad things can happen during pregnancy. As one mother put it:

Part of the shock of his death was that anything so con- sciously planned and worked on could not have not worked, and something that was so . . . that had a technical aspect right from the beginning . . . there was nothing at the end to do, clinically, that would have saved him.

The experience of the death of their baby did not fit with the mothers' imagining how it would be to be a mother to a child. Mothers asked, "Why me?" without getting answers. Only gradu- ally did they learn to live with the fact that the child had died. The mother described above, whose baby was stillborn, experienced a second loss in early pregnancy, following artificial insemination. She found herself very angry following the second loss. It was just "too much." She said:

So I got pregnant again. It didn't feel right from the start, the symptoms were weak and then it went away completely, and as soon as it started feeling not right, I got terrified. It was like standing in front of the car with the headlights on. Like a deer caught in the headlights of a car. Being pregnant made me feel so exposed and terrified. Then at seven weeks it was clear that it was not right. The doctor said it was a blighted ovum, so I had a D&E. That was the point at which my depression seriously deepened and my friends got even more distant. I think they were really freaked out by how angry and depressed I was. They couldn't take it. I think they were mad at me for trying to get pregnant again, for being so upset. I had been pretty polite, but after the miscar- riage, I was not.

Another mother, following the birth of a girl a year and a half after the death of her baby son, said, "I still cry. I have her but I still cry." She recalled when her lost baby was in the hospital, im- mediately following delivery:

And who knows? You don't know. You have no idea. You
wonder if you made the right decisions. Or am I doing the
right thing? . . . dealing with the stress of this poor child
being so ill and not being able to do anything, not being able
to touch him, not being able to hold him . . . .

The mother in the row house, described above, was able to
withstand tremendous social pressure and made the decision to
carry her second baby to term even though she was almost certain
that the baby suffered from the same genetic defect as her first
child, who had died. This mother thought that the first loss had
prepared her for her second experience of loss.

The Narcissistic Injury

One of the primary differences between late pregnancy loss and
other types of loss is in the degree of the qualitative experience of
loss. Late pregnancy loss is viewed by the mother as a personal loss
constituting a narcissistic injury to her self-esteem, her identity as
a mother, and her ability to provide protection for her child. As
one mother stated:

I felt as if part of me died, too. The first week after she died
I was really numb. I was in a lot of pain. I hadn't been able
to go to the bathroom yet, and I had a big episiotomy. They
wanted me to go home, but I said I wasn't ready. If my baby
had lived they would not be sending me home. I told the doc-
tor that and he didn't know what to say. I felt rejected, de-
prived. I had a little bouquet of flowers from my husband's
work and nothing else. I didn't have a baby. I didn't have
flowers. I didn't have anything.

Another mother stated:

I don't remember how I functioned during the day. I don't
remember it at all. I do remember going to bed at 5:00 P.M.
My best friend had given me a stuffed animal when I was in
the hospital, so that was my security blanket. So, I'd get into

bed with my stuffed animal and my nightgown, and the
kids would come in and I would read to them in bed.
I didn't want to read to them in their rooms. I don't have
much memory about it.

As one mother said, "I couldn't understand what was wrong
with me. The depression comes from the narcissistic blow." This
mother articulated how she found herself seriously depressed, not
because of loss but because of the narcissistic damage of the experience, which she confronted long after the agony of the acute
grieving period was over.

The death of the child also represented the death of the world
of being-a-mother to that lost baby, at that time. The mothers ac-
quired almost reflexive thoughts about having another baby immediately. Four of the mothers, and the pilot mother, began actively
planning for another baby within the first few months after the
death. One mother, after finding herself pregnant again, began the
long anticipated prospect of becoming a mother to another baby.
All of the mothers described their anticipation, planned or otherwise, of conceiving another baby within a few months of the
death. All of the mothers had subsequent pregnancies following
the perinatal death of a wished-for baby.

After two pregnancy losses, one mother is actively engaged in
accepting the possibility that she will not become a mother again.
For her, the losses possibly represent the death of any future world
of mothering. She states that this prospect is beginning to feel
"more and more all right" with her. This mother has found renewed interest in work and in intimate relationships. For all participant mothers, the death represented death of the world of
mothering that particular baby.

THE FINALITY OF THE DEATH OF THE BABY

The ultimate loss for mothers who experience the death of a
wished-for baby involves (1) the loss of the particular child, (2) the
loss of being-a-mother to that child, and (3) the loss of a future relationship with that child. The finality of the death is only gradually

experienced and accepted. Even though the realization is gradual, each mother described living through the process and her poignant acceptance of the finality of the death. Some mothers were unable to explain why it was so gradual and what was wrong, but, at the time of the interviews, all five mothers and the pilot mother had learned to "live with" the idea of the death and the finality with which it had struck. One remembered:

> *It happened like a blow. He was dead. There was no way to deny it. My baby was dead. He would always be dead. There was nothing I could do but live with it.*

Another mother stated:

> *It was incredible, really. In the midst of the most horrible thing that had ever happened to me, I was thinking, planning, doing it by the book. I was devastated, really.*

Living Through and "with" Death

In the preceding discussion, it was discovered that mothers were able to use isolation as a protective world for themselves; it provided the space and time needed for personal expressions of mourning. The experience of being in another world enabled mothers to live through their loss and be "with" the dead baby. In this other world, mothers were able to prepare for reentering and then being in the larger social world without their babies. The experience was accompanied by a changed relation with the world, a changed and still-altering view of the world, and a choice of continuing to live within the world and of being a mother to another child:

> *There was nothing I could do about it. I had no choice. I just moved through it day-by-day. Time seemed suspended. I had my pictures, my privacy, and my memories. I could close my eyes and see the experience all over again. I could be pregnant . . . before it all came crashing down. I was afraid I'd forget what he looked like. And in time it became more and more OK.*

One mother described her experience as being in a "cocoon" for nine or so months. She had not read about this perception nor heard other mothers talk about mourning in this way.

Altering World Views

The experience of having a baby die greatly affected the views the mothers had of the world before and during the crisis and after the death. The changed and still-altering world view is related to the meaning the mother gives to the experience—a meaning that is temporal, connected to people, and bound in the context of experience in the mother's world.

Mothers varied in their mourning experiences, but there were some common features. Variations were in the degree to which the mothers had (1) integrated the experience into other aspects of their lives, (2) incorporated the experience into life stories and histories, and (3) allowed the experience to change their world and their relationship to their world. However, each mother voiced change in the following areas: change in *what* she connected with, *how* and *why* she connected with it, and with *whom* she was now connecting. In addition, the sense the mothers made of the experience differed, but they all reflected a more heightened awareness of values regarding life and death and of the value of the wished-for baby. The mother of the baby who was stillborn following conception by artificial insemination stated:

> *I know that no matter what's going on now, whether it's good or bad, that it's going to change. Something else is going to happen. That's really comforting, because I don't think that I had that longer range vision before. . . .*
>
> *This was so bad that it put everything else in perspective. It was one of my worst fears. Now that it's happened, I feel freed up. I had always wanted to write. I can be comfortable alone. Relationships are more important to me, but I'm less desperate. . . .*
>
> *I'm not as easy as I used to be. I think I was much more obliging before. I don't feel as much like a cheerleader. I've incorporated the idea of evil and disaster into my view of life and through that have gotten more interested in my*

spiritual life. My perspective has altered violently. The whole idea of good and bad are both part of the same swing. I'm much more [confrontational] than I was before. I've gotten interested in death and loss.

Some mothers possessed world views that were especially helpful in the aftermath of the death of a baby. Mothers whose experiences furnished them with a sense of coherence—a reasonable expectation that life would turn out positively—were able to weather the storm of the acute grieving period with more use of social and relational connections and resources. They found greater comfort within immediate relationships with husbands and partners, family, friends, and social support systems, and they entered actively into a decision about having another baby.

The effect of a wished-for child's death on a mother's world views was related to her coping with the experience and aftermath of the loss and its temporality, the context of the loss in her life, and the quality of her connected relationships prior to, during, and subsequent to her experience. In this area particularly, the researcher found that the temporality of the experience, the mourning of the loss, the personal meaning, and the qualitative contextual aspects of the mother's life in general all affect the construction of a world view following the loss.

Further, from the first to the last interviews, changes were noted in the mothers' world views. Several mothers are interested and willing to continue interviews so that the unfolding of their loss can be explicated and observed over time. The interest of the researcher and the mothers in continuing inquiry after completion of the current study was thought to be (1) significant to validating the process of inquiry and (2) related to the need to explore the phenomenon as it unfolds over time.

Death Overlaid with Life

The theme that death of a loved one is overlaid with new life and rebirth was discovered to be very present, very strong, and unanimous in mothers' experience of loss. This, along with the theme of loss, was a persistent, consistent, and recurrent theme in the data.

It was present from the first piloted interview, throughout inquiry, and into the final interviews. The existential descriptions found in artistic, literary, and creative findings are supportive, especially excerpts from Enright (1987) and from Eliot (1963) poem in *The Waste Land,* entitled "The Burial of the Dead" (1955).

The themes of death overlaid with life and rebirth took varying forms as interpreted by the mothers studied. The pregnancy and birth of the baby who died were connected in mothers' minds with loss of a loved one—a father, for one mother; a brother who died in adolescence; a favorite cousin for whom the baby in utero was named and referred to during the pregnancy. Perinatal loss was related to:

1. Subsequent pregnancies, some ending in further pregnancy loss and some ending with delivery of healthy, live babies.
2. A multigenerational family history of maternal death, maternal failure, and use of a drug by the mother of a participant. The drug had a subsequent impact on the participant's cervical difficulties in carrying a baby to term.
3. Each mother's interest, following the perinatal death, in having another baby.
4. An attempt to become a mother again, either with a conscious plan or otherwise (four of the five mothers have had subsequent live babies).
5. Renewed respect for the value of qualitative aspects of the mothers' lives.

Several stories in which mothers' views of the death of a wished-for baby are connected with life are very touching:

> *My cousin was killed in a car accident that May, ... She had been named for my father. So when I got pregnant we named this child for her. We called our baby by name throughout the pregnancy.*

Another mother described how the pregnancy was like a breath of fresh air during a period when her husband's father was terminally ill; the pregnancy and wished-for new baby helped them cope during a period of stress.

My husband's father died that January and we went to the viewing. A pretty awful time in terms of illness and death. But, the pregnancy kind of kept me going. There was a memorial service and people were commenting that at least there was one bright spot. We had told him we were expecting a baby before he died. We were so glad he knew about the baby.

A mother whose brother had died in an accident told how her baby was buried with her brother:

My brother and baby are buried together in the same cemetery plot my father bought when my brother died. My dad visits the cemetery daily. He plants spring pots and a little window box in front of the tombstone each year. He plants all kind of pretty spring flowers and when they bloom and die off he puts in summer flowers that will last throughout the summer. It's nice. It's pretty. We bought a tree and planted a tree on the side of the tombstone.

Each mother in the study discussed the ritual memorial service, funeral, or burial of the wished-for baby. One mother, whose parents are both deceased, had a friend purchase the plot where her baby is buried. She visits the plot only occasionally and never alone, because the city cemetery is unsafe. One mother and father of a stillborn baby scattered the baby's ashes, along with flowers, over a beautiful remote spot in a Philadelphia park that has a stream. Another family scattered ashes over common ground. The mother and father of two baby daughters who died because of genetic problems buried both babies in the town where the mother's parents live.

Failing and Trying Again

This theme pervades the data of the lived experience of mothers' loss. As stated above, each mother had an almost reflexive focusing, even during the acute grieving period, on beginning another pregnancy immediately. The transition into the world of being-a-mother was largely incomplete with the death of the baby. One mother stated: "Once a mother, always a mother." The mothers' view of the world as a mother, the mothers' identity, necessitated another attempt at being-a-mother.

One mother who experienced guilt during mourning, thinking that she had been responsible for the death of her baby, was pregnant within three months of the death. Guilt was not an essential theme for mothers in this inquiry, but guilt was experienced most acutely by this mother. The anniversary year was spent in mourning, even as she prepared for her new baby's birth. She delivered a healthy baby girl almost a year to the day of her baby boy's stillbirth. The poem, "Mother's Day," spoke about being a mother for a little while. This mother's desire to be a mother had been a carefully considered decision over the tenure of her relationship with her husband and was a very strong force in her life. She continued to mourn and parent at the same time, taking care to use her judgment and thoughtful processing of experience to consider whether she would have another child. At the writing of the dissertation, this mother was pregnant again, a little over three years after her loss.

Summary of Shared Themes in Mothers' Experiences

The essence of the meaning of the mothers' experience is that mothers find themselves abandoned by the infant and the larger social world following the death of a wished-for baby. Existential meaning of the experience of being-a-mother in another world is described as an experience in temporality, connection, and relatedness, bound within the context of mothers' lives. In addition, the shared themes, the "essences" of meaning that emerged from mothers' experiences of their babies' death were: essences of loss, reflective pulling back, recovering, and reentering the social world; embodiment of mourning; narcissistic injury; finality of death; living through and "with" death; altering world views; death overlaid with life; and failing and trying again.

SIGNIFICANCE OF DISCOVERY AND KNOWLEDGE OF MOTHERS' EXPERIENCES

The most significant result of the investigation into mothers' experiences and the discovery in this inquiry is that direct practice implications can be immediately addressed for caregivers as well as for mothers and families. Care must be taken to not overgeneralize from the findings, but mothers' mourning care can be guided and shared by all those who share the human mourning experience. The researcher believes that a mother's mourning care nurtures and provides mourning care for those around her who are also mourning. Nursing care in particular must go beyond the establishment of protocols and must provide a nursing presence throughout the mother's and family's experience, in order that decisions regarding the mother's experience of being-a-mother to her dead child may be explored in detail.

At the time I was writing this chapter, a relative experienced the death of her 16-year-old son following a motor vehicle accident. The mother had not been with her son when he was taken off life support. (He had been kept on life support to provide time for arranging for recipients of organs.) She had not experienced being-a-mother by being present when he died. She was very disappointed that, despite attempts to arrange for organ donation, only bone and skin were able to be used.

Like other mothers, she needed human care grounded in knowledge and understanding. I called her and allowed her to discuss her needs and wishes regarding being-a-mother to her son and being "with" him before he was buried. On the day of the funeral, she assumed she could not see him again because the funeral director had closed the casket. This mother wanted to see her son one more time; a phone call arranged a last viewing, her last opportunity to be with her son before he was buried later that morning. She continues to struggle with her loss even as she acknowledges her continuing need to mother her other three children. The meaning of the experience for this mother is, out of necessity, guiding her mourning.

If a mother feels supported, many mothering ways can make it possible for her to be "with" her child in death. Slowing the time from the death to the funeral, or from the death to transfer of the baby to the morgue—perhaps even taking the baby home briefly— will allow time for the mother to explore what she wants and needs from the experience. These considerations are crucial to using the experience to become more fully human, which is the ultimate goal of this research. Taking the time to talk through decisions is so simple, yet so profound. It transforms the mourning activities and processes from passivity to activity and helps in discovering the dictates of mothers' needs and wishes. Daring to ask what a mother wants and needs implies a wish to be "fully and humanly present" for the answers. Exploring possibilities and choices introduces a fuller awareness of the meanings of human experience. Findings from this inquiry need to be placed in the hands of the mothers themselves, to empower them to carve out in their mourning, a path that reflects their values and philosophies, especially in the absence of informed care.

Early in this century, when death was removed from the home to the hospital and funeral parlor, it became marked by distance and shrouded with increasing silence. People found it difficult to "know how" to mourn, so they did so alone. Bringing it out into public awareness, as a normal human experience, assists the mother in carving out her individual mourning experience. The author heard many stories about how mothers "never got over it," and discussed with mothers their concern about "how" they "were going to be," especially in the beginning. Mothers in the study, like other mothers, are very resourceful when confronted with overwhelming grief. The nature of their grief requires that they care for themselves. This self-reflection enables mothers to cope with trying to become a mother again, with mothering again, and with continuing to mother their other children in the face of tragedy.

Following one of the presentations of this doctoral research, a faculty member told me about an experience of one of her students that day. The student had been assigned to care for a mother who had experienced her baby's death. The baby had been taken to the morgue, and the mother wanted to see and hold the baby again. The nursing staff had discussed the request. When the student became involved, it was apparent that the staff were hesitant and were probably not going to arrange it. The student nurse, with the help of her instructor, took the mother to the morgue to be "with" her baby who had died.

Both this mother whose baby had died and my relative who lost her son felt much better following the experience of being-"with" the child. Often, this care is present; but when it isn't, it directs the focus of the mothers' mourning to what was *not* done, to who was *not* there, rather than to her sorrow, which seems for a long time as a "never-ending story." If such a simple act of being "with" provides so much comfort, one wonders why it is not facilitated.

The needs and care of mothers change over time, following the death. In the immediate aftermath, taking pictures before and after the death of the baby, alone and with the parents and nurses, has been found especially helpful to mothers. Video and audio taping and active participation in the memorial services are some of the mothering activities that mothers find helpful.

Of particular interest after loss of a child is the period needed for the acute mourning to subside. (After the death of an adult, this period ranges from nine months to three years.) Some mothers describe an intensity in mourning that takes them by surprise. Because of the social responses engendering silence, this period is most difficult. The mothers again worry about their mental health and wonder how to proceed. There is need for continuing study of maternal mourning over time, in order to better guide mourning within an adequate time frame. Of particular assistance to the mother is the establishment of a visible memorial or remembrance of the child. The social world underestimates that time and further negates the feelings of loss by commenting, "Oh, I didn't realize you are still feeling bad." The implication is that a mother who has other children will harm them by "dwelling" on the death.

In addition to this discovery, which is validated over and over by those with experience of the phenomenon, mothers who participated in this study welcomed the opportunity to reflect on their experience. They voiced personal benefit and increased understanding from participating. At the same time, they knew their contribution to knowledge would benefit others.

Sartre (1965), a leading existentialist, stated that the goal of literature is:

. . . to reveal the world and particularly to reveal man [sic] to other men [sic] so that the latter may assume full responsibility before the object which has been thus laid bare. (p. 18)

He also stated:

If you name the behavior of an individual, you reveal it to him [sic]; he [sic] sees himself [sic]. And since you are at the same time naming it to all others, he [sic] knows that he [sic] is seen at the moment he [sic] sees himself [sic]. (p. 16)

It is hoped that, through writing and sharing research findings with many audiences, "essences" of the human experience of mourning the death of a baby will be experienced fully, within all of the life worlds surrounding the baby, the mother, and the family and friends. It is hoped that through this fully human experience, when guided with knowledge, understanding, and caring connections, those involved will be assisted in becoming even more fully human because of, not in spite of, the experience, and that the phenomenon will no longer continue to be buried in silence. As with this study, removing some of the silence allows direct practice implications.

Implications from this research also speak to a need for nurse researchers to commit themselves to inquiry into phenomena for which there is great professional and/or personal knowledge and interest. Reflection on experience facilitates understanding and assists in critical analysis of experience. In my view, the discovery in this study was connected to a relative goodness of fit among the phenomenon of interest, the availability and richness of human experiences with the phenomenon, the particular phenomenological perspective and methodology used, and the human commitment of all involved in the inquiry. I hope it will enable those who receive the results to be more fully human within the many worlds within which we are involved as human beings.

EPILOGUE

I'd Rather Be Buried in a Small Country Graveyard

I'd rather be buried in a small country graveyard . . .
Where mothers and fathers have gone on before,
Nurturing life and land in death,
As they tilled and toiled the earth in life.

I'd rather be buried in a small country graveyard . . .
Where baby has been mother to me in her absence,
Helping to see what was had in what was lost,
And to have it anyway, in spite of and because of her
death.

I'd rather be buried in a small country graveyard . . .
Where love for sandy farmland, pines, ti-ti swamps
*   lay barren,*
Quietly waiting . . .
Awakening and nurturing meaning and understanding.

Sarah Steen Lauterbach, written in May 1993,
one year after father's death, and almost
12 years after Amy's death.

REFERENCES

Campbell, J. (1973). *The power of myth.* New York: Doubleday.

Eliot, T. S. (1963). *Collected poems 1909-1962.* New York: Harcourt, Brace, and World.

Enright, D. (Ed). (1987). *The Oxford book of death.* Oxford, England: Oxford University Press.

Heidegger, M. (1962). *Being and time.* (J. Macquarrie & E. Robinson, Trans.) New York: Harper & Row. (Original work published 1927.)

Lauterbach, S. (1992). *In another world: A phenomenological perspective and discovery of meaning in mothers' experiences with death of a wished-for baby.* Unpublished doctoral dissertation, Teachers College, Columbia University, New York.

Merleau Ponty, M. (1962). *The phenomenology of perception.* London: Routledge & Kegan Paul.

Munhall, P. (1992). Unpublished manuscript.

Munhall, P., & Oiler, X. X. (in press). *Nursing Research: A Qualitative Perspective.* New York: National League for Nursing. In press.

Sartre, J. (1965). *What is literature?* (B. Frechtman, Trans.) New York: Harper & Row. (Original work published 1949.)

Untermeyer, L. (1964). *Robert Frost's poems.* New York: Washington Square Press/Holt, Rinehart and Winston. (Original work published 1930.)

van Manen, M. (1984). *"Doing" phenomenological research and writing.* Alberta, Canada: The University of Alberta Press.

van Manen, M. (1990). *Researching lived experience.* New York: SUNY Press.

ABOUT THE AUTHOR

Named for my mother, I was nicknamed Selen as a little girl and have always gone by this name. I grew up in the rural backwoods of northern Florida, in the community of Shady Grove. Most of my childhood was spent on a farm with my family. Of five children, I was the second child and first daughter. My grandparents' families were early settlers in the area, and I expect to return to this farm when I eventually retire.

My parents were not farmers in the usual sense. My mother was college-educated and during most of my childhood was a school teacher in a four-classroom country school which I attended until the eighth grade. We were all taught by my mother; a brother spent several years in her class. My father was in the Army and lived apart for most of my formative years; we lived with him in Fort Benning, Georgia, and in Germany when I was in the fifth grade. He tried farming briefly after his retirement.

The professions of my parents and their emphasis on education set us apart from the country people around us, even though each summer we worked in the tobacco fields and on our family farm. My high school years were marked by increasing competency, exploration of talents, and activity in a variety of youth organizations during which a leadership potential was discovered and nurtured. In my senior year of high school, I was elected and served as Florida State 4-H Club President. Mastering the skills and crafts of both my grandmothers always gave me something interesting to do. In my junior and senior years, I raised Angus steers for show.

I was fortunate to have attended University of Florida with a nursing major under the direction of Dean Dorothy Smith, a nurse educator who had begun a nursing curriculum that was revolutionary for the time. The nursing educational experience nurtured my interest in people and in the world of ideas and academics. It provided an atmosphere for personal and professional development that has been the foundation of my adult life.

My early professional experience included both academic and clinical practice in psychiatric/community mental health nursing. These interests have kept me connected to university life and education throughout my adulthood, in teaching roles or pursuit of education.

I lived and traveled in England for three years with my husband, and moved to Philadelphia following a job search. Shortly after we became parents, we were confronted with children's health issues, so I took a career break and became a "stay-at-home mother." Upon my reentry into teaching 11 years later at La Salle University, I commuted to New York to begin the doctoral cohort nurse executive/nurse educator program at Teachers College, Columbia University. I taught full-time for the first year of doctoral study and then took a year of academic leave to complete the research. The concentration provided by full-time study lent a focus and intensity that contributed to my viewing doctoral education and the completion of my dissertation as the most complete learning experience of my life. It continues to give a focus to my scholarly work. With a colleague, my work on "Caring for Self" has been concurrent with the dissertation.

I have lived with my family in the diverse urban community of University City in Philadelphia for 20 years. Our children are adolescents now and have had a varied education in public and private schools. Marlow, my older daughter, is 17 and attends West Catholic High School. Jared, our son, is 15 and is a sophomore at Central High School, a public school. Alexandra, our surviving twin daughter, is 12 and is newly enrolled in the seventh grade at Germantown Friends School having spent her earlier school years in a neighborhood public school. Her twin, Amy, died nine days after a birth emergency and is buried in the Hendry family's country graveyard at Shady Grove, close to where my grandfather was born.

My mother still lives on the farm, and my four siblings and their families all live in northern Florida. My children and I enjoy our journeys each year to a part of the country that I love and to the experiences with family that continue to provide the taproot of my life.

8

The Transformation of Anger into Pathology

Patricia L. Munhall

ON *THELMA AND LOUISE*

I am a film addict. I admit I'm powerless to skip even bad films. Somehow, even they hold interest for me. As I start this chapter, I know how it's going to end. That is what it's like when you have finished a study and are going to write a chapter on it. So, I'm telling you about films for a very specific reason. Yesterday I saw *True Romance*. I won't tell you about it from beginning to end, but only the parts relevant to this chapter.

The female character is a call girl who gets "beat up" by her pimp of four days. Later in the film, she gets slashed with glass, kicked in the "guts" and face, and more or less thrown through a glass shower door. We are led to think she is dead: She is seen bleeding profusely.

Her boyfriend kills her pimp, then mistakenly takes a luggage bag of cocaine, which causes him only to be hunted by "the mob." They torture his father and then kill his father. It doesn't really matter why.

Then the "cops" are involved, as are Hollywood drug abusers, innocent bystanders, and, of course, the mob. They all kill each other. Why they do this really doesn't matter. It's called entertainment. It's violent.

Some other recent films I've seen were also entertainment and violent: *Single, White Female, Point of No Return,* and *Kalifornia.* But for the most blood and violence, there was *Reservoir Dogs,* written by the same fellow who wrote the aforementioned *True Romance. Reservoir Dogs* even had a warning attached to the movie posters about the extent of the violence. And can we forget *Silence of the Lambs?* I could go on.

Why do I mention these films in a chapter on anger? Because of the very mixed message our society gives us about anger. On the screen, it is taken to the extreme. Yet, let a woman show she's angry and people cringe. Does it bring back childhood fear—perhaps fear of a mother or a mother's anger, or fear of making a father angry?

I've heard people respond to a woman's getting angry in very negative terms. They never say: "That's good. She's good at expressing her emotions," or, "At least she won't get sick," which, by the way, is the major point of this chapter. Instead, they say: "She's a first-class bitch!" When a woman gets angry often, "What a bitch!" is the usual response to what may be an initial expression of anger. Even when a woman is not overtly angry, but anger is present, the veiled hostility burdens people. "She's so hostile," they will say. Or they figure out that she is hiding her anger behind passive aggressive behavior. Witch or bitch, an angry woman inspires fear.

Yet, remember the film, *Thelma and Louise?* If you haven't seen it, I suggest you should; even if you have seen it, view it again from the perspective of the expression of anger. Women, at least the women I know, loved the film; men were scared of it, a reaction that was to be expected. Men didn't come right out and say so. Film critics (most are male) superanalyzed it as a fairy tale that would never, could never, come true. Women don't leave their abusive husbands, women don't curse, smoke, drink, and do similar "stuff." Women don't steal, have sex, blow up trucks, kill. If they do, they will drive off a cliff and die.

Let me tell you something personal. I have a bumper sticker on the back of my bedroom door that says, "Thelma and Louise Live"; and I believe that. In that last scene, the car actually landed comfortably after a five-foot descent onto a road to freedom. The film's concluding with their suicides pulls the mask off the reality behind the film: Women like Thelma and Louise cannot survive.

Many women went on that joyride with Thelma and Louise. In the real world, most women won't express such anger. They exchange it for something more acceptable—often, in the process, doing harm to themselves and, paradoxically, to others.

WHY AREN'T MORE WOMEN LIKE THELMA AND LOUISE?

Outside of being called a "bitch" for expressing anger and a "first-class bitch" for characteristically expressing anger, there are reasons why women will not or cannot express anger. But what kind of anger am I talking about? I am talking about anger expressed in rational ways—not explosive rage, where anger was held in for too many hours, days, years; not yelling, screaming, hysteria. I am talking about expressing to another human being feelings of anger toward someone, or something, and telling that person face-to-face. I am talking about knowing and feeling anger and verbally expressing it. A person who "throws a fit" rather than express anger rationally has waited too long. Why do women *withhold* anger or *hold* it inside until it burns a hole in their stomach, or they become depressed, or their key relationships deteriorate. Some women set someone up to act out their anger for them. None of this does them much good, and none of this is healthy. Why is holding anger in so pervasive? Fear of expressing anger is, women have told me, why they hold it in. Women say they not only suffer from anger, but they are not allowed to outwardly experience it. Society, or those people who make up society, has not given permission for women to be angry or to express this emotion. The mixed message, therefore, is not so mixed after all. Anger for entertainment is acceptable. Some people even think we can "get rid" of our anger vicariously in this way. The message that is not mixed here is simpler: Do not express anger outwardly, in reality; if you do, the consequences may be severe. Consequently, women fear anger—the anger of others as much as their own. But most women are not even aware of their anger. There anger is held way in, down deep—*repressed* describes it perfectly.

REPRESSED ANGER

I have treated numerous women in therapy and have had countless conversations with women. I have also had group therapy sessions with women. I have known women, of course, all my life—friends, a sister, my mother, myself. Yet they all seem to have difficulty with anger. There are many reasons. Primarily, women repress their anger. Then women transform it. You may say, "I know about that! People somatize." You are right, they do, and it is very serious. It is not an answer, however; it is a problem. Transformation of repressed anger is a very big problem (Munhall, 1993).

TRANSFORMATION OF ANGER INTO WHAT?

Repressed anger in women, and, to some degree, in men as well, is transformed into a pathological condition that society can name and therefore tolerate. The sad part of this is that the transformed pathology is far, far worse than a healthy expression of anger.

THE CRUELEST PARADOX

I want to make one important statement here. I will come back to it later in the chapter. *Women are so censored in the expression of their anger, and the anger is so repressed, that they do not leave situations that make them angry.*

Women who are angry about a particular situation do not first try to change it, or, when the situation does not change after "giving it time," they do not leave the provoking situation. This means that the transformation itself veils the real situation. It is a smoke screen; it is a solid wooden door.

TRANSFORMATION OF ANGER INTO PHYSIOLOGICAL DISORDERS

Susan, a religious woman, turned 50 years last month. Susan is not a fictitious person. Susan never gets angry with anyone or anything. She prays and fasts. She also does very good things for people. She is thoughtful and considerate, and she never forgets anyone's birthday. As a matter of fact, she makes a big "to-do" about friends', children's, and her husband's birthday.

So, turning 50 and having this milestone birthday, I suspect Susan might have thought there would be a certain celebration for her. Her husband had a friend whose wife was also going to turn 50 around the same time. The men got together and planned a surprise party for the two wives; they called it a hundredth-year birthday party.

The party was planned for the Sunday after Susan's Wednesday birthday. Vicki, one of my friends, visited Susan on her birthday. Susan had received flowers and a cake from her husband and children.

I was outraged at this set of events. I said to Vicki, "That's terrible; isn't she angry?" I added that I thought Susan's husband was passive aggressive and cruel. The sharing of the party was more passive aggressive stuff and the hundredth-year concept was just plain insulting. I know I own these ideas. Vicki's reply was: "No, Susan didn't get angry. She went to bed at 9 P.M. with a terrible migraine."

This outcome is not unusual. No one seemed aware that possibly Susan was angry. "The cruelest paradox" has a part here: Susan herself was not aware of her anger. She did not express anger to anyone, or even feelings of disappointment. Everything was fine, except on her 50th birthday she was in bed before 9 P.M. with a headache that literally prevented her from seeing. As part of her migraine, she had blinding lights in the way of her vision. Because she could not see, she could not say anything without compounding the pain. *Pain:* now that's the real transition. The emotion felt—anger—is often so painful, for so many reasons, that it converts to another kind of pain; a pain that can be spoken about aloud; a pain that may even prompt sympathy and, with women, empathy, like the pain of a migraine.

Susan performed well at the party (which *was* a surprise), but then went home with yet another migraine. Perhaps several things contributed to that: sharing the party, for one; and being five days into her pain at how Wednesday had passed. Either situation could have triggered the blinding light. Or maybe when her family and friends sang, "Happy 100 years to you," at a party for which "100 years" was the decorative theme, maybe it was all too much.

Because anger is not well-tolerated—except by those intrigued by images of anger in film or literature, for example—it is largely discounted, disconfirmed. It goes underground.

REASONS FOR GOING UNDERGROUND

This is a complex event that has become embedded in history and in our culture. Anger is depicted in literary works and in films, including those that represent history, and our perception of history, as destructive, murderous, aggressive, fearsome, intolerable to feel, and impossible to express. Society attempts to forbid the direct expression of anger; in some forms, such directness is practically illegal. Imagine that you were angry enough to yell at someone and you actually raised your voice, perhaps at a neighbor whose dog barks all night and keeps you awake. Suppose that, previously, you had discussed this situation quietly and constructively with your neighbor, who just ignored you. During one sleepless night, you wake up your neighbor and say, "I'm not going to take this anymore." Now you have broken the law about expressing anger. In this instance, you may have disturbed your neighbor's peace, and you may even have implied a terrorist threat. Not to leave a stone unturned here, let's say that prior to the night when you "took the law into your own hands," you had called the police precinct. The officer who took your call responded, over the phone, that nothing could be done beyond issuing a warning to your neighbor.

The point here is how anger is perceived. The icons of anger are destructive. Society would rather not permit women to express their anger directly because of the fearsome nature attached to it. Women who dared to express it might be abandoned, hurt, or ostracized. Many women I have spoken to believe that the expression of anger is a sin; a few women believed one of the ten commandments prohibited anger. Recall the oft-repeated compliment, "She has the patience of a saint."

There is much to be learned from that compliment. *Many saints who had all that patience were killed.* Getting oneself killed could even be construed as the epitome of self-destructive behavior. Many abused women fall into this pattern. It serves no purpose to push anger underground.

Sending anger underground, or repressing it, is encouraged by the idea that anger expressed is aggressive and is destructive to society. In reality, it is the other way around. The destruction, if that is the way the anger is expressed, is turned against the self unconsciously. Because the perception of anger is so negative, women tell me that they are either unaware of its presence or, if aware, they keep the anger underground in other ways because they fear the consequences of expressing anger. They know that some people will get mad at them. Others may leave them. Others may hurt them. This is another paradox: The ways in which women seem to go underground with their anger often produce the consequences they were trying to avoid. They are left. They get hurt. They hurt themselves.

MORE ABOUT TRANSFORMATION OF ANGER IN PHYSIOLOGICAL DISORDERS

Before proceeding here, let's return to why women do what they do. After discussing Susan, I realized I could address the question, because there is so much transformation of anger still to discuss.

In a 1993 article, I termed many of the conditions that lead to or evidence transformation *psychosomatic*. I still believe in the wholeness of the body, but, for discussion here, I have separated the part from the whole. I've done that so that when we recognize psychosomatic disorders in ourselves, or in others, we will not be so quick to dismiss them. It seems unfortunate that the label, *psychosomatic,* has become an adjective that describes a condition that is not all that important. The word has a dismissive quality, as if the person is responsible for the psychosomatic disorder and can do something about it independently. This view is part of the cruelest paradox: The individual does not have such knowledge. The repressed anger seeks its expression as a psychosomatic disorder.

What are the origins of some other physiological conditions for which I now have a better understanding? Women have come to me for vague feelings of unhappiness or, in deep misery, have asked for therapy. They do not speak often about physiological conditions; I suppose they think I am not the appropriate person to treat those conditions. Often, what emerges, in words or through gestures, are conditions such as frequent headaches or gastrointestinal disturbances such as "pain" in the stomach. Many of these women hold their abdomens where they feel their pain; they describe being "doubled over in pain." This is rage repressed, and we can prevent women from being doubled over in pain. Animals do not repress, they howl at the moon if need be. Are women permitted to do that, and, if so, with what consequences?

Women with weight problems (for purposes here, I will speak mostly of what we call *obesity*) come to mind. Janet Greenson, in her 1993 book, *It's Not What You're Eating: It's What's Eating You,* writes about the way individuals "stuff" down their feelings with food. Sound familiar? Women who substitute eating or cooking for more direct expressions of anger sooner or later return to it. They feel it again, in the same context; they are fearful and still prohibited from expressing the feeling. The unexpressed anger can even grow more painful. The pleasurable preparation and eating that momentarily relieved their pain fade into memory. The anger remains. Afterward, the woman comes to direct her anger at

herself. She becomes her own victim. And she may very well repeat this cycle again and again.

SUBSTANCE "ABUSE" AS A PHYSIOLOGICAL DISORDER

Food is the most easily accessible substance to "abuse" when ex-
changing momentary pleasure for the expression or recognition of
anger. Many women in this study—and, of course, described in all
forms of media—are medicating their pain with food, alcohol, and
drugs. The remorse that follows is often alleviated only by continued use of whatever it takes to relieve the pain.

I believe that the word *abuse* is erroneously used here. The
abuse is not so much of the substance, but because of the use of
the substance. Self-abuse is just another way of channeling anger
toward self. Recall the painful result of repressing anger. Common
sense dictates trying to remove oneself from a situation that is contributing to pain. In this regard, the use of various pain-relieving
substances is understandable even though it is quite detrimental to
health.

It is important to understand women who try to save others
from their perceived destructive anger at their own expense. I
hear women being critical or judgmental about other women who
are manifestly "abusing" a substance but are actually in hidden
pain.

Another critical element I have come to understand well is that
health care professionals focusing on weight, alcohol, or drug
problems are not always successful in their treatment. Often, these
problems are called *stubborn* and that awful word *obesity* is sometimes modified by the word *morbid.* Phrases like "She is going to
kill herself if she keeps going like that" are, unfortunately, very
true. Intervention, I would propose, should certainly not be at the
behavioral level. Insight and intervention need to be where the
pain is, and that pain is often repressed anger. If this seems knotty,
it is. The emotion of anger needs expression in ways that will
shortly be discussed.

I knew this before beginning this study, and I am now even more focused on its appearance. I realize how moralistic and judgmental we all can be, and particularly when repressing while transforming anger. It seems that the quieter the pathology, the more acceptable it is. In fact, quiet repression is almost regarded as a virtue.

QUIETER, LESS VISIBLE PATHOLOGY

There are more hidden ways to announce to those around you that something is wrong. Because the woman herself may not know what that something is, once again she might seek treatment for the symptom that is disguising what is wrong.

Women, far more than men, seek treatment for conditions of "unknown origin"—constant headaches; gastrointestinal problems; neck, back, chest, and joint pains. The "unknown origin" label immediately closes off further probing. We don't know where this disease, disorder, or symptom comes from, so women are treated for their symptoms, little more.

ACCEPTABLE TREATMENT FOR TRANSFORMATION

Treatment of symptoms-only is a serious failure. The following excerpt is from a daily newspaper. Oddly, this kind of recognition seems more or less *not* to influence the medical mindset of treating the symptom.

> *If Anger Ruins Your Day, It Can Shrink Your Life*
>
> *Chronic Hostility—A Hazard to Health*
> - *Affects sympathetic nervous system fiber endings.*
> - *During anger, the sympathetic nervous system raises pressure and heart rate, among other effects.*
> - *Angry people often produce too much of the "fight or flight" hormones but not enough hormones to counter them.*

- *In the chronically hostile, the parasympathetic system fails to restore them to normal. Stiffened arteries, a weakened heart, and other problems can result. ("Health," 1990)*

If a health care practitioner—in this case, a medical doctor—has a hunch that some of these conditions are psychosomatic (which, as I mentioned, almost means they are imaginary), the treatment of all the transformative disorders is fairly standard. For the headaches, backaches, stomach pains: *Rx: Valium* (or a derivative; doesn't matter much)

We have come to accept that angry women are very difficult. Perhaps, as in *The Stepford Wives,* tranquilizing these annoying women is seen as good, real good. If Thelma and Louise had been properly tranquilized, it might have prevented their "crazy" behavior. That's just a film. But a qualification is in order. With women who "act out" their anger, tranquilizers can prevent unacceptable behavior.

Many women understand that they are being placed on mind-altering substances. The relief provided is temporarily satisfying for them. Yet, it is important to know that such medication further represses anger and even allows women to stay in situations that often produce altering states of fury, rage, and anger.

And yet, in the same article, a subheading read:

Constantly boiling
over in anger could
be as bad as
smoking.

and still more

Suppressing Anger Is Lethal

Following up on the group 19 years later, Dr. Julius found that the women who had reported that they would feel anger but would not express it were three times more likely to have died than those women who said they would feel less angry or those who said they would express their anger.

Another excerpt, published earlier that year, announced (Blakesler, 1990):

The First of Its Kind

The study is provocative and interesting, said Dr. Stephen Weiss, chief of the behavioral medicine branch of the National Heart, Lung and Blood Institute, which financed the project. It is telling us that some people who have been diagnosed with heart disease and who make behavioral changes may be able to prevent subsequent heart attacks.

Weiss added that it had not been proved that such changes would help all heart patients. He said the study needed to be repeated before the general public could be given general recommendations on the importance "*of anger and anxiety in heart disease.*" Depression, the other side of anger, will be discussed later.

To return to the prediction that people "who make behavioral changes may be able to prevent . . . ," this phrase is often used along with the treatment of the symptoms. It includes behavioral changes such as: *Rx: Work less, exercise more, change diet, and get out more. Rarely is the patient advised: Avoid certain people, get out of the situation you are in, reflect on control issues and expectations, see a therapist to "work through" your anger (anger* is rarely spoken aloud). Rarely, if ever, does anyone want to acknowledge the anger of a woman.

To repeat, for emphasis: When a woman is perceived as angry within this physiological dimension, a drug is frequently prescribed. If a woman becomes "out-of-control," she's drugged more, arrested, or perhaps institutionalized. Not a pretty scenario.

THE SCENARIO FOR TRANSFORMATION INTO PSYCHOLOGICAL DISORDERS

Let's begin with an extreme in understanding anger. There can be violence done to the self, or a rage against the self that takes up residence in the psyche. A woman named Lily, who came to me for therapy as a last resort, put it this way:

I have nothing to live for. I want to die. Then I can't do it. I think to myself, I can't do it because of my children, who are now grown up. Or maybe I can't do it because I don't have the courage. I simply hate myself [cries here for a period]. I feel nothing but self-hatred. I don't think I could kill myself, but I know I don't want to go on like this. Feeling nothing, dreading everything. I do not experience pleasure about a thing. It's almost like I am dead.

DEPRESSION

Most readers will recognize the previous excerpt as depression, yet most women who are depressed like Lily rarely consider the possibility of repressed anger or rage. When Lily directs her anger inward, against herself, a tragic loss of living time is involved. The anger that presents as depression, much like a physiological disorder, is safely secured somewhere. She will not be angry, rageful, or a murderer of herself or others, but, in a way, she is already dead and feels powerless about that. Without using medical terminology, *anger is often diagnosed as depression* when depression shows its face as persistent sadness, anxiety, hopelessness, and pessimism. In addition, decreased energy, sleep disturbances, and thoughts of death all keep the anger from surfacing into full-blown rage.

Repressing anger into depression hardly makes life worth living. In *A Brilliant Madness*, Patty Duke (1992) tells her story of being diagnosed as manic-depressive. After the manic phase, in which she felt out-of-control, she would suddenly slip into "debilitating, suicidal lows, periods of depression that found her cowering under the covers for weeks on end."

That particular book tells the story of pain and anguish—and anger. But again, *Rx: Lithium.*

This is not to be construed as an antimedication crusade. Medications can hold people together. However, I must emphasize two points: (1) the *treatment of a symptom does only that* and (2) the appearance of a symptom is often the concealment of another problem.

Women taking such medication might be affected positively. Yet where is consideration given here to their anger response to possible contributing conditions: physical and sexual abuse, poverty, biases, unhappy marriages, or being poor? There is black humor in the line, "I was depressed because I was poor, but now with this medication I don't care that I'm poor, abused, or even unhappy." Many women have told me that. The situation doesn't change, but the medication they are taking changes the way they "feel" about the situation. They tell me of now feeling indifferent to, or empty about, the very things that would provoke anger, *if they could express it.*

MORE ON PSYCHOLOGICAL TRANSFORMATION

Julie, a 28-year-old married woman, came to me with the following story:

I was an only child and my mother really didn't want me. She was living with a musician and she was an artist. I was what she called an "accident." They kept me, but ignored me. I was seven years old and I thought about taking a knife and doing something to myself to get attention. I don't know why I didn't. I didn't have any friends. I tried everything to escape being so lonely, but no one seemed to care. I found something I liked and that was dancing. So I became a dancer.

You might accept here that Julie finally was able to take care of her needs for attention, but don't be fooled that easily. At long last, the dancing had put her in the spotlight, but, like medication, the anger from her childhood eclipsed this creative attempt to get what she needed. Julie came to me depressed, crying with feelings of self-hatred, low self-esteem, self-doubt, sadness, and a pervasive sense of loneliness. She sat with me unknowingly filled with the rage of being an "accident" and unparented. The admiration she received as a dancer did not cure her lack of self-esteem or lack of self-worth.

Feelings of low self-esteem and others' opinions of low self-worth contribute much to women's anger. A woman can be angry at society for second-classing her, or, as in Julie's case, she can be angry at not getting what she needed when she needed it.

Medication does not alter feelings deeply embedded from childhood. Medication may alter the mood of the person, by creating indifference, but Julie needed therapy to learn how to give up her internalized parent and begin to separate from her mother. She learned what it would take for her to live her *own* life. Medication doesn't do that. If a woman cannot do that alone, therapy with a therapist who has worked through much of his or her own anger will.

I say this from experience. Julie, after a year or so, was able to say, "How dare she call me an accident" and "Even if I was not planned for, what kind of mother would tell her daughter that?"

COMFORTABLY NUMB

"Nonfeeling" (which could be part of depression) is another state exhibited by women with repressed anger. I have a friend, Elle, whose affect is, as they say, "flat." Flat? I've known her long enough to see her enraged. And when Elle becomes enraged, it scares me.

Much of the time, Elle sublimates her anger; she does this well, but it is not enough. Her anger, which captures more of her energy than her sublimation does, can suddenly explode. Elle goes from being comfortably numb in a subliminal state to being fiercely scary. I know that part of my view of this has to do with my own fear of encountering rage. I'm all right with it in the therapeutic setting, but, because of my own internalized mother, Elle scares me. Her explosion is out of proportion. But then I think of her history. Somewhat like Julie, Elle was an "accident." Worse, her mother gave her up for adoption, then changed her mind and took her back.

Is there a medication for rejection by parents? No, but there is for the *symptoms* rejection produces. Within this psychological transformation of anger to comfortably numb—whether through denial, physical symptoms, or medication—there is ever-present for women the transformation of anger onto their social world.

ANGER TRANSFORMED INTO
SOCIAL PROBLEMS

Again, these are not mutually exclusive categories; there is an intrinsic wholeness to this process. Teasing out some parts for discussion here is necessary to help in understanding the transformation of anger into other entities, such as child abuse, disrupted work, affiliative relationships, or murderous feelings if not murder itself. An excerpt from a piece of fiction follows. Is this story very different from the real-life event of Jean Harris and the Scarsdale diet physician?

> *Francesca was a young girl about to marry and living a rather idyllic life. She was out taking a walk with her youthful enthusiasm, placing flowers in her hair, and walking to her fiance's cottage. She was pleased to see his truck parked outside the cottage and looked through the window. This is what she saw and did:*
>
>> *At the small table in the center of the room, Louisa Natale sat naked except for her swan hat, drinking champagne.*
>>
>> *"To your great beauty," Colin said, pouring his glass of cool champagne between her long and tawny legs.*
>>
>> *"To your great freedom," Louisa smiled . . . .*
>>
>> *Then a hot stream of adrenaline began its swift voyage through Francesca's body and she was convulsed with rage.*
>>
>> *She was going to kill him.*
>>
>> *She had taken her father's .22 revolver from the desk drawer . . . .*
>>
>> *Nothing else in her mind but killing Colin Mallory.*
>>
>> *She fired the revolver. (Shrever, 1986, p. 66)*

Woman as murderer, as worked out in films and novels, is probably less prevalent than in real life. Becoming enraged to the point of violence is a potential for all women who are repressing anger, however. The urge to kill is there. Most do not act on it; they do these other things:

- Sabotaging self and others.
- Allowing violence in the home—in this instance, the woman might not actually inflict pain herself, but allow a partner or a sibling to act out violently on a member of the family.
- Seeking and staying in abusive relationships.
- "Unconsciously" contributing to "accidents" in the home or workplace.
- Being mean to others, holding grudges, practicing horizontal violence.
- Seeking out and remaining in destructive relationships.

When women talk about anger slipping into their social and family worlds, they often speak of relationships as paramount. The relationship must stay intact even at a cost. Fragile as relationships are, they must be protected.

The literature has been replete with research findings that speak to women in relationships. These findings stress the importance women place on connection and attachment. Right behind these are responsibility and caring—the foundations for the connection and attachment.

Confrontation—or, on the lea side of confrontation, even a wisp of anger—might disturb the equilibrium of a relationship. The outcome of this powerful dynamic is that women often do things when they don't want to do them. They do things for the sake of a relationship. They go along with something purely to maintain peace and harmony.

What's wrong in this scenario is that, backstage, the anger, resentment, and hostility keep mounting. Acting as though one is without needs, just to keep harmony and peace within a relationship, will eventually cost a high price. Giving up "self" for the sake of a relationship, in any context, is literally "self-destructive." When that term is taken apart, one can think of self and negate the very idea that a woman would give up that self. It is a murdering of the self, and those murderous feelings toward self are not bearable indefinitely. Before long, eruptions occur.

There is a certain recognition of this process in relationships with a woman's partner if she has one. Numerous self-help books, for instance, are published to assist women in understanding and taking action. Unfortunately, for many women, dismantling such relationships, if that is the course of action chosen, may not be the best solution. In effect, their situations do not lend themselves to recipe-like, "self-help" formulas. Yet, these formulas should not be completely dismissed. Some women, following advice in self-help books, have succeeded very well in disentangling themselves from destructive relationships and the by-products of constant anger. Still other women transform their anger elsewhere.

TAKING IT TO WORK

Women who are having a tumultuous time at home and are feeling powerless to remedy it act out their anger in the workplace. This is inappropriate. I have yet to have a patient or friend say to me, "I'm a bitch to work with," yet I have had patients and friends complain about a "bitch" at work.

Debra, a participant in this study, said:

> I hate going to work. I don't care if Fran's [her boss] anger is projection. It is unbearable to feel it and to be subjected to her outbursts. She is constantly demeaning me and there's not a thing I can do about it. I have to stay in this job for at least a year.

This is an interesting situation. Fran, her boss, projects anger inappropriately in the workplace, and Debra has to repress her anger to keep her job. Both women are experiencing anger through social interactions.

And the Children

Many women seem to equate good mothering with a conflictless situation. All conflicts must be avoided even if the avoidance causes the mother to be furious. Psychologizing has taken the place of saying to a child, "Your behavior is driving me crazy." Saving the mother–child relationship at all costs to self is another example of self-destruction. The relationship itself is doomed. Lack of anger will not keep the child attached. The task, in fact, is for the child to learn to separate from the parents. Rebellion offers an initial road. The more a mother withholds her anger about her rebellious child, the more rebellious the child will become. Whether it occurs in grammar school, high school, or college, children must detach. Ideally, the process is accomplished without anger or malice, but this is difficult. Women who do this best seem to relinquish the need to control their children.

Let's return to anger. I want to summarize what has been said thus far and then discuss further how women seem to handle anger. The most successful cases are quite interesting in their dynamics.

REVIEW: HOW ANGER IS TRANSFORMED

Through the body, anger takes up *residence* as:

- Headaches, migraines
- Gastrointestinal problems
- Coronary problems
- Weight difficulties
- Other conditions, often labeled as psychosomatic.

Anger is transformed into other *feelings or thoughts.* It *resides* as:

- Depression
- Low self-esteem
- Self-doubt
- Feelings of emptiness and powerlessness
- Self-hatred.

Lastly, it seems that anger is also transformed *in social interaction or in relationships.* Here it *resides* and appears as:

- Horizontal violence
- Child abuse
- Abuse in the home
- "Self-destructive" relationships
- Wish to "control" others.

The list goes on. What is critical here is that all these conditions or situations involve a transformation of anger. Often, the emotion of anger is not in the awareness of women's psyche, because the taboo of expressing anger is so ingrained. This is what happens. Or so it seems.

REPRESSION OF ANGER

Throughout this study, one dynamic has particularly stood out:

If anger goes unrecognized, it is left in silence. Repressed into recesses of the unconscious, it reappears transformed into something society finds more acceptable. Then society is spared the "fury" of a woman and the condition can be treated. Even child abuse, it seems, is something less frightening than a woman's rage. We fail to see that child abuse is a woman's rage, that migraine headaches are an expression of anger, and that fury, as in furious, is at the heart of destructive relationships.

In propositioning that women transform anger into other pathology, I could be more concrete perhaps and say this is what happens:

1. Anger makes women sick.
2. Anger then is quickly converted to another condition.

3. That condition is often treatable. Rx: Tranquilizers, antidepressants.
4. The anger is not resolved.
5. The cycle begins again and the transformed condition, or a variation thereof, returns.

Are not these conditions that I have discussed cyclical and pattern-like? We see a pattern, and that pattern is the camouflage of anger.

IS THERE A WAY OUT?

I saw the film *Sleeping with the Enemy*. As on a roller coaster, the leading man is nice to the leading lady one day, abusive the next. In the end, she had to kill him. In another film of the same genre, the woman kills the man too. In real life now, such murders often stand up in court as self-defense.

Murder is not the answer, but it is definitely a warning. Repressing anger is dangerous to your health and the health of those around you.

Theories exist on how one handles anger. These theories change. Not too long ago, it was thought best to "let it all hang out," say everything, don't keep anything inside; direct the anger toward the person provoking you. That led to many problems. Another problem is described by Lerner (1985) in *The Dance of Anger*—a pattern of ineffective fighting, complaining, and blaming that only preserves the status quo.

Books about how to deal with this emotion are unknowingly predicated on the idea that "something" (in this case, anger) is transformed. Other books sell on how to be with the transformed conditions: diet books, how to raise your children, how to be successful at work, how to make your relationship "work," and so on. The anger is masked. It remains in silence.

In my practice and research, I am constantly amazed as to how anger emerges through talking. Talking leads to recognition. Recognition can lead to the realization that the transformed condition *conceals* the dreadfulness of anger.

TWO POSSIBLE WAYS OUT

There are two possible ways out: one is research-based and the other is practice-based. That other ways exist as well does not change the fact that these two ways seem to aid women in encountering their original condition of anger. I would like to add one other caveat. If women are taking medication for other conditions transformed from anger, it is probably best for them to stay on the medication until the anger is more understood. If the medication masks the anger, then that could be problematic.

THE *PRINCE OF TIDES* WAY OUT

I call this the *Prince of Tides* way out. The film and book of this name demonstrated the tenacity of repression and the painstaking way one goes about reaching inward to the core. This story had to do with repressed rage—repressed way, way back.

Part of the recognition of that kind of anger has to do with the realization that what happened in the past cannot be changed. However, in this study, and in my personal life and professional practice, when it comes to anger at parents, this much I have learned: If this anger is repressed, it shows up each day and in ways that one might not even be aware of. *That* can be changed; the anger from and about childhood can be verbalized rather than rejected. Verbalizing is more complex than can be summarized here, but it still remains an important outcome and one I will stand by. Women who repress the anger from their childhood repeat it continuously and in transformed ways. The process is like peeling the layers of an onion: verbalizing to remove layers of the mask; therapy; the therapeutic process; the talking "cure." Contrast this to spilling out one's "guts" to the person or people with whom one is angry. Therapy is a process in which a transformed condition can be traced back to its source. Does this always work? No. But when it does work, all sorts of changes are possible. The headaches may be changed back to anger, and there it is: anger. Now a woman is talking, with a therapist, expressing anger, rage, and fury in a safe environment.

If this route is chosen, the woman needs to find a therapist who has worked through his or her own experiences with anger. A clue: *If the therapist discourages expressions of anger,* or dismisses them, *this is not the way out with this therapist.* The energy that is anger needs to be discharged. Slamming doors, telling other people what's wrong with them, or self-attacking themselves is not helpful to women. Yet, talking is discharging, and talking with someone who will accept a woman's anger and encourage its expression does help.

This sounds simple, but, in my experience it seems the hardest or most difficult resistance to overcome. The taboo against expressing anger is strong. Better to be physically ill. During this study, however, women told me that it was this therapeutic process that led them out of their quagmire—at least those who had the good fortune to be ready and who also found a therapist who not only could tolerate anger, but gently pressed for its expression. In these instances, the silence of anger was over.

RECYCLING—A RATHER LARGE RECOGNITION—THE SECOND WAY OUT

Some women I interviewed told of recycling without have therapy; others spoke about it coming because of therapy. With or without therapy, recycling produces one of life's greatest learnings: You cannot control the behavior of another person.

Yet, participant after participant, discussing their experiences with anger when it was not expressed, spoke about other individuals or situations. These individuals or situations were about to change, and then they, the women, no longer would be angry. These women believed, or perhaps wished to believe, the promises: "I'm going to change" or "It won't happen again."

When the anger was transformed, they unfortunately blamed themselves for whatever was occurring. However, when some women were able to be specific about the reason for their anger, they often did believe the promises made to them. We need to remember this response. We see women in terrible situations. Perhaps we should understand that, even in such situations, they are hoping and waiting for the promises to come true. Wanting attachments and relationships, women find it difficult to do what they need to do: *to let go of the illusion of control.*

Sally, in growing awareness, told me:

I let him and my children treat me like garbage. I made up all sorts of excuses for their behavior. They didn't even have to do that! I forgave their treatment of me based on ideas that I construed to justify what was going on. Mostly I blamed myself. I was not good enough.

Then after years of this emotional abuse I realized that it wasn't me, and they weren't going to change and I let go. I stopped wishing for change. I stopped making excuses for them. In fact I told Robert [her boyfriend] that it was over. It was the most difficult decision but I realized that if he didn't go, this situation was going to go on forever. I could not control him.

Sally's situation cannot be fully understood from this one vignette. What can be understood is the recognition that she could not change the person who made her angry. Odd, or not so odd? I knew Sally well. I believe it took two more Robert types before she accepted that realization viscerally. Here again was the repetition compulsion.

The point is: Women must try to locate the source of their anger and, instead of transforming their anger, get the source of their anger out of their lives. That *is* a way out. Another woman presenting said that her teenager was making her angry. But that is not entirely possible; it was more than that. She could not control her teenager; her anger was an issue of control. She was angry that she was *indeed* losing control over her son. She was actually losing control (having rages) over losing control. Removing the source of her anger, thereby reconceptualizing that source, could benefit her—for instance, with her wish to control others. At this point of recognition, we realize that we are angry; we mull over it, we reflect on it until we actually realize it. We realize the truth in it. I used to say, as a way of being humorous: Lower your expectations and you won't be so disappointed or angry. "Removing the source" could also take on reflection of our expectations.

One of the best prescriptions for anger is: Remove the source of your anger. Do not transform it. Recognize it as a communication. Talk to it, talk about it with someone—a friend or therapist—and dwell a bit with it. Participants and patients who think and talk about their anger seem to understand it better. Those who react to anger, in the moment, are often those people who have become accustomed to roller-coaster highs and lows.

Before I end this chapter, I'd like to address that latter idea. For some people, the experience of anger—perhaps in adrenalin-producing arguments with another person, especially a significant other—can be addictive. The addiction is to excitement, and it is difficult to give up. In some instances, it becomes a way of living. However, this way of living is actually dangerous to physical and mental health. When anger is transformed into excitement, two expressions come to mind: (1) "He is always looking for a fight" and (2) "Kiss and make up." For some couples, fighting and anger are exciting; they work (or the couple wishes them to work) like aphrodisiacs. They use their anger to seduce each other—a major difficulty in changing this transformation of anger.

So far, I have presented two ways some people effectively deal with anger. They are not actually exclusive. Often the first, talking with a therapist, leads to the second, eliminating the source of anger.

OTHER WAYS OF KEEPING ANGER AS ANGER

Remember the primary result of this research: women transform anger into other pathology. Too often, that pathology is treated and the anger returns. Participants and patients have also described other ways in which they handle their anger. Not all anger need go through the first two suggestions. As emotional energy, a response to anger needs to be *in proportion.* When a situation is self-limiting—an incident and not a condition of life—women seem to transform it. Someone who angers a woman or someone doing something that makes her angry does not always cause headaches, intestinal problems, or an evening of brooding.

Women say that, whenever something angers them, they walk, they jog, they do something physical with that energy. This also seems to give them time to put into perspective whatever happened to anger them. Women write in journals, saying whatever they would like to say. Some psychologists or nurses would call this outlet a discharging of anger—"getting rid of it." If it works, it is far better than the larger thematic content of this chapter. These women are not transforming anger. They recognize it and do not disguise it.

THE CRUX IS THE CONCEALMENT

In coming to a close, I think of a patient, Lisa, who told me:

I can't believe it took me four years of therapy to really feel anger toward my parents. I could not bear to have anything but loving feelings toward them. I could not say that they hurt me and caused me great pain and I was pissed off as hell. Why didn't you tell me?

The taboo not to be angry was so strong in Lisa that she never heard me. When she was ready, she not only said it all but felt it all, after being treated for anxiety attacks, depression, and two surgical procedures. Transformation of anger into pathology takes its toll.

If the Thelmas and Louises of the world are portrayed in films as doomed because they left their sources of anger, the taboo becomes more entrenched. Helena, in *Boxing Helena,* another film, was honest, but a bitch, too. As a result, the audience was prodded to think that dismemberment of her body was appropriate. Is there any wonder? The medium is the message and the message is quite clear: Keep anger silent. There's a better way: Transform it.

The taboo against a woman even feeling anger deserves some reflection—*before* she gets sick; *before* there is violence; *before* there is self-abuse. Silent collusion among ourselves needs to be opened up.

We need to talk, especially about anger. We need to let anger out of our inner recesses and feel it as communication. The consequences of silencing it can be metaphysically likened to *Silence of the Lambs.* We are not lambs, nor do we wish to be.

ABOUT THE STUDY

Purpose

A human response critical to the ideas of women's holistic health promotion is the response of anger. The simultaneity of psychological, physiological, experiential, cultural, and historical interactions when anger is felt, displayed, or repressed clearly demonstrates a holistic all-at-once response with the environment. The purpose of this phenomenological study was to explore the following phenomenological questions:

- What is the existential experience of anger for women as they live it?
- What is the meaning of anger to women as they reflect on it?

Method

A phenomenological method derived from the work of Max van Manen (1990) was used to answer the research questions. Steps in this method include turning to the nature of the lived experience, existential investigation, phenomenological reflection, and phenomenological writing. Women in and out of psychotherapy were participants in the study.

FINDINGS AND CONCLUSIONS

The findings and conclusions of this study have important implications for women's health promotion and clinical practice. The existential experience of anger for women, as they live it, includes (1) psychosomatic occurrences such as headaches, insomnia, ulcers, back pain, and obesity, which are often treated as though no preexisting condition exists and (2) experiential feelings: emptiness, helplessness, fear of losing control, fear of losing relationships, withdrawal, and "nonfeeling." Some essential themes include anger held inward or repressed, inability to express anger, powerlessness, disrupted work and affiliative relationships, and decreased self-esteem. Guilt, self-concept distortions, and self-destructive life processes and patterns also emerge strongly from the data. The implications for women's education and health care intervention have to do with bringing to the patient's consciousness both the underlying dynamics of anger and the healthy versus the "unhealthy" expression of this powerful human response.

REFERENCES

Blakesler, S. (1990, September 20). *Study links emotions to second heart attack. New York Times.*

Duke, P. (1992). *A brilliant madness.* Bantam Books.

Greenson, J. (1993). *It's not what you're eating: It's what's eating you.*

"Health." (1990, December 13). *If anger ruins your day, it can shrink your life. New York Times.*

Lerner, H. (1985). *The dance of anger.* New York: Harper & Row.

Shrever, S. (1986). *Queen of hearts.* New York: Simon & Shuster.

van Manen.

ABOUT THE AUTHOR

I understand that anger is a frequent response. But, I also know there is a taboo against expressing it. Today, I did not feel anger. Probably an odd day. It's not over yet! I am working as the Associate Dean of the Graduate Program at Barry University in Miami. In my today world I say I found an excellent Dean, Judith Balcerski, and with as much fortune, a loving, patient secretary, Karol Geimer. I am working with wonderful faculty, students, and staff.

My two sons, Dennis and Craig, have grown. Dennis will be graduating from NJIT this Spring and Craig may be transferring to Barry next Fall. They taught me a lot about anger, especially the part about control; a hard lesson. We're doing better now. The attachment is more of love and acceptance.

I went into analytic training and slowly began to work with my own anger and the anger of others. More hard lessons.

Good lessons, because I'm learning. And through sharing this learning I hope some recesses, mine and others, open a bit more each day . . . and maybe we will howl at the moon.

9

Motherhood and
Women's Development

Dula F. Pacquiao

*[The study of mothers] . . . is of particular interest for the
psychology of love, holding in it the promise of elucidating a
love that combines intensity and wisdom, a love that is neither exclusive nor finite but at once constant and changing." [The study of women] . . . may bring to psychology a
language of love that encompasses both knowledge and feelings, a language that conveys a different way of imagining
the self in relation to others. (Gilligan, 1984, p. 91)*

The experience of mothering two children has undoubtedly created profound changes in my being and in my views about people
and things around me. Knowing that I have changed has not eased
my feelings about the way things are and how I deal with them. As
my daughter finishes her sophomore year in college and my son,

his third grade in elementary school, I am faced with renewed feelings of confidence and tentativeness about the future. The pain and fears associated with my daughter's leaving home for school are insidiously being replaced by concerns about her choice of career: Will it capitalize on her strengths and at the same time assure her a stable future and some sense of fulfillment? On the other hand, the push to determine and achieve a sense of clarity in my son's capacities presents a nagging strife in completing his homework and supporting his involvement in extracurricular activities so he can "find himself."

I have come to realize the existing differences between my two children. My experiences when my daughter was growing up have not made it any easier to deal with my son. Each child presents different situations, challenging previous ways and necessitating innovative modifications of the treasured past. I am baffled by the changes within me, by my gaining a sense of confidence that "things will turn out well" my moving toward unconditional acceptance of my son, and my being less preoccupied with his academic achievement so long as "he is happy." Many times, mixed feelings of apprehension and guilt jolt me, prodding part of me to expect more from him, as I did from my daughter. Yet, I am disturbed by the thought of rejecting his childish spontaneity and denying myself the chance to relish his cute antics. These are too precious to be ignored.

The case of a Michigan couple who adopted a newborn from Iowa has been prominent in the media in recent months. I was pained to witness the anguish of "Baby Jessica's" adoptive mother, Jan Deboer, over the inevitability of giving her toddler back to her biological parents after the courts declared that the adoption process had been fraudulent. Jan Deboer has maintained that the court failed to recognize the special bond and intimacy between Baby Jessica and the Deboers since birth. She insisted that they have become her parents; since birth, they have shared a life of mutuality and reciprocity that can never be replicated in another time and space.

Indeed, most of my friends who have children stress the fact that parents should enjoy every moment with each child because they "grow up so fast." Each developmental phase is unique and its differences from the next phase can only be fully appreciated within the context in which it occurs. Deprived of this direct experience of the events surrounding each phase, a mother loses the chance to appreciate the rich dimensions and contextualized meanings of that particular life stage.

As a mother, my worries about the prospect of old age are replete with fears of neglect and abandonment by the younger generation. The value premises of self-reliance and independence, which I have carefully nurtured in my children, may someday haunt me when I myself can no longer adhere to them. As children gain more capacities for self-reliance, their sense of respect and gratitude toward their elders presumably lessens. On the contrary, my experience with my daughter since she went to college has been quite positive. We have become friends, confiding our inner secrets to each other. She speaks her mind and is quick to remind me of her rights. I am astounded by my ability to make adjustments, accommodating her imperiousness and feeling less denigrated by it. I am often stunned, disbelieving that I have not reacted in the same way and with the same intensity as I would have in the past. Part of me is ridden with fear and apprehension for abandoning values that have been proven effective and have safely guided me up to this point. Yet, a sense of subtle assurance is fed from within, stifling those doubts with guarded optimism in following my intuitions.

I resonate with the theme of the movie, *Terms of Endearment.* The relationship between the mother (Shirley MacLaine) and her daughter (Debra Winger) evolves from a highly protective and nurturant stage when the child is young to an adversarial and conflict-ridden temporal stage during adolescence and early adulthood when the child begins to assert her own perspective. In fact, the rift between them has resulted in Shirley MacLaine's conspicuous absence at the wedding of her only child. As mother and daughter live apart, experiencing difficulties and self-realizations about their own lives, they become more aware of their similarities and the strength that each one provides the other, and how these are predicated on a long-standing intimacy that existed between them. After being told of her terminal illness and having accepted the prognosis, Debra Winger is convinced that her mother, rather than her husband, should become the primary caretaker of her two young sons. He confirms that the nurturant capacity of his mother-in-law mirrors the capacity he has often observed in his wife. He agrees that his wife's desired arrangement is best for his young children.

Terms of Endearment effectively portrays the potential for growth in both mother and child that can flourish within the context of mothering. It is testimonial to the supremacy of women's affiliative and caring prowess in promoting the welfare and protection of others. The film demonstrates what authors have identified as a central achievement of motherhood: the creation of a relationship of equality, collegiality, and intimacy between daughters and their mothers. Transformation to this type of relationship is made possible by a mother's understanding that the initial inequality between parent and child is only temporary (Feuerstein, 1980; Hobbs, 1982; Shure & Spivack, 1978). Such a relationship results in the instrumental enrichment of those involved.

My Question

Delving into my own experience with mothering, I have uncovered more mysteries and complexities about the phenomenon instead of clarifying or validating my life as a mother. Hence, my quest in knowing "what's it like being a mother" is prompted by listening to other mothers' experiences. Through their thoughtful reflection on these experiences, they in turn can validate the existence of others like myself and find affirmation of their own lives.

THE MEANING OF MOTHERHOOD: WHAT'S IT ALL ABOUT?

The experience of giving birth to a child is replete with new meanings that encompass changes in defining one's self-image, values, roles, priorities, and purposes in life. This episode is accompanied by a reconceptualization of one's past; a host of insights are given birth by the mothering experience. A more realistic valuation of oneself is prompted by a simultaneously occurring panoply of responsibilities. Some are new, others are recurrent but perceived differently in both meaning and intensity.

Carol (mother of three boys, aged 15, 13, and 8 years) described her experience with the birth of her first son:

It changed everything. Initially I had a lot of difficulty. When I was pregnant the first time, I received a Mother's Day card and I didn't like it at all. It took me sometime after he was born to even refer to myself as a mother. It was not at all part of my identity. The responsibility of caring for someone that is continuous, it is always there, you can't quit. I think of my initial adjustment to the loss of freedom, loss of time, but it was also very nice to have a child. I was surprised right after he was born how maternal I felt in terms of how thrilled I was to have a baby . . . it is so hard to describe.

Carol's experience supports Rubin's (1984) findings regarding maternal psychological adaptations to pregnancy. Women are found to move from an initial stage characterized by ambivalent feelings about the pregnancy and self-attentiveness to a stage of realization of the baby's existence as a separate being, prompting attention to its successful preservation. As pregnant women face imminent birth and signs confirming presence of another being inside them, concerns begin to focus on the prospective child. Rubin believes that this is a necessary adjustment that prepares mothers to assume their caretaking role after birth.

Motherhood is considered to be one of the most significant developmental tasks of adulthood and indicative of an individual's reaching maturity (Dion, 1985; Hoffman & Manis, 1979). Mothering tasks require unwavering commitment toward responsibility, advocacy, and generosity for others, and these are recognized as hallmark attributes of adult maturity.

A great awakening to this strong sense of responsibility was echoed by the mothers in this study after their first child was born. Marion described her first encounter with her daughter (her only child) after delivery:

She [the nurse] took so long to bring her to me. When she came, she was the cleanest child I have ever seen. She had a little bit of blood, she had bangs. That's what took her [the nurse] so long. Things were just viewed differently after that. Here is responsibility. It's not me-and-my-husband anymore. This is another life that needs to be nurtured, that needs to be protected. I can't put it into words. She became more or less the center of what we did.

Several studies contend that central to the conceptualization of morality in women is the understanding of responsibility and relationships (Chodorow, 1978; Gilligan, 1982; Lyons, 1983). Responsibility orientation is rooted in a sense of connection and relatedness with others. Among women, the principle underlying the ethic of care is a psychological logic of relationships in which moral problems are defined within the context of obligation to exercise care and avoid hurt (Gilligan, 1982).

Mothers I spoke with associated a child's birth with tremendous feelings of joy, pride, a sense of accomplishment, a sense of continuity, and an opportunity to recreate a better life for themselves. Similar findings by other studies are noted in the literature. Chodorow (1978) believed that, among women, motherhood in part regains a sense of being mothered. Descriptions offered by this mother support these findings:

This is the best thing I've ever accomplished. I'm doing something for the future. I am enabled to give them opportunities that I did not have. It's a feeling of accomplishment, an extension of myself to the future, also of pride that they are a part of me.

Chodorow (1974, 1978) posited that female identity formation, in contrast to that of males, takes place in an ongoing relationship because girls are generally parented by the same gender. Because female identity formation involves continuity in the daughters' relationships with the same mother since birth, mothers correlatively see their daughters as extensions of themselves. One mother put her birth experience within the context of her previous life:

I come from a very large family; I have five sisters and four brothers. There were a lot of things in my background that I felt could have been different. If I were growing up now, there are some things that I wish I could have experienced that I would like my daughter to experience. And, pretty much, she has.

Attempting to understand why she wanted a baby, Slater (1977) wrote:

When I am feeling cheerful and OK, I see it in a different way: that having a baby has been a way of exploring and recovering part of myself, of somehow reliving and reshaping my own childhood and, through it, perhaps getting a bit mature. (p. 12)

An Irish-Catholic mother of ten discovered (Fairweather, McDonough, & McFudyean, 1984):

. . . it was breast feeding that first really made me aware of my body, the pleasure and pride it could give me. When I fed my first baby, I felt the most intense emotion, and sense of happiness and pride, that I'd ever felt in my life. (pp. 161–162)

For many women, being a mother provides profound experience in human connection. Both their childhood and their adult experiences contribute to the evolution of this sense of connection. Women are found to have a much greater sense of the pleasures derived from close connection with children's physical, emotional, and mental growth than men (Miller, 1986). Reflective of the sense of connection that has been identified by Gilligan (1982), motherhood is an opportunity to establish one's legacy and shape a better life for oneself by building a positive future for others. Central to mothering are the formation and sustenance of affiliations and closeness with others.

New Ways of Relating with Others

Motherhood ushers in a state of flux affecting relationships with others. Among the mothers studied, their conversations reflected

profound changes in their present relationships and reformula-
tions of their past affiliations with others. Judith Ballou (1978)
contended that reattachment of rapprochement with one's mother
is an important task of pregnancy and motherhood. It enables the
new mother to see herself as a competent adult capable of fulfilling the responsibilities of giving birth.

*Mary aptly elucidated this phenomenon: "I finally began to re-
alize that children love you unconditionally, and your parents
love you unconditionally."* Margaret admits that having gone
through motherhood herself has made her more appreciative of
her own mother: *"I didn't realize how hard she worked until then
because she always stayed home. Everything was always in order
and she was always available."*

Young girls are noted to transform and internalize their mothers' values, ideas, and ethics in developing their own model and
standards of mothering (Berg, 1986). Ballou (1978) stated that the
developmental tasks associated with pregnancy and motherhood
include feeling and behaving like a mother, especially like one's
own mother. Emergence of positive feelings toward one's mother
indicates development of empathic understanding of others as separate from oneself.

The mothering experience fosters the development of empathy
and the sensitivity necessary for taking the role of the particular
other (Gilligan, 1982). Philosopher Nel Noddings (1984) concep-
tualizes caring as a type of "generous rationality." Empathy, according to Noddings, "does not involve projection but reception
. . . receiving the other into oneself," hence being able to see and
feel with the other (pp. 1, 30, 186).

Mothers depict the reciprocity and mutuality of closeness, the
sensitivity, and the feelings of happiness that develop between
them and their children. Motherhood also connotes inevitable personal sacrifice (Nuttbrock & Freudiger, 1991) as well as added responsibility and difficulties. These are balanced by a greater sense
of fulfillment and productivity.

Sue went back to full-time employment a few weeks after her
children were born. She reported feelings of profound pleasure
when her young sons react with great anticipation to her coming
home from work. *"I cannot imagine what's it like coming home
to an empty apartment after work. They make me feel important*

and needed." She related the early difficulty of commuting from New Jersey to Brooklyn, where both she and her husband work.

My children did not like to sleep. It was like one continuous, sleepless night. One time, I was coming home and I was extremely sleepy, so when I saw one car parked by the curb, I did exactly that so I [could] take a nap. Do you know that it was my husband in the other car? He too, was taking a nap. We still laugh about this incident.

Belenky, Clinchy, Goldberger, and Tarule (1986) have identified constructed knowledge as the highest level of cognitive achievement among women. Constructivists are found to have the ability to reassert themselves by integrating their subjective, personal knowledge with their rational, abstract knowledge. Akin to Gilligan's (1982) responsibility orientation, women constructivists' moral response to conflicts is a caring response. They try to resolve conflicts within the context of each person's perspective, needs, and goals, in order to come up with the best possible solution for everyone. Problem solving is based on an empathic understanding of everyone involved.

Sue's anecdote reflected her ability to view hardships as mutable and within the framework of caring for her young children. The caring principle she invoked in this situation becomes the basis from which all other aspects of her life at that particular time and space are placed in perspective. Hence, she finds humor and hope in an otherwise pitiful and desperate situation. The process of promoting the growth and development of children is an important source of growth and development for parents as well (Galinsky, 1981; Loevinger, 1976). Sue's experience elaborates the meaning of growth in her capacity for empathy and caring as a consequence of her maternal practice.

MOTHERS' VIEWS OF THEMSELVES

Redefinition and reconceptualization of oneself occur with motherhood. The experience of mothering evokes different sensitivities and qualities in one's being.

After her marriage and the birth of her children, philosopher Sara Ruddick (1984) found herself dislocated within the world of intellectuals in academe where she had robustly thrived previously. Upon discovering solace in rereading Virginia Woolf, she explicated these changes within her.

I seemed to learn new ways of attending to the natural world, and to people, especially children. This kind of attending was intimately concerned with caring; . . . the more I attended, the more deeply I cared. The domination of feeling by thought, which I had worked so hard to achieve, was breaking down . . . I allowed feeling to inform my most abstract thinking. (pp. 150–151)

Motherhood involves resetting one's priorities in life. Resurgence of previously suppressed values displaces and rearranges one's goals and purposes. The mothers studied described attention to the affiliative, affective, and relationship-oriented tasks in contrast to the deeply instrumental, career-oriented objectives that were formerly regarded as important. They spoke of relearning the world, reliving their own childhood in their experiences with their own children.

Mary, the youngest mother in the cohort, has a 12-year-old son. She remembered:

It made me slow down and appreciate the process of life more. You go through your own childhood and when you're a young adult you get so involved with your school and your career, making an income, and then suddenly when you have a baby, you have to slow down. Your time is now divided. I began to relive a lot of what I enjoyed growing up. I got to do it again with my son.

The tasks associated with mothering entail different abilities, and mothers are confronted with new challenges that cast doubts on their previous achievements. They understand that motherhood roles cannot be proficiently met by the same skills that have been successful in the past.

Margaret (mother of two daughters, aged 19 and 17 years, and a 12-year-old boy) who just finished her doctorate, described her feelings:

It is a humbling experience. It's the one thing I've done in which I feel I have not done so well as my other accomplishments. It is difficult to even know when you have done a good job of it . . . the outcomes are not as easily measurable.

Similarly, Sue (mother of two boys, aged 12 and 8 years) noted: *"I was disappointed with myself trying to be a good mother and a professional. Finally, I realized that I can't be as good in both of these roles at the same time."*

Ruddick (1980) stated that a wisdom is gained through maternal practice and maternal thinking: the capacity for empathy. She defines empathy as the ability to imagine and be sensitive to the interior life of others. Self-awareness is the prelude to empathic development. For Margaret and Sue, self-awareness has aided them in setting the ground rules for their interaction with others and their definition of themselves. They are also able to bring their unconscious thoughts into the conscious realm by legitimating their subjective feelings about themselves within the objective realities of motherhood.

MOTHERS' VIEWS ABOUT THEIR CHILDREN

The pleasures associated with motherhood are not limited to concrete, obvious accomplishments or deeds by the children. Rather, they are inclusive of the ambiguous, almost mystical qualities in their children, which can only be appreciated by a mother who has been embedded within an intimate relationship with the child.

Jean (mother of three; two are in college and one is in high school) identified this situation as one of her happiest as a mother:

When my youngest daughter was in elementary school, she wanted to get the singing solo part in a school play. She wanted this very badly and she practiced and practiced. And it came down between her and a girl who was a good friend of hers. She did not get the part. When we went to the recital, my daughter was one of the background people in the chorus. And when her friend started singing the solo, I looked at my daughter to see if she would get disappointed because I know how badly she wanted this. And I remember looking at her, and her face was just shining, looking at her friend and mouthing words of encouragement for her friend. That really made me very happy. It made me see what a really good, strong person she was that she can have the strength at that age . . . not to feel diminished or cheated.

Jean's proud smile and moist eyes were apparent as she related this incident. She admitted that she has repeated this story many times.

Carol narrated an incident involving her youngest son:

He was four then, and we had a lot of company that day. He was just running about when he ran into me and said, "Oh, you're just what I need." It made me feel good. He just needed to connect. He was not upset or anything. He needs that sometimes . . . some reassurance. It was so spontaneous and he looked so relieved when he said that.

Motherhood provides profound experience in human intimacy, which, in turn, initiates epistemological revolution (Belenky et al., 1986). Maternal practice has enhanced these mothers' sensitivity toward their children. Their empathic skills permit an interpretation of the situations within the perspective of their children. These mothers have essentially become the voices of their children by elaborating the meanings of the experience from the vantage point of the child. Through maternal thinking, they have gained intimate knowledge of their children and become enabled to understand them in their own terms.

Ruddick (1980) identified the primary concerns of maternal thinking as preservation of the vulnerable child and fostering of its growth. A mother, according to Ruddick, "must shape natural growth in such a way that her child becomes the sort of adult that she can appreciate and others can accept." In the anecdotes provided by Margaret and Carol, it is apparent that the qualities exhibited by their children in these situations manifest the same values they uphold.

Similarly, Gilligan (1982) argued that women's definition of moral problems is based on the principle of obligation to exercise care and avoid hurt. Miller (1986) theorized that women's position in society has encouraged them to concentrate on the emotions and reactions of others. In turn, this concentration has developed in them, more than in men, a greater sensitivity to the pleasures of close connection with their children's physical, emotional, and mental growth.

Mothers with grown daughters described an intimate, friendly relationship with them. Jean went back to get her baccalaureate degree when her two daughters were attending high school and middle school. Because she did not know how to use a typewriter, her daughter would type her papers (and would be fascinated by what she learned about nursing and psychology). Jean recalled:

We used to study together. They come to me when something bothers them, when they're upset. The other day, the youngest asked me, why do people douche? I want your opinion as a nurse. My son will likely go to his Dad more.

I resonate with Jean's experience. One evening, I received a frantic call from my daughter, who attends college. She sounded very upset; she had been diagnosed as having a vaginal yeast infection. She said, *"I did not know what it was, so I went to the clinic and they did a Pap smear"* (her first time). I remember asking her if she wised to speak with her Dad after our conversation, and she replied, *"No."* My daughter has always enjoyed her Dad's "fun" company and considers him a "nice" man. When it came to intimate, womanly subjects, however, she always approached me.

In contrast to fathers, mothers tend to interview and ask questions rather than lecture their daughters. Question posing is at the heart of maternal practice, which draws out children's feelings and latent knowledge (Shure & Spivack, 1978). In fact, woman talk is characterized by Spacks (1982) as focused on small shared truths conducted through "gossip." Gossip, according to Spacks, concerns the personal and the particular in exchanges that penetrate the truth. Woman talk is self-revealing rather than probing; it is indicative of knowing in a collaborative manner, which achieves trust building among intimates.

Unlike that of most men, women's caring is likely to be provided in a connected mode. Most daughters have indicated that their mothers valued them on the daughters' own terms, characterizing their relationships with the mothers as built on trust (Gilligan, 1982; Lyons, 1983). One primary task of maternal practice is the creation of mother–daughter relationships that are underscored by equality, collegiality, and intimacy (Feuerstein, 1980; Hobbs, 1982; Shure & Spivack, 1978). This kind of relationship is an elaboration of women's connected mode of knowing, which promotes fusion and acceptance.

By contrast, tales of lingering unhappiness in adulthood, among daughters who were deprived earlier of maternal attention and nurturance, have been documented in the literature. They have underscored each child's need to be looked on with joy and basic approval by a delighted parent. Daughters who suffered maternal neglect expressed feeling unreal to themselves (Bassoff, 1992). Virginia Woolf (1985), who was a victim of sexual abuse at an early age, wrote that she was:

> . . . not being connected to her own experience . . . living behind a screen, lying in a grave and seeing through a film of "semi-transparent yellow," being wrapped in cotton wool, deadened and disembodied.

She described her mother as a "general presence." De Salvo (1989) has depicted Virginia Woolf as a prototype of an unprotected child whose early experience with sexual abuse affected her sense of integrity and worth as a human being. Personal accounts of incest victims were also noted to be filled with portrayals of distant, unavailable mothers, and the children's hunger for maternal nurturance (Herman, 1981).

Rose Wilder Lane's diary relates her underlying unhappiness and persistent lack of a sense of wholeness as a result of her harsh, stoic childhood. Her mother, Laura Ingalls Wilder, insisted on strong instrumental expectations from her daughter and gave very little emotional nurturance. Throughout her life, Rose continued to yearn for closeness and intimacy with her mother—a yearning that drained her emotionally in the end (Fellman, 1990).

DEALING WITH SOCIETY AND DEVELOPMENTAL CHANGES IN CHILDREN

Because the tasks of mothering are constantly changing, they require innovations for each phase in the child's life. Motherhood deals with transformation of human beings. Growth involves change, which in turn involves learning. Raising children exemplifies a totally different kind of learning. What mothers learned yesterday is not good enough and does not apply today (Miller, 1986). Thus, the work involved in mothering necessitates a different kind of learning—a complex, evolutionary, and inclusive learning of all facets of human potential.

Mothers clearly identify illness in their children as a source of stress. They are disappointed when children do not live up to their potential. The mothers are aware of changes and different challenges associated with each developmental phase of life. Caretaking and nurturance of a helpless human being, which is the priority in infancy, shifts toward value inculcation, discipline, and school achievement as the child progresses through the succeeding growth stages.

Marion stated: *"When they're little, my word is enough. But as they get older, they will be exposed to other things which I have no control over."*

Fear that their children will become involved with drugs or will contract AIDS was verbalized by these mothers. They were aware that problems are developmentally related and they fully anticipated dealing with different problems as they appear. Ellen (mother of two boys and a girl) admitted to having:

> *. . . extreme difficulty letting go, especially with my teenage daughter. I know that this culture is different from*

where I was brought up, but I am always fearful that she will get pregnant or get AIDS. It is harder to take care of girls.

Mothering is not limited to the confines of one's home. As their children move toward teenage years, these mothers are confronted by outside forces beyond their control, in addition to the naturally emerging developmental changes in their children. Promotion of value continuity is made more difficult by media influence, which tends to depict values contradictory to those espoused at home. Voicing the same concerns as these mothers, the National Teachers' Association and Tipper Gore have initiated political pressure on the media to elevate standards in children's programs.

Carol related her dilemma with her eldest boy:

[He] hits the second one when he is upset. He still does it up to now. We (my husband and I) tried so many things to stop it but it just took so long until we found something that worked. We get worried when something like this is left on its own and becomes a pattern. We let him sit progressively longer. He did not like to do it at all. It was a way of showing him a nonviolent way of punishment. It was difficult because I did not want to hurt his feelings and at the same time we have to teach him a sense of fairness. His younger brother is much smaller . . . .

Carol's concerns reflect Ruddick's (1980) supposition that the primary tasks of maternal thinking and practice are (1) to protect the vulnerable child and (2) to foster the child's growth. Similarly, Galinsky (1981) has stated that adult development regularly proceeds in the direction that supports the developmental progress of children. Both these findings underline the inherent responsibility orientation among females, which operates around the ethic of care (Gilligan, 1982).

Other studies have found that reciprocal influence on each other is exerted by the behaviors of mothers and their children. Children, through their characteristics and behavior, exert influence on parental behavior and parent-child interactions, thus contributing to their own development (Bell & Harper, 1977; Belsky,

1984; Stern, 1977). Correlatively, responsiveness on the part of the mother has been shown to relate to child behavior in interpersonal domains (Roggman, Langlois, & Hubbs-Tait, 1987). Some mothers in the group studied admitted to deliberately creating a pathway for successful adult life, which they perceived as realistic gender expectations in society.

Carol is worried that her 15-year-old son's academic abilities are not adequately defined in terms of his future career. Unlike the second son, who excels in math and science, the older boy's aptitude is geared toward English and history. She believes that they *"are more nebulous in terms of career choices." Society still "expects men to have a good job."*

Mothers provide early guidance, to ensure their children's survival outside of the home environment. Knowledge of the individual child's unique needs is addressed within the same value premises that the parents uphold. Continuity in a value orientation that transcends developmental phases is apparent.

Identifying herself as a feminist, Mary believed that it is just as important for girls to achieve as boys: *"If I had a girl, I would do the same thing, like I'd try to make sure she had a good job."*

Marion, an African American who lives in an upper-middle-income section in a suburb, reflected on the difficulty of bringing up a son instead of a daughter. She would *"worry more about his safety . . . it is tough for a Black male teenager to be walking, even in a nice, White neighborhood. People tend to be suspicious and afraid of them."*

Concern with violence among boys was shared by Jean, an African American who is married to a White theologian. Speaking about her son, Jean argued: *"We have to make a conscious effort since their toys are geared to [violence]. We would talk to him regarding violence with guns. He liked model toys so we would ask him to make a cargo helicopter that would help transport people. We also did not have television. We read a lot."* Jean and her husband have attempted to provide shared toys for their son and two daughters, but she has noticed that *"they tend to be attracted and play more with sex-stereotyped toys."*

Sports involvement is one area into which mothers steer their sons, because of societal expectations or because their sons indicate a strong interest in sports. Sue, who has two young sons, pointed out: *"We have to since they ask for it. Their peers are all playing in these games, so they also want to join."*

The significance of childhood play has been underscored in terms of its effects on the child's emotional, moral, cognitive, and social development (Piaget, 1952, 1965). Sex differences in children's play have been found to exist and to foster development of gender-related behaviors (Lever, 1976). Parent–toddler dyads during play depict more positive nonverbal reactions when the toys involved are stereotyped for the child's and parent's gender (Caldera, Huston, & O'Brien, 1989). Greater incidence of violence has been demonstrated in men's stories than in women's, which are projected into situations of personal affiliation (Pollak & Gilligan, 1982).

CONCEPTS OF AN IDEAL CHILD

In defining characteristics of an "ideal child," mothers in this group identified attributes that nurture connectedness and responsibility orientation. They viewed these qualities as gender-independent, elucidating Gilligan's (1982) supposition that women's definition of morality hinges on the caring principle. These values, which transcend both gender and age of children, support sustenance of relationships and connectedness with others.

The mother of a 12-year-old boy embellished these qualities:

I hope that he becomes a good person, that he is ethical, truthful, and can get along with others. All the education, all the money, it just won't mean a thing.

Jean, a registered nurse whose two children are attending Ivy League colleges, made this point:

I want them to be happy, fulfill themselves. I want them to love, not coopted by material norms. I want them to do something because they love it. I don't want them to pick something because of prestige. I don't want them to become physicians because in our culture they are looked up to. I want them to find what they love to do. Happiness is satisfaction with yourself, professionally and personally. And the love of life that comes from that.

Another mother who has three sons commented that her goal for each of them was:

. . . a child [who] is confident and considerate, well-behaved but not constricted to be his own person. I don't think my conceptualization of a good child will be any different if she is a girl.

Studies of dyadic interactions between mothers and their young children revealed correspondence between mothers' internal models of relationships and children's behavioral and developmental status (Crowell & Feldman, 1988; Leichter, 1984). Correspondence between mothers' self-reported and observed childrearing strategies has likewise been demonstrated (Kochanska, Kuczynski, & Radke-Yarrow, 1989).

Mothers in interracial marriages characterize their children to be sensitive and tolerant of ethnic differences because of their natural exposure to both cultures at home. Some believe that their children perceive the world as "colorless" because of what they observe at home. An atmosphere of respect and mutual tolerance exists between spouses and children who are deliberately exposed to both cultures. Jean, who has the oldest children in the cohort, is an African American married to a White southerner. She noted that her children:

. . . are able to move cross-culturally with ease. I saw this with my son. He went to Elizabeth High School. He had Black friends, White friends, smart and not-so-bright friends. He was an athlete so he had friends who were not so intellectual. I have seen him move in and out of the Black dialect. He'll joke about it. When he went to Dartmouth, he said, "Well, up here with all these White people in New Hampshire, they don't think us Black folks know how to

*talk." He can be very intellectual and articulate, very bicul-
tural and aware of how to behave in different situations.
My daughter in Harvard feels the pressure of polarization
in campuses. She has absolutely resisted this and she found
a group called SHARE which is looking into cross-cultural
dialogue.*

Mothers encourage strongly their children's awareness and appreciation of their ethnic heritage. When the spouse is from another cultural group, they expose their children to both groups.
Mary prefers her husband to talk to their son in Chinese at home.
Carol, who is married to a Filipino, believes that her children
should be exposed to the Filipino way of life in the Philippines and
looks forward to their summer vacations there. Sue, a Filipino married to a Jewish American, is grateful that her children had the opportunity to know both sets of grandparents before both their
grandfathers died. Marion decorates her home with African art,
subscribes to African American magazines, and encourages her
daughter to play jazz pieces at the piano.

Motherhood builds on affiliative relationships that promote
continuity and create legacy. Ruddick (1980) explained that, typically, a mother shapes the natural growth of her children in such
a way that they become adults whom she can appreciate and others can accept. The criterion of her success is the production of a
young adult acceptable to her group. Mothers within interracial
marriages demonstrate strategies that promote their children's
survival and acceptance in both ancestral groups.

GOING BACK TO WORK

Mothers who went back to full-time employment soon after their
children were born described their initial difficulty with this decision, the continuing hardships this arrangement posed on them,
and their struggle with persistent guilt.

Berg (1986) has cited evidence of profound guilt consuming
women who combine employment and motherhood, to the extent
that these internal conflicts thwart their drive for achievement

(Horner, 1972). In a survey by *Working Woman* magazine, men and women predominantly disapproved of mothers' working outside the home when their children are young (Hewlett, 1983). Increasing enrollment of women in higher education in other countries such as Germany and Japan has proportionally delayed their marriages and first childbirth, confirming the perception that women who are actively pursuing college degrees are not ready to have children (Blossfield & Jaenichen, 1992; Kumagai, 1984). College women's thrust toward expansion of their careers has not resulted in a change in their childbearing expectations (Baber & Monaghan, 1988). Young college women have been found to perceive marital and parental roles as interactive with a woman's job performance (Etaugh & Poertner, 1992).

In fact, motherhood has remained the greatest dilemma to the feminist movement in terms of achieving consensus regarding its responsibilities and effects on gender equality issues (Rowbotham, 1989; Trebilcot, 1984). Although the movement has adequately raised women's consciousness to ask questions relevant to motherhood, which had previously been accepted and taken for granted as the primary role of women, it has not achieved consensus regarding the role of motherhood in women's lives, the effects of motherhood on achievement of gender equality, and the delineation of effective strategies for addressing the responsibilities of motherhood while maintaining one's career.

Sue expressed her frustration at her inability to make plans: *"There are times that you just have to drop everything because of the children, like when they have school activities I have to attend or the babysitter does not show up."*

Margaret spoke of her unhappiness at home—the relentless "lack of order," her children's "constant complaining," and her inability to resolve conflicts. Both her mother and her mother-in-law had stayed home with their children.

The fact that I have been working and being the primary breadwinner was thought of as strange. Nobody said it was a good thing to do (going back to school to obtain my doctorate). Like, when I finished my doctorate, I was not as happy as I thought I would be. My mother-in-law said, "Oh,

it was hard on the family." She never indicated the hard
work I did. My children always thought I was strange, I was
never like the other mothers. I am always in school, always
doing something. I never fit in.

I resonate with these mothers. My young daughter in elementary school blurted out one day, *"Why can't you be like Michael's*
mother? She is always at home with him." She used to stay at
Michael's house after school and on those mornings when I had to
report early to work. My 9-year-old son just recently requested
whether I can be a "lunch aide" at his school like his "Grandma
Bernie" (his baby sitter after school). I turned speechless every-
time they made those statements. There were not many good reasons to argue against their positions without putting them or
others down. I have always felt out-of-place standing in school, not
knowing anyone, while waiting for the bell to ring for my children's dismissal.

However, since my daughter started college, she thinks it's
"cool" that I have a doctorate. In contrast, when I sent a letter for
my son to be excused from school so he could attend my graduation, he said, *"My teachers were congratulating me. I had no idea*
what's it all about. They were asking me what your degree was
so I told them, you're a nurse."

Fairweather et al. (1984) formulated that the feminist movement's failure to understand the issue of motherhood is rooted in
its inability to recognize that women themselves bring a psychological dimension to motherhood that needs to be explored instead of just being looked on as a social phenomenon. The
experiences of these mothers with active careers need to be examined phenomenologically within their own uniquely situated
context.

Margaret was angered and hurt when her daughter refused to
decorate their Christmas tree with her younger brother. She
wanted to bake cookies at her friend's house instead. Margaret
confessed: *"I don't know how to bake cookies. Or she tells me her*
friend has a nice garden. I don't like gardening."

Indeed, young children communicate their own formulation of
what a mother should be, which often compounds guilt feelings

in their working mothers. Berg (1986) defined guilt as an "excoriating interface between women's conflicting roles which is hidden, erupting, disguised, insidious and insistent" (p. 23). Guilt, according to Berg, affects mothers in four dimensions: (1) relations with their children, (2) jobs, (3) marital relationships, and (4) their sense of self. Guilt exists regardless of whether the woman was forced to work for financial reasons.

Mothers in this group described varied patterns of mothering, which require reflective decisions in balancing motherhood and career roles. Working mothers communicate a special influence on their children.

Margaret, who identifies herself as a nurse and lawyer, aptly stated:

I think they learned from me that they can do whatever they want to do. I don't think they're limited because they have always seen me do a variety of things. Like they would never think that a woman could not do that. It would never occur to them. My kids really know how to write a real good term paper and I guess I did show them that. If their friends have a term paper, they come over here and work on it.

Mothers who stayed home when their kids were younger and went back to work gradually afterward, felt no regrets about giving up their jobs for their children. Retrospectively, they discovered some reservations about their decision. Thus, combining roles of motherhood and career poses difficulties for both groups of mothers. For instance, Mary wished that her family could move into a house (from an apartment in the Bronx) by the time her son was a bit older. Because she did not work, it took the family longer to save for a house. Nevertheless, she rationalized that if she had not gotten pregnant so soon, she would have been able to get a house before her son was born.

Carol, who was working full-time until her first baby was born, admitted that she should not have stayed so long away from work. She has worked part-time since the youngest of her three sons started elementary school. She feels strongly against leaving "small" children to someone else "full-time." She did not have to work in order for their family to survive (she is married to a physician).

It would not have been as difficult to get back to work if I worked part-time sooner. Most of the people I have worked with have left this area and it is difficult even just to get references.

Studies of mother–infant attachment point out the critical influence of early interactions between mother and child that tend to persist and become stable in adulthood (Belsky, 1984; Bowlby, 1980; Stern, 1977). Internalized models of attachments are found to guide future behaviors and to formulate expectations and adaptations (Bretherton, 1985). If women's priorities are geared toward nurturance and promotion of attachments with others, it is understandable that decisions relevant to balancing career and mothering tasks will remain as sources of perennial conflicts and guilt for mothers. As Ruddick (1980) pointed out, if the primary task of maternal practice is the protection and preservation of the child, leaving a young, vulnerable child presupposes deep soul-searching with concomitant heavy guilt feelings on the part of the mother.

DEALING WITH DISAPPOINTMENTS

The mothers studied demonstrated a strong capacity to reformulate episodes of disappointments with their children into epics of incredible humanistic growth and character development. Mothers appear to have infinite resources to bring out the positive aspects in their children in times of difficulties. They have the capacity to stretch and accommodate, recycling a negative event into opportunities for reconciliation and healing.

One mother's sadness and disappointment were evident as she spoke of the time when her oldest son was counseled out of the university he was attending. He was advised to go to a junior college because of poor academic performance in his freshman year. She always believed that the pathway to success, which parents can provide for their children's future, is through "good education" and ensuring the children's success in school. Initially, she was as devastated and embarrassed as her son was. Her anger was transformed to an empathic understanding after she observed some positive progress and satisfaction in her son. That experience changed her perspective about the nature of success:

> *A successful child is a happy child. Success is not just getting good grades. It is being contented and at peace with oneself. In fact, I was never an outstanding student but I was always happy growing up.*

Jean narrated the transformation in her son, the eldest of her three children. *"Being a bright, minority student in high school,"* he was sought after by Ivy League schools such as Dartmouth University. His future postsecondary school seemed assured; yet, after two years in college:

> *[He] fell in love, the girl got pregnant so they got married. My husband and I did a lot of soul-searching, wondering if we should have done something different. At the time, we were very upset. But he has made a good life for himself. They could have gotten an abortion which they did not. He quit school and work. His wife went back to school right after the baby was born and we are attending her graduation next week. She will go to work and he will go back to college, and this time he makes it on his own. They'll do it themselves, the hard way.*

Jean spoke with pride and admiration for her son:

> *His in-laws, who had initial difficulty accepting him (they're French Canadians), are also very impressed of my son.*

Women's emphasis on sustenance of relationships with others allows them to describe events in a language of intimacy that is characteristic of the close connections they develop with their children. These mothers show profound capacity for empathy by understanding their children in the children's own terms during episodes of extremely disappointing situations. Disappointments are perceived as times for strengthening other qualities in one's being. These mothers' personal knowledge about their children, marked by intimacy and caring, enables them to fully appreciate the transformation in their children—a transformation that is all-inclusive rather than fragmented into distinct components such as scholastic achievement.

THE NATURE OF MOTHERING

This group of mothers confirmed a unique role they perform for their children in contrast to their husbands. They described how the special relationship they have with their children flourished through their maternal practice.

Mary explained her perception of the differences between herself and her husband pertinent to child care:

> *I think I nurture my son more than my husband does. I try to take him where he wants to go . . . and not have these expectations ahead of time that he has to meet. I try to be responsive to his cues rather than . . . it's the nurturing piece. I just seem to be more involved, more in tune to what's going on in his life.*

Mary described a "good mother" as someone who "really cares and she's there . . . like, the kid is ready for school the next day. He has a clean shirt to wear. I know that some of these things are so materialistic but they count, in a way."

Miller (1986) contended that women's development is organized around building and maintaining affiliations, which predisposes their equating loss of relationships as tantamount to loss of self. Hence, attention to the total well-being of the child, both affective and instrumental, is inherent in the connected ways of knowing typified by these mothers.

Mothers who worked full-time depicted the all-encompassing, ambiguous roles they perform. Comparing themselves with their spouses, these mothers reflected the nature of this caring and attentiveness toward their children:

I think fathers are task-oriented. It is the mother who knows what size underwear everybody wears, constantly knowing when a kid has to go up a certain size, or when to put away the summer clothes . . . just having a broad picture of everything. I could be at work but if it's, like, mid-October, I could be thinking about their Halloween costumes. My husband tells me I worry too much. When the kids need immunization, I would research and find out what side effects they have. I look into everything and it is exhausting.

Another mother voiced her inability to stop being *"controlling. I need to know all the details, making sure everything is in order."*

One mother explicated her role during times when her children were ill: *"My husband participated but I took more care of the children. I was the one who took off from work when the kids were sick, not him."*

In delineating the nature of their maternal practices, these mothers confirmed the centrality of responsibility orientation, which emphasizes the caring principle. Relationship orientation is underlined by their attending to details, giving care in a connected mode whose primary purpose is the understanding of the child on his or her own terms, and placing the child's best interest before their own. Maternal practice, in this sense, creates empathic attention to the totality of the child's being, through heightened sensitivity toward every aspect about the child.

The mothers indicated strong involvement in their children's education. They shared common expectations that learning should take place in a safe, nurturant environment. When situations had required drastic measures, they had taken decisive action on behalf of their children. Mary offered this anecdote about her son:

He went to Catholic school for kindergarten and I decided to put him in public school for first grade, thinking that they have more resources. The emphasis in Catholic school at that level was on socialization while [in] . . . public schools [the emphasis] was on phonics. It was playing catch-up with him all year. I was angry because he was going into a system totally unprepared and here I was, a teacher and supposed to know something about education. I taught him how to read myself. The teacher kept telling me that he needs to mature. I just wouldn't buy that. Then his wristbands were stolen and he was beaten one day after school. So I had him taken out and put back in a Catholic school. He's been there ever since.

Margaret recalled her frustration in dealing with the school and health care system involving her children. *"I was not prepared for the mediocrity, the incompetence of teachers, and the lack of discipline in public schools. I felt that my children were treated insignificantly."* She too transferred her children to a Catholic school.

It has been empirically documented that early childhood experiences influence the social, emotional, and cognitive development of children (Maccoby & Martin, 1983). Secure mother–child attachments have been found to nurture cognitive development in children as measured by their reading abilities. The role of the mother as the early, primary caregiver has been strongly implicated in childhood school achievement (Bruner, 1985; Bus & Van Ijzendoorn, 1988; Heath, 1983; Pelligrini, Brody, & Sigel, 1985; Sulzby, 1986). Education is considered a critical pathway toward growth achievement, which is one of the fundamental purposes of maternal practice.

Patience and tolerance of their children are echoed by full-time mothers, especially when they compare themselves with their husbands. Simone de Beauvoir spoke of patience as *"one of those feminine qualities which have their origin in our [women's] oppression but should be preserved after our liberation"* (De Beauvoir, 1976, p. 153). Mothers in this study validated this observation in their experiences. Comparing herself with her husband, Carol explained:

I allow things to go on before I do anything. He does not. He will stop it as soon as it gets started. He is looser in other things than I am. He is easier to ask permission from about going out. He does not question about who will be there, what time he will come home, who will drive . . . these things I need to know.

Another mother reiterated the theme:

My husband calls me the staff sergeant. Since I spend more time with the kids, I provide the consistency in their discipline. My husband gives in to them easily since he is not with them all the time. He admits that and he accepts it. He just wants to have fun with the children when he is around with them.

Mothers recognize the mutuality and symbiosis existing between them and their husbands in providing a wholesome atmosphere for their children. They have learned to accommodate the initial differences between them and to work toward a relationship in which they respect each other's strengths and vulnerabilities. For the most part, they have identified greater synchrony with their husbands on issues pertaining to childrearing and their children's future.

Sue discussed the evolution in her relationship with her husband:

In the beginning, we would have many discussions between us about how to deal with our children's misbehavior. Now, we don't have to consult each other often since we generally agree with each other on this aspect.

Collaborative decision making and congruence in their expectations of their children were emphasized by Carol:

My husband expects them to go to a good school and I like them to go to a good school but I feel that so long as they get a good, solid education, I am not so concerned about it. His expectation of them in school is also much higher and I'm glad at that because it is positive. However, putting a lot of pressure on the child can also have negative effects. I also expect them to do well but I find it difficult to put pressure on the child. I do not equate success in life with career status. So long as they are happy, well-adjusted, and have a productive career.

Differences that exist between spouses are interpreted within the context of each other's past experience; hence, mutual tolerance and sensitivity develop. Empathic understanding of their husbands was noted in these mothers' conversations.

One mother, who is married to a Chinese American born in Hong Kong, recognized the differences between them and, most significantly, their agreement on important issues:

One is the standard of living. He always thinks that I'm spoiling my son since he grew up with a struggle and did not get his fair shake as a child. He does not care so much about the spoiling but he expects things in return, I think. You've got to do well because you have been given too much. He was brought up not to answer his parents but kids pick up even on television how to argue, how to debate. But we share the same values of honesty, hard work, motivation to work. The values are the same but the approaches may be different.

Carol believes that her husband's tolerance of physical expression of anger in their sons and of "noise" originates from his growing up in a family of eight (he had four brothers and three sisters). In contrast, she is the youngest of three girls and stayed home mostly by herself when her two older sisters were in college.

As has been stipulated by Gilligan (1982) and others, relationship and responsibility orientation pervades women's thought and behaviors. Maintenance of affiliations requires correlative empathic development with emphasis on accommodation rather than competition, sensitivity rather than objectivity, and movement toward increased fusion and intimacy rather than separation and autonomy. Miller (1986) stressed that, as a consequence of women's oppression, they have been diverted from expressing their own emotions and encouraged instead to concentrate on the emotions and reactions of others. This inequality heightens women's sensitivity and nurturance, placing them at the core of directing real changes in the child.

MATERNAL ROLE MODELS

A new perspective about their past relationships, reconstructed within the context of their present experiences from which new meanings are derived, was heard in these mothers' conversations. They painted images of "good mothers" as unselfish, self-sacrificing, available, gentle, and nurturant women. Their formulations of a "good mother" were largely reconstructed from pleasant memories about their own mothers.

One mother admitted: *"It hurts me when I am unable to help them when they have a problem. My mother somehow managed to help me out when I had problems."* Another mother recalled her mother as the one who *"gave the hugs and kisses when we got hurt. She made the hurt disappear."*

Marion depicted her mother as *"good. She was always there. You can come into my mother's house even as an adult without having to have a key, because she [is] always home."*

Young girls have been found to transform and internalize their mother's values, ideas, and ethics, to develop a model of proper behavior and a standard of mothering (Stone, 1979). Parents' childhood memories and their subjective conceptualizations of their childhood experiences have been empirically shown to influence subsequent parental behavior, providing a filter through which parents view and respond to their own children (Belsky, 1984; Maccoby & Martin, 1983; Ricks, 1985).

Sue recalled that, during her childhood in the Philippines, she used to go to the marketplace with her mother. *"By day's end I would be so exhausted and hungry from the heat. Then my mother would hold me, look at me and smile. I remember her smile . . . it was reassuring and comforting . . . it was enough to tell me that everything will be fine."*

Marion spoke of her mother as a gentle woman who taught her restraint in dealing with little children. *"Mother said, 'You know why I don't hit you when I'm mad, because as an adult I could really hurt a small child.'"*

A striking similarity among these mothers was their positive sense about their past. They viewed their own childhood with both subjectivity and objectivity, identifying easily both parents' admirable and not so tolerable traits. If there were attributes in their parents that were negatively regarded, an empathic understanding of past events evolved.

Mary spoke of her father as someone with a *"lot of energy"* who *"always managed to make time"* for her. Her mother was admired for having a *"lot of sound, logical reasoning . . . a realist."* Her practical sense provided stability for Mary as a young girl. However, both parents did not *"plan. Everything seemed to be always done at the last minute, very spontaneously and impulsively."*

To Carol, her Dad's sense of humor and his ability to deal with different kinds of people with ease were most admirable. Her mother was the organizer, good with money, but had a temper. Carol was amused to find more and more of that temper resurrected in her.

Sue admitted that more traits of her parents are surfacing in her as she grows older. She always hated her father's controlling attitude, yet her strong focus on knowing the details, making sure that everything is in order, is more a reflection of her father than her mother. Her mother is viewed as the nurturant one who easily gave in to her father's strong will. Sue related the time when both her parents stayed with her after her father retired. They applied for work. Only her mother got accepted, and she turned down the job offer because her father had told her that *"he would feel bad if she got it and he did not."* Her mother did not inform her father that she had been accepted and declined.

Jean remembered that her dad was:

> . . . *[a] very controlling man, very bright, very smart despite the fact that he only completed fifth grade. He joined the merchant marines and lived all over the world. He has a great love of books and politics. He always discussed politics at the dinner table with us. He was the disciplinarian.*

In contrast, Jean portrayed her mother as warm but too sub-servient to her father. *"In a lot of ways, I don't know how she re-ally thinks about things. Oftentimes, she would reflect my father's views."* Most of all, she admired her dad's being a strong family man despite the fact that he had no role model or support system in that role. Jean noted her understanding and acceptance of their life-style:

> *My mother grew up in a rural, southern state, very strict up-bringing, while my Dad had exposure to different things. It worked well for them that she remained that way. I would not want that for myself. My husband and I are more egali-tarian with each other and with our children.*

In describing women constructivists, Belenky et al. (1986) stressed their ability to blend their subjective feelings with their objective, rational understanding. The voices of the mothers stud-ied illustrated their adeptness in reexamining their past, bringing into the open their personal and subjective perspectives within the objective realities of past and present events. They have gained in-sight from the strengths and weaknesses of their parents, clarify-ing their parents' behaviors within the context of their parents' own time and space as well as their relevance in the present situ-ated context of their own lives. These women are able to criticize their past in a positive sense, which enables them to recreate a bet-ter life for themselves. They express great tolerance of differences and ambiguity, which are milestones of empathic learning and con-nected knowing.

Except for one mother, all of the group credited qualities of their fathers as influences in their own achievement. These at-tributes were distinctly identified as instrumental to their own achievement. Interestingly, attributes in their mothers, such as be-ing warm, affectionate, and nurturant, although perceived as posi-tive, were not considered to be as influential as the qualities they cited in their fathers.

Miller (1986) argued that most of women's work is not recog-nized as real activity because of the very nature of the work itself.

It is geared toward helping others' development, rather than toward self-enhancement. Men, on the other hand, are engaged in what society clearly designates as economically productive roles with clear-cut outcomes. Miller proposed that what women do every day of their lives in raising children involves real changes that foster the most important growth of all—the realization of human potentials.

PUTTING IT ALL TOGETHER

Mothers in this study communicated their increased confidence as they gained more experience with their children. Although the job of caretaking did not get easier with their succeeding children, these mothers gained heightened confidence in themselves through maternal practice.

They denied deliberate, formal attempts in learning their mothering roles. One mother stated, *"You just know when it works. Experts just confused me further so I decided to just do what I thought I should do."*

Caregiving, as described by Stern (1977), is a creative art characterized by spontaneity. Mothers' interactions with their infants have been observed to be reciprocal; their peculiarities are determined by the individual potentials that participants bring into the interactions. Stern further stated that mothers pretty much create their own caregiving art. The outcomes depend on the manner in which the art is rendered. The impact of caregiving requires its delivery in its entirety. It loses its potency when given as separate components of its whole. Thus, the art of caregiving is more than the sum of its parts. Caring involves a great deal of learning and creativity, that transpire in a highly spontaneous, unstructured, and nurturant manner that is supportive of infinite growth in children.

Often, mothers' informal consultations with friends and colleagues about their problems yield satisfactory results. One mother, who was concerned about her increasingly negative feelings toward her son (he *"seems to know just the right buttons to pull, to get me angry and lose control"*), felt worse after talking with her husband, who asked her:

How can you hate your own son? And then when I talked to my neighbor, she said, "Oh, my daughter, I hate her all the time when I am snitched." I found it very helpful to know that it is OK to have a horrible relationship with your child when you are upset with him. It took a lot of pressure from me.

Indeed, women are found to learn better in an atmosphere of collaboration rather than by adversarial discourse. The preceding episode illustrates how collaboration with another mother permitted affirmation of this particular mother's subjective, personal feelings in dealing with an objective and seemingly rational situation. One mother's shared experience created comfort and confidence in the other.

Belenky et al. (1986) identified constructed knowing as the epitome of women's epistemological development. A critical prerequisite in the acquisition of constructed knowledge is the affirmation of one's subjective/personal knowledge. Subjective knowledge is a perspective that conceives truth as personal and intuited. It is rooted in the discovery that personal experience is a valuable source of knowledge. Connected knowing, as conceptualized by Gilligan (1982), builds on subjectivism, which fosters the ability to gain access to other people's thoughts and feelings. This is recognized as the pathway to development of empathy. Constructed knowledge is marked by a woman's ability to integrate her subjective, personal, and intuited knowledge with rational, abstract, and intellectual knowledge. It presupposes integration rather than subordination of one type of knowledge to another. Constructed knowledge legitimizes women's predilection toward the connected mode of knowing, which upholds experiences, feelings, and subjective interpretations as bases of knowledge.

The experience of motherhood promotes this pattern of epistemological development by elevating a woman's subjective knowledge to the level of importance given to rational knowledge. As

Ruddick (1980) has argued, maternal practice breeds maternal thinking by enhancing a mother's attentiveness and sensitivity to simple everyday happenings. Her careful attention and reflection about the universe in which she lives cultivate the mother's capacity for empathic understanding of others. Weil (1951) defined empathy as the ability for "attentive love" that places the welfare of others before one's own. Attentive love, according to Weil, is careful attention to every facet of growth potential in others.

Du Bois (1983) has asserted that passionate scholarship is derived from personal knowledge (Polanyi, 1958) because of the intimate participation of the knower in the act of knowing. Hence, the knower develops strong commitment in the knowledge gained—knowledge that merges both feelings and thoughts.

The educational philosopher, Paulo Freire (1971), compared traditional teaching with "banking" wherein the knower is a mere passive depository of information that remains the sole property of the teacher. This type of education, according to Freire, "anesthetizes and submerges the consciousness." Belenky et al. (1986) supported Freire's contention and emphasized the concept of "midwife-teacher who draws out the feelings and latent knowledge from the learners' head, giving birth to their own ideas, making them explicit and elaborated."

As pointed out previously, mothers talk to their children and pose questions rather than lecture. Question posing that transpires in an atmosphere of intimacy and trustful relations unleashes the latent potential in children. The art of gossiping, so characteristic of woman talk, is trust building whose objectives are: to reveal oneself and to know the innermost feelings and thoughts of others about the world as they experience it in everyday life. Women's gossip penetrates the truth in a collaborative sense and supports their natural predispositions in learning.

Motherhood awakens the innate capacities for wisdom in women in an active, connected fashion through a high degree of intimacy and a relatedness that is congruent with their innate propensity for this type of knowing. Maternal practice validates the significance of mothers' intuition and experiential perspectives. Thus, mothers begin to recognize themselves as sources of great wisdom.

Because the everyday tasks of mothering involve changes and learning, they are complex and transformational. As Miller (1986) has posited, maternal practice deals with the most important change of all—development of human potential. Growth promotion in this sense is holistic, encompassing the physical, emotional, moral, social, and cultural capacities into a single being. Motherhood entails reciprocal learning and involves real changes in both mother and child. These changes tend to be mutable rather than static, nurturant rather than stifling, contextual rather than fixed.

The following poem resonates this profound capacity of women in promoting growth in others:

Girls

Others on healthy wanderings
to the darksome poets are forced to fare;
must always be asking a traveler
if he's not seen one singing there
or laying his hands on strings.
Only girls will never ask
what bridge leads to images;
will smile merely, brightlier than necklaces
of pearl against silver bowls unfurled.

All doors from their lives are entrances
into a poet
and into the world.

(Rilke, 1977, p. 9)

Indeed, motherhood gives birth to infinite possibilities in each child. The everyday work of mothers occurs in a nondescript sort of way, seemingly ambiguous because of its vastness and inherent complexity and inseparable into distinct and definable parts. The salience of womanhood, with its associated warmth, nurturance, and attentiveness, unleashes latent knowledge and abilities in others. The essence of mothering can be conceptualized as the art of giving birth. It opens the gates to discovery, development, and sustenance of the total being. Rilke's analogy of the child as a poet denotes the unique, infinitely creative capacities in the young that can be given life by maternal practice.

As health care professionals, we need to be sensitized to women's conversations, their lived experiences, their thoughtful reflections about themselves and the world in which they thrive. Empowerment of these women lies in the recognition of their personal knowledge, which is subjective and intuitive. As has been formulated by many scholars, integration of subjective and personal knowledge with objective and rational knowledge allows women's inner voices to be heard. Women's integrated voices validate their innate ways of knowing, which are mediated by principles of relatedness, responsibility, and care. Women thrive in an atmosphere of trust rather than doubt; their confidence and self-esteem flourish in intimate rather than adversarial relationships.

The thrust toward professionalism, with its demands for a high degree of objectivity and rationality, must not abrogate the very nature and essence of womanhood—and, for that matter, motherhood. Women's ways of knowing are elaborated by maternal practice in caring for their children. Women's knowledge is connected with their experiences with the world, merging both their feelings and their thoughts in achieving empathic understanding of phenomena. This type of knowing, which is constructed from the inherent relationships between personal and objective knowledge, has been found to be liberating for most women. Their minds are freed from the oppression of highly abstract, disconnected, unmeaningful facts. Rationalism devoid of contextualized meanings tends to limit the transformation in women and children. Affirmation of their intuited knowledge gives life to their profound capacity for wisdom, which has been documented as most supportive of the growth and development of the young child.

ABOUT THE STUDY

As a mother who is engaged in an economically productive career, I do not have the choice of staying home with my children. Maintaining both motherhood and career roles poses tremendous difficulties for everyone involved, not to mention the guilt that I try hard to ignore. On the other hand, staying home with my two children during summer vacations only intensifies my desire to get back to work. I relish different experiences with my family, colleagues, and friends. I dread the thought of losing a portion of what I love to do despite the sacrifices all of these experiences entail.

Recently, my ponderings made me realize that I have three categories of intimate women friends. One group provides the collegial and professional support, called upon regarding problems with work and about nursing, in general. Another group, which tends to be in small numbers, consists of mothers who have children, roughly the same ages as my own. This group I consult with when I encounter problems with my children. A third group, close-knit family members whom I have known most of my life, renders advice about dilemmas pertinent to my husband's and my own families of origin. I find that these groups of friends address different dimensions in my needs. They are not interchangeable nor responsive to problems they cannot relate with.

My husband finds humor in my overuse of the telephone. With little time left to myself, the phone is my primary mode of connecting with these friends. These calls have done wonders for my well-being. I find pleasure, sustenance, and understanding from these women.

This study was undertaken essentially to gain insight into myself as a mother and career woman. The subjects were ten mothers with children, who have maintained careers before and/or after their children were born. Only one mother, who worked for many years in her profession, has not returned to full-time employment. Except for one, the rest have more than one child. The women are between 40 and 50 years old, married and living with their spouses. All of these women have college degrees.

Phenomenology has been chosen to discover the contextualized meanings of the motherhood experience. It is rooted in the philosophical belief that reality is constructed within the framework of an individual's life experience. Reality in this sense is derived from an individual's highly subjective perceptions and reflections on the meanings of his or her lived experience (Munhall, 1989). In contrast to quantitative research methods, phenomenology stems from the existentialist philosophical belief that human beings have the capacities to interpret and derive meanings from their experiences, which are highly individualized and contextualized. These meanings cannot be superimposed by others' preconceptions about the experiences. Van Manen (1990) has explicated the existentialist philosophy behind phenomenology. It is:

[the] study of the life world—the world as we immediately experience it pre-reflectively rather than as we conceptualize, categorize or reflect on it. . . . It attempts to gain insightful descriptions of phenomena.

Munhall's paradigm of the four existential life worlds was utilized in examining the phenomenon of motherhood. Mothers' phenomenological descriptions of their experiences were analyzed in terms of the four situated contexts Munhall suggested: (1) spatial, (2) temporal, (3) corporeal, and (4) relational. Their revelations and reflections were analyzed for emergent themes within the context of the time and space of their experiences and their own perspective about the phenomenon, taking into account the interplay of all the particulars within that situation.

Thematic conceptualizations were derived from the mothers' phenomenological descriptions, which constituted the major data source for the study. Verbatim recording of mothers' conversations was done to capture the essence of their own interpretations of their maternal experiences. Literature pertinent to motherhood was reviewed and "bracketed" to prevent preexisting assumptions about this phenomenon. Other sources of data to augment the mothers' descriptions were comprised of media and literary works. Supplementary sources were tapped after thematic analysis of the mothers' descriptions was completed. The review of the literature was used to find validation of mothers' perspectives about their life experiences.

The themes presented reflect the recurrent patterns of meanings derived from these mothers' experiences. These were constructed from the mothers' own descriptions and interpretations. The most recurrent theme mothers identified involved changes associated with motherhood and maternal practice. Motherhood, in its day-to-day sense, created a revolution in the way they feel and think about phenomena. These changes affected their self-image; feelings and thoughts about the world around them; relationships with others; values and priorities; and reconceptualizations of past, present, and future events.

The underlying rationale for these changes was found to be the evolution of their special way of knowing. Maternal practice affirmed their experiential and intuitive knowledge as a source of great wisdom. Mothering promoted the discovery of a high level of thinking that is constructed from the connectedness of their experiences with their intellectual knowledge, thereby giving full meanings to abstract phenomena.

Mothers' thought process emphasizes the inherent relatedness and wholeness of events, the same paradigm they used in caring for their children. Constructed knowledge translated into their relationships with their children, which operated within the principles of affiliation, responsibility, and care. This mode of operation was found to be most supportive of growth in the young child. The kind of growth nurtured by maternal practice was marked by total transformation in the child's well-being.

Listening to these mothers' conversations has given me profound insights about myself. Their reflections provided affirmation of my own experiences as mother and career woman. I found reassurance from their validations about the pleasures and disappointments associated with mothering. Most of all, I have found renewed confidence in my own intuitions about situations.

REFERENCES

Baber, K., & Monaghan, P. (1988, August). College women's career and motherhood expectations: New options, old dilemmas. *Sex Roles, 19,* 189–203.

Ballou, J. (1978). *The psychology of pregnancy.* Lexington, MA: Heath.

Bassoff, E. S. (1992). *Mothering ourselves: Help and healing for adult daughters.* New York: Penguin Books.

Belenky, M. F., Clinchy, B. M., Goldberger, N. R., & Tarule, J. M. (1986). *Women's ways of knowing: The development of self, voice and mind.* New York: Basic Books.

Bell, R. Q., & Harper, L. V. (1977). *Child effects on adults.* Hillsdale, NJ: Erlbaum.

Belsky, J. (1984). The determinants of parenting: A process model. *Child Development, 55,* 83-96.

Berg, B. J. (1986). *The crisis of the working mother: Resolving the conflict between family and work.* New York: Summit Books.

Blossfield, H., & Jaenichen, U. (1992, May). Educational expansion and changes in women's entry into marriage and motherhood in the Federal Republic of Germany. *Journal of Marriage and Family, 54,* 302-315.

Bowlby, J. (1980). *Attachment and loss, Vol. 2: Loss.* New York: Basic Books.

Bretherton, I. (1985). Attachment theory: Retrospect and prospect. *Monographs of the Society for Research in Child Development, 50* (1-2, Serial no. 209), 3-35.

Bruner, J. (1985). Vygotsky: A historical and conceptual perspective. In J. V. Wertsch (Ed.), *Culture, communication and cognition* (pp. 21-34). Cambridge, England: Cambridge University Press.

Bus, A. G., & Van Ijzendoorn, M. H. (1988). Mother–child interactions, attachment, and emergent literacy: A cross-sectional study. *Child Development, 59,* 1262-1272.

Caldera, Y. M., Huston, A. C., & O'Brien, M. (1989). Social interactions and play patterns of parents and toddlers with feminine, masculine, and neutral toys. *Child Development, 60,* 70-76.

Chodorow, N. (1974). Family structure and feminine personality. In M. Z. Rosaldo & L. Lamphere (Eds.), *Woman, culture and society.* Stanford, CA: Stanford University Press.

Chodorow, N. (1978). *The reproduction of mothering.* Berkeley: University of California Press.

Crowell, J., & Feldman, S. S. (1988). Mothers' internal models of relationships and children's behavioral and developmental status: A study of mother–child interaction. *Child Development, 59,* 1273-1285.

De Salvo, L. (1989). *Virginia Woolf: The impact of childhood sexual abuse on her life and work.* Boston: Beacon Press.

Dion, K. K. (1985). Socialization in adulthood. In G. Lindzey & E. Aronson (Eds.), *Handbook of social psychology,* Vol. II (pp. 123-148). New York: Random House.

De Beauvoir, S. (1976, October). Interview by A. Schwarzer in Marie-Claire. Reprinted in E. Marks & I. de Coutivron (Eds.) (1981), *New French feminisms* (pp. 151-153). New York: Shocken Books.

Du Bois, B. (1983). Passionate scholarship: Notes on values, knowing and method in feminist social science. In C. Bowles & R. Duelli-Klein (Eds.), *Theories of women's studies* (pp. 105-116). London: Routledge and Kegan Paul.

Etaugh, C., & Poertner, P. (1992). Perceptions of women: Influence of performance, marital and parental variables. *Sex Roles, 26,* 311-321.

Fairweather, E., McDonough, R., & McFadyean, M. (1984). *Only the rivers run free.* London: Pluto Press.

Fellman, A. C. (1990). Laura Ingalls Wilder and Rose Wilder Lane: The politics of a mother–daughter relationship. *Signs: Journal of Women in Culture and Society, 15* (3), 535-561.

Feuerstein, R. (1980). *Instrumental enrichment: An intervention program for cognitive modifiability.* Baltimore: University of Maryland Press.

Freire, P. (1971). *Pedagogy of the oppressed.* New York: Seaview.

Galinsky, E. (1981). *Between generations: Stages of parenthood.* New York: Berkley.

Gilligan, C. (1982). *In a different voice: Psychological theory and women's development.* Cambridge, MA: Harvard University Press.

Gilligan, C. (1984). The conquistador and the dark continent: Reflections on the psychology of love. *Daedalus, 113,* 75-95.

Heath, H. B. (1983). *Ways with words: Language, life and work in communities and classrooms.* Cambridge, England: Cambridge University Press.

Herman, J. L., with L. Hirschman. (1981). *Father–daughter incest.* Cambridge, MA: Harvard University Press.

Hewlett, S. A. (1983, July 27). Working mothers: Effect on children. *New York Times,* 15.

Hobbs, N. (1982). *The troubled and troubling child: Reeducation in mental health, education and human service programs for children and youth.* San Francisco: Jossey-Bass.

Hoffman, L., & Manis, J. (1979). The value of children in the United States: A new approach to the study of fertility. *Journal of Marriage and the Family, 41,* 583-596.

Horner, M. S. (1972). Toward an understanding of achievement-related conflicts in women. *Journal of Social Issues, 28,* 157-175.

Kochanska, G., Kuczynski, L., & Radke-Yarrow, M. (1989). Correspondence between mother's self-reported and observed childrearing practices. *Child Development, 60,* 56-63.

Kumagai, F. (1984). The life cycle of the Japanese family. *Journal of Marriage and Family, 46,* 191-204.

Leichter, H. J. (1984). Families as environment for literacy. In H. Goelman, A. Oberg, & F. Smith (Eds.), *Awaking to literacy* (pp. 38-50). London: Heinemann.

Lever, J. (1976). Sex differences in the games children play. *Social Problems, 23,* 478-487.

Loevinger, J. (1976). *Ego development.* San Francisco: Jossey-Bass.

Lyons, N. (1983). Two perspectives on self, relationships and morality. *Harvard Educational Review, 53,* 125-145.

Maccoby, E. E., & Martin, J. A. (1983). Socialization in the context of the family: Parent-child interaction. In E. M. Heatherington (Ed.), *Handbook of child psychology, Vol. 4* (pp. 1-101). New York: Wiley.

Miller, J. B. (1986). *Toward a new psychology of women.* (2nd ed.). Boston: Beacon Press.

Munhall, P. (1989, Winter). Philosophical ponderings on qualitative research methods in nursing. *Nursing Science Quarterly,* 22-28.

Noddings, N. (1984). *Caring.* Berkeley: University of California Press.

Nuttbrock, L., & Freudiger, P. (1991). Identity salience and motherhood: A test of Stryker's theory. *Social Psychology Quarterly, 54* (2), 146-157.

Pelligrini, A. D., Brody, J. H., & Sigel, I. E. (1985). Parents' book-reading habits and their children. *Journal of Educational Psychology, 77,* 332-340.

Piaget, J. (1952). *The language and thought of the child.* London: Routledge & Kegan Paul.

Piaget, J. (1965). *The moral judgment of the child.* New York: Free Press.

Polanyi, M. (1958). *Personal knowledge.* Chicago: University of Chicago Press.

Pollak, S., & Gilligan, C. (1982). Images of violence in thematic apperception test stories. *Journal of Personality and Social Psychology, 42* (1), 159-167.

Ricks, M. H. (1985). The social transmission of parental behavior: Attachment across generations. *Monographs of the Society for Research in Child Development, 50* (1-2, Serial no. 209), 211-227.

Rilke, R. M. (1977). *Possibility of being: A selection of poems.* (J. B. Leishman, Trans.) New York: New Directions.

Roggman, L. A., Langlois, J. H., & Hubbs-Tait, L. (1987). Mothers, infants, and toys: Social play correlates of attachment. *Infant Behavior and Development, 10,* 233-237.

Rowbotham, S. (1989, Spring). To be or not to be: The dilemmas of mothering. *Feminist Review, 31,* 82-93.

Rubin, R. (1984). *Maternal identity and the maternal experience.* New York: Springer.

Ruddick, S. (1980). Maternal thinking. *Feminist Studies, 6,* 70-96.

Ruddick, S. (1984). New combinations: Learning from Virginia Woolf. In C. Asher, L. DeSalvor, & S. Ruddick (Eds.), *Between women* (pp. 137-139). Boston: Beacon Press.

Shure, M., & Spivack, G. (1978). *Problem-solving techniques in childrearing.* San Francisco: Jossey-Bass.

Slater, T. (1977, October). Why I decided to have a baby. *Spare Rib, 63,* 12.

Spacks, P. (1982). In praise of gossip. *Hudson Review, 35,* 19-38.

Stern, D. (1977). *The first relationship: Mother and infant.* Cambridge, MA: Harvard University Press.

Stone, E. (1979, May 13). Mothers and daughters. *New York Times Magazine,* 17.

Sulzby, E. (1986). Writing and reading: Signs of oral and written organization in the young child. In W. H. Teale & E. Sulzby (Eds.), *Emergent literacy* (pp. 90-115). Norwood, NJ: Ablex.

Trebilcot, J. (Ed.). (1984). *Mothering: Essays in feminist theory.* Totowa, NJ: Rowman and Allanheld.

van Manen, M. (1990). *Researching the lived experience: Human science for an action-sensitive pedagogy.* New York: SUNY Press.

Weil, S. (1951). Reflections on the right use of school studies with a view to the love of God. In S. Weil (Ed.), *Waiting for God* (pp. 105-106). New York: Harper (Colophon Books).

Woolf, V. (1985). *A sketch of the past: Moments of being.* (J. Shulkind, Ed.) Unpublished autobiographical writings. New York: Harcourt Brace Jovanovich.

ABOUT THE AUTHOR

Dula F. Pacquiao is Assistant Professor of Nursing at Kean College of New Jersey. She obtained her baccalaureate degree in nursing from the University of the Philippines, her Master of Arts degree from Teachers College, and her doctoral degree from Rutgers University.

Her expertise is in the area of anthropology of education. She has conducted two ethnographic studies on cultural influences in the aging experience of Filipino and Anglo elders. Through a faculty research grant, she has recently completed a study on sociocultural influences in cognitive styles of African American, Filipino, and Hispanic nursing students.

Dr. Pacquiao has presented numerous lectures about the Filipino culture and its application in health care delivery and nursing education. She has been conducting review courses especially designed for foreign nurse graduates and ethnic minority nurses for the RN licensure examinations.

Since leaving her home country of the Philippines, Dr. Pacquiao has resided and taught nursing in Toronto, New York, and New Jersey. She has been an active member of the Philippine Nurses Association of New Jersey, now serving as its President-elect and Chairperson of the Research Committee.

Dr. Pacquiao resides in New Jersey with her husband and two children. She was recently appointed by Governor James Florio to the New Jersey State Board of Nursing and was designated Chairperson of the Education Committee.

10

Seeking Harmony: Chronic Physical Illness and Its Meaning for Women

Zane Robinson Wolf

SEEKING BALANCE

A woman who lives with chronic physical illness seeks balance in her day-to-day life. She is more aware of the need for this stability than most women, for she is well-acquinted with the disequilibrium brought on by the major and minor crises that accompany disease. A life with a chronic disease is a personal journey for each woman who tries to keep the disorder in perspective and to live life in the best way possible.

I just deal with things on a daily basis. That's what you have to do. There are good days and there are bad days.

There are days when I frankly feel or sense that I am really going to have a bad day breathing. I get into work and find that they are varnishing doors. I leave the area. . . . Sometimes you get so depressed and into the "Why me?" But there are worse diseases to have.

Knowing that it is possible to again achieve equilibrium is encouraging to a woman. Stability is sought in the face of the facts of disease. However, most of the time, many of the symptoms of the disease subside as do some of the effects of treatments; life goes on, relatively unencumbered.

I vowed that I was not going to let it interfere with my life.

NOT WANTING A CHRONIC DISEASE

At first, a woman hopes that she does not have a chronic disease. She wants it to go away and is acutely aware of an uncertain future. Her wish converts to denial of the illness despite the evidence.

My first hospitalization was precipitated by repeated passing out. My hemoglobin had dropped to 7 (Gm) and I was living alone. I had passed out and slid down in the shower, but I couldn't fall because I was wedged. My brother walked in and found me. It was enough for him [to see me this way].

In this woman's case, diarrhea and weakness were evident for some time, but she could not accept the possibility of disease. In other words, a woman ignores common everyday symptoms that could be nothing because she is accustomed to them or does not think she could have a disease.

A woman seeks other explanations for the symptoms that she notices. She blames symptoms on the allergy season, knowing that allergies are easier to live with and more socially acceptable than some diseases. But her hopes and denial get pushed aside brusquely as physicians confirm that there most likely is a problem.

The first thing he did was to look at my eyes. He said, "We'd better have some tests." Two days later he called and said, "I don't want you to get upset or anything. I think we have a case of hepatitis."

Up to this point, having no diagnosis allows a woman to stand on a threshhold where "not knowing" helps her to pretend that she is well.

I would try to pretend that I wasn't short of breath. I didn't even know that I had the disease. I thought, "Maybe you really do need to get back into shape."

DAWNING AWARENESS

The onset of a chronic illness is gradual, allowing each woman the opportunity for its warning signs to settle in a bit and to become familiar.

My husband died, and I took walks with my daughter when I went to California to visit her. But I noticed that I just couldn't do it. I would go a couple of blocks and she would tell me to sit down and then come back and pick me up. It [chest pain] was really scary, because I thought I was getting threatened [sic] with a heart attack.

A woman becomes accustomed to not feeling well. For example, one woman noticed that drinking an alcoholic beverage became repugnant when it never had been before. She stopped drinking and later accepted her physician's warning that even one drink of an alcoholic beverage was out of the question for the remainder of her life. Additionally, fatigue is a companion for many women prior to a definitive diagnosis. Finally, physicians treat some women for minor symptoms in some cases, failing to look further for more serious problems. All of these reasons contribute to why it often takes quite a while for some women to be diagnosed.

Essentially, a woman often notices that something is "not right," but needs a crisis to prompt confirmation by family, friends, and health care providers.

> *I couldn't lift my arm or even move my leg. I didn't feel like doing anything and my face was numb. I felt nothing on my right side at all.*

> *It was my heart attack which I thought was my gall bladder; we went to the doctor and he sent me to the hospital.*

> *He [the physician] recommended that I join an exercise club. So I went to the club at work and had a workup, but they never checked my pulmonary function. They never even checked me. So I exercised for the whole summer and as it progressed into the fall I noticed that I got a lot of dizziness upon exertion.*

A woman knows that something serious is happening to her. However, she needs someone to confirm this for her, to have her symptoms endorsed and legitimized with a diagnostic lable. When this happens, some women are shocked. Some become depressed and suicidal.

> *I wanted to go jump in front of a car, and I can remember one day staying home. I was just so depressed that my husband got very alarmed and took off a day of work to stay with me because he was concerned about what I might do. As I thought about jumping in front of a car, I thought it would be my luck just to be maimed.*

She sees herself changing. She knows that her depression is not typical and realizes that she is herself, yet not herself, and that the chronic illness is taking hold.

RECEIVING THE OPINION

Subsequently, a woman makes an appointment to see a physician. The response of the physician varies; if the woman is an acquaintance of the physician, he or she may not believe that the complaints of the friend are serious. This disbelief delays treatment. Or, the physician may downplay the symptoms and blame them on the aging process. Because women know that they are most likely cared for by competent physicians, they accept a doctor's opinion tentatively, when actually the doctor's personal relationship with the woman clouds his or her judgment. Said one chronically ill woman, "They [physicians] don't want to find something wrong with you because they know you." The physician's inability to see the disease in a friend could end in negligence. "They should have sent me to PT [physical therapy] when I was in the hospital. They never did that. My doctor didn't know how to deal with it. He had a hard time. He couldn't get over the fact that I had a stroke." This woman suffered permanent muscle and nerve damage.

Physicians' inability to identify disease in a patient-friend protects them. It hurts a physician to see a friend, whom he or she may be very fond of, suffer. Physicians often are angry with women who succumb to a disease. In addition, a woman patient knows that physicians minimize the symptoms of women. For one woman, this delayed diagnosis many months. She was labeled as getting old. "The woman, who is 38, is getting old, and needs to get in shape. So I was annoyed after I was diagnosed with sarcoidosis."

Finally, the chronically ill woman is diagnosed and the physician begins to treat her. She reluctantly accepts the extent to which experiences in hospitals, with technology, and with medications are involved in her care. Physicians support their female patients throughout the crises of the disease. They check in periodically in order to keep the woman informed. "He would call me on the phone and ask me how I felt. When the tests came back he would be on the phone. I didn't have to wait until the next time." When another woman's insurance would not cover her physician's fee, the physician wrote off a $10,000 fee. Physicians care for and protect their own and their patients' interests in the fight against disease. Their concern is manifested when they stay with the woman during crises, remissions, and exacerbations.

When physicians confront their own personal lack of expertise in a female patient's care, they do not hesitate to consult with another doctor. The complexity of the disease challenges their knowledge and skill. "They [internists] sent me right away to the pulmonary doctor. I had a biopsy of the lymph nodes and that was when they diagnosed that I had the disease." Another physician called in a consultant to do a liver biopsy. He was having difficulty with the biopsy during his caring for the patient with hepatitis.

The physician's concern is shared with office staff, who also get acquainted with the patients over the long course of a chronic illness. They tell jokes and encourage her. Registered nurses help.

She would just hold my hand and tell me that the biopsy was important to me. She told me to think of pleasant things.

THE PROBLEM WITH DIAGNOSTIC TESTS

Physicians, nurses, and office staff provide continuity of care and human connection during the disturbing as well as the routine times, such as the frequent visits for diagnostic testing. They share in the illness experience. Women meet caregivers in outpatient settings, physicians' offices, clinical laboratories, and hospitals.

The second biopsy was horrible. I thought that they were going to keep me overnight because my blood pressure dropped. I had a nurse with me the whole time. I had to lay flat on my back for four hours. Then I could go on my side for four more. I had to stay quiet for two days after the biopsy.

The women are subjected to many diagnostic tests which help health care providers to monitor the course of the disease and make decisions regarding treatment.

Women also come to understand that health care providers do not always act responsibly and sensitively when caring for them.

Examples are not hard to find: when a nursing student informed one woman that she could not handle the stresses in her life, the woman asked the student to leave the room; when a physician forgot to send his patient's chart to a specialist, the woman traveled to an appointment and virtually wasted her time and that of the consulting physician; when a nurse told a woman who was hospitalized with ulcerative colitis that her IVs were turkey and pie on Thanksgiving, the woman said of the incident, "I almost took the IV bag and wrapped her up in it." Being lectured to and yelled at by a physician or nurse does not change a woman's behavior.

SEARCH FOR CAUSE

Blaming themselves or their family for the disease, women search for its causes in their diet ("Some of it may be food-related, from what I'm reading"), emotional stress ("It started out at an emotional time, a break-up of a longtime relationship"), and family history ("It's hereditary for me; my mom had a couple of strokes and my dad and grandparents had hypertension"). Concern about the family history prevails in the search for causation.

Another reason why I used to be worried about my heart was because of my family history of heart trouble on my mother's side and my father died of a heart attack. I had two brothers who died of massive heart attacks, and my other brother died of a stroke; that's practically the same thing. So when I started feeling bad and having the angina, I thought, "Here I go."

She may not be certain of the exact cause.

All that they could say was that it was a form of hepatitis.

BEING PERSISTENTLY AWARE

Living with a chronic illness changes a woman's life. She may finally live companionably in the knowledge of it, accepting it along with the people at work and her loving family and friends at home. She seeks a truce with the disease, manages symptoms, and regulates activity levels. A woman adjusts to the changes, aware of the reality of disease on a daily basis.

> *It's changed my life. The only way I have is to realize that I have to stop and think about when I'm getting short of breath, to question what is the reason behind it. I have changed. It slowed me down.*

The disease at some point penetrates a woman's life; its presence cannot be ignored.

> *I've had it for 21 years. It's always a presence, always a part of my life. Sometimes it is more pervasive than others. I've been hospitalized twice for an extended period of time. When it started it was not nearly as serious. It was just an intermittent discomfort or annoyance. But I've been on medications for the last 15 years.*

BEING IN THE VORTEX

At the time of diagnosis, a woman sees the seriousness of her situation.

> *I couldn't sit up and I couldn't do anything. I just lay flat in bed. My blood pressure wouldn't come down. It took a while before it came down.*

Time and experience add detail to her perceptions. She visits many physicians, becomes friendly with office staff and nurses, learns the name of laboratory technicians, and consults with neighborhood pharmacists. She learns the ropes of the health care delivery system. The disease refuses to go away. However, she refuses to succumb to it.

> *Like many sick people, I had begun to realize that my illness was not so much a state of being as a process of*

transformation. My body was changing, losing weight, lus-
ter, and vitality, while assuming an ethereal tenor, just as
my interests and preferences were shifting dramatically. I
yearned for some kind of map or diagram that could de-
scribe, and even predict these strange mutations of charac-
ter I felt myself undergoing. (Duff, 1993, p. 78)

KNOWING THE PATTERNS

Often, the disease has a pattern of its own. It introduces its id-
iosyncratic disruptions to a woman's life, changing its course in
unwelcome directions.

The flare-ups run in cycles. I have not had any in the past
six months. For the previous year and a half before that, I
would be miserable for weeks at a time, maybe have two
weeks' respite, and then it would start up again. It was al-
most continuous for a long period of time.

Remissions and exacerbations switch places. They take turns and
come and go rather erratically. The flare-ups stimulate the woman
to become more compliant with medication regimens and other
treatments. The remissions lull her into complacency and immerse
her in the attractiveness of control. She lives in the moment and
revels in the tranquillity of feeling better. Later crises convince
her that this terrible disease was predetermined. She contracts her
world. Uncertainty about the timing of flare-ups reminds her of
how ill she can become.

I started with the vomiting two weeks before we moved. I
didn't call the doctor. I didn't want to go to the hospital. I
ended up with (keto)acidosis. I spent time in the intensive
care unit.

———

I've hit a couple of emergency rooms, which is not fun. They
give you a little bit of epinephrine and that clears it [wheez-
ing, shortness of breath] up.

MEETING UNCERTAINTY

There is a lot of uncertainty implicit in a woman's experience of living with a chronic physical illness. The period of waiting and not knowing is loaded with uncertainty as the woman holds her position on a threshold of not being sick but knowing that she is not well. Her symptoms inform her something is not right. Later, she is not reassured by the formal sanction and label of a specific disease. Once she knows she has the disease and becomes a patient, there is uncertainty about what variation of disease she has. In some cases, the cause of the disease is not readily identifiable.

All that he could say was that it was a form of hepatitis B. When the autoimmune doctor came in, he said that it changes the whole picture and could have been the beginning of it all. I don't understand all of this. I may have had autoimmune hepatitis.

For a while, she inhabits limbo. She hesitates to make plans with friends and becomes extremely tentative. She begins to appreciate what a split personality feels like. When stability returns, symptoms subside and she becomes less of a patient. She wonders about what patterns the disease will assume in the future.

I had an eye examination and that was OK. I think, "What else is it (sarcoidosis) going to progress to?" And then with the respiratory aspect of it, "Will it resolve?" If it leads to pulmonary fibrosis, that is a whole other ballgame.

She worries about when exacerbations will come.

I can go three, four weeks and then all of a sudden I have a problem and I have no idea why. This goes along with rheumatoid arthritis where some days you cannot predict it.

When the flare-ups come, she wonders when she will feel better and whether the disease will go away.

Some days I feel great and other days I don't feel so well. I don't have a lot of energy and I'm really tired and get GI symptoms.

Or, a physician tries to reassure her that this specific symptom does not mean an exacerbation.

He [the physician] said that the shortness of breath could be the adjustment of my system to the medicine.

She responds and begins to fit as much as possible into her life. She knows that there is no cure for her disease, and that treatments, surgery, meditation, and medications are only buying her time.

I noticed that I couldn't do enough. It was like I had so little time and I had to get it all in, everything in, because you never knew when it was going to fail again. That's the same feeling that I have today.

She loathes wasting time and is impatient with those she works with and lives with. She tries to be sensitive to the fact that her impatience to live, to get on with it, irritates people. Time is an important commodity, and she knows that less is available.

PREFERRING ONE DISEASE OVER ANOTHER

When she considers the possibility of having other diseases, a woman admits that having a certain disease is preferable to having another. If she has two or three chronic illnesses, the preference is definite.

I can deal with the asthma. Maybe it's because I've had it longer than the arthritis. The arthritis is debilitating. The worst thing that could ever happen to me would be having a leg amputated because I wouldn't be able to walk.

Walking brought her joy, so the immobility that arthritis could bring in the future would be worse than her shortness of breath. Having sarcoidosis is better than having lymphoma. She is always able to look outside herself and say, "There but for the grace of God go I."

A woman is grimly aware that following the treatment plans of one disease might interfere with another. Acquiring an acute illness could threaten the stability of the chronic illness. "If I have a respiratory infection, the joints, the back and the knees flare up and they stiffen if there's fever involved."

FORCED ACCEPTANCE

A woman shuttles back and forth between accepting and refusing to accept her disease. Her disbelief finally relents in the face of the evidence provided by symptoms and through the confirmation of this evidence by blunt physicians. "After me asking 20,000 times, they said, 'Why don't you just accept that you have it. . . . You got it.'" Situational crises that she might have been going through for years delay acceptance that she has a serious chronic illness. One woman's angina and coronary artery disease was put on the back burner as she cared for a difficult, chronically ill husband. "I had this for three years before my husband died. And then after that, it did get worse. Now I think that maybe it was just time for it to get worse." She compartmentalizes her own problems, serving the needs of the other. She is able later to allow her symptoms to come to the surface. The timing is right for the onset of disease.

A woman tries to avoid acknowledging the actuality of the disease because she senses in the beginning, and later lives with, the major impact that it has on her life. A major change in life-style follows unwilling acceptance. It permeates the present and the future. Tears dramatize her impotence and depression.

Once again I spent the whole weekend crying because of my fears related to the uncertainty about the progression of the disease and the control of the pain. I'm also afraid this is affecting my husband more than I'd like it to, and that he

*will eventually decide he can't handle it any more and de-
cide to leave me. I don't know what I'd do without his love
and support. I'm just afraid he is supportive out of duty and
not out of love or caring.*

The disease shapes her. For example, she imagines discussing sarcoidosis with a boyfriend and tries to project his response; she
considers the effects of the disease on having children. Vacation
plans change because very cold and very hot days stir asthmatic
symptoms. She chooses jobs carefully because having a bathroom
in the vicinity is essential when one has ulcerative colitis. She
avoids social situations because of the disease, making excuses
and giving other reasons, not the real one.

FIGHTING AND WINNING

Once she accepts her given diagnosis and moves past the confusion
and denial of the early days, a woman begins an active fight against
the disease. This is a distinctive part of her illness experience.

*I just never gave into not doing, because I kept thinking, "If
I go backward . . . I can't! I have to fight all the way."*

---

*Well, I just had to get better, that's all. That was a pain in
the neck. I'm very impatient.*

A woman may choose to fight the facts as presented and shape
her life aggressively. Although she was warned not to have children before her impending marriage, because of diabetes, she
chose to have three children. Physicians had presented her with a
bleak picture—for example, problems during pregnancy. She experienced difficult pregnancies, but is happy to see that her children are healthy.

Women's voices join to resist the enemy, chronic illness. Knowing another fighter who has a chronic illness encourages women
in their own resistance.

I had known an asthmatic at work, one who could just about breathe and yet carried out her daily activities. So I fought it. I continue to fight it and I still fight it to this day.

KNOWING THE ENEMY WITHIN

A woman's fight against her disease is a fight against herself. Some of her anger is directed inward and she hates, temporarily, that part of her that has gone awry. She finds that the energy expended during her illness journey is worth using, but realizes it is lost and cannot be recouped. She views the disease process as disgusting because of the secretions produced, the fatigue experienced, and the limb weakness noted. In addition, the disease may force her to use therapies that change or kill off some of her, rejecting the good parts of her body along with the bad. Consequently, she recognizes her own disloyalty to her body in her choice of specific treatments.

BEING VULNERABLE

A woman who lives with chronic physical illness implicitly acknowledges a heightened sense of vulnerability. The implications of having a chronic disease are many; the potential assaults to her body, mind, and spirit are frightening. The uncertainty of the course of the disease also stimulates fear. While control of life and experience is an illusion for many people, a woman who has a chronic illness holds less of that illusion.

There's a certain degree of control, but some if it is not controllable. The implications are scary because it [ulcerative colitis] increases the risk of cancer and also the sequellae. The arthritis goes along with it as do the long-term effects of prednisone.

Taking prescribed medications increases the risk of having other problems.

Chronic illness also makes a woman susceptible to infectious disease. The diseases themselves and corticosteroid drugs such as prednisone add to the risk of infection and the arthritic flare-ups. "He [the physician] said everything was so low that I could pick up anything." Contact with other infected people may be dangerous to her, bringing the potential of harm, adding insult to injury. "It was a concern about what I was exposed to. I still keep it in the back of my mind, especially now with the new strain of TB and other respiratory diseases." She moves more cautiously at work and at home.

Additionally, sensitivity to the rejection of people who learn she has a chronic disease, especially one that many associate with contagion, increases a woman's personal vulnerability. "I would never tell my neighbor; she would move if she thought I had hepatitis." She provides another incident:

> *I had to take four penicillin before I went to the dentist. I explained everything to him and he called the doctor. He took the tooth out and the girls came in to clean up. And he [the dentist] said, "Leave everything there. Just leave everything there." You could see that it [clean-up] just wasn't routine. I could feel it, I'm not dumb. I thought, "Why don't you wait until I leave?" It agitated me, he was going to take every precaution because there was bleeding. . . . I learned not to tell anybody [about having hepatitis].*

HIDING BEHIND THE STIGMA

She is embarrassed to be sick. She blames herself and tries to protect herself from facing that something is wrong by pretending not to be ill. She hopes that the people she works with will not notice intrusive symptoms.

> *I was really embarrassed so I was trying to pretend that I wasn't short of breath. So I'd get up and turn around for a minute so that they wouldn't see. When I finally caught my breath, I'd start lecturing again.*

She hides evidence of the disease from family, friends, employers, and teachers.

It's like I'm trying to cover it up. It's hard.

I hid the inhaler in my pocket and went to the ladies' room; I always hid it from my employer and my teachers.

I was in the hospital over Thanksgiving and my birthday; I made sure my mother didn't know.

She hides her medications to prevent others from discovering her disease. Doctors' appointments are scheduled on days off and during vacations. She carefully plans ahead when meeting people socially, so that no one will notice her symptoms. The planning gets tedious, because she finds herself spending a lot of energy trying to appear symptomless so she will not have to explain herself. Additionally, the memory of experiencing the lack of compassion and sensitivity haunts her. She remembers being ridiculed many years ago. Said one woman, "We would go to parties and he'd say, 'Oh, look at the two diabetics sitting there, not eating any cake.'"

Not only is the compunction to hide the disease associated with a need to protect others from witnessing the woman's discomfort and pain, it is also related to her awareness of the fact that sick people are frequently stigmatized in society. The symptoms and suffering tend to set chronically ill women apart. "I just said I had a liver infection. . . . People back off." The women do not wish to be pitied, ostracized, or criticized.

I never wanted to be stigmatized as someone who has a chronic respiratory problem or who is labeled as a chronic disease-type person. I've known people who just call out sick. I never wanted to be stigmatized as one who abused sick time in that way.

Having the diarrhea that goes with ulcerative colitis makes the woman keenly aware that her symptom is not discussable in public. She moves aside, pulling back from life. She is isolated and lonely. Part of this may be reinforced by the unfeigned curiosity of acquaintances. "They look at you and say, 'Why are you short of breath?'" Often, family and friends help her to feel less different, less dirty. However, diseases are like dirty words for some people. Because of this, women are embarrassed at being found out.

One woman finally felt well enough to treat herself to a manicure. The manicurist noticed the rash on her hands and arms, caused by one of her medications that fights transplant rejection. The manicurist treated her as though she were contagious, in spite of her reassurances. The manicurist put on a mask and gloves and finally groomed her nails. She has never made an appointment for a manicure since.

Feeling dirty is equated with having an infectious disease. Often, the precautions to protect oneself and others are not well explained to the woman by health care providers. As a result, the woman feels like a pariah, afraid that everything and everyone she touches will be contaminated and possibly hurt. After a while, this fear subsides, chiefly because no one is hurt after contacting her.

At the time, I felt dirty. I think that is the word. I washed the doorknobs with Lysol. Every day I would wash the doorknobs and the phones. I did everything. I asked about sex, and I asked about food, and I asked about people. And I asked about going to the store and touching things. I asked the doctor if I could go to church. He said, "Yes, you just don't have to shake hands." All of these things were in my mind.

She finally accepts that she cannot do anybody any harm, even though the disease remains in her body and the path of the disease may take a long time to travel. Her acceptance of herself and her disease within reveals a self-regard for a newer, changed woman. She wants to be thought of as a person, not a disease.

KNOWING FEAR

Fears originate from many sources and contribute to the separateness that the chronically ill woman perceives. Recognizing her differences as compared to other women, she does not wish her experience to be open to public scrutiny.

The imminent possibility of a heart attack stirs fear of dying, fear of the actual disease itself, and fear of disability. "According to the doctors, I was ready for a major heart attack when I was operated on." Many members of this woman's family had died from heart disease. Similarly, the symptoms brought to another woman by her disease are frightening.

The longer I was up, the worse I began to feel. I was tired and now felt nauseated. I could do nothing but sit in a chair and hope I did not have to even talk to my husband. By the time we got home I was experiencing pain from my waist to my feet in the back of my body.

Finally, fear of being disabled worries another.

I didn't like that, in my early 30s, that I was starting with a chronic disease. I didn't want to end up like my mother who had chronic lung disease . . . having a disability secondary to asthma.

Additional impairments are feared, on top of already existing disabilities. Having already experienced severe osteoporosis resulting from taking prednisone for hepatitis, a woman fears falling in the shower and suffering fractures.

Fears also center on the effects of the pathologic course of disease in the woman's body. She carefully considers the different parts of her body it can afflict next, and wonders where it will strike.

My fears are [for] the future and what is going to happen to me. I don't know. I see myself as a person who has broad shoulders. But I wonder if I'm going to have a weak point.

At the end, when a woman has a chronic illness, death is always a possibility, and the need for control of dying and death is important. She wishes that an investigational drug will come along to stop the disease like a magic bullet. At the same time, she doubts that a medication could ever relieve all of the pain and decrease the effects of the disease process. Finally, she fears having repeated laboratory and diagnostic tests, not only because of the associated discomfort from the procedure but also because of what the results could mean.

He said, "We should go back in [have another biopsy]." I said, "Can we wait six months?"

CONTEMPLATING FUTURE LOSSES

A woman captures her ever-present fear of kidney transplant rejection and renal failure in her dependency on the serum creatinine numbers reported on the results of a laboratory study. Many things could threaten her equilibrium, causing the values to change; for example, an immunologic insult resulting from an infection or from forgetting to take a medication could tip her delicate balance.

I just always felt as though my life hung on a decimal point. They told me that my creatinine was 12 . . . the [hospital] lab had forgotten to put in the decimal point. I had it repeated and it was 1.2. They screwed up on a transplant [recipient]! I really felt like I was literally hanging on a decimal point.

The losses that accompany chronic illness are many. Clothes do not fit the same when you have peritoneal dialysis treatments. New clothes are purchased because the old ones not longer fit. Dress size changes after osteoporosis follows long-term prednisone therapy, and with this adjustment goes part of her identity and self-confidence. Drinking an alcoholic beverage, once enjoyed before dinner each day, has to be abandoned. Rigorous aerobic exercises are out of the question. Persistent shortness of breath and annoying weight gain are inescapable. A slower pace is resented, as is permanent nerve and muscle damage to a shoulder. Flowers are not planted, weight is gained, friends are not visited, certain favorite foods are not eaten, and a relationship may not be encouraged. Depression sets in at the realization that a woman may not see her children grow because of her chronic renal failure:

They were about three years old when I started getting sick. I tried to make my time with them quality time. I was not going to be their mother. I was not going to live to raise them.

A woman predicts the possibility of additional losses. She anticipates greater damage to her body resulting from irreversible changes, the progress of disease to other organs, and the effects of treatments, medications, and tests that go with the illness. "The fact will always be in the back of my mind, 'What else is going to develop?'" Dreams of marriage and having children are set aside. She worries about nonspecific problems. These are heralded by premonitions that something is going to happen before changes in status are evident.

A woman may be terribly angry as she sees women her own age, as well as everyone else around her, moving about easily, going out, and doing the things she cannot do. "I was the tender age of 27."

RECOGNIZING SYMPTOMS

Even before I went to the doctor's, it bothered me that the urine was very dark.

Before a woman admits that she is sick, she has been living with the symptoms that eventually help to confirm her disease.

I noticed that I could not walk as fast as I used to, that I got out of breath. I had angina for three years before I was operated on. It progressed to where I got pains in the chest and my left arm. It got so bad that I couldn't even eat a meal without getting a pain. Except for the pain I was all right.

When symptoms start to gang up on her, she focuses her attention inward. She recalls them with precise detail:

I didn't feel good. It felt like somebody was taking a hammer and just hitting me on that one side. I had blurred vision. I couldn't focus well and my concentration was really off. I found myself sitting down a lot, trying to get myself together. When I got home, the dizziness had gotten worse and my legs had started to drag. I called the doctor and didn't tell her about the numbness. I just told her my head was hurting.

She is very sensitive to body and mind cues that signal changes in her condition. Imperceptible changes warn her to pay attention to herself. She tries to tune into the cues and notices that she might not have been getting enough rest or has been stressed by work or family matters. A woman might realize that something is going to happen and she should pay attention: her breathing is becoming more labored.

Soon after diagnosis and the beginning of treatment, a woman notices that the disease brings other symptoms. Fatigue is hard to ignore: she sleeps much longer than usual. Eyes and skin reveal that they are sick. She aches all over. Her respiratory secretions disgust her. She has migraine headaches and bruises easily. She suffers joint pain and back pain. She becomes nauseated and vomits. She cannot eat or sleep. The array of symptoms that she lives with slows them, but she tries to put each symptom into perspective.

The arrhythmia would create what felt like a dramatic flipping of my heart in my chest and literally take my breath away. The sensation was that of feeling hollow. Yesterday and today I have had the worst total body pain I have ever had. It brings me to tears often. My back hurts, my anus hurts, my arms ache so much I feel sick, the bottoms of my feet have sharp pains every now and then. My stomach hurts and feels full of gas. I began to feel depressed and very unsure about a lot of things going on around me. I was paranoid and thought that people must think I'm stupid. I could not control my crying.

The symptoms settle in and change a woman's everyday life. Even walking down steps makes her short of breath "on a bad day," so she avoids this. She analyzes each symptom, trying to figure out what made it become more severe. She adapts. Eventually, the symptoms improve for a while. Still, she hates the symptoms and the treatment. "I hate the pain with a passion and I hate taking medicine for it." She continues to be afraid of the disease and the symptoms; she notices subtle changes, such as color changes in her hands as a result of her asthma. It is difficult to separate the symptoms of an acute illness, such as a strep throat, from the chronic illness. Symptoms that seem to be related to the disease are fit into the pattern. Said one woman, "On my bad days I feel really sleepy, really tired: just no energy."

Symptoms test the limits of a woman's endurance. She suffers for a while and uses standard medications before calling the doctor for the big guns (a stronger prescription). She also combines remedies and treats herself.

I can deal with the pain for about three to five days, and then I can't deal with it. I have to take something and have the rheumatologist inject it [her knee]. If I can't relieve it with exercise or with hot showers, I live on liquid Heet. It burns like fire, but it feels so good. I paint the joint with Ben-Gay. Extremely hot water makes it feel better.

TAKING MEDICATIONS: PROBLEM AND SOLUTION

Many agree that the cure can be worse than the disease. For example, the corticosteroid drugs that are so essential to treat sarcoidosis or hepatitis bring more difficulties to the women taking them. Cataracts form and vertebrae crumble because of these medications. What helps also causes harm.

Three years ago I had a terrible backache. They put me in the hospital and decided that the side effects of prednisone had left me with osteoporosis. I lost five vertebrae. I was in the hospital nine days and they put me in a brace. Then they sent me home with medicine. I gave myself a needle. It's called Calciferol.

Women may take a large number of medications during flare-ups of their disease. "I took 26 pills a day, and now I'm down to about six or seven." One woman takes four to five injections each day to manage her diabetes. She said, "You don't dwell on it, you just go ahead and do it." She might worry about how strong or potent generic medications are, preferring brand names. She blames the medications for how bad she feels and for many other things.

Medications are convenient targets of frustration and anger, but women recognize their dependency on the drugs. They fear dependency and potential addiction just as they know that symptoms sometimes improve dramatically, chiefly because of prescribed drugs.

The worst thing is the medication—I really don't like the steroids. It helps to relieve the symptoms.

A gradually decreasing number and dosage amount of medications proves that a woman is getting better. Chest pain subsides; depression disappears, as does sleeplessness; shortness of breath goes away temporarily; and blood pressure goes down. It may take time for her and her physician to adjust medications so that severe symptoms are eliminated and comfortable levels are achieved. However, many women will never be free of taking medications.

It is difficult to remember to take medications as prescribed; four-times-a-day medications get in the way of a busy schedule. Many times, women are reminded to do so by their symptoms. They create reminders to help them comply. It is also difficult to take medications that cause side effects such as tremors and weight gain. People may think the woman is an alcoholic or cannot control her appetite. Women are also sensitive to the changes medications wreak on the serum values reported on laboratory tests.

UNDERSTANDING THE DISEASE

A woman appreciates it when her need for facts about her progress and her disease are shared freely by physicians. They do not always get the answers they seek: there are many unknowns with chronic illness. One woman brought a list of questions to a hepatitis specialist and was happy to get some answers. She continues to want more details, however, and does not seem to be getting the information she desires. Although she hates to complain about her lack of understanding of her disease and treatment, she does, and she seeks answers from a variety of people. She consults with a sage woman friend and a nurse acquaintance. She asks her friend to look up information in textbooks. She actively enlists her female network to figure things out. She becomes an expert, at least in her case. Her understanding of the disease deepens in a way that health care providers appreciate to a limited extent. She lives with it; she knows it. She knows herself in her disease.

Whether it was the chemical, a combination of chemicals, or pollens in the air that I was becoming susceptible to a respiratory ailment . . . I knew it was not going to get better as time went on, based on articles that I read in journals.

FOLLOWING A PATH OF SELF-CARE

A woman follows many paths to keep herself as healthy as possible following her diagnosis. This does not mean that she ignores some of the other changes in her health that are not related to chronic illness.

I just feel that all my hormones have been really messed up with this. I wonder how long I've had this. I started a few

*years ago with menstrual and hormonal irregularities
. . . I wonder how long I've had this sarcoidosis and if this
caused the menstrual irregularities.*

She also pays attention to other bodily changes that are associated
with her disease, such as noting the color of her urine long after
the acute stage of her hepatitis.

Self-care efforts proliferate and are carefully followed. For
example:

*I changed my life as far as eating habits. I try to eat very
little fat. Once or twice a week I have a little meat, but I very
seldom have beef. I eat mostly chicken and I don't fry anything. I eat fish, broiled. I drink decaffeinated coffee. When I
bake I use cannola oil and I always have skim milk.*

Women do many things to take care of themselves: drink a lot of
water, walk more, stop smoking, adjust medication dose and frequency, eat prunes, use heating pads, avoid spicy food, get more
rest, and attend a cardiac rehabilitation program. Sometimes they
stray from the path but return to it when they have a flare-up or
notice subtle changes. They recognize that they could "do a better
job and stay on top of it." Most of the time, they avoid trouble, if
possible, and consequently avoid more symptoms and acute
episodes of the disease.

Taking care of herself also means that she keeps on going. She
may change her patterns, alternate her work and rest periods. But
she resumes her life after the acute phase of the illness passes. "I
didn't stop doing anything. I run the house, I cook, I clean, I do the
wash, I hang it out, I take three or four walks on the lawn." A family member advises her not to go too far. But she determines her
own level of activity. For some women, the disease results in a
transformation of their social selves. They move outside of their
circumscribed worlds by becoming more active and meeting a lot
of friends. They look at life differently.

However, activity is tempered by fear of overdoing it, of doing
something that could be harmful. She avoids allergens, cold
weather, and stressful situations. Even her avoidance of activity is

selected carefully and pursued actively. It is aimed at protecting and promoting her health.

COPING

In spite of the many stresses and setbacks intrinsic to her illness, she manages to cope. Her sense of humor and her ability to distract herself or to go along with others' distractions soothes her. She doesn't slow down. She keeps busy. She laughs.

> *There's a funny side to it. I became frustrated. I threw out everything that I touched, Vaseline and cream for my hands. I threw everything out of my bed. I ripped it apart. I took the rug off the floor, the curtains down, everything in there . . . the soap. Everything went.*

Another woman smiles:

> *I remember that I got a card that joked about life after 40. You go to bed with Ben-Gay and you wake up with Rice Krispies where you snap, crackle, and pop. There's a lot of truth to that.*

Watching a funny movie or having fun with friends and family helps. This help mixes well with the disease and dissolves some of the anger she feels about being ill.

CONNECTING TO OTHERS

She looks outside herself even when challenged by chronic physical illness. She continues to perform many roles. Among them are: wife, mother, daughter, sister, aunt, teacher, and friend. She ignores her own disease as she cares for another.

> *I had to take care of him. And I know it was a little bit hard because he really got so bad toward the end. I didn't get much sleep then.*

She is inclined to protect others. "I said to the lab technician, 'Did you read my chart?' 'Why?' she asked. 'Because I have hepatitis.'" A woman is still concerned about her sister who has the same family history of heart disease as she does. She tries to protect her by giving advice about lowering her cholesterol and reducing her weight. A wife protects her husband by not telling him everything that she knows about her disease. ". . . because of his diabetes and then he had a stroke." A daughter keeps her mother from worrying as she begins to realize that she may be having a stroke. "I didn't tell my mother because I didn't want to worry her. I told her I was going to lie down because I was very tired. I didn't tell them about the numbness and that my leg was bothering me."

She seeks to control the events in her life. But it is difficult for her to be comforted and protected. She sees it as reverting to the child within and prefers being in command of herself and others. But the illness derails these hopes and forces a temporary reliance on others. Fear of being alone at night stimulates a woman to move in with her son after his wife leaves him to file for divorce. The protection and companionship turns out to be mutually beneficial to mother and adult son. The arrangement goes on for a while, until she is stronger and less afraid and he starts dating again.

The reactions and support of family members, including husbands, uncles, children, and mothers, show in many ways. Some loved ones just accept the disease; they take it in stride. They contribute to her cause by helping her: they cook, clean, visit the hospital and home, pick up the prescriptions, bring food, and drive her to appointments. They take on some of the woman's work. "If the family wants me to do something and if I don't feel good and the asthma acts up, they usually don't push me. They know, just leave it be." After a while, loved ones grow tired of hearing about the disease. She becomes more isolated with this insight and turns to other chronically ill women, seeking support. They enjoy talking to one another; they are like sisters, or members of a special class.

Sometimes a woman's preoccupation with her illness and her children limits the amount of attention she pays to her husband and their relationship. She attempts to give her children everything. She puts herself and her disease after everything else. She is able to raise them and accomplishes the only thing she wanted to succeed at during her life. But in this accomplishment she realizes that her husband needs attention and she cannot provide it along with everything else. Relatives and friends tire of her situation. In spite of reassurances that they are there for her, sometimes they are missing.

The impact of the disease is felt most in the nuclear family. They ask after her and pray for her. When a mother is sick and her child is aware of this, the mother worries about the child's reaction. "My son had a hard time because he couldn't deal with me being sick." The children of one woman are independent and flexible. She attributes their resilience to her illness, although she shielded them from much of it during their childhood and adolescence. Concern spreads to the extended family. When family and friends fuss and try to control what the woman does, she may ignore them.

If the woman and members of her family are alienated, the chronic disease may place additional stress on an already troubled relationship. Divorce results. Or, the illness may provide an opportunity to fix things, especially if she takes advantage of the opening provided by the illness or a related crisis, after having considered her possibly earlier, more certain, more easily visualized death.

Friends stay connected. They help her through the illness experience just as her family does—by shopping and visiting. "I had only been diagnosed [with hepatitis] a couple of days. She rang the doorbell and said, 'I came for a cup of tea.'" They encourage her to reconnect after diagnosis and to stay connected to them and to life. They come back, again and again.

I was very sick at the time, but my friend had heard from my son that I wasn't supposed to do anything. I came home and they had dinner. She has been such a part of my life, almost like a sister.

Being a part of her life means sharing the illness experience. Friends share the history and have special knowledge of each other's lives. They are available to the woman's children, spouse, and other friends to relate some of this history.

Pets contribute their unconditional love to the chronically ill woman. They help to get her moving in the morning, reminding her of her obligation to the care of the pet and to her own exercise program.

The dog helps me to move. I've got to take care of the animal because of a sense of responsibility. I worry about other things rather than just flopping on the sofa worrying about me all of the time.

Animals help women see the humor in the everyday and experience the common joys. The women are indebted to them.

A woman who contemplates her death, first at a distance and then close-up, plans for the welfare of those she will leave. She tells her wishes to a child, husband, father, mother, sister, brother, or friend. She looks beyond her needs and tries to devise strategies to accomplish what she thinks is best for those she loves.

KNOWING A DISEASE

A chronically ill woman's death is more predictable than others. She is told this by her physician. Chronic disease equates with a death sentence for some. For example, even if transplanted organs, hemodialysis, surgery, and medications delay death for a time, women reluctantly accept the fact that their death will most likely come sooner than their imagined time.

The first time, hemodialysis was not available. A transplant was unheard of. So for me, that [chronic renal failure] was a death sentence.

Her life is changed dramatically. She cannot retrace her steps. A woman affirms that her disease has caused a major disturbance in her life.

I couldn't believe that I could go through so many traumatic events and still be alive.

A woman lives the many consequences of having a chronic illness for over 25 years. Some of these events are specifically health-related and seem to cluster during a one- or two-year time period. Organ transplantation, immunosuppressant drugs, skin cancer, cardiac arrests, vascular access surgery and revisions, and peritoneal dialysis and hemodialysis contribute to a life punctuated by the persistent and intermittent upheavals of chronic illness. Depression and hope take turns. The variety of treatments for the disease does not provide a cure. The treatments bring other symptoms and discomforts. Blood pressure fluctuates. The dialysate instilled during peritoneal dialysis causes cramps, and hemodialysis is "horrible." For another woman, the chemotherapy for recurrent breast cancer poisons the good cells along with the bad and results in nausea, hair loss, changes in the sensation of taste, and overwhelming fatigue.

BEING INCREASINGLY AWARE

Once a woman lives with a chronic physical illness, she is intimately aware of what being physically ill means. She knows that her "own suffering serves but to wake memories in friends' minds of their . . . aches and pains that went unswept" (Woolf, 1948, p. 12). She notices others who, she hears, have such a disease and echoes their experience. She is especially attentive to the details of their lives and her sensitivity to these other persons is more acute than most. She resonates with their experience. Sometimes she feels their pain and worries about the impact of the disease on the many facets of their lives. She finds someone to commiserate with.

I have a good friend at work who was just diagnosed with asthma. So now she's joined the chronic club.

A woman knows that the illness, rather than being the end, opens up possibilities and new growth along with the suffering.

She cherishes the opening up. "I have become more immersed in my life and wish that for [her]. I have just really begun to be in relationships with women that are caring and affirming." She seeks friends and family, hopes for new relationships, and goes after life.

The longer death casts a shadow, the faster you need to dance. (Wadler, 1992, p. 5)

Her fragility is balanced with her ability to fight and to live. "He said to me and he keeps saying to me, 'You must remember, you're fragile.' I know I am." She knows that she has a lot of power. It keeps her in the here-and-now, connected to the people in her life. It enables her to reach out to others and to new experiences.

Even though she is not certain of her future, a woman plans for it. She might dream of moving to a warmer climate. She carefully considers how she will function at work there. Her vision of the future is not free of the present worries that her disease brings. She knows of the uncertainties in an intimate way. She recognizes that sometimes, no matter how emotionally steady she may be or how well she is caring for herself, the unexpected can happen. Her disease reasserts its powerful presence. She believes in fate.

Knowing that the future could bring more limitations and adjustments, she recognizes how much she values her own independence. Her ability to move freely in her world cheers her. She sees the beauty of her world, and she cherishes it even as she has visions and dreams of what is not to be in her life.

I have a Peace rose and small red roses; a thornless red rose. I have about five bushes. They're beautiful. I have some grapes. I have a beautiful Concord grape.

The beauty of her world soothes her worries.

Her sense of responsibility to family and friends and to the people at work is acute. She plans which rooms she will clean at home, and when, so as not to neglect the house. She is so responsible at work that people quickly notice when she is not feeling well. Worrying about what the disease will do to all of the jobs she performs gets her attention. She is compulsive—almost fanatical—about her attendance record at work. She worries about personal finances and about keeping a job.

If the woman is lucky, she is seen by her employer to be a good worker. A stroke changes her ability to perform at work. It is reassuring to hear that she will not lose her job, that it is secure. At the same time, she is attuned to the hazards at work. Some work is so demanding that her body is unable to keep up the pace. She notes her limits and paces herself. "You have to stop. You have less energy. You are really tired."

Work performance suffers. She fears being unemployed. A woman may be asked to leave her job because coworkers and administrators consider her a liability. In retrospect, she may wonder how she managed to work as long as she did. But she feels the sting of others' discrimination against chronically ill people.

They finally forced me out, and they said, "If you don't go out on disability, there are other ways we have of getting rid of you." She did, she told me that.

Work may be dangerous for her: she could become infected by her contacts. Furthermore, her resistance may decrease so that she is more susceptible to respiratory infections.

Women also worry about their health, and they worry about their death. Occasionally, these worries advance to anxiety.

I was beginning to feel unusually anxious, continuously. I'd get a nervous sensation in my solar plexus. I would find myself taking deep breaths to try to get rid of the feeling. I'd lie down in the bed and the feeling would overcome me. I'd feel my heart beating and would wonder if all of this was related (to my disease).

Seeing into the uncertain future stirs her worries.

A woman does not relish being a burden to society; she enjoys independence. She has seen the limits that disease has placed on her, and realizes its present impact. She asks about her future, her death. However, she gets few satisfactory answers.

I said, "What will it do to my life?" He said, "Shorten it." I said, "None of us knows our life span. Can you put a time limit on it?" He said, "The first five years are difficult. Up to then, we don't know."

Religion serves as a base for some women. They depend so much on their beliefs that it would be difficult for them to face illness without them. Women explain their good times and successes as being part of God's plan. Their roots in religion enable them to take things as they come. If not very spiritual before being diagnosed with the disease, they are soon afterward. They trust the rest of their time here to God. However, there are times that they rail against God, demanding why they were sent more than they could handle.

A chronically ill woman prepares many gifts for the ones she loves. Her legacies are her children, the love of her husband and friends, her fragility, her strength. She shares her perspectives of what it is to be a woman, to be sick, to recover, and to get sick again. Her experiences are an everyday legacy, one of living with the symptoms, medications, and other accompaniments of chronic illness. She instructs other women through her own journey.

ABOUT THE STUDY

The meaning of chronic physical illness for women has been found to have the following patterns. Their sequence here does not necessarily indicate a chronology of occurrence.

Seeking Balance: Keeping the Disease in Perspective

Not wanting to have a chronic illness; denial of disease and searching for a minor cause of symptoms; confirmation of disease and not having a diagnosis

Dawning Awareness of Having a Chronic Disease

MD's disbelief she is sick: protects himself; MD minimizes the symptoms of a woman; MD treats her; MD confronts his or her lack of expertise; MD's referral to other physician due to complex, chronic nature of disease; MD support and surveillance; MD concern; RN support during illness; MD office staff support and humor; seeing technology involved in care; health care providers' less than sensitive/responsive care

Identifying the causes of the disease: why she has the disease; family history; another part of health history

Having to be subjected to many diagnostic tests, which often result in problems

Chronic awareness of chronic disease; pervasive nature of chronic disease

Vortex of Chronic Illness

Patterns of disease; minor and major remissions and exacerbations; uncertainty about chronic disease

Preferring to have one disease rather than another; having more than one chronic or acute illness

Forced acceptance of disease; major impact of disease on life; fighting disease and winning; admiring another woman who is a role model

Finding Disease Repugnant

Pretending not to be sick so others will not know; hiding the disease from others; stigma of disease; isolation; feeling dirty

Fear of disease; fear of having the disease made public; fear of increased disability; fear that disease will progress; fear of diagnostic tests and procedures; fear of altered future and dying

Losses resulting from disease; fear that chronic illness will progress and more losses will occur; anger at seeing healthy people

Disease brings symptoms; enduring symptoms; body-mind sensitivity to cues; symptoms are frightening; symptoms improve; symptoms intrude on life; analyzing symptoms; hating symptoms; limits of endurance living with symptoms

Regimen designed to treat disease brings additional problems; reactions to drugs; fear of medications not being potent; dosage of medications; blaming medications for feeling bad; dependency on medications; difficulty living with medications; interaction of medications and blood values and other systems

Understanding of Disease

Promoting health postdiagnosis; worry about effect of disease on other aspects of health; self-care; poor self-care; attention to bodily functions; avoiding trouble; maintaining activity; modifying activity; fear of hurting self

Humor and Distraction; Humor Used to Cope

Women have many roles; caring for other person causes her to ignore her own disease; protecting others from disease; family support; family concern; chronic disease as a crisis that adds stress to already crisis-laden relationships; friends and family help to make her feel less dirty; animal support; female friends continue to help, despite possibility of contracting infectious disease; friendship between two women over the years is a gift and a legacy to each other and to children

Vulnerability: to other infections; to people's rejections

Crisis and Upheaval

Having chronic illness heightens awareness to others' experiences; having female friends with chronic physical illness

Fragile survivor; sense of self; future planning; insights; taking pleasure in beauty

Worrying; working; worry about death; confronting an early death; fear of dying made public: violating intensely private event of death gifts to those she loves, such as having a child and other legacies

The demographic characteristics of the interview participants are as follows:

Participant No.	Age	Race[a]	Religion[b]	Marital Status[c]	Living Status	Diagnosis/ Surgery	Age at Diagnosis
1	76	W	C	M	With spouse	Autoimmune hepatitis; osteoporosis	70
2	75	W	C	W	Alone	Coronary artery disease; coronary artery by-pass graft	62
3	72	AA	P	D	Alone	Noninsulin-dependent diabetes mellitus; hypertension; thrombophlebitis	71
4	38	W	C	S	Alone	Sarcoidosis	37
5	45	W	C	S	Alone	Asthma; osteoarthritis; rheumatoid arthritis	31
6	46	AA	P	S	With family member	Hypertension; cerebrovascular accident	44
7	46	W	J	S	With family member	Ulcerative colitis; osteoarthritis	24
8	82	W	J	W	With family member	Coronary artery disease; myocardial infarction	78
9	49	W	P	M	With spouse	Fibromyalgia	42
10	53	W	P	D	Alone	Chronic renal failure; renal transplantation	23
11	38	W	C	M	With spouse	Insulin-dependent diabetes mellitus; hypothyroidism; pernicious anemia	18
12	59	W	C	M	With spouse	Breast cancer with recurrence; osteoarthritis; fractured hip repair	53

[a] W = White; AA = African American
[b] C = Catholic; P = Protestant; J = Jewish
[c] M = married; W = widowed; D = divorced; S = single

REFERENCES

Duff, K. (1993). *The alchemy of illness*. New York: Pantheon Books.
Wadler, J. (1992). *My breast: One woman's cancer story*. Reading, MA: Addison-Wesley.
Woolf, V. (1948). On being ill. In V. Woolf, *The moment and other essays*. Orlando, FL: Harcourt Brace Jovanovich.

ABOUT THE AUTHOR

I am Zane Robinson Wolf, PhD, RN, a Professor of Nursing at La Salle University and Associate Director of Nursing for Research at Albert Einstein Medical Center in Philadelphia.

I am interested in helping nurses to use research findings and methods as tools to strengthen nursing practice. I hope to continue to develop skills in using qualitative methodologies. My areas of interest are medical surgical nursing, rituals, medication administration, and nurses' and patients' experiences in hospitals.

I learned a great deal from the women in my life, and from my husband, children, students, colleagues, patients, and participants in my research studies. My children taught me most about myself, my husband and friends have steadied and validated me, and my parents, grandmother, sisters, and brothers helped me get in touch with what is important in life. Writing about women's experiences brought me back after difficult times to people and thoughts to be cherished.

Index